Guilford County North Carolina Will Abstracts

***

1771-1841

Compiled, Indexed & Published

By

Irene B. Webster

Southern Historical Press, Inc.
Greenville, South Carolina

Please direct all correspondence and orders to:

www.southernhistoricalpress.com
or
SOUTHERN HISTORICAL PRESS, Inc.
PO BOX 1267
Greenville, SC 29601
southernhistoricalpress@gmail.com

ISBN #0-89308-352-6

Printed in the United States of America

FOREWORD

GUILFORD COUNTY, NORTH CAROLINA WILL ABSTRACTS, 1771-1841 was compiled mostly from Microfilm Reel No. C. 0460001 which was ordered from North Carolina Department of Cultural Resources, Division of Archives & Records, Raleigh, N. C. (hereafter called Archives). The reel was photographed from the recorded wills in 1964 in the office of the Clerk of Superior Court in Guilford County in the county seat of Greensboro.

The reel covers Will Books A, B, and C--time span 1771 through 1859. This volume could not cover the whole time span of the reel because of index space needed.

NO PAGE NUMBERS - The numbers of the wills are not page numbers; they are File Numbers. The page numbers are rather dim on some pages and the first 12 pages of Book B are missing. It appears that some years after the wills were recorded, someone went through Books A, B, and C marking each will with a File Number in very heavy black ink. One should be able to order a copy of a recorded will from the courthouse by furnishing the name of the testator or devisor, name of Will Book, and File Number.

ORIGINAL WILLS of Guilford County are filed at the Archives alphabetically by county and surname (address on page 143). In ordering a copy, name of the county, name of testator, and the probate date of the will should be given. If there is no probate date, give date the will was written.

PROBATES - Wills were usually received for probate at the next Term of Court after the death of the testator. Court in Guilford County was held the third week of the given months.

UNRECORDED ORIGINAL WILLS - Abstracts of those from Guilford County that fall within the time span of this volume are included. A list of all unrecorded wills of Guilford County that are stored at the Archives are listed on page 143 with the Box Numbers in which they are stored.

THE PHONETIC SPELLING of the names is copied in the abstracts most of the time, though the several different spellings of the same name within the will is not always given. ONE WILL NEED TO EXAMINE THE INDEX OF NAMES VERY CAREFULLY so as not to miss one of the various spellings. As to the other content of the wills, an effort was made to interpret the phonetic spelling, leaving just a trace of its "flavor".

ABBREVIATIONS - "dw" for during widowhood is probable the only one not recognizable and it is spelled out when there is room on the line. However, when "bed, cow, and horse" are listed among bequeaths, this usually means that a bed & furniture, a cow & calf, and a horse, saddle & bridle were bequeathed. "Prb" is used throughout the book for probated. Occasionally "w/o" is used for wife of, as "d/o" equals daughter of, etc.

TITLES - One never used his title (Captain, Colonel, Esquire, etc) in signing as witness to a will, but if the Clerk used a title of a witness in the probate, that title was added in this volume for further information on that person.

GUILFORD COUNTY was formed from Orange and Rowan Counties in 1771. It is now bounded on the north by Rockingham County which was formed from Guilford in 1785; on the east by Alamance County; on the south by Randolph County; and on the west by Davidson and Forsyth Counties.

CLERKS OF COURT - Thomas Henderson was the first Clerk of Court in Guilford County. He then became the first Clerk of Court for Rockingham County at the first session held in February 1786.

According to OLD GUILFORD, NORTH CAROLINA COURT MINUTES 1781-1788 (1978) by Nancy Hawlick Stein, it was on 21 February 1786 that the Guilford Court of Pleas & Quarter Sessions elected Thomas Searcy as Clerk of Court with William Dent and Thomas Henderson as sureties for his bond.

Based only on the signatures appearing on the probates at the end of the wills contained in this volume of abstracts, John Hamilton must have been the third Clerk of Court, serving from 1790 until 1816 when John Hanner became Clerk of Court.

W. W. Woodburn first signed as Clerk of Court in wills probated during the August Term of Court 1833. A. E. Hanner was Clerk beginning with the May Term of 1834; then W. W. Woodburn was serving again during the May Term of 1836.

John M. Logan began his service as Clerk of Court during the November Term of 1837, serving for the duration of this volume and many years beyond.

DEPUTY CLERKS - Joseph Davis was the first mentioned, serving under John Hamilton. A. E. Hanner served during the time that John Hanner was Clerk of Court. After this period, the Deputy Clerk rarily co-signed the probates with the Clerk of Court. In one instance, N. B. Houston co-signed as Deputy Clerk with John M. Logan.

WILLS PROBABLY NOT RECORDED UNTIL 1816 - It appears that no wills were recorded until John Hanner became Clerk of Court in 1816 and that he divided out the accumulation of wills alphabetically and then arranged the wills under each letter chronologically and then started two books--one for the old wills and one for the current wills. If this is correct, a few intended for Book B are among the wills in Book A, as there are several in the first book probated in 1816, 1817, & 1818. There are 418 wills in Book A, so it must have taken quite a while to record this backlog. How many had been lost???

APPRECIATION - I wish to thank friends who have been of great help. There would be no publication without production manager Mary Louise D. McCollum.

Linda C. Vernon, Lenora W. Sutton, and Hassell B. Gann have been kind enough, on their trips to Raleigh, to secure zeroxed copies of original wills at the Archives when needed; and, also to search for probate dates when they were not recorded in the Will Books.

The staff at the Madison Library has given of its time in helping to decipher illegible names.

Irene B. Webster

Mrs. S. F. Webster
206 W. Hunter Street
Madison, N. C. 27025

TABLE OF CONTENTS

A:01 - JAMES ARCHER - 2 Jan 1799 - Prb Aug 1799
Son DAVID - 150 ac where he lives, negro girl Phillis
Wife CATHERINE and dau SARAH - plantation, negroes Jacob, Jenny, Jack, Peter, and Dick. Son JOHN - negro boy Isaac
Dau MARY HAMILTON - negro woman Jude
Dau ELIZABETH HAMILTON - 20 shillings & what she has received
Son THOMAS - 25 shillings plus what he has already received
Exrs: John Hamilton, Carolus Jenkins
Wits: Carolus Jenkins, Joel Jenkins, John Stevens

A:02 - JAMES ANTHONY - 25 Jan 1796 - Prb Aug 1799
Wife MARY - Bay mare, stock, third of linnens, 5 pds hard money
Son OBED - land on Hickory Creek where he lives, clock
Son JONATHAN - 140 ac bought from John Wilfer where he lives
Daus CHARLOTTE, PHEBE, MERAT, RUTH, JUDAH - residue of property
Exrs: Son OBED ANTHONY, Stephen Gardner, Jr.
Wits: Abigail Gardner, Stephen Gardner, Jr., Stephen Gardner

A:03 - ISAAC ARMFIELD - 20 Dec 1780 - No probate.
Wife ELIZABETH - home plantation during widowhood
Two oldest sons WILLIAM & JOHN - to inherit home plantation
Other ch: SARAH ARMFIELD, ISAAC, ANN ARMFIELD, JOSEPH, JACOB, and ELIZABETH ARMFIELD - to inherit personal property
Exrs: Son WILLIAM ARMFIELD, brother WILLIAM ARMFIELD
Wits: Enoch May, William Armfield, Nathan Armfield

A:04 - JONATHAN ARMFIELD - 24 Jan 1801 - Prb Feb 1801
Wife ELIZABETH - negroes Lier, Cuz, Hannah & Sarah
Brother SOLOMAN - tract bought from John McBride
Sarah Standley's son Jonathan Standley
Exrs: Wife ELIZABETH ARMFIELD, SOLOMAN ARMFIELD
Wits: John Roper, Henry Stuart, Thomas Newlin

A:05 - CHARLES ADEAR - 16 Jan 1785 - Prb Feb 1786
Wife MARGARET - home plantation; equally divided after her death
Ch: MARY, CHARLES, ELIZABETH, SARAH, WILLIAM, JANE, JOHN, and MARGARET. Ch of first wife: ESTER, JAMES, ELLINER and CATHERINE - each five shillings
Exrs: Wife MARGARET ADEAR, John Readduck
Wits: John Readduck, Joseph Brown

A:06 - MARTHA ALLISON - 23 June 1810 - Prb Feb 1811
Major Jeremiah Forbis - negro woman Lucretia Martin
Isabella (w/o John Finley) and Martha (w/o James Wilkey)
Samuel & John Allison - negroes Sam, Martin & Walker
Isaiah Allison's son Samuel and dau Martha, as they come of age
Esther Grimes, dau of Jain Allison - proceeds from sale
Exr: Samuel Allison
Wits: Isaiah McDill, Joseph McBride
Codicil 9 Dec 1810 - Legatees: Jane Britton, Ann _____, James Allison, Martha Allison (dau of John Allison), Mary Forbis, Jane McDill, Elizabeth Allison, Mary Allison, Ann Allison.

A:07 - JOSEPH ALEXANDER - 28 Mar 1799 - Prb May 1799
Wife MARTHA - 150 ac adj Andrew McGee, Robert Galbreath, Thomas Landreth, James Doak

Son GEORGE - to inherit home plantation, stock, blacksmith tools
Exr: Wife MARTHA ALEXANDER - Wits: Robert Hannah, John Doak

A:08 - JOHN ALLEN, Sr. - 8 Feb 1780 - Prb Aug 1781
Son DANIEL - all my land to maintain my wife and daus
Wife SARAH - a separate tract of land if she wished
Daus: SARAH, ANN, JEMIMA, MARY, and KEZIAH
Sons BENJAMIN (cow & calf), JOHN, & JOSEPH - each five shillings
Exrs: Josiah Settle, William Clark
Wits: Daniel Allen, Joseph Clark, Rebecca Clark, William Clark, John Allen, Jr.

A:09 - JEREMIAH ANDREWS - 19 Dec 1799 - Prb May 1800
Wife MARY - choice of furniture, saddle, dish, seven plates, etc
Son BENIT - balance of property except Rodger Willises
Gr dau MARY WILLIS - feather bed & furniture, cow & calf
Exrs: Wife MARY ANDREWS and Rodger Willis
Wits: James Touchstone, Burgess Delacy

A:10 - WILLIAM AKIN - 27 May 1799 - Prb Aug 1799
Sons WILLIAM & JOHN - home plantation
All my daughters - one good feather bed when they marry
Exrs: Thomas Wiley, John Thom - Wits: John Thom, James Sloan

A:11 - WILLIAM ARMFIELD, Sr. - 28 Mar 1804 - Prb May 1812
Wife LYDIA - all my estate while she remains my widow
Son WILLIAM (10 sh), dau MARY BROWN, sons NATHAN, SOLOMAN, dau ANN FIELD, son DAVID - each 20 shillings
Son JOSEPH - all my estate at decease or remarriage of wife
Exrs: Wife LYDIA ARMFIELD, son SOLOMAN ARMFIELD
Wits: William Armfield, Joseph Armfield

A:012 - BENJAMIN AYDELETT - 3 Sept 1813 - Prb Nov 1813
Wife TABITHY - use of home plantation and negro man Pompey
Son PARKER, dau MADAY SPRUCE 20 sh. Son LEVEN - 10 shillings
Son SHADRACK - to inherit home plantation from wife
Daus LUCY & SARAH AYDLETTE - negro girls Tenis & Tamar, beds
Exr: Son LEVEN AYDELETT - Wits: Daniel Donnell, John Hancock

A:013 - JAMES ANDERSON - 25 Nov 1814 - Prb May 1815
Sons: ISAAC - one cow; JOHN - Home place at wife's death; WILLIAM - one bed. Dau SARAH SULLAVEN - my chest
Wife SARAH - all she was possessed of when she became my wife
Exrs: Wife SARAH ANDERSON, William Harvey
Wits: John Finley, Elizabeth Finley

A:014 - JOHN BLAIR - 22 Sept 1777 - Prb 28 Sept 1778
Wife JEAN - a good horse & saddle, her bed & spinning wheel over and above the third part or whatever the law allows
Four sons: THOMAS, JOHN, ANDREW, JONATHAN (all under 21)
Two daus: JEAN and MARTHA BLAIR
Proven by oaths of Thomas Blair, William Gowdy, Hugh Blair

A:015 - ALEXANDER BREDEN - 26 Oct 1793 - Prb Nov 1793
Wife - use of land to raise and educate my children
Oldest son WILLIAM - the land when he becomes of age

My older daus - a bed and furniture to each
Exrs: Daniel Gillaspie, Senr., John Donnell
Wits: D. Caldwell, John Orr

A:016 - JOHN BEALS - 21 Apr 1809 - Prb May 1809
Wife SUSANNAH - use of plantation & personal estate
Sons JOHN, CALEB and WILLIAM BEALS - land on which each lives
Son JESSE - 100 ac of plantation on which I live on Deep River
Son ELEAZAR - 50 ac adj Bethuel Coffin and Isaac Cook
Daus SARAH (wife of John Carter) and Margaret (wife of Benjamin Milliken) - each $5. - Exrs: Son JOHN BEALES, Bethuel Coffin
Wits: Joshua Dicks, Nathan Dicks

A:017 - BENJAMIN BARNARD - 7 Sept 1792 - Prb Nov 1792
Wife EUNICE - property during widowhood; third if she marries
Son TIMOTHY - 8 pds worth of stock, 1/5 of household furniture
Sons LIBEN, FREDERICH, SHUBAL, ELISHA - divide land and stock
Dau EUNICE - to be supported by brothers inheriting the land
Daus MARY, LYDA, LUSINDA, MATILDA - each 1/5 household furniture
Exrs: Wife EUNICE BARNARD, son LIBIN BARNARD
Wits: Stephen Gardner, Abigail Gardner

A:018 - ROBERT BREDEN - 12 June 1777 - Prb not recorded
Wife MARY - a home and provisions on my plantation
Son CHARLES - home plantation
Dau MARGARET BREDEN - her bed & furniture, 1/3 movable estate
Son ROBERT - 100 ac of home plantation, 1/3 of movable estate
Son ALEXANDER - 20 pds value of movable estate before division
Exrs: Stepson JOHN DONNELL, John Rankin
Wits: John Donnell, Thomas Donnell

A:019 - JESSE BEALS - 24 July 1811 - Prb Aug 1811
Wife ANN - use & profits of estate after my mother SUSANNAH BEALS is through with it, movable property she had at marriage
Son JOHN BEALS (minor). Bros JOHN, WILLIAM, CALEB, and ELEAZER
Exrs: John Hoskins, Bethuel Coffin
Wits: James Thornburg, John Beals

A:020 - JOHN BARNETT - 1781 - Prb Aug 1781
Wife ELIZABETH - third of estate & use of negro fellow Glasgow
Ch: MARGARET BARNETT, JOHN, MARY BROWN, ANNE, ELIZABETH, WILLIAM, and JOSEPH (silver watch)
Exrs: William Barnett, James Robinson
Wits: William Plunkit, Elinor Robinson

A:021 - WILLIAM BARNHILL - 23 Sept 1791 - Prb Nov 1791
Wife SARAH - 18 ac of land with provisions, choice of stock, etc
Son WILLIAM and his children - 200 ac of home plantation
SARAH BARNHILL (dau of WILLIAM) - my young bay mare
Dau MARY STUART - stock and mother's part after her decease
Son-in-law WILLIAM JENKINS - 30 pounds
WILLIAM (son of ROBERT BARNHILL) - five pounds
Exrs: Robert Hannah, Thomas Landreth
Wits: George Forbis, Isaac Hayes, Margaret Blair

A:022 - WILLIAM BEARD - 11 Sept 1794 - Prb May 1795

Wife LEVINA - profits of estate dw; if she chooses to marry, no more than one good horse and saddle and one good feather bed
Son DAVID (under 21) - hatter's tools
Son BENJAMIN - 88 ac bought of Richard Glover & William Roper
Son WILLIAN - home plantation at mother's death or remarriage
Daus LYDIA BEARD, RACHEL BEARD - stock, furniture, feather bed
Exrs: Stephen Gardner, John Talbot
Wits: Stephen Gardner, Barnabas Coffin

A:023 - JOHN BENSON - 17 Sept 1793 - Prb Nov 1793
My four ch: JANE SHELLY, JOHN BENSON, Jr., AILEE MENDENHALL, REUBIN BENSON - estate to be divided equally; pewter to daus
Exr: George Manlove
Wits: James Caldwell, Richard Glover

A:024 - NATHANIEL BROWN - 1 Jan 1790 - Prb May 1790
Dau ELIZABETH MCMURRY - 15 pds.
Gr dau MARY MCMURRY and NATHANIEL MCMURRY - each four pounds
All my grand children - estate divided equally between them
Exrs: John Brown and William Brown
Wits: James McMurry, Thomas Brown

A:025 - RICHARD BOURTON - 17 Dec 1799 - Prb Feb 1801
Wife - plantation, negro boy Tom, use of plantation, stock, etc
Son RITCHARD - negro boy Bobb
Son WILLIAM - Negro man Ben, woman Henny, boy Joe, 1/3 of land
Daus ELIZABETH SIMONS (20 pds in money), MARY MILLIKEN (negro boy Sam), DORCAS BOURTON (negro Nell, horse, bed & furniture)
Dau MILIKAN - third of land after decease of wife
Gr ch: RITCHARD REAVES, MARTHA REAVES, THOMAS REAVES - 1/3 of land after decease of wife
Exrs: Sons RICHARD BORTON, and WILLIAM BORTON
Wits: Thomas Lowe, John Hallum, William Hallum
Proved in court by John Hallum Esq of Rockingham County

A:026 - CATHERINE BOYD - 12 Jan 1783 - Prb 17 Feb 1783
Dau MARGARET WASON and son ANDREW BOYD - personal property
Exr: John Hallum
Wits: Robert Boak, John Hallum

A:027 - JACOB BOON - 17 Jan 1795 - Prb Feb Court 1796
Son-in-law ADAM WHITESELL - 50 ac adj Andrew Gibson and Michael Charles
Dau MARGARET WHITSELL - my bed and furniture
Gr Ch: ANNE BOON, JACOB BOON, JOHN BOON - 90 pds when of age
JOHN BOON (son of MARTIN BOON, dec'd) - 25 pds provided he shares his father's land when sisters & brothers become of age
Ch of MARTIN BOON dec'd: DANIEL, MARTAIN & CATHERINE BOON - 25 P
Exrs: Adam Whitesell, JOHN BOON, Senr
Wits: William Ramey, Benjamin Ramey

A:028 - JOHN BURNEY - 22 Aug 1794 - Prb Nov 1794
Wife CATHERINE - negro Jeffrey, plantation while she lives
Eldest dau ELIZABETH - one horse & saddle, bed & furniture
Dau REBECKAH - one horse & saddle, bed & furniture, chest
Son ROBERT - 200 ac where he lives adj son WILLIAM

Son JOHN - home plantation at decease of his mother
Gr sons: JOHN (son of WILLIAM), JOHN (son of ROBERT), and WILLIAM (son of JOHN) - remaining lands
Exrs: Wife CATHERINE BURNEY, son ROBERT BURNEY
Wits: John Gilchrist, George Denny, William Denny

A:029 - JOHN BLEAR - 8 Oct 1770 - Prb Feb 1772
Wife MARTHA - all my property during her widowhood
Son JOHN - to receive property at decease or remarriage of wife
All my children - five shillings sterling each
Exrs: Wife MARTHA BLEAR, son JOHN BLEAR
Wits: James Cunningham, William Gowdy

A:30 - JAMES BILLINGSLEY - 5 Jan 1776 - Prb May 1776
Wife MARY - land until youngest sons WALTER & BARZIL come of age
Ch WILLIAM (bed & furn), MARTHA, WALTER, BARZIL - share equally
Married ch: JAMES, ELIZABETH, CLARENCE, SAMUEL, JOHN J. - 2 sh
Exr: Wife MARY BILLINGSLEY
Wits: Tidwell Lowe, William Homer

A:031 - JAMES BLAIR - 1 Mar 1776 - Prb May 1776
Wife MARY - child's share and home dw, third of movables
Son JOHN - mill & tools, land, horse & saddle, third of movables
Dau AGNES - 50 pds money, third of movable estate when of age
Exrs: Wife MARY BLAIR, son JOHN BLAIR
Wits: Moses Campbell, Francis McBride, Adam Lackey

A:032 - WILLIAM BROWN - 10 Aug 1794 - Prb May 1795
Wife and son JAMES - tract of land whereon I live
Son ELIAS - plantation of my mother & father after their decease
Daus NANCY, REBECKAH - each a bed & furniture, cow & calf
Exrs: Wife and Edward Bullock
Wits: George Brown, John Eadsley, William Gray

A:033 - WILLIAM BRITTAIN - 1 Jan 1794 - No prb date
Son HENERY - land adj Joseph Unthank on Murfries Branch
Son JOSEPH - land adj William Coffin on Murfries Branch
Son WILLIAM - remaining land
Daus: HANNAH HUNT, MARY WITTY, REBEKAH ROBINSON, NAOMY ROBINSON, RUTH BRITTAIN, ANNE BRITTAIN - each five shillings
Wife REBEKAH BRITTAIN - remaining part of estate dw
Exrs: Wife REBECKAH BRITTAIN, Joshua Dix
Wits: Daniel Baldwin, Uriah Baldwin, Thomas Terry

A:034 - MATTHEW BROWN - 3 Feb 1787 - Prb May 1787
Sons JOHN, ROBERT, & THOMAS - money from 343 ac on Ready Fk Cr
Son WILLIAM - 300 ac west of home plantation
Son MATTHEW - 340 ac east of home plantation
Daus JEAN RAIL, MARGARET SHRIFT - twenty shillings
Exrs: Son WILLIAM BROWN, Col. John Peasley
Wits: Sampson Stewart, Andrew Stuart

A:035 - ISAAC BEESON - 3 Mar 1802 - Prb May 1802
Wife PHEBE - all of estate during widowhood
Son ISAAC - to inherit home plantation from wife
Son NATHANIEL - tract of land adj George Mendenhall

Daus MARY, CHARITY, PHEBE, and MARTHA - five shillings
Sons BENJAMIN, SAMUEL, EDWARD, and WILLIAM - five shillings
Two children of dec'd son RICHARD - five shillings
John Ades, boy living with me - to have a horse at age 21
Exrs: Wife PHEBE BEESON, son ISAAC BEESON
Wits: Hezekiah Starbuck, Joshua Hains, BENJAMIN BEESON

A:036 - JOHN BARNES - 16 May 1801 - Prb May 1802
Wife ELIZABETH - feather bed & furniture during her life
Son JESSE & son-in-law PURNEL CHANCE - remaining estate, if they pay the following: Sarah Hutton - one heiffer
Grandaus ELLISEBETH, LUCY, and RODEY SWIGETT - one heiffer
Son JOHN, Joshua Gullett, and son-in-law ELIJAH BALDLY - 5 sh ea
Exr: Son JESSE BARNES
Wits: Joseph Glenn, Benjamin Dixon, Benjamin Nettler
Probate was caveated by Elijah Rumley and Joshua Gullett at August Court 1801

A:037 - JEAN BARNETT - 13 Feb 1804 - Prb Feb 1805
Polly McCalhatton (dau of Wm.) - my bed & furn, spinning wheel
Polly McCalhatton (w/o William) - one milch cow
Exr: Friend Polly McCalhatton (Spelled McKilhatton in probate)
Wits: L. Dilling, James Cook

A:038 - WILLIAM BALDWIN - 11 Feb 1808 - No probate date
Bros JOHN, JESSE, & DANIEL (minor) - carpenter and Joiner tools
Sisters ELIZABETH, JANE, and SARAH BALDWIN - notes due me
Father JOHN BALDWIN - residue of estate
Exrs: Father JOHN BALDWIN and Barnabas Coffin
Wits: John Sanders, Joseph Mills

A:039 - JAMES BROGDON - 17 Jan 1810 - Prb Feb 1810
Wife ANN - all my estate & negro boy Charles
Daus PATIENCE and KESIA - negroes Cleria and Allex
Dau RELIANCE - increase from slaves
Exrs: John Walker, John Dinkins
Wits: William Brown, John Walker, Jr., William Lucas

A:040 - EDWARD BULLOCK - 20 Jan 1813 - Prb May 1813
Sons WILLIAM, DAVID, JOHN, EDWARD, JAMES, & LEN - 5 shillings
Daus ELIZABETH RALPH, SUSANNA LONEY, SARAH STAFFORD, and WINNEFRED - 5 shillings each
Wife ANN DOGGED BULLOCK - all my estate for her natural life
Son GEORGE - estate after decease of wife
Exrs: Wife ANN DOGGED BULLOCK, William Starbuck
Wits: Hezekiah Starbuck, Latham Starbuck, Joel Hunt

A:041 - THOMAS COX of Richland Creek - No date - Prb Nov 1771
Wife - side saddle, third of personal estate, live with Thomas
Sons THOMAS, JOSHUA, DANIEL, JOHN, ABNER - plantation at age 21
Daus SARAH and MARTHA - each a feather bed at age 18
Exrs: Soloman Cox & William Moreman qualified in Court
Wits: William Garner, Stephen Jussey, John Hussey

A:042 - THOMAS CRAWLEY - 16 Jan 1778 - Prb May 1778
Wife FRANCES - my whole estate during her lifetime

All my children - divide estate at decease of wife
Son THOMAS - 200 ac on Hickory Cr. Son JOHN - 1 sh starling
Exr: None named Wits: James Jackson, Jr., James Jackson, Sr.

A:043 - MOSES CAMPBELL - 9 July 1782 - Prb 19 Aug 1782
Wife REBECKAR - third part of estate for life
Sons WILLIAM and JAMES - to inherit land on which I live
All my children, including all my daus - personal property
Exrs: Thomas Blair, Peter King
Wits: Joseph Dill, Mary Dill, Charles Bruce

A:044 - ELINOR CHAMBERS - 2 June 1781 - Prb Aug 1781
Dau STUART - cotton cloth for gown, quilted petticoat, apron
Dau ELINOR MOUNT and son THOMAS - 30 gallon still & utensils
Son FREDRICK FULKERSON and dau MARY FULKERSON - residue of est
Exr: Son ABRAM FULKERSON (Note: son THOMAS was CHAMBERS)
Wits: Notty Jordan, Elizabeth Jordan, Leven Ellis

A:045 - JACOB CHRISTMAN of Reedy Creek - 1 Apr 1779 - Aug 1785
Eldest sons JOHN & JACOB - 10 pds less than remainder of ch
Wife BARBARA - plantation dw, bedding, large iron pott, horse & side saddle, best cow, spinning wheel, two sheep, pewter, etc
Other ch: DANIEL, BALSHASER, JOHN, GEORGE, ABRAHAM, JOSEPH, HENRICK, DAVID, CATHERINE, BARBARA, ELIZABETH, REBECCA, and ANNA MARIA - share and share alike
Exrs: Friend Jacob Drog, son JACOB CHRISTMAN
Wits: John Matthew Mucksh, Ludwig Meining

A:046 - JOHN COFFEE - 19 July 1783 - Prb May 1785
Ch: MICHAEL COFFEE, ELIZABETH MILFORD, NANCY BELL, JOHN COFFEE, SOPHIA BAINES, SARAH BEACH, MARY DIMON, & REBECCAH NORMAN - one shilling each
Son THOMAS COFFEE - 220 ac tract of land whereon I now live
Son THOMAS, daus MARGARET & LUCY COFFEE - residue of estate
Exrs: Sons JOHN COFFEE, THOMAS COFFEE
Wits: Charles Bruce, David Peoples, Hubbard Peeples

A:047 - CHARLES CURTIS - 3 Apr 1781 - Prb Aug 1781
JOHN MORTON - 248 ac tract of land in Spotsylvania County, Va
Son PETER CURTIS - 400 ac of land on south side Dan River
Gr sons GEORGE MORRIS & CURTIS MORRIS - 240 ac adj above land
Wife MARGREY - one negro fellow Isaac, remainder of estate
Daus NANCY JOHNSON & JUDY MORRIS - slave Isaac at decease of wife
My other children - one shilling each
Exrs: Wife MARGREY CURTIS, George Johnson
Wits: George Peay, Moses Lillard, William Lovil

A:048 - JAREMIER CROWDER - 28 Jan 1795 - Prb Feb 1795
Son ISACK - one black colt
Wife MARTHY - all my estate during widowhood
Ch: SARY PRINCTHIT, FANNY WILSON CROWDER, ELIZABETH CROWDER, PATSY CROWDER, JOHN CROWDER, WILLIAM (? blot) CROWDER, ANDERSON CROWDER, and JAREMIER CROWDER
Son PLEASANT CROWDER - five shillings
Exrs: Wife MARTHY CROWDER, son-in-law JOSEPH PRICHET
Wits: David Gilliam, William Crowder

A:049 - JAMES CUNNINGHAM - 24 Sept 1791 - No probate date
Sons JEREMIAH, MATHEW, and dau ISEBEL CUNNINGHAM - land to boys and all furniture, cattle, hogs, sheep divided equally
Son WILLIAM and dau ELIZABETH BURNEY - each five shillings
Exrs: Sons JEREMIAH CUNNINGHAM, MATHEW CUNNINGHAM
Wits: Drury Peeples, Eder. Long

A:050 - ANTHONY COBLE - 24 May 1790 - Prb Nov 1793
Son GEORGE COBLE - 150 ac where I live on head springs of Bever Creek as described in deed dated 10 May 1788
Son LUDWICH - 150 ac tract north of the home tract
Son DAVID - 150 ac south of home tract on Shockles Creek
Daus: BARBARA GLAS, LISABETH SMITH, EVE GLAS, MOLLY SHUTTERLING, CHARITY GRAVES, and MARY GRAVES - thirty pounds
Wife - to receive payments from GEORGE, LUDWICH, & DAVID
Youngest dau CATARENA CORTNER - 30 pds value in moveables
Exr: Son JOHN COBLE
Wits: George Cortner, Jacob Coble, David Coble

A:051 - THOMAS CHARLES CRAFT - 27 Oct 1794 - Prb Feb 1795
Wife CHARLOTTE - one third part of land & movable estate
Son JOHN CHARLES CRAFT - remainder of land
My seven ch: MARRY, JOHN, SARAH, NELLE, REBECKA, LYDIA, and GEAN CHARLES CRAFT - divide remaining estate
Negro girl Betty to be sold
Exrs: Wife CHARLOTTE CRAFT, son JOHN CHARLES CRAFT
Wits: Robert Donnell, James Weatherly, Thomas Johnson

A:052 - ALIJAH COFFIN - 20 July 1793 - Prb Nov 1793
Wife - Sorrel colt, saddle & bridle, kitchen & household furn
Dau MARY - all lands and estate my father may leave me
ALIJAH COFFIN (son of bro LIBSON) - land whereon I live, at 19
WILLIAM COFFIN (son of bro WILLIAM) - land if ALIJAH dies
My seven bros: LIBIN, WILLIAM, SAMUEL, BARNABAS, MATTHEW, BETHUEL, and LEVI
Daus PRISCILLA and MARY - personal estate, MARY at age 18
Exrs: Brother MATTHEW COFFIN, friend Allen Unthank
Proved by Jacob Boyers, John Howel, and Richard Williams

A:053 - BENJAMIN COFFIN - 1 Dec 1789 - Prb May 1790
Wife ELIZABETH - use & profit of half my estate
Son AARON - estate I inherited from my father on Nantucket in New England, also what descended from my grandfather, BATHALDER HUSSEY at Winter Harbour
Son ADAM - my estate in N. C. after decease of his mother
Dau ELIZABETH BARNARD - one pot, one skillet, one pewter plate
Dau PHEBE COFFIN - to have support by ADAM if he remains single
Dau RACHEL COFFIN - to have support by ADAM until she marries
Exrs: Wife ELIZABETH COFFIN, son AARON COFFIN
Wits: Daniel Worth, James Dick, Job Worth

A:054 - JAMES CALHOUN - 20 Jan 1795 - Prb Feb 1795
Wife JINNET - maintenance, bedding, horse & saddle, stock
Son JOHN JONSTONE CALHOUN - land on which I live
Son SAMUEL - to be paid 15 pounds by John J.
Dar Elsaman - 20 ac of land on Hogans Creek

Son JAMES - the young mair
Ch: ELIZABETH CALHOUN, MARY CALHOUN, ANN CALHOUN, ROBERT CALHOUN, SARAH CALHOUN, ELSEERMAN CALHOUN, NANCY CALHOUN - remainder
Exrs: Son JOHN JONSTONE CALHOUN, son SAMUEL CALHOUN
Wits: Abner Bowen, Samuel Calhoun

A:055 - DAVID COOPER - 20 June 1791 - Prb May 1792
Wife - to have command of my estate until children are raised; then a third and one negro woman
Son JOHN - a mare colt Dau ANA - two cows and calves
Sons: JOHN, DAVID, THOMAS, and WILLIAM - whole of my lands
Exrs: Wife and son JOHN COOPER. No witnesses

A:056 - HANCE CLARK - __ Mar 17__ - Prb May 1791
Wife MARY - all my lands, good, and chattels
Daus ANNE, MARY, CATHORINE, and JEAN CLARK - each 20 sh, Bible
Exrs: Wife MARY CLARK, John Stuart
Wits: James McBride, "& somebody else"

A:057 - WILLIAM CHARLES - 4 Apr 1796 - Prb May 1796
Sons WILLIAM & SOLOMAN - each a horse worth 14 pounds
Daus SARAH, MARY, ANNA, and LEAH - bed & furniture, 14 pds each
Wife LEAH - plantation whereon I live during widowhood
Eight children: REUBEN, ISAAC, WILLIAM, SOLOMAN, SARAH, MARY, ANNA, & LEAH - proceeds of estate at end of widowhood of wife
Exrs: Wife LEAH CHARLES, Elijah Charles
Wits: Matthew Coffin, Elijah Charles, Tarlton Johnson

A:058 - JOHN PHILIP CLAPP - 8 Sept 1797 - Prb Nov 1798
Eldest son VALENTINE - 200 ac on the Alamance where he lives
Son ADAM - 412 ac on waters of Rock fork (?), ten shillings
Sons JOHN & LUDDERWICK - land on which each lives
Ch of dau BARBARY SWING, dec'd, former wife of MATHIAS SWING - one negro woman named Jenny, five shillings each
Dau CHRISTINA, w/o PHILLIP ALBRIGHT - negro boy Franck, 10 sh
Dau MOLLY, w/o CONRAD HAGNEY - tract on which they live, 10 sh
Dau CATHERINE, w/o ADAM BROWN - land where Holoman Brown lives
Dau EVA, w/o EPHRAIM BURROW - negro girl named Nancy, 10 sh
Wife BARBARY - remaining lands, negroes, stock, furniture, etc
Wits: Samuel Lindsay, John Job, Junr., John Cooper

A:059 - WILLIAM COFFIN - 4 May 1796 - Prb Nov 1796
Wife ELIZABETH - use & profit of plantation whereon I live until son WILLIAM becomes 21; then half
Son WILLIAM - home plantation and land bought of William Britton
Son ELIHU - land bought of John Hunt on Brush Creek
Dau ESTHER COFFIN - feather bed & furniture, half of pewter, half of chairs, a good walnut chest, a good suit of clothes incl bever hat, horse & saddle, etc - at the age of 18
Dau ACHSA - feather bed & furniture, 10 pounds in money
Sons VESTAL, NATHAN, & JOB - land bought from Thomas Hunt, land bought of Bethuel Coffin, & land bought of Robert Gilbreath
Sons WILLIAM & ELIHU - remaining lands, desk, book case, books
Exrs: Brother BARNABAS COFFIN, Brother MATTHEW COFFIN
Wits: None. Proved by William Starbuck, Samuel Coffin, Jacob Rogers, and Bethuel Coffin

A:060 - THOMAS CRANOR - 5 Apr 1795 - Prb May 1796
Wife HANNAH - all my estate as long as she remains my widow
Son JOSEPH - gun left to me by my father
Son MOSES - gun now at Henry Ford's. All my children.
Exr: Brother MOSES CRANOR
Wits: Winsmore Houren, Matthew Macy, Benjamin Trotter

A:061 - JOHN CLARK - 6 Sept 1790 - Prb Nov 1790
Wife MARY - one half of my possessions in this country
Brother CHARLES CLARK - five shillings
Nephew JOHN CLARK, here with me at this time - remaining half of my estate, also my right and claim in Ireland
Exrs: Andrew Wilson, William Scott
Wits: Sarah Ried, Hannah Denny

A:062 - ABRAHAM COOK - 29 Apr 1792 - Prb Feb 1793
Daus RACHEL JESOP and MARY STEPHENS - five shillings
Youngest daus SARAH & RUTH COOK - all the household goods, stock, their Mother's clothing
Son ISAAC - 131 ac on SW of my tract on Deep River
Son JOHN - 131 ac tract of land adj ISAAC
Son ABRAHAM - tract adj his brothers on the north, my gray horse
Son NATHAN - land whereon I live, my sorrel horse
Exrs: Sons ISAAC COOK, ABRAHAM COOK
Wits: Enoch Macy, Daniel Baldwin, James Thornburg

A:063 - SAMUEL COFFIN - 4 Jan 1799 - Prb May 1799
Wife MARY - use of plantation for 4 years if she remains my widow; then half to be divided between:
Sons JOHN, SAMUEL, DAVID, THOMAS, JETHRO, and WILLIAM COFFIN
Dau MARY - feather bed, cow & calf, looking glass, pewter, etc
Dau PRISCILLA - feather bed. Dau LYDIA - ten shillings
Daus DEBORAH STARBUCK, MARY & PRISCILLA COFFIN - remainder of household goods
Exrs: Brother BARNABAS COFFIN, MATTHEW COFFIN
Wits: Jesse Standley, Abel Coffin, John Stuart

A:064 - JOSHUA COFFEE - 1 Sept 1797 - Prb Feb 1798
Son JOHN - choice of five slaves being sold to procure land
Wife ELIZABETH - land for life; then land goes to JOHN
"On Mr. HARRIS, my son-in-law, returning such property to my estate as he has received, the whole estate to be divided between my loving wife ELIZABETH and my two children JOHN COFFEE and POLLY HARRIS...at decease of wife property to be shared by JOHN COFFEE and POLLY HARRIS"
Exrs: Wife ELIZABETH COFFEE, son JOHN COFFEE

A:065 - LUDWICK COBLE, Planter - 17 May 1809 - Prb Aug 1809
Wife EVA - full power of my possessions during widowhood; then
Sons JOHN and ELY - share the estate
Daus SARAH, ANNE, SOPHIA MAY - good horse when of age, furniture
Son DAVID and dau MARY CLAP - share in division of residue when other ch have received as much as they have already received
Exrs: Wife EVA COBLE, son JOHN COBLE
Wits: George Cobble, William Corsbie

A:066 - NATHANIEL CLARK - 15 Nov 1802 - Prb Feb 1803
Wife ANN - my estate both rayle & personally, during widowhood
All my children - proceeds of sale at decease of wife
Exr: Wife ANN CLARK
Wits: Justain Knott, Soloman Warren, Nancy Knott

A:067 - THOMAS CUMMONS - 2 Sept 1808 - Prb Feb 1816
Daus RACHEL & ANNY - 230 ac on Rock Creek, negro boy Auston, negro girl Amice and her two ch: Sally and Thankful
Dau JANE & her children - 200 silver dollars
Dau MARGARETHA - negro boy named Isac
Dau MARY - 150 silver dollars
Step-dau BATCEY BELL - forty silver dollars
Sons ROBERT & SAMUEL - remaining part of property
Exrs: Sons ROBERT CUMMONS, SAMUEL CUMMONS
Wits: Robert Low, John Cummons

A:068 - HENRY COMPLIN - 22 Feb 1805 - Prb Aug 1805
Wife REBEKAH - all my estate during widowhood
Eldest son JAMES - 2 pds & no more as I have given him
Daus DOLLY WILLIAMS and SOPHIA WILLIAMS - five shillings
Sons HENRY & HOOPER - tract whereon I live
Daus BRITTAIN COMPLIN & ANNANETTE COMPLIN - each 5 sh & no more
Exr: Wife REBECKAH COMPLIN
Wits: George Swain, James Wilson

A:069 - TOBIAS CLAPP, Senr. - 23 Jan 1800 - Prb Feb 1800
Son DANIEL - 137 ac where he lives & 65 ac from adj tract
Son VALENTINE - 200 ac of land on which he lives
Son PHILIP - 114 ac on which he lives; as I value the land at $2 an ac, remainder of his inheritance be made up to him in money
Wife CHRISTINA - third of remainder of land, 1 heifer, 1 steer, 1 horse, 12 hogs, 3 beds, spinning wheel, plough & geers for two horses, etc; and negro Anny & her child Ishmel
Son TOBIAS - $400 to make up for land I didn't give him
Daus ELIZABETH, MARGARET, MAGDELIN, & BARBERY - $400 each
Sons GEORGE & ISAAC - remaining land bought of Osbon, spring colt and stock of bees
Remainder of slaves valued as follows: Dick - $200, Frank - $300, Bill - $200, Nelly - $200
Exrs: Son-in-law HENRY KECK, friend Adam Starr
Wits: Adam Starr, Jacob Grisson

A:070 - MARY CAMPBELL - 4 July 1805 - Prb Feb 1806
Gr son JAMES (son of ARCHIBALD CAMPBELL) - my gold watch
Gr dau POLLY (dau of JAMES CAMPBELL) - suit of my best wearing clothes, half of my cupboard furniture, two cows and calves
Niece SARAH COVEY - half of cupboard furniture, all my geese
John Thorpe (son of Aaron) - $20, still I bought with his father
Sons ARCHIBALD & JAMES - each a fourth of residue of estate
Nephew EDWARD EDWARDS - fourth; also Leven Covey - fourth
Exrs: Leven Covey, Abraham Peeples
Wits: J. Moore, Richard Bortan

A:071 - THOMAS COOK - 1 Feb 1805 - Prb May 1805

Wife MARY - use of plantation, farm tools, 2 mares, 2 cows & calves; but if she marries, 1 bed and her wearing clothes
Sons THOMAS & JOSEPH - ten dollars
Son JOHN - blacksmith tools, horse, feather bed & furniture
Son JACOB - mare called Polla
Son WILLIAM - two year old colt and fifty dollars
Sons TEMRI, ISAAC & NATHAN - estate at dec or remar of wife
Dau SARAH STUART - $10. Gr dau ELIZABETH COOK - bed & furn
Exrs: Sons JOSEPH & THOMAS COOK
Wits: Barnabas Coffin, John Stuart, Jr., Jonathan Mills

A:072 - JEAN CRISWELL - 7 Oct 1794 - Prb Feb 1801
Eldest dau MARGARET WORK - five shillings
Eldest son JAMES, youngest son WILLIAM, youngest dau MARY - each one third of all my estate
Exrs: Sons JAMES & WILLIAM CRISWELL & dau MARY CRISWELL
Wits: John Larkins, John Gilchrist

A:073 - SARAH CRANOR - 15 July 1797 - Prb May 1801
Gr son JOSHUA (son of MOSES CRANOR) - one pewter dish
Son MOSES - my Bible, one pint tankard, one dollar
Gr son JOHN - one cow and one bed
Gr daus PRUDENCE & PHEBE - half gal pewter bason, bed & furn
Gr son JOSEPH LISTOR & gr dau MARY LISTER - cow, cotton cards
Dau ELIZABETH FORD - Saddle, half gallon bason
Gr dau PRUDENCE FORD - my chest, counterpain, gallon pot
Son THOMAS CRANOR'S estate - $1 & my account against the estate
Gr Sons WILLIAM, MOSES & THOMAS FORD - rest of stock & furniture
Exr: Son-in-law HENRY FORD
Wits: Winsmore Houren, Sarah Houren, Mary Hemry ?

A:074 - FRANCIS CUMMINS - 30 Oct 1792 - Prb Feb 1800
Wife JANE - estate dw to bring up & school my children
Daus ANN, MARTHA, & THANKFUL CUMMINS - each $55 value, to consist of Horse & saddle valued at $25, bed and furniture
Sons THOMAS & ELIJA - all my land divided between them
Exrs: Jeane Cummins, John Fowler, Thomas Black

A:075 - PARIS CHIPMAN - 30 Jan 1797 - Prb May 1801
Wife MARGARET - full privilege of house & land for life, $100
Sons JOHN & PARIS - land called Farlow, each third of estate
Daus HANNAH HORNEY & MARY HORNEY - divide one third of estate
Exrs: Sons JOHN & PARIS CHIPMAN
Wits: Obadiah Harris, Manlove Wheeler, Henry Wheeler

A:076 - WILLIAM COFFIN - 31 July 1803 - Prb Nov 1803
Son LIBIN - thirty pounds of the currency of North Carolina
Son WILLIAM - five shillings
Heirs of son SAMUEL - forty pounds to be divided among them
Sons BARNABAS (35 pds) and MATTHEW (90)
Son BETHUEL - 25 pds, land contract valid if fulfilled
Son LEVI - tract from Michel Mason, clock, great Bible
Gr dau PRISCILLA COFFIN (dau of ALIJAH) - 150 pounds
Son LIBIN'S son ALIJAH

Dau DEBORAH TERRELL - 10 shillings with what I have given her
Gr son LIBIN HUNT & gr dau MIRIAM HUNT - 10 pounds in money
Exrs: Sons BARNABAS COFFIN & MATTHEW COFFIN
Wits: Ann Hodgson, Thomas White

A:077 - CLAIBORN CURTIS - 16 Sept 1803 - Prb Nov 1803
Wife SARAH - my whole estate
Exr: Wife SARAH CURTIS
Wits: Joshua Underwood, James Smith, Mary Smith

A:078 - JOHN COE - 23 Oct 1807 - Prb Nov 1807
Daus MARY AYDELETT, NANCY CAUSEY, HANNAH GAMBLE - each 40 sh
Dau HULDAH COE - bed, cow & calf, saddle, cotton & flax wheels
Wife SARAH - land whereon I live, household goods, riding gear
Sons AVERY & JOSEPH - $1,108 owed by Thomas Webb, $100 each
Son JOHN - $60
Exrs: Wife SARAH COE, son JOHN COE, Junr.
Wits: James Galbrath - Proved in Court by Andrew McGee

A:079 - GEORGE CUMMINS - 9 Dec 1805 - Prb Feb 1808
Wife SARAH - 250 ac on Cumberland on waters of Half Pone Creek
Son JOSEPH - 250 ac being on each side my dwelling house and on both sides Haw River betw Thomas Cummins & Hugh Cummins
Heirs of son JOHN, son THOMAS, son GEORGE, dau ELISABETH, son JAMES, dau SARAH, dau MATHEW, son CHARLES, son HUGH - 5 sh ea
Exrs: Wife SARAH CUMMINS, son JOSEPH CUMMINS
Wits: Justain Knott, William Anthony, Elizabeth Cummins

A:080 - MARY COVEY, widow, of Rowan Co - 20 June 1799 - Feb 1807
Nowel Sapp - my part of the waggon
Step-dau SARAH SAPP - chest, fourth of my wearing apparel
Sister ELIZABETH THARP - remainder of my wearing apparel
Children of my brothers & sisters - remainder of my estate
Exrs: Brothers MARTIN PEGG, VALENTINE PEGG
Wits: Abel Knight Ye third, Samuel Couch

A:081 - JOHN CHAMBERS - 8 Apr 1788 - Prb May 1800
Wife ELIZABETH - estate for life, negro woman Ails, 1 of her ch
Son-in-law ANDREW WILSON - twenty shillings
Gr ch by dau AUGNESS, dec'd: DANIEL, ROBERT & CHARLES WILSON-60 pd
Dau JENNET RANKIN - slave Ails at decease of her mother
Son-in-law WILLIAM RANKIN, husb of JENNET - remainder of estate
Exrs: Son-in-law WILLIAM RANKIN, friend William Scott
Wits: John Anderson, John Donnell, William Scott

A:082 - JEAN CALHOUN - 10 June 1804 - Prb May 1805
Daus ELIZABETH FLEMON, MARY WHEATLEY, ANN HOLIDAY, SARAH LOVE, ALSE THORPE, NANCY READ - all my wearing clothes
Son JOHN - five shillings
Son SAMUEL - bed, stone jug, for paying my burial expenses
Son ROBERT - five shillings
Gr dau EASTER CALHOUN - bed, bolster pillows, 5 sheets, 2 quilts, four head of cattle, herd of sheep, pewter plates & spoons
Exr: Benjamin Barham
Wits: Charles Barham, Nathan Barham

A:083 - BARNABAS COFFIN - 11 Nov 1814 - Prb Aug 1815
Wife PHEBE - use of home plantation during widowhood
Son JOSEPH - $100, third of my books
Son ABEL - 4 ac & house bought from Joseph Mills, my four books of Arts science
Son BARNABAS - $200, what he has received, third of my books
Son STEPHEN - $300, third of books, use of my large Bible and other family journals, that wagon he took to western country
Daus HULDAH STANLEY, PHEBE HUNT, ELISEBETH HUNT - $150
Dau PRISCILLA COFFIN - feather bed, table, chest, trunk, $130
Gr sons: BARNABAS HUNT, BARNABAS COFFIN, BARNABAS STANLEY - $1
Son-in-law JESSE STANLEY - all the notes I have on him
Sister DEBORAH TERRELL - may occupy a room at my house
Exrs: Brother BETHUEL COFFIN, sons JOSEPH & ABEL COFFIN
Wit: Matthew Starbuck

A:084 - SIMON CHRISTOPHER, late of Franklin Co., Va. At this time at the house of my friend, Aleayer Kersey
Exr (not named) to take all from wife NANCY and son JANETT to pay doctor's bill and debt to Walker Carter & Robert Coaling.
Wits: none; Prb Feb 1812

A:085 - THOMAS CUMMINS - 1 Aug 1813 - Prb Nov 1813
Wife ELIZABETH - plantation & all my lands, but if she remarries
Sister ANN MAYBEN - my part of books Uncle THOMAS CUMMINS left to her and me
Children of my bros & sisters - land sold and divided
Exrs: Friend David Mayben, Wife ELIZABETH CUMMINS
Wit: James Millis, James Ozment, Joel Sillivan

A:086 - HENRY CAPP - 13 Dec 1809 - Prb May 1812
Wife CATRANENA - $200, horse & saddle, 2 cows, bed, etc
Daus ELIZABETH, DONLEY, MAGDALINA - each $200
Son JOHN - $40 to balance the land given to other sons
Dau MARGARETHA - $200
Sons HENRY & FALTY - have received $200 in land
Dau BARBARA and dau HAINES - each $200
Son JACOB - 150 ac on south side of plantation
Exrs: Son JOHN CAPP, Daniel Whitsel
Wits: John Chrisman, Fatty Waggoner

A:087 - JOHN COBLE - 3 May 1813 - Prb Nov 1815
Son MARTIN - 125 ac adj his land, wagon, cow, bed & furniture
Dau MARY - balance of tract I live on, two cows
Exrs: Son MARTIN COBLE, son-in-law ELISHA BENNETT
Wits: Jonathan Hadley, Andrew Shatterly

A:-88 - JAMES DENNY - 26 Sept 1774 - Prb Nov 1774
Wife MARY - negro Tom, negro Dina at my father's death, use of plantation until sons JAMES & WILLIAM come of age - dw
Exrs: Wife MARY DENNY, Alexander Caldwell, William Gravely
Wits: Abraham Makellhatten, Alexander Breden, James Wilson

A:089 - PHILEMON DEATHERAGE - 24 Jan 1778 - Prb May 1778
Wife ELIZABETH - third part of my real & personal estate; rest to be divided equally between my children:

GEORGE, SARAH, BIRD, ACHILLIS, SOLOMAN, JAMES, MARY - all minors
Boy John Davis, alias John Hand, now bound to me - same education as my children
If any of my sons shall misbehave and not be governed by my mother, he shall be bound out to learn a trade until age of 20
Exrs: Brother GEORGE DEATHERAGE, son GEORGE DEATHERAGE, friend Joshua Smith, James Joyce
Trustees: Friends Alexander Martin, Charles Galloway
Wits: James Cook, Alexander Smith, James Galloway

A:090 - THOMAS DAVIS - 16 Mar 1780
Wife HEPZIBAH - all my estate during her widowhood; then to:
Daus DEBORAH, LYDIA, and ELIZABETH
Sons JOHN, TRISTRAM, PETER & THOMAS
Exr: Wife HEPZIBAH DAVIS
Wits: Nathaniel Macy, Paul Macy, William Coffin
"For probate see Minute Docket No. 2, page 27"

A:091 - THOMAS DENNIS - 24 June 1774 - Prb Feb 1775
Gr son JOHN, s/o EDWARD DENNIS, dec'd - 100 pds when of age
Wife SARAH - in partnership with son THOMAS - all my estate
Exr: Son THOMAS DAVIS

A:092 - DANIEL DAUGHERTY - 28 Aug 1786 - No prb
Wife ELIZABETH - maintenance by the estate and her room
Wife & dau HANNAH - each a horse, all my cows except two
Son JOHN - 8 pds, the steers, bulls & hogs, use of the house
Sons WILLIAM & DANIEL - two cows, remainder of furniture
Son JAMES - 1 sh sterling, repairs of house and plantation
Exrs: Sons WILLIAM & DANIEL DAUGHERTY
Wits: Adam Walker, Daniel Dillon, Jr., Joseph Thornbrough, Jr.

A:093 - ROBERT DWIGGINS - 6 Feb 1789 - Prb May 1789
Wife LIDIA - all estate except 400 ac bought of Jean Netherly
Ch: SARAH, ELIZABETH, DANIEL, ANN, ROBERT, JOSEPH & MARY - bond against William Dodson be used for their schooling
Son JOHN - 200 ac of land
Son JAMES - 200 ac of land at 21
Son SAMUEL - remainder of land at his mother's death
Exr: Son JOHN DWIGGINS
Wits: Edward Bowman, John Dwiggens, James Dwiggins

A:094 - JAMES DENNY - 10 Dec 1790 - Prb Feb 1795
Married ch: MAY DUCK, ANN BASS, MARYANNE PEASLEY, GEORGE, JANE HAMILTON, AGNESS & ELIZABETH DONNELL, & JAMES DENNY - $1 each
Son JAMES - loan of 5 pds without interest for eight years; then the 5 pds be paid to gr son JAMES, son of GEORGE DENNY
Dau HANNAH - her horse & saddle, 2 cows, bed, 6 sheep, pewter
Wife AGNES & son WILLIAM - equal interest in remainder of estate
Exrs: Son WILLIAM DENNY, John Donnell
Wits: John Rankin, Charles Wheeler, Joseph McGanghy

A:095 - FREDERICH DEAN - 15 Mar 1798 - Prb May 1798
Wife FRANCES - all my estate; child's part if she remarries
Sons THOMAS & SOLOMAN - five shillings
Daus MARY & ELIZABETH - five shillings

Unmarried daus: SARAH, FRANCES, REBEKAH, NANSEE, CHARITY, and JEAN DEAN - each at time of marriage feather bed & furniture, Cow & calf, 3 pd 17 sh worth of my household furniture
Sons ISAAC & FREDERICH - home place at wife's decease (minors)
Exrs: Wife FRANCES DEAN, son-in-law RICHARD BOURMAN
Wits: Hezekiah Starbuck, William Gray, James Whicker

A:096 - ABRAM DUFF - 6 Mar 1789? - Prb May 1791
Wife MARY - Bay mare, her own saddle, 2 beds, best milch cow, etc
ABRAM DUFF, son of bro SAMUEL - cow or that much in money
Bros JAMES, WILLIAM, SAMUEL, JOHN & ROBERT - rest of estate
Exrs: Bro WILLIAM DUFF, father SAMUEL DUFF
Wits: Ralph Gorrel, Thomas Brown, Ann Kerr

A:097 - PETER DILLON - 15 May 1796 - Prb Aug 1796
Daniel Dillon, Jr. - riding horse, saddle & bridle, my clothes
Wife CHARITY - home place and remainder of my estate
Exrs: Wife CHARITY DILLON & Daniel Dillon, Junr
Wits: Strangman Stanly, Beroni Mills

A:098 - PETER DICKS - 13 Dec 1795 - Prb Nov 1796
Son JAMES - land east of Davis Creek
Gr son WILLIAM DICKS - land adj Lamb, Coffin & John Beal
Wife ELIZABETH - remainder of my land
Gr son PETER DICKS - land at decease of wife, desk, clock
Exrs: Son JAMES DICKS, Grandson PETER DICKS
Wits: Salathiel Stone, Zachariah Dicks

A:099 - ROBERT DOAK - 24 Sept 1796 - Prb Nov 1796
Wife HANNAH - home plantation, negro girl Sisley, mare, beds, dw
Son JOHN - 150 ac bought of James McCuiston, negro Ned, bed
Son JAMES - 150 ac, negro boy Jim, horse, bed & furniture
Son ROBERT - 100 ac on the Alamance, negro Jonas, bed & furn
Son WILLIAM - 100 ac on the Alamance, negro Mol, one colt
Dau HANNAH - 1st child of Mol, filly & saddle, bed, $50
Dau ELISEBETH - 2nd child of Mol, filly & saddle, bed, $50
Son-in-law ROBERT GORRELL
Son DANIEL - property of wife at end of widowhood
Dau MARY DOAK - negro girl Luce, bed & furniture, saddle, $50
Exrs: John Gillaspie, John Doak, wife HANNAH DOAK
Wits: William Doak, James Doak, Anne Doak

A:100 - WILLIAM DENNIS - 20 Feb 1791 - Prb May 1791
Sons-in-law: OBEDIAH CALLOWAY, JONATHAN CALLOWAY & MATHIAS DENNIS - 75 ac bought of James Barnum on Mans Fork
Wife - above mentioned land and home plantation during widowh
Sons WILLIAM & DANIEL - remainder of my lands
Youngest ch: LEAH, WILLIAM, DANIEL, LEVINAH - home plantation
Wits: Mathew Brown, William Rayl, Aaron Mendenhall

A:101 - PATRICK DIAMOND - 24 Oct 1790
Wife SARAH - third of estate, bound ch named SARAH MEDLIN
Son JOHN - five shillings starling
John Morrison - five shillings starling
Son STUART - third of personal estate
William Pritchett - five shillings starling

Dau MARY DIAMOND - five shillings starling
Son WILLIAM - two-thirds of land; all at wife's dec, personal est
Exrs: Sons STUART & WILLIAM DIAMOND
Wits: Valentine Mileham, Walter Mileham
"See Minute Docket No. 2, page 112" (for probate)

A:0102 - ROBERT DAUGHERTY - 15 Feb 1804 - Prb May 1804?
Samuel Stewart - land I bought from him
WILLIAM DAUGHERTY, SAMUEL DAUGHERTY, and Holdeberry - tract on Spring Creek in Wilson County, State of Tennessee
Brother SAMUEL - lands of my father's estate
Mother VAN DAUGHERTY - one hundred dollars
Sister SUZAN FLACK - Sixty dollars
Brother JOHN DAUGHERTY - my saddle
Sister BETSEY DAUGHERTY - remainder of my property
Exr: Brother JOHN DAUGHERTY
Wits: John Starrett, John Alcorn, Benjamin Wilson

A:0103 - WILLIAM DOAK - 1 Sept 1807 - Prb Nov 1807
Wife ANN - 120 ac of plantation during widowhood, bed, mare,saddle
Youngest sons RODDY, JOSIAH & JONATHAN - divide the negroes
Son JOHN - ten dollars
Son WILLIAM - 200 ac bought of Robert Anderson, sorrel mare, saddle, 2 cows, bed & furniture
Son ROBERT - 200 ac, bay colt & saddle, bed & furniture, 2 cows
Son RODDY - 100 ac, bay colt & saddle, bed & furniture, 2 cows
Son JOSIAH - 100 ac, saddle, bed & furniture, 2 cows
Son JONATHAN - plantation from his mother, saddle, bed & furniture
Dau MARY - 50 pds hard money, horse & saddle, bed, 2 cows
Dau MARTHA - 50 pds, horse & saddle, 2 cows, bed & furniture
Roddy Hannah's son Bill - $3, still wagon, blacksmith tools
Exrs: Wife ANN DOAK, son WILLIAM DOAK, Robert Hannah, Sr.
Wits: Roddy Hannah, Sr., John Alexander

A:0104 - JOHN DUNLAP - 27 Jan 1794 - Prb Aug 1805
Son JOHN - 106 ac, working tools, mare, saddle, my wearing clothes
Dau MARGARET DUNLAP - household furniture, 100 pds in bonds on Col. John Gillaspie and his son Daniel Gillaspie
Son ROBERT - 106 ac with improvements, where I live
Gr dau MARY ARMFIELD - one cow
Exrs: John Armfield, Daniel Gillaspie, Margaret Duniap

A:0105 - DANIEL DILLON - 20 Aug 1805 - Prb Feb 1806
Youngest son ISAAC - balance of old survey on Reedy Fork, land on south side of Beaver Creek
Gr daus SARAH & ELIZABETH WALLACE - ten dollars
All my children: MARTHA, NATHAN, WILLIAM, PETER, JESSE, DANIEL, PATIENCE, & ISAAC DILLON - share remaining property
Exrs: Sons NATHAN & PETER DILLON
Wits: Silvanis Gardner, Jonathan Hodgson, William Baruch

A:0106 - ELISEBETH DONNELL - 5 Jan 1802 - Prb Feb 1802
Brother THOMAS DONNELL - all my cattle
Sister MARY DONNELL - half of certain money owed me, my bed, etc
Brother SAMUEL DONNELL - half of money, divide my books with MARY
Bro-in-law JAMES DENNY - money owed by George Biner, walnut chairs

Exr: Brother-in-law JAMES DENNY
Wits: Thomas Denny, John Donnell

A:0107 - CHARLES DEER - 30 Apr 1811 - Prb Aug 1811
Son BRADLEY - South end of plantation, share negro Phil with wf
Wife ELISEBETH - 2/3 of land, dwelling house, negro Vilot
Son REUBIN - his horse & saddle, bed & furniture, black colt
Dau FANNIE NORMAN - bed & furniture
Gr son CHARLES (s/o BRADLEY & CATHERINE) - bed & furniture
Gr sons JOSEPH, HINUN & CHARLES NORMAN (sons of JOHN & FANNIE)
Exrs: Sons BRADLEY & REUBIN DEER, John Norman
Wits: William Brown, Mathew Brown

A:0108 - JAMES DOAK - 8 Dec 1805 - Prb Feb 1806
My ch: ALEXANDER MCKEEN & MARY his wife, THOMAS BLAIR & ELEANOR his wife, JOHN DOAK, MARTHA DOAK, WILLIAM F. DOAK, ROBERT DOAK, & JAMES W. DOAK - my land in Tenn on west bank of Stones River
Wife MARY - to have first choice of the land
Exr: Wife MARY DOAK, son JOHN DOAK
Wits: William Tease?, John Moore

A:0109 - WILLIAM DICK - 22 Jan 1810 - Prb Nov 1810
Wife REBECCA - use of plantation, moveable effects, live stock
Gr son WILLIAM DICK (son of JAMES) - part of plantation adj Hance McLaine, the courthouse, and Obediah
Son SAMUEL - $500 note I have on Obediah
Son THOMAS - the plantation whereon I live adj William Dick, Smith Moore, widow Gibson & widow Hutchinson
Sons JAMES, THOMAS & OBEDIAH - proceeds from sale, residue
Gr dau POLLY DICK (son of JOHN) - $100
Exrs: Sons JAMES DICK, THOMAS DICK
Wits: Walter McCuiston, Tho. Dyakill, Robert McCuiston

A:0110 - CHARITY DILLON, Widow of PETER DILLON - 28 Sept 1797
Son BENONY MILLS - all my lands, goods, & chattels
Gr dau CHARITY MILLS - six pewter plates
Exr: Son BENONY MILLS Prb Nov 1811
Wits: Strangman Stanley, Hugh Hodson, Jesse Stanley

A:0111 - GEORGE DENNY - 29 Feb 1816 - Prb May 1816
Wife REBECCAH - household goods
Oldest sons: JAMES, THOMAS, GEORGE & WILLIAM - one dollar each
Daus MARY ANN WILSON, PEGGY DENNY - one dollar each
Youngest son ALVAN - balance of my land
Exrs: Wife REBECAH DENNY
Wits: Robert Donnell, William Denny

A:0112 - ROBERT ERVIN - 24 Feb 1796 - Prb May 1796
Wife MARY - all moveable property
Sons SAMUEL & JAMES - land whereon I live, one bay horse
Son GEORGE - ten pounds in money
Exr: Wife MARY ERVIN, William Montgomery
Wits: Richard Hodson, Rebeccah Montgomery

A:0113 - ABRAHAM ENDSLEY - 27 June 1808 - Prb Feb 1818
Wife SARAH - home, Roan spotted mare, one spotted cow, bed and

furniture, pewter, delph ware knives & forks, Psalm book, etc
Son SAMUEL - 180 ac on south side of plantation, provided he distills the brandy in a diligent and lawful manner
Son JOHN - 180 ac in middle of the tract, family Bible
Son ABRAHAM - 180 ac north of plantation, $12 for his schooling
Dau AYDS NELSON - one dollar
Dau HANNAH MCGEE - eight dollars
Dau SARAH ENDSLEY - $8, bed & furniture, third of pewter, cow
Dau MAHALA ENDSLEY - $40 when she comes of age, $12 for schooling
Dau ELISEBETH ENDSLEY - eight dollars
Exrs: Wife SARAH ENDSLEY, friend Wyatt Peebles
Wits: Jeremiah Cunningham, John Lomey, John Endsley

A:0114 - JOHN EUBANKS - 8 Sept 1812 - Prb Feb 1818
Wife KATHERINE - all estate during widowhood - tract in Orange County to be sold to pay debts
My nine ch: ELISEBETH, RICHARD, FRANCES, POLLY, PHILIP, GEORGE, JOHN, RACHEL, and CATHERINE
GEORGE, JOHN, RACHEL, and CATHERINE to live with their mother
Exrs: Joseph McCain, James Holman
Wit: Henry Hart

A:0115 - WILLIAM FORBIS - 8 Dec 1771 - Prb 1772
Sister ANN FORBIS - horse I bought from John Smith
Brothers JOHN & ARTHUR - remainder of my estate
Exrs: Brothers JOHN & ARTHUR FORBIS
Wits: Thomas Morgan, John M. McClean, Thos. Wiley

A:0116 - ARTHUR FORBIS - 2 July 1780 - Prb Aug 1781
Wife ELIZABETH - command of my plantation and family; if she marries, third of moveable property
Son JOHN - lands of the old place & land on Burch Creek
Son ARTHUR - home plantation at wife's decease or remarriage
Daus ANN, ELIZABETH, MARY, & MARTHY (minors) - proceeds of land
Exrs: Son JOHN FORBIS, Thomas Wiley, Wife ELIZABETH FORBIS
Wits: Michael Burke, Matthew Russell

A:0117 - THOMAS FLERE - 20 July 1781 - Prb Aug 1781
Wife JANE - half of moveable property, half of house & lot in Willmenton, #52 on Front Street, negro woman Nancy
Dau JUDITH FLERE - other half of what her mother receives
Exrs: Wife JANE FLERE, James McCuiston
Wits: William Kennedy, Ann McCuiston, Thomas McCuiston

A:0118 - JOHN FIELD - 12 Dec 1787
Wife MARY - home plantation of 150 ac during widowhood
Son WILLIAM - five pounds
Daus ELESABETH, ANN, & HESTER FIELD - fifteen pounds, one cow ea
Son JOHN - three pound note on John Worthenton
Son THOMAS - one horse colt called Ranbo
Son ROBERT - one pound
Son JOSEPH - 100 ac near where David lives
Son JEREMIAH - 100 ac of middle of tract
Son JESEY - home plantation when his mother dies or remarries
Dau JANE JONSON - one pound
Mother ELISEBETH POWEL - to live here at her pleasure

Exrs: Wife MARY FIELD, brother JEREMIAH FIELD
Wits: William Field, Lidoak (her mark) Field
"For probate, see Minute Docket No. 1, page 327"

A:0119 - ARTHUR FORBIS - 10 Apr 1789 - Prb 1794
Daus LIDIA DONNELL, ELISABETH & ANN FORBIS - proceeds from sale
Son-in-law & dau: HANCE & JENNET MCCANE - 70 shillings
Exrs: Step-sons JOHN & ROBERT RANKIN
Wits: John Anderson, Henry Rose, William Gowdy

A:0120 - WILLIAM FAIRBANKS - 13 Aug 1797 - Prb Aug 1797
Wife MARY - land & household property for raising my children
Ch: SUSANNAH, DAVID, WILLIAM, & SARAH
Sister-in-law SIDNEY SPENCE & her son JOHN to have free living provided she assists in supporting my family
Exrs: Wife MARY FAIRBANKS, brother-in-law NATHAN SPENCE
Wits: Ezekial Duweese, Nathan Spence

A:0121 - DANIEL FISHER - 12 Nov 1797 - Prb Feb 1798
Son MOLLOSTON - 100 ac tract bought of Levin Wright provided he rears and schools son JOHN and dau SARAH
Son JONATHAN - home place provided he rears & schools:
Sons DANIEL, THEODORIS, & NATHAN; daus MARY & HANNER
Son THOMAS - 50 ac of land, colt of my black mare, some more learning to sifer as far as the rule of three
Exrs: Friends William Starback, Strangman Stanley
Wits: Hezekiah Starbuck, Michael Stanley, Susannah Dillon

A:0122 - DAVID FOURHAND - 6 July 1802 - Prb Aug 1802
Ch: GORDIN, GARISIES, OWING, dau MOLEY, & JOHN - ten shillings
Wife PRUDENCE - home plantation for use of her & my eight ch
Son THOMAS - one colt
Exrs: Roger Kirkman, Nehemiah Causey
Wits: Roddy Hannah, David Swift

A:0123 - ELISHA FLACK - 18 Jan 1795 - Prb Nov 1802
Bro ELIJAH - 390 ac of land to take special care of my mother
Sister DORCAS - 18 pounds. Sister HANNAH - one gray horse
Bro ANDREW - 150 ac on upper part of land adj Sols Fulton
Bro THOMAS - my saddle and wearing apparel
Exr: Brother JAMES FLACK
Wits: Claiborn Curtis, Thomas Ross

A:0124 - JANE FLACK - 15 Jan 1802 - Prb Nov 1802
Son THOMAS - all my lands - 300 ac
Andrew Flack, son of Elisha - my black horse
Samuel Daugherty's dau Jenny - my saddle
Dau JENNY - two coverlids
John Daugherty's dau Polly - my great pot
Dau DORCAS - my bed and furniture
Andrew Flack's dau Jenny - my wheel
James Flack's son Elisha - one cow
Sons THOMAS & ELIJAH - my cattle & sheep
Exrs: Son JAMES FLACK - to divide property
Wits: Andrew Flack, Elijah Flack

A:0125 - ROBERT FLEMING - 26 Sept 1806 - Prb Nov 1806
Daus ISBEL ARNETT, SARAH FLEMING & MARY COX - five shillings
Sons SILAS & ALEXANDER - five shillings
Sons ROBERT & JAMES - to divide my land, each a colt
Youngest ch BETSY & BONIAK - personal property
Exr: Friend Henry Brannock
Wits: William Brannock, Benjamin Shearman

A:0126 - JOHN FORBIS - 16 Sept 1793 - Prb May 1806
Wife MARY - sole management of plantation during widowhood
Sons JEREMY, WILLIAM, ELI, & JESSEY - to inherit the land
Daus LIDDY, REBECCAH, POLEY & ANN FORBIS - personal property
Son HUGH - 100 ac adj his land on Buffalow Creek
Exrs: Hugh Forbis, Jeremy Forbis, William Forbis
Wits: Daniel McMin, Hugh Wiley

A:0127 - JOSIAH FINLEY - 21 Mar 1801
Wife ALCEY - home plantation during life or widowhood
Wife, sons GEORGE & JAMES - to divide 370 acres of land
Dau BETSEY - negro woman Poll at death or remarriage of wife
My five daus: BETSEY FINLEY, RACHEL FINLEY, LETTIS FINLEY, POLLY FINLEY & ABEGAIL FINLEY
Exrs: Wife ALCEY FINLEY, friend John Cunningham
Wits: John Coe, Senr., George Finley, Aaron Causey
"For probate see Minute Docket No. 3, pps 125-6."

A:0128 - WILLIAM FIELD - 24 Mar 1815 - Prb Aug 1815
Wife NANCY - third of land during widowhood, negro woman Leah, bed, household furniture, kitchen utensils, geese, sheep, etc
Dau JANE HANNAH - twenty shillings
Son JEREMIAH - negro woman Dinah that Jesse Hannah had
Son JONATHAN - two thirds of lands, farming tools, two cows, hogs
Dau NANCY - negro girl Beck, two beds, two cows, horse & saddle
Exrs: Bro-in-law WILLIAM ARMFIELD & NANCY FIELD
Wits: Nathan Armfield, Jeremiah Field

A:0129 - EDWARD GUILBERT - 10 Oct 1782 - Prb Nov 1782
Wife - dwelling house, negro woman Nice, maintenance dw
Sons JOHN & WILLIAM - lands, desk, still; WILLIAM to maintain his mother on the home plantation
Dau ELIZABETH - one cow, to inherit negro Nice from mother
Gr ch JEAN, MARY & ELIZABETH COMING
Wit: Robert Marley

A:0130 - WILLIAM GOWDY - 15 Nov 1786
Sons JAMES & WILLIAM - home plantation & 90 acres more
Sons ROBERT & JOHN - land on Russell's Branch
Sons WILLIAM & JOHN - if either or both incline to learning, let it be done if Rev David Caldwell, William Scott & Henry Ross think their land sufficient to pay the cost
Dau SARAH - 20 pds, mare, saddle, bed & furniture
Dau ELIZABETH BILLINGSLY - the black mare, cow & calf
Exrs: Son JAMES GOWDY, William Scott, Henry Ross
"No witness being present, call upon Thomas Henderson, Esqr., Henry Ross & Hezekiah Rhodes to prove the handwriting, accord- to a law passed 22 Oct 1781." Probate Minute Docket No. 2, page 143.

A:0131 - JONATHAN GIFFORD - 17 Feb 1793 - Prb Nov 1793
Wife EUNICE - third of personal estate, 20 ac of land dw
Son WILLIAM - tract bought of Joshua Chadwick, silver buckles
Daus SARAH & EUNICE - each twelve pounds
Son JONATHAN - 100 ac whereon I live, Bible
Four daus SARAH, EUNICE, MARY & HANNAH - one good ewe sheep
Exrs: Friends William Bourland, Barnabas Coffin
Wits: Obadiah Harris, Barnabas Coffin, Phebe Coffin

A:0132 - WILLIAM GRAY - 10 June 1794 - Prb Aug 1794
Eldest son JAMES - land he lives on adj Samuel Beeson
Son WILLIAM - 100 acres whereon he lives
Son ISAAC - 110 acres whereon he lives
John - 50 ac adj William Ballard and Abraham Cook, part of a deed from Williamson Brown
Son JESSE - 100 ac as it is laid off for him
Son JOSEPH - 120 ac whereon he lives
Son THOMAS - land between WILLIAM & ISAAC
Son SAMUEL - remainder of my lands after widowhood of his mother
Wife - her part of land for maintenance and support dw
Daus ELIZABETH RAPER & MARY BROWN - five shillings each
Youngest dau LYDIA when she comes of age - two cows & calves, bed & furniture, young horse creature
Youngest sons JOSEPH & SAMUEL - cow & calf at marriage
Exrs: Sons WILLIAM & ISAAC GRAY
Wits: Williamson Brown, William Simmons

A:0133 - GEORGE GULLET 14 May 1796 - Prb Aug 1796
Gr son ISACK JESTER - 26 pds he is already possessed of
Dau NANCY SMITH - 26 pds she is already possessed of
Dau MARGET CLIFTON - 10 pds she is already possessed of
Rest of my children to have equivalent
Exrs: Sons JOHN & GEORGE GULLET
Wits: Thomas Buckner, Aydlett Buckner, Stephen Huddleston

A:0134 - CHARLES GREEN - 20 May 1798 - Prb May 1798
Brother JOHN GREEN - my mare, saddle & bridle, hogs
My near cousin JOHN BEESON - a new saddle in the hands of Peter Searbuck, my still and tubs
Wits: Benjamin Beeson, James Sanders

A:0135 - STEPHEN GOUGH - 1 Dec 1798 - Prb Feb 1799
Wife JEAN - third of lands & movables, horse, saddle & bridle
Son DANIEL - five shillings in full
Son JAMES - 100 ac where he now lives
Son SAMUEL - 100 ac that I cleared last year
Son STEPHEN - ballance of my land
Daus NANCY & POLLY - bed and furniture, cow & calf
Exrs: Wife JEAN GOUGHF, Thomas Kirkman
Wits: Jonathan Tatum, Clarles Spence

A:0136 - ROBERT GWYN - 10 Sept 1801 - Prb Nov 1801
Wife RACHEL - negro Sall, grey mare, saddle & bridle, beds
Son JOHN - tract of land, negroes Luce & Ben
Daus ISOBEL, NELLY & POLLY GWYN - negroes Easter, Geace, & Patie
Exrs: Wife RACHEL GWYN, John Cunningham

Wits: Patrick McGibbony, John Cunningham

A:0137 - JOHN GILLASPIE - 13 June 1806 - Prb Aug 1806
Wife ELIZABETH - $50, home place, farming tools, negro girl Nance, four head of Horned cattle, household & kitchen furniture
Son DANIEL - $300, negro woman Pat, 2 head of cattle
Son JAMES S. - $300, my bay horse, two head of cattle
Dau BETSEY STARRETT - $100, three head of cattle
Dau ANNE HANNAH - $150, negro Mill, 3 head of cattle
Nephew Rev. JOHN GILLASPIE - $100
Gr son JOHN GILLASPIE, son of DANIEL - home place at dec. of wife
Gr son CHARLES JOSEPH, son of JAMES - land on both sides Muddy Br
Gr son ALFRED HANNAH - 100 ac adj John Hannah, Jessie Weatherly
Lands adj Thomas Crouch to be sold
Exrs: Son JAMES GILLASPIE, son-in-law JOHN HANNAH
Wits: Thomas Black, Daniel Gillaspie, Margret Gillaspie

A:0138 - JAMES GOWDY - 22 Jan 1809 - Prb May 1810
James Billingsley, son of Henry, and Joel Murry - my home tract
Sister BETSEY BILLINGLSEY - my white cow
Rebecah Murry, dau of Joel Murry - my cow named Starry
Rebeckah Ros, dau of John Ros - my desk
Brother ROBERT GOWDY - my rifle gun
Brother JOHN GOWDY - my watch and sleeve buttons
Sister SARAH ANDERSON - my large and small Bibles
Thomas Wilson, son of Archibald Wilson - $20 for schooling
Henry Billingsley's children excepting James Billingsley and Jean Murry - when they come of age...
William & James Billingsley - my wearing apparel
Exr: Hance McCain
Wits: John Thompson, Archer Wilson

A:0139 - NATHAN GLADSON - 24 Mar 1810 - Prb Aug 1810
Wife ANN - my plantation & stock
Eldest son DANIEL - five shillings
Sons LEVIN, JOHN, JOSHUA, and NATHAN - to divide my land at the decease of their mother; also at her decease:
Daus MINTE GULLETT & ELIZABETH HACKET - my movable estate
Exrs: William Killingsworth, Leven Gladson
Wits: John Dinkins, Edward Weatherly, John Gilchrist

A:0140 - ROBERT GWIN - 14 Nov 1771 - Prb Feb 1772
Wife ISABELLA - third of my estate; all land for her use whilst she is unmarried and raising and schooling all my children
Son ROBERT - at 21 to have southern part of home plantation
Daus MARTHA & ISABELLA - remainder of estate when 21
Brother JAMES GWIN - one of my best suits of apparel
Robert Gwin Porter, son of William Porter - five pounds
Exrs: Wife ISABELLA GWIN, Henry Work
Wits: Henry Work, William Wallace, David Morrow

A:0141 - PHILIP GLESS - 17 Feb 1773 - Prb May 1774
Sons GEORGE & POWEL - the land whereon each lives
Gr son GEORGE, son of CHRISTEN GLESS - 200 ac on Alamance
Dau CATREN, wife of JACOB COBLE - thirty pounds
Dau BARBERY GLESS & dau MARY, wife of TOBIAS CLAP - thirty pds

Dau INLAND PHILPENAH GLESS, w/o CHRISTEN GLESS - two shillings
Wife MARY - home, all ready money, one bay mare, brown horse
Son PHILIP - remainder of estate
Exr: Son PHILIP GLESS
Wits: James Hunter, George Gobal, Tobias Clap

A:0142 - RALPH GORRELL - 31 Aug 1812 - Prb May 1816
Wife MARY - whole of farm while son JAMES & two daus live with her, to leave to any child she pleases
Sons DAVID & JAMES - west side of plantation
Son WILLIAM - 100 pds on note he owes me, in full
Son DAVID - negro Bob, 450 ac on South Buffalo Cr adj Gillaspies
Son ROBERT - $50 and discount of what he owes me
Son RALPH, living in Ireland - tract I purchased of brother ROBERT in Kingdom of Ireland, County of Doney
Son JAMES - home place after his mother dies, negroes Peter Smith, Kevey & Tom, 594 ac adj Greensboro, watch, bookcase
Grandson RALPH, son of DAVID GORRELL
Oldest dau ELIZABETH FORBIS - negro Hannah, five pounds
Dau CATHERINE - 250 ac bought of John Doak, negroes Bill & Lee, horse, saddle & bridle worth $150
Daus MARY MAXWELL & AGNESS STEWART - $250 each
Dau ANN TOM - $320, 255 ac adj Joab Weatherly, her sister MARGARET, & James Ozment
Youngest dau MARGARET - remainder of tract adj her sisters
Gr son RALPH GORRELL, son of WILLIAM - $50, tract on Reedy Creek
Gr son ROBERT GORRELL, son of ROBERT - tract bought of John Boak
Other gr ch in America: RALPH FORBIS, RALPH, son of ROBERT GORREL, DAVID, son of RALPH GORRELL, MARY MAXWELL, RALPH, son of RALPH & AGNESS STEWART, RALPH, son of DAVID GORRELL, JOHN, son of ROBERT GORRELL
Exrs: David Gorrell, Samuel Thom, John Stewart
Wits: S. Gwin, J. H. Starrett, Joseph Davis

A:0143 - MOSES GORDY - 24 Oct 1795 - Prb Aug 1802
Wife EUNICE - home plantation during widowhood
Eldest son MOSES - 75 ac & my home when he becomes 21
Youngest son ISAAC - 75 ac south of MOSES' land
Daus ELIZABETH OLIPHANT, NANCY TRIDEN, PRISCILLA ELLIOTT - have received their share
Dau POLLY - one cow and one ewe
Exrs: Wife EUNICE GORDY, John Gilchrist
Wits: Joseph Elliott, John Gilchrist, Edward McGlamery

A:0144 - MATTHEW GRIER of Alamance Settlement - 15 July 1802 - Prb Aug 1802. Wife MARY - home, third of land, furniture, stock
Son THOMAS & son-in-law SAMUEL FLEMING - five shillings
Daus NANCY GANNON & ELONEAR GRIER - each a third of the land
Exrs: Thomas Hamilton of Buffaloe, Thomas Grier
Wits: S. Stewart, Thomas Gill

A:0145 - CRISLEY GLESS - 7 Dec 1771 - Prb Feb 1772
Wife - three cows, bed & furniture
Son GEORGE - 100 ac of land with improvements
Exrs: Wife & Peter Julen
Wits: William Davis, Jacob Gobal, Philip P. McMin?

A:0146 - SAMUEL GILCHRIST - 5 Mar 1816 - Prb May 1816
Eldest son JOHN - all his land on the branch, my negroes
Son PATRICK DAVIDSON GILCHRIST - land on west side of branch when he comes of age, my hard money for his schooling
Exrs: Brother ROBERT GILCHRIST, Thomas McNeely
Wits: William Gilchrist, Delilah Heath, Sarah Heath

A:0147 - JOHN HUNTER - 29 Aug 1777 - Prb Feb 1778
Son EDWARD - negroes Charles, Julia, Jupeta, Will, Felix, Alex, house furniture, stock
Gr sons JOHN & ALEXANDER HUNTER, sons of EDWARD - land, negroes Siser & Tom, mill tract
Daus ALLAY TATE & ELIZABETH WALKER - to have their corn ground free at the mill; ALLAY to have negroes Cate & Jimmy; Elizabeth to have negroes Tom, Ross, Cisley, and Isham
Gr sons JOHN HUNTER, DAVID, JOEL, & WILLIAM WALKER, sons of JOHN & ELIZABETH WALKER - negroes in possession of JOHN WALKER, Sr.
Dau SARAH MAY - negroes Lucy, Nathan, Sukey - which they have
Sister JANE MARTIN - negro Pheby
Gr ch ROBERT, JOHN, ELIZABETH & FRANCES LEE and ch of EDWARD HUNTER - increase of negroes Lucy & Judy, residue of property
Alexander Martin - negro boy Ben
Exrs: Alexander Martin, James Martin, James Hunter, John Tate
Wits: George Peay, Senr., Giles Carter, Agnes Hoggatt

A:0148 - GEORGE HODGSON of Rowan Co. - 5 June 1864 - Prb Aug 1774
Son GEORGE - 200 ac of home plantation & improvements I bought of Robert Lamb
Sons ROBERT & JOSEPH - remaining part of home plantation, tract bought from William Ozburn
Son JOHN - five shillings
Dau SARAH, wife of FORD HIETT - five shillings
Dau SUSANNA, wife of WILLIAM HIETT - five shillings
Wife - to divide remainder of land and money with sons
Exrs: Robert Lamb & Nathan Dicks
Wits: Thomas Wilson, Jeane Wilson, Margaret Williams

A:0149 - JOSEPH HINDS - 14 Apr 1772 - Prb Aug 1772
Wife SUSANNA - all my estate during widowhood
Son JOSEPH - five shillings
Wife's dau ANN MCCONNEL - cow and calf
Prudence Roberts - cow & calf if she lives with wife until 18
Sons SIMEON, LEVI, JOHN - estate at death or remarriage of wife
Exrs: Wife SUSANNA HINDS, Jeremiah Reynolds, Isaac Beeson

A:0150 - CHRISTOPHER HUSEY - 1 Apr 1773 - Prb May 1774
Wife ANNE - third part of my estate
Sons STEPHEN & CHRISTOPHER - remainder of my plantation
Son-in-law ROBERT HODGINS - another tract of land
Daus ELIZABETH COMER, NAOMEY COX, ANNE HODGINS
Exrs: Son STEPHEN HUSEY, Soloman Cox, Joseph Comer
Wits: William Wierman, Samuel Hendrix, Mary Hendrix

A:0151 - THOMPSON HARRIS - 15 Oct 1775 - Prb Nov 1775
Sons ROBERT & JOHN - divide land where John Sanders lives
Wife HANNAH - half of home plantation, stock

Son THOMPSON - half of home plantation
Son CHRISTOPHER - half of plantation when wife dies
Exrs: Wife HANNAH HARRIS, son ROBERT HARRIS, George Vaughan

A:0152 - WILLIAM HOGGATT - 5 Sept 1771 - Prb Nov 1771
Wife HANNAH - third, use of plantation while rearing children
Sons WILLIAM, JOSEPH & STEPHEN - estate after decease of wife
Dau MARGARET - horse, side-saddle, ewe & lamb, cow & calf, 10 p
Son JOHN - horse & saddle, 2 cows & calves, 2 ewes & lambs
Note of Sefenus West for land on great Pee Dee to be divided among all my children
Exrs: Brother JOHN HOGGATT, John Beals, Jr.
Wits: Michael Swain, Stephen Cesney, James Land

A:0153 - ISAAC HILL - 28 Feb 1781 - Prb Aug 1781
Wife ELIZABETH - fourth part of my estate
Ch: SARAH HILL, RICHARD, ISAAC - remainder of estate
Exrs: Friends Archibald Yarbrough, John Dabney
Wits: Susannah Thrift, Abraham Thrift

A:0154 - PHILIP HOGGATT of Deep River in Rowan Co. - 9 Sept 1763
Prb Feb 1783. Wife MARY - half of my improved land & dwelling
Eldest son PHILIP & 2nd son DAVID - five shillings
Dau JEAN, widow of HENRY MEINER - 10 pounds, my Bible
3rd son WILLIAM - five shillings
4th son - five shillings, pair of cart wheels, rifle gun
5th son ANTHONY - five shillings, pot in his possession
Youngest son JOSEPH - my plantation & adjoining lands
Children to divide proceeds of 200 ac in Albemarle Co., Va. on Phil's Creek
Exrs: Sons WILLIAM, ANTHONY, and JOSEPH HOGGATT
Wits: Walter Thornburgh, Henry Thornburgh, Nathan Dicks

A:0155 - WILLIAM HAMILTON - 26 May 1785
Wife MARY - house and plantation during widowhood, negroes Hanna, David, Luse, half of household furniture & tools
Nephew GEORGE HAMILTON, son of brother THOMAS - half of my land in Cumberland
Niece HANNAH GRIER, dau of sister JOANNA - other half of land
Niece HANNAH COOTS, dau of brother JOHN COOTS - five pounds
Exr: Wife MARY HAMILTON
Wits: John Oats, Joseph Hamilton
Will of William Hamilton received in court 21 Feb 1786 and set aside; George Hamilton, legatee, & his lawyer Spruce Mc Coy. 27 Nov 1781 - MARY MCELHATTON, widow of WILLIAM HAMILTON & wife of WILLIAM MCELHATTON, protest legacies and are made Administrators.

A:0156 - NATHAN HIATT - 6 Oct 1786 - Prb May 1787
Wife MARY - my bay mare and side saddle, household and kitchen furniture, four year old heifer
Son CHRISTOPHER - my stockings, black handkerchief, neck stock, my buckle
Exrs: Uncle WILLIAM HIATT, brother-in-law JOSEPH THORNBURGH
Wits: Jesse Williams, Joshua Dicks, Asher Hiatt

A:0157 - FRANCIS HARTLEY - 19 Dec 1788 - "For probate, see Minute Docket No. 2, p 84." Wife SARAH - all personal estate
Exr: Charles Bruce
Wits: Jane Sepratt, Parnel Blessard

A:0158 - PETER HARRIS - 29 July 1790 - Prb Nov 1790
Wife HANNA to have her living off the cleared land during widowhood, stock to be sold for raising of my children
My three sons - equal division of land
Dau NELLY - one large bason, two spoons; other household goods to be appraised & divided between wife and five youngest girls
Exrs: Wife HANNAH HARRIS, George Rayl
Wits: James McMurry, James Barham, Henry Mitchell

A:0159 - PATRICK HAYS - 17 Aug 1790 - Prb Nov 1792
Wife REBECAH - my whole lands & all household goods during widowhood and then to Rubin Land & Drokes Denny
Brother JOHN - five shillings
Exr: John Lane
Wits: Robert Calhoun, James Calhoun, Alee Griffin

A:0160 - THOMAS HOULSTON - 25 Sept 1792 - Pro Feb 1793
Wife - third of the movables & sorrel horse during widowhood
Brother SOLOMAN - sorrel horse if wife remarries
Sons of my wife - JOHN, JONATHAN, & MOSES STUART
Exr: Leven C. Charles
Wits: Bartholomew Williams, John Forguson, Jeremiah Shelby

A:0161 - CHRISTOPHER HIATT - No date - Prb Feb 1793
Wife LYDIA - maintenance during widowhood, horse, saddle & bridle
Sons JOHN, ASHER, AMOS, CHRISTOPHER - land equally divided
Dau ESTHER - feather bed & furniture, white cow & calf, colt
Exrs: Wife LYDIA HIATT, son JOHN HIATT
Wits: Joshua Dicks, William Hiatt, Jesse Evans

A:0162 - JACOB HOFHAINS - 24 July 1793 - Prb Aug 1793
Wife MARY ELIZABETH - dwelling house, spring house, stil house, books, Bible, two cows & calves, etc., redy money
Son JACOB - 150 ac west of my land - to give to his mother yearly: 12 bu wheat, 6 bu corn, 150 lb port, 50 lbs beef, 10 lbs sugar, 3 gal molasses, 5 gal brandy, 10 lbs flax, 5 lbs wool, 1/2 lb spice, also to feed her horse and cows
Son DAVID - 100 ac of land. Son CHRISTIAN - 70 pounds money
Sons DANIEL & PHILIP and daus MALLISON, CHRISTINA, BARBARA, and ELIZABETH - remainder of estate
Exrs: Wife MARY ELIZABETH HOFHAINS & son DANIEL HOFHAINS
Wits: Jacob Christman, John Osias

A:0163 - SETH HUDDLESTON - 7 Mar 1791 - Prb Nov 1794
Wife LYDIA - all my estate to bring up my children
Son JONATHAN - half of my real estate when he becomes of age
Daus SARAH, LEVINAH, MARY, ELIZABETH, HANNAH, & RACHEL - half of estate at death or remarriage of my wife
Exrs: Wife LYDIA HUDDLESTON, William Beend
Wits: Philip Horney, George Mendenhall, Eliab Gardner

A:0164 - JAMES HILTON - 5 Aug 1796 - Prb Aug 1796
Wife MARY - 100 ac of land and improvements during widowhood
Son STEPHEN - to inherit his mother's property
Son ELEXANDER - 25 ac of land where he lives
Ch JOHN, ABRAHAM, HANNAH, PRISSALA, & ANN ELEXANDER - div. 200 ac
Sons WILLIAM, PETER, JAMES - five pounds
Son JOHN - my rifle
Exrs: Wife MARY HILTON, Michael Willson
Wits: John Hilton, Michael Wilson, Hezekiah Gardner

A:0165 - NAOMI HARGROVE - 14 Apr 1799 - Prb May 1799
Son SAMUEL & dau MARTHA - land whereon I live
Other sons and daus - one dollar each
Exrs: Son SAMUEL & dau MARTHA HARGROVE
Wits: George L. Brown, Jesse Hargrove

A:0166 - JOSEPH HOSKINS - 4 July 1799 - Prb Aug 1799
Wife HANNAH - rights of plantation, mare & saddle, bed & furniture
Dau ELIZABETH - mare & saddle, spinning wheel, bed & furniture
Son JOHN - 100 ac south of Thomas White, stock
Dau HANNAH - $75, spinning wheel, one cow, tea kettle
Son ELI - $300; desire that he be put to a trade
Dau ANN - $80, one large pot with hooks & pot rack
Sons JOSEPH & ELLIS - all the tract whereon I live
Dau MARY - $100
Exrs: Friends Thomas White and Jesse Williams
Wits: Thomas Benbow, Jesse Evans, Phebe Stanley

A:0167 - ARNOLD HOSKINS - 10 June 1797 - Prb Nov 1799
Wife ELIZABETH - whole use of my land during widowhood
Sons ARNOLD & JOSEPH - to inherit land from wife
Daus NELEY & JEAN - mare, saddle & bridle, 6 pewter plates
Exrs: Friends James Tharp & John McMurry
Wits: John McMurry, James Tharp

A:0168 - JOHN HENDERSON - 28 Mar 1800 - Prb May 1800
Youngest sons DANIEL & THOMAS - 200 acres whereon I live
Sons JOHN & WILLIAM - remainder of land
Wife - land adj Harper & Bark
Dau REBECKAH - her mare & saddle, feather bed and furniture
Exrs: Friends John Rudock, Samuel McMillican
Wits: John Mordock, James Smith

A:0169 - DAVID HARRIS - 18 July 1800 - Prb Nov 1800
Father OBADIAH - the horse I bought from him & saddle & bridle
Sister ELIZABETH - residue of estate
Exrs: Father OBADIAH HARRIS, Barnabas Coffin
Wits: Joseph Mills, Hannah Mills, Elisebeth Baldwin

A:0170 - STEPHANUS HAWORTH - 16 Apr 1804 - Prb May 1804
Wife ELIZABETH - mare, saddle & bridle, bed & furniture, dishes
Dau RACHEL - her saddle, bed & furniture
Son SOLOMAN - my anvil now in his possession
Son RICHARD - 200 ac whereon I live, tools, feather bed & furn
Dau JANE - a saddle, bed & furniture belonging to her
Dau PHEBE - one dollar more than she has already received

Dau HANNAH - saddle, feather bed and furniture
Exrs: Friend John Howell and son RICHARD HAWORTH
Wits: Micajah Haworth, George Haworth, Mary Haworth

A:0171 - JOHN HODGSON - 3 May 1804 - Prb Nov 1804
Wife MARY - home, furniture, cow, maintenance, 15 pds in money
Son JOSEPH - my land and working tools
Dau SARAH LOVET - $10 or a cow worth that much
Gr son AMOS HODGSON - five shillings
The rest of my living children
Exrs: Sons JOHN and GEORGE HODGSON
Wits: Joseph Thornburgh, William Thornburgh

A:0172 - LEWIS HOLTON - 27 Dec 1800 - Prb Aug 1805
Gr son LEWIS RENNOLDS - $12.50
Dau DINAH - support for her live time
Friend John Coe, Senr - ten pounds
Daus DOLLY CESENEY, NANCY RENNOLDS, RACHEL BARTLEY and gr dau HANNAH HOLTON alias COE - my personal estate
Exr: John Coe
Wits: James Doak, William Doak, Junr

A:0173 - CHARLES HARDIN - 7 May 1806 - Prb Aug 1807
Wife JEAN - mare named Nance, saddle & bridle, maintenance
Dau REBECKAH - $50, sorrel colt, saddle & bridle
Son STEWART - 120 ac of land, including improvements
Sons JOHN (190 ac), CHARLES - 190 ac & mare named Sall
Dau CATHARINE - $25, colt, saddle & bridle
Son-in-law DAVID BRIGGANCE - $5
Exrs: Sons JOHN & CHARLES HARDIN
Wits: Thomas McCulloch, Senr., Thomas McCulloch, Junr.

A:0174 - JOHN HUNT - 21 Sept 1809 - No probate date
Wife POLLY - maintenance, household furniture, cow & calf, etc
Sons JACOB, STUARET, & WILLIAM - plantation & land on Joseph Brittain's Meddow Branch; sons to be put to trade at 19 yrs if they desire
Dau SALLY - feather bed & furniture, chest, 4 ac of land on Moon's Creek adj James Harris
Exrs: Jehugh Stewart, William Brittain
Wits: Nathan Cannady, Hannah Stewart, Henry Esterig

A:0175 - GEORGE HUTTON - 7 Sept 1810 - Prb Nov 1810
Ch of Arnold Hutton: Mary, Elizabeth, William, Jemima, Ruthy, James & Lydia - proceeds of sale when all are 18 yrs old
Exr: Arnold Hutton
Wits: Samuel Lindsay, John Elliott, William Grimes

A:0176 - JOHN HARVY - 2 Aug 1811 - Prb Aug 1811
Wife NANCY - all my estate, to dispose of personal property as she wishes
Cousin ISAAC LAMB - my land after death of my wife
Exr: Wife NANCY HARVY
Wits: John Howell, Samuel Lamb, Robert Lamb

A:0177 - WILLIAM HITCHCOCK - 22 Aug 1806 - Prb Aug 1811

Wife HANNAH - all my estate and debts, horses, cattle & sheep
Wits: William Piggott, David Snoley

A:0178 - JABEZ HUNT - 28 Sept 1812 - Prb Nov 1812
Wife PRISCILLA - all my estate during widowhood
Father NATHAN - my half the land we bought of Josiah Gilbert
Dau SEMIRA - estate after death or remarriage of wife
Springfield Monthly Meeting - $5 for use of building Meeting house. Exrs: Father NATHAN HUNT, Father-in-law MATTHEW COFFIN, Zebulon Hunt, Phenibas Albertson
Wits: David North, Joshua Moore

A:0179 - GEORGE HODGSON, living on Waters of Pole Cat.
1 Jan 1808 - Prb Feb 1813
Wife RACHEL - maintenance of plantation while my widdow; if she remarry - 1 horse beast worth $40, her bed, cow & calf
Dau PHEBE OZBORN, son WILLIAM, dau MARY WARD, son GEORGE, dau RUTH BENNETT - five shillings each
Daus SUSANNAH, RACHEL, & DEBORAH HODGSON - cow, bed & furniture
Son ISAAC - 50 ac north of the plantation
Son ZACHARIAH - plantation divided with ISAAC
Exrs: Sons WILLIAM & ISAAC HODGSON
Wits: Job Worth, John Williams

A:0180 - JOHN HEALY - 1 Dec 1809 - Prb Feb 1813
Aaron Rick - 150 ac of land, negro Harry
Wife PHEBE - all I possess during life, and at her death:
Son JESSE - home plantation, negroes Sam & Ned
Mary Healy - negro Jacob, bed & furniture, corner cupboard, desk
Phebe Healy (d/o Hugh Healy who receives $10) - negro Mary
Patrick Healy - my watch & rifle gun
John Brown - bay colt, saddle & bridle
Wits: Manlove Horney, Samuel Horney

A:0181 - WILLIAM HIATT - 30 June 1814 - Prb Aug 1814
Wife - maintenance of land while my widow, grain now growing for maintenance of her and the family
Son AARON - 50 ac
Oldest sons JOEL, BENNAJAH, ISOM - balance of land
Dau REBECCA - bed & furniture, cow & calf
Balance to go to wife and daughters
Exrs: Sons BENNAJAH & SILAS HIATT
Wits: Richard Williams, Jesse Evans, Samuel Kellam

A:0182 - PHILIP HAM - 4 Mar 1814 - Prb Aug 1814
Son HEZEKIAH - five shillings & what I have already given him
Son JOHN - plantation if he pay $100 I owe to Isaac Beeson
Daus ELISABETH JOHNSON & ANN JOHNSON - residue of estate
Exrs: Son HEZEKIAH HAM, son-in-law WILLIAM JOHNSON
Wits: Barnabas Coffin, Ebenezer Hunt

A:0183 - JOSEPH HOGGATT - 3 July 1803 - Prb Aug 1815
Wife PHEBY - maintenance during widowhood, mare & saddle, bed
Sons STEPHANUS (oldest), PHILIP, JOSEPH, WILLIAM, NATHAN, and MALEN - each one dollar
Sons ZIMRI and ISAIAH - all the lands I now possess

Daus PHEBE NEELEY and SARAH HOGGATT - divide $108
Exrs: Zimri & Isaiah Hoggott
Wits: Thomas Moore, Samuel Hunt

A:0184 - SMITH HEATH - 18 July 1805 - Prb Feb 1816
Wife TABITHA - plantation, house, & movables, during widowhood
Sons HENRY, JOHN, & SAMUEL - to divide land
Gr son THOMAS SLICK - equal share in movable property
Exrs: Wife TABITHA HEATH, son JOHN HEATH

A:0185 - WILLIAM HEATH - 16 Feb 1816 - Prb Feb 1816
Wife DELILAH - my whole estate and all that I am possessed of
Exrs: Wife DELILAH HEATH, friend James Priden
Wits: Samuel Gilchrist, Robert Gilchrist

A:0186 - GEORGE HIATT - 2 Jan 1793 - Prb Nov 1793
Daus RUTH DICKS & URSLEY STEPHENS - my iron pots
Gr daus SUSANNAH HIATT & MARTHA HIATT (daus of JOHN HIATT, dec'd) the little pot and to MARTHA - all my estate
Exrs: William Armfield, son WILLIAM HIATT
Wits: William Armfield, James Wilson

A:0187 - JOSHUA HANES - 21 July 1813 - Prb Aug 1813
Wife HANNAH - all my estate; third if she remarries
Son JOSEPH - $50
Son JEREMIAH - $10 a year as long as he improves the land for his mother
Bound boy Jonathan Millar, bound girl Rebekah Gisped - indenture to be complied with if they serve their time
My ch: Sons JOHN, JOSEPH, JACOB, JOBE & JEREMIAH and ELIZABETH, and Sarah Eddins - remainder of estate
Exrs: Wife HANNAH HANES, Sons JEREMIAH HANES & William Eddins
Wits: None. Will proved in court by Hezekiah Starbuck

A:0188 - ROBERT HODSON - 7 Apr 1813 - Prb May 1813
Sons RICHARD, JONATHAN, DAVID, THOMAS, ROBERT, & JESSE - 5 sh
Daus ELIZABETH, RACHEL, REBECCA, MARY, & MARTHA - each 5 sh
Wife SARAH - third of proceeds of my land & stock
Son HUR and dau SARAH - remaining two thirds; SARAH to have third of stock when she marries
Exrs: Wife SARAH HODSON, William Harvey
Wits: Thomas Swain, Paul Beard

A:0189 - DAVID HODSON - 8 Mar 1816 - Prb May 1816
Wife HESTER - my house, lands, and stock during widowhood
Daus RACHEL ($4), ANNY ($5), MARGARET ($5), CHARITY ($4), HESTER ($30, chest), ELIZABETH ($30)
Sons DAVID & SIMEON - inherit lands & property from wife
Exrs: Wife HESTER HODSON, Jesse Hodson
Wits: N. Millis, Joash Reynolds, William Harvey

A:190 - JOHN HALL - 5 Mar 1816 - Prb May 1816
Son JAMES HALL - all my lands, farming tools, Bible, clothing
Daus AGNES & BECKY - their mother's clothes, bed curtains, books
Exrs: Son JAMES HALL, Robert Gillaspie
Wits: John Pritchett, Eli Hall

A:0191 - JOHN HEATH - 11 Feb 1816 - Prb May 1816
Sister ELIZABETH - one loom and one heifer
Wife CHARLOTTE - all my land & movable property
Daus NANCY & LEVINA - estate divided after widowhood of wife
Exrs: Wife CHARLOTTE HEATH, Moses Gilchrist
Wits: Joseph Braley, William Burney

A:0192 - SAMUEL HEATH - 29 Mar 1816 - Prb May 1816
Wife JESTIN - plantation & movable estate during widowhood
Son JOHN - plantation when he reaches 21 years of age
Daus MARY, SARAH, & KEZIAH HEATH - to inherit movable property
Exrs: Brother RALPH HEATH (Smith tools), Wife JESTIN HEATH
Wits: Robert Heath, Delilah Heath, John Gilchrist

A:0193 - JACOB HEATH - 22 Mar 1816 - Prb May 1816
Wife MARY - plantation & movable property during widowhood
Eldest son SAMUEL - land he now lives on
Sons ROBERT & RALPH - tracts they now live on
Eldest dau EDELY PILKINGTON, daus KEZIA & REBEKAH HEATH - $300 ea
Exrs: Wife MARY HEATH, son RALPH HEATH
Wits: Delilah Heath, Levin Woolen, John Woolen, John Gilchrist

A:0194 - LODWICK ISLEY - 26 July 1788
Wife ELIZABETH - estate during widowhood or until oldest child becomes of age
Exrs: Peter Summers, Christen Isley
Wits: Andrew Gibson, Palliser Isley, T. Maguar
"For probate, see Minute Docket No. 2, p. 7."

A:0195 - GEORGE INGLE - 17 Sept 1797 - Prb Feb 1801
Wife MARGARET - 150 ac plus plantation, stock, tools, money
Youngest son ADAM - his mother's property at death or remarriage
Eldest son BARNABAS - 200 ac on which he lives
Sons GEORGE & JOHN - 108 ac on east & south of Plantation, my saw & grist mills
Son JACOB - 100 ac to be struck from north side of old tract
Son LUDWICK - 165 ac on which he lives
Youngest daus PHILIPINA, LOVINIA, SOPHIA - each 2 cows & calves, 2 sheep, bed & furniture, chest, 2 iron pots
Dau MARGRET, wife of WILLIAM CHRISTO - five pounds
Grand dau EVE SWING, dau of BARBARY SWING, dec'd, & her father GEORGE SWING - five pounds
Daus CATHERINE (wife of JOHN HUFFMAN), MARY (w/o JOHN CLAPP), CHRISTIAN (w/o AARON FIPPS), TURLEY (w/o ISAAC GREESON), PHILIPINA, LOVENA, & SOPHIA - residue of estate
Exrs: Wife MARGRET INGLE, friend Jacob Coble, Senr.
Wits: Samuel Lindsay, Jacob Clap

A:0196 - THOMAS JENKINS - Prb Nov 1771
Wife LETTIS - third part of all my estate, goods & chattels
Son HUR - remaining part of estate
Ch: ANN SMITH, DANIEL JENKINS, MARTHA COX, & THOMAS - 1 sh
Son JOHN - residue of estate
Exrs: Sons HUR JENKINS, THOMAS JENKINS
Wits: Samuel Ozburn, Joseph Ozburn

A:0197 - MICHAEL JORDAN - 8 Mar 1775 - Prb May 1775
Wife MARY - my house & lot in Wilmington, house in Guilford near Courthouse. Exr: Wife MARY JORDAN
Wits: Waightstill Avery, Robert Nidirbal, Robert Agnew, Jacob Mayer

A:0198 - ALEXANDER JOYCE - 3 Mar 1778 - Prb May 1778
Wife JANE - negroes Ned, Sue, & Pegg, 240 ac in NE corner running down the river
Son ROBERT - when 21 land adj his mother, slaves Harry & Cate, 100 p
Sons THOMAS (10 pounds) & JOSEPH (100 pounds)
Son JOHN - 526 ac in Pittsylvania Co., Va. on Sandy River, negroes Dick & Jenny
Son JAMES - negro Bill, 100 pounds in money
Son ELIJAH - 200 ac on NW corner, negro woman Hagat, my still
Son ALEXANDER - 100 pounds in money, negro Casar
Son ELISHA - 100 pds, tract including the mill, negro Jude
Son ANDREW - 200 ac lower tract on both sides of river, negro Sam, 100 pds in money
Dau SARAH - negro Nan, two cows, 10 pounds in money
Dau MARGARETT - negro Amy, horse & saddle, bed & furniture
Dau ESTHER JOYCE - negro Dinah, horse & saddle, bed & furniture
Dau ELIZABETH JOYCE - negro Jenny, horse & saddle, bed & furniture
Dau MARY JOYCE - negroes Jacob & Agness, horse & saddle, etc
My little children: ELISHA, ANDREW, ROBERT, MARGARETT, ELIZABETH, & MARY - to be educated
Exrs: Sons JAMES & ELIJAH JOYCE, brother THOMAS JOYCE
Wits: James Holderness, Charles Gates, James Vernon, Alexander Smith

A:0199 - PLEASANT JOHNSON - 8 June 1787 - Prb Aug 1787
Wife ELIZABETH - all of my estate during widowhood to raise my ch
Exr: Claiborne Curtis
Wits: Joel Johnson, Nickolas Smith, Mary Huse

A:0200 - JAMES JACKSON - 24 Mar 1785 - Prb May 1789
Eldest sons JAMES & DAVID - all my estate
Youngest son GABRIEL - 100 ac on which he lives
Exrs: William Armfield (son of Isaac Armfield), Joseph Thornburg
Wits: William Armfield, John Armfield, Nathan Armfield

A:0201 - WILLIAM JACKSON - 1 Oct 1792 - Prb Nov 1792
Son ANDREW - all my real & personal estate
Wife MARGARET - to live with ANDREW, be helped & maintained
Son-in-law JOSEPH SUMMERS - ten shillings
Exr: George Wilson, Esqr
Wits: James Wilson, Mary Ross

A:0202 - ALEXANDER JOHNSON - 3 Dec 1790 - Prb Nov 1793
Dau ELIZABETH - 4 cows, 2 heifers, 2 calves
Son JOHN - one gunie (guinea = British coin worth 21 shillings)
Dau MARY - my own bed & furniture, mare colt that came of Pol
Son THOMAS - one gunie. Dau SARAH JOHNSON - one dollar
Dau MARGARET BEARD - 1/2 joe (small Spanish coin)
Dau AGNESS ALEXANDER - one dollar
Dau JENNETT JOHNSON - 2 cows & 1 calf, 1 heifer, 7 sheep

Dau ESEBEL JOHNSON - 2 cows, calf, 9 sheep, roan colt named Jack
Son GEORGE - 3 mares, colt, my dwelling plantation, tools
Gr son JOSEPH ALEXANDER - one heifer
Exr: Son GEORGE JOHNSON
Wits: David Sherwood, John Stephenson, Samuel Sherman

A:0203 - GEORGE JAMISON - 21 Mar 1794 - Prb Aug 1796
Wife ELIZABETH - my land (100 ac), other goods & chattels
Exr: Wife ELIZABETH JAMISON
Wits: Silas Pearce, Joseph Hiatt, James Dunning

A:0204 - DAVID JACKSON - 7 Apr 1800 - Prb May 1800
Bro JAMES - one grown cow or value thereof in money
Bro GABREL - dark brown mare that he received as a loan
Nephew JOSEPH (son of GABREL) & DAVID (son of GABREL) - my land
Exrs: Maj Patrick McGibbony, Col Daniel Gillaspie
Wits: William Jenkins, Daniel Gillaspie, Patrick McGibbony

A:0205 - WILLIAM JACKSON - 16 Sept 1804 - Prb Nov 1804
Wife SARAH - all my stock & household furniture, land
Son JOHN - to inherit from wife at her decease
Son JOSEPH - tract adj Elijah Manship, Joseph Jackson
Exr: Son JOHN JACKSON
Wits: James Fraizer, Nicholson Millis, Andrew Williams

A:0206 - JAMES JOHNSON - 24 July 1800 - Prb May 1809
Sons JOSHUA & CALEB - wearing apparel, wagon, cross cut saw
Son SOLOMAN - ten dollars
Son-in-law JOHN BEALS & wife SUSANNA - 10 sh, duck knife
Heirs of dau MARGARET CLARK & heirs of dau ELIZABETH WILLIAMS - ten shillings
Ch: JOSHUA, CALEB, SARAH WICKERSHAM, HANNAH HOWELL, and MARY HOWELL - residue of estate
Exrs: Caleb Johnson, Allen Uthank, John Howell
Wits: Robert Brittain, Joseph D. Barriett, Reuben Beard

A:0207 - EPHRAIM JENKINS - 2 Sept 1811 - Prb Nov 1811
Friend Hans Pettegrew - all my estate; also my executor
Wits: James Gibson, William Ray

A:0208 - JAMES KIRKMAN 25 Mar 1790 - Prb May 1791
Son GEORGE - one cow & calf - in full part of his porshun
Son WILLIAM - twenty pounds, in full
Son ELIJAH and son ELISHA - negro boys Charles & Daniel
Gr son JAMES HENDRICK (son of MARY HENDRICKS) - 60 ac purchased of Wm Dick adj Wm Forbis, John Forbises Creek, negro girl Levah
Sons THOMAS SHERWOOD & RODGER - 400 ac tract whereon I live
Wife MARY - dwelling house, third part of cleared land, firewood
Exrs: Wife MARY KIRKMAN, Hendnay Henricks, Robert Hanna
Wits: John Forbis, Daniel McMin, Catherine Ludenima

A:0209 - PETER KIRKMAN - 20 Nov 1800 - Prb Feb 1801
Wife ELEANOR - mare & saddle, 2 cows, her bed & furniture
Dau SARAH - bed & furniture, desk, other furn. when of age
Eldest sons JOHN & GEORGE - the plantation
Sons WILLIAM & PETER - remainder of estate

Exrs: Brother WILLIAM KIRKMAN, Wife ELEANOR KIRKMAN
Wits: W. Jackson, James Millis, William Adams

A:0210 - DAVID KERR - 19 Nov 1802 - Prb May 1804
Wife CATHERINE - dwelling house, negro Sall & her 2 children
Son WILLIAM - plantation, working tools, $100
Sons-in-law RALPH GORRELL, JOHN TOM, DAVID WILEY, THOMAS BROWN, WILLIAM WILEY, GEORGE DONNELL - $100 each
Exrs: Wife CATHERINE KERR, Ralph Gorrell, John Tom
Wits: George Donnell, Thomas Wiley, John Thom, William Wiley

A:0211 - JOHN KELLAM - 29 Sept 1804 - Prb Aug 1805
Sons CUSTUS & SAMUEL - all my lands, feather beds
Son HENRY - the colt that my mare is with
Daus ELIZABETH & ESTER KELLAM - feather beds
Ch: JOSHUWAY KELLAM, SHADROCK KELLAM, JOHN KELLAM, JOHN TUMBLESON, SARY CLAKS, ESTER KELLAM, ELISEBETH KELLAM, HARVY KELLAM, CUSTUS & SAMUEL
Exr: Son JOHN PURSEL KELLAM
Wits: Henry Potter, Zadock Potter, Mary Potter

A:0212 - ELIZABETH KERR - 9 Sept 1809 - No probate date
Dau MARGARET KERR - bed & furniture, chest, delf plates, the crop of cotton to be divided with her younger sisters
Son DAVID - colt, half the crop of corn
Dau ISBELL KERR - bed & furniture
Son JAMES - One chaff bed, sheet, quilt, our chest
Dau CATHERINE KERR - skillet, teapot & cups & saucers
Son JOHN and dau MARY ROSS - ten shillings
Ch CATHERINE, ELIZABETH, WILLIAM - residue of estate
Exr: John Wharton
Wit: Andy Weatherly

A:0213 - ABEL KNIGHT - 2 Sept 1804 - Prb May 1810
Son ABEL - 125 ac on SW corner of my tract
Gr son SAMUEL KNIGHT - 120 ac on SE corner of my tract
Eldest son THOMAS - plantation where I live & remainder of land
Son JONATHAN - 60 in lieu of land
Exrs: Gr son ABEL (son of THOMAS KNIGHT), William Hunt (son of William Hunt, dec'd)
Wits: Joel Hiatt, Andrew Knight

A:0214 - CATHERINE KERR - 25 July 1807 - Prb May 1816
Son WILLIAM ($150) & to his daus KETTREN & GRACE - negro Villet
Son-in-law RALPH GORRELL & wife MARY (my bed & furniture) and their dau KETTRIN - negro Eads
Son-in-law JOHN THOM & wife ELINOR - negro Sal
Son-in-law WILLIAM WILEY & wife ANN - negro girl Roas
Son-in-law DAVID WILEY - $20. Son THOMAS - my house Bible
Son JOHN & heirs - $10. Son DAVID ($10) & his son DAVID - $50
Son-in-law THOMAS BROWN & wife AGNES - $50
Son-in-law GEORGE DONNELL & wife ISABELLA - $50
Son WILLIAM & my daus - residue of estate
Exrs: Sons-in-law RALPH GORRELL & JOHN THOM

A:0215 - WILLIAM LOMAX, Carpenter - 4 Aug 1772 - Prb Feb 1773

Wife ANN - third of estate money after sale, bed, cow, pewter
Son WILLIAM - half of my working tools
Dau ANN FERRINGTON - one heifer called Pretty
Son THOMAS - half of working tools, cow & calf
Son TERRENCE - one roan mare & colt
Sons ROBERT & JAMES & dau ELIZABETH LOMAX - money from sale
ROBERT & JAMES to be bound out until 21 if they choose
Exrs: Wife ANN LOMAX, son THOMAS LOMAX
Wits: Samuel McCracken, Samuel Cowan

A:0216 - SAMUEL LORIMER - No date - Prb May 1774
Wife MARY - child's part of movable property, lifetime on land
Eldest sons JAMES & HUGH - the land. Four youngest children.
Exrs: Wife MARY LORIMER, son HUGH LORIMER
Wits: John Nelson, Alexander McKeen

A:0217 - PHILIP LEWIS - 25 May 1797 - Prb Aug 1797
Wife MARY ELIZABETH - third of my land as long as she liveth
Son PHILIP - to inherit land from his mother, remainder of land
My dau BARBERRY - as much of moveable property as one of the others (Note: Dau of a former wife?)
Exrs: Wife MARY ELIZABETH LEWIS, John Swisher
Wits: John Starr, Jacob Swisher, Joseph Winegardner

A:0218 - JOHN LAKEY - 19 Jan 1794 - Prb Feb 1794
Wife RACHEL - my whole estate, goods & chattels and then to:
My children
Exrs: Wife RACHEL LAKEY, son WILLIAM LAKEY
Wits: William Byford, Hezekiah Wheeler, Quillen Byford

A:0219 - DAVID LOW - 17 May 1787 - Prb Nov 1794
Son SAMUEL - 250 ac except for the 5 ac I gave to the Meeting House which stands thereon, land valued to 300 pds & negro valued to 100 pds
Dau LISABETH - 100 pounds, 50 ac of land, negro girl
Dau EVE - 100 ac where I live on waters that run into Stinking Quarter. Son CUNROD - 200 ac on north side on waters that run into Bever Creek
My wife - to be supported by CUNROD
Exrs: Adam Starr, Jacob Clap
Wits: George Cortner, Christopher Lockman, Peter Cortner

A:0220 - EDWARD LOVEY - 10 Oct 1795 - Prb Nov 1795
Wife SARAH - her living on the plantation, mare, saddle, bridle
Daus SARAH & MARY - third of stock if wife remarries
Son JOHN - 150 ac, horse & saddle, cow & calf, 6 sheep, etc
Son JAMES - 150 ac, good horse & saddle, to be learned to read and write and sypher to the Rule of Three
Dau SARAH - mare & saddle, cow & calf, 4 sheep, pigs, flax wheel
Dau MARY - same as SARAH, to learn to read and write
Dau ELIZABETH CUMTON - cow, flax wheel
Exrs: Wife SARAH LOVEY, son JOHN LOVEY
Wits: Abner Endsley, Jeremiah Cunningham

A:0221 - THOMAS LANDRETH - 18 June 1800 - Prb Nov 1800
Eldest son FRANCIS - 100 ac off west end of plantation

Son THOMAS - 210 ac of land bought of Isaih Weatherly
Son JOHN - 92 ac bought of John Doak, to be given household furniture as she has furnished her other sons at marriage
Son SEMOR - $125 of an obligation on Bennoni Clayton, all his school books
Son JEDIDIAH - balance of Clayton's obligation, $193 on Robert Hannah, and $50 on John Elliott
Wife MARTHA - whole of plantation, moveables during widowhood
Son ASA - to inherit from his mother
Exrs: Wife MARTHA LANDRETH, son JOHN LANDRETH
Wits: John Finley, John Elliott

A:0222 - ADAM LACKEY - 8 Dec 1800 - Prb Feb 1801
Wife MARTHA - home, negro girl Fillis, half of books, 2 horses
Brother ALEXANDER'S son ADAM - plantation at death of wife
Robert Stuart's son named Adam Lackey - $50
William Curney's son, grandson of John Curney, named Adam Lackey
Walter McConel - for friendship - $70 ($50
William Lackey, said to be son of bro SAMUEL LACKEY - 5 shillings
Allimance Congregation - $40
Children of sisters CATRIN BURNEY, MARY BURNEY, JANE PORTER
SAMUEL BURNEY, son of sister MARY BURNEY - clock
Exrs: Wife MARTH LACKEY, Col Daniel Gillaspie, Ralph Gorrell
Wits: Robert Gorrell, Daniel Gillaspie

A:0223 - JOHN LAWRENCE - 20 Feb 1800 - Prb May 1804
Wife ANN - one bed & furniture
Son CALEB - the remainder of my estate
Exrs: Wife ANN LAWRENCE, Joel Harris
Wits: Harman McGee, Edward Tatum Taylor, Noel Parrish

A:0224 - ANDREW LAW - 31 Mar 1807 - Prb May 1807
Ch: RACHEL, JAMES, ROBERT, ANDREW, & ELIZABETH - each $1
Mentions land already received by ANDREW, ROBERT, & JAMES
Wife MARGARET - remainder of all my estate
Exrs: Wife MARGARET LAW, Nephew JOHN SMITH
Wits: Hezekiah Wheeler, John Forbis

A:0225 - HENRY LEE - 2 July 1803 - Prb Aug 1808
Son HENRY - negro boy Peter, my distill
Son JOHN - 20 shillings & what I have already given him
Son JOSHUA - negro boy Dick
Dau ELIZABETH HARRELL - negroes Selah, Sam, & Bob
Dau ABEGAIL KING - negroes she has received: Dinah, Penny, Jacob
Gr son HENRY KING, son of JOSHUA LEE - negro girl Creese
Wife SARAH - support, both negroes, & household furniture dw
Exrs: Joshua Lee, William King, David Harrell
Wits: John Dougherty, John Coffey, James Chilicut, Michael Coffey

A:0226 - ADAM LOMAN - 6 June 1814 - Prb Aug 1814
Wife ELIZABETH - third of plantation next to the river, Ready Fork to the rock leading across George Wagner's ford
Son ADAM - plantation he has adj my wife
Sons ANDREW & GEORGE - to inherit land from wife
Son ANDREW - 80 ac on other side of road adj John Coleman, Junr

Wife & children now at home - household furniture, stock etc
Dau SALLY HUGHS - one cow
Exrs: Son ADAM LOMAN, John Smith
Wit: William Weatherly

A:0227 - ROBERT LAMB - 1 Feb 1814
Sons SAMUEL, SIMEON & JOHN - land & stock already given them
My four daus & gr dau: ELIZABETH WHITE, DEBORAH HOGATT, ESTER HODSON, ANN REYNOLDS & MARGRATE BALDEN - property they have
Wife - household furniture, live stock
Exr: Yeno Worth. Wits: Daniel Worth, Benjamin Hall
"For probate, see Minute Docket No. 4, p. 409."

A:0228 - SAMUEL MILEHAM - 25 Feb 1795 - Prb May 1795
Wife ELIZABETH - third of land, mare called Peg, one bed
Sons JOHN, SAMUEL, EBENEZER - remainder of land
Daus SARAH & MARY - horse & saddle, cow & calf, bed & furniture
Exr: Wife ELIZABETH MILEHAM
Wits: Ezekial Deweare, William Simpson

A:0229 - JAMES MONTGOMERY - 26 Mar 1797 - Prb May 1797
Son JOHN - all my land. Son WILLIAM - yearling colt
Daus JANE, ELIZEBETH, LYDIA, CHARLOTTE, MARGRET & MARY - each $60; all are minors and he wishes them all to live together until MARY becomes of age
Exrs: Sons JOHN & WILLIAM MONTGOMERY
Wits: Matthew Macy, John Walton, Nathaniel Walton

A:0230 - CHARLES MEDARIS - 15 Mar 1793 - Prb Aug 1793
Eldest son THOMAS - horse & saddle, cow & calf, bed & furniture
Son JOHN - all my lands, sorrel mare & saddle
Wife ELIZABETH - all my lands during widowhood, personal prop.
Exrs: Wife ELIZABETH MEDARIS, son JOHN MEDARIS
Wits: Edmund Jean, John Dwigins, Mary Dwigins

A:0231 - DINAH MACY
Dau ANNA MACY - large looking glass, leather trunk, pewter, etc
Dau ABIGAIL STANTON - my worsted gown, two new handkerchiefs
Gr dau DINAH MACY - handirons, fire shovel, two Histories, etc
Dau-in-law HANNAH MACY - duffed blanket, round table, billows
Gr dau ANNIE OZMENT - one garlick sheet, weaving pan, apron
Gr son THADEUS MACY - one black heifer 4 years old
Gr dau HEPSEYBAH RUSSELL - half the feathers out of my bed, etc
Gr dau MARION SWAIM - one checked apron
Gr sons ISAAC MACY & DAVID MACY - carpenter tools, cattle
Daus ABIGAIL & ANNIE MACY - each a lamp, silver spoon, bed, etc
Dau SARAH MACY - my pewter cup
Exrs: Son-in-law ENOCH MACY, dau-in-law HANNAH MACY
Wits: Thadeus Macy, Deanna Jog

A:0232 - ROBERT MITCHEL - 6 Nov 1775 - Prb Nov 1775
Wife MARGARETE - third of land & tenements, half of chattles
Son ADAM - remaining land
Daus MARY ROSS, JEAN ANDERSON - each five pounds cash
Gr son ROBERT MITCHEL - eighteen pounds in money
Youngest dau REBECCA - half of chattles, viz: stock & money

Exrs: James Denny, Robert Rankin
Wits: Adam Mitchel, Alexander Caldwell

A:0233 - WILLIAM MONTGOMERY, Sr. - 14 July 1796 - Prb Nov 1796
Wife HANNAH - plantation & third of moveable estate dw
Eldest son WILLIAM, eldest dau FRANCES BUCKANON, 2nd dau ELIZABETH BAILEY, dau HANNAH MCKNIGHT - each one silver dollar
Dau MARY - horse & saddle, bed & furniture
Son JOHN - all my smith tools
Son DAVID - to inherit from his mother plus 45 ac between Edmund McGlamor, John Gilchrist & myself
Gr dau JEAN, dau of REBECCA - 50 pounds at age of 18
Exrs: William Scott, John Gilchrist
Wits: John Gilchrist, Samuel Gilchrist, Robert Gilchrist

A:0234 - AARON MENDENHALL - 19 Nov 1789 - Prb Feb 1794
Eldest son JAMES - 100 ac off east end of my tract, smith tools
Son MOSES - 100 ac off west end of tract
Wife MIRIAM - house & rest of land to support the children
Daus DINAH, MIRIAM & CHARITY - share moveable estate
Exrs: Wife MIRIAM MENDENHALL, BETHUEL COFFIN
Wits: George Rayl, John Thomas, Molly Thomas

A:0235 - JAMES MARTIN - 16 Oct 1793 - Prb Feb 1796
Wife MARY - whole of my estate during widowhood
Son JOHN - 77 ac off NE of tract at death or remarriage of wife
Son JAMES - 100 ac off SE of tract, the same he lives on
Son HENRY - residue of land after at decease of wife
Daus FRANCIS MARTIN, MARY BEESON - all household furniture
Dau HANNAH SILLIVAN - five shillings
Exrs: Nathaniel Macy, Paul Macey
Wits: Joseph Iddings, Nathaniel Moore, Samuel Lamb

A:0236 - ZEDOCK MEARS - 16 Nov 1789 - Prb Feb 1790
Wife - lands, chattles, household furniture during widowhood
My children
Exr: Wife E_____ MEARS (Name not in will and not all appeared on microfilm in the probate--probably ELIZABETH)
Wit: James Mills

A:0237 - THOMAS MENDENHALL - 8 Oct 1782 - Prb Feb 1785
Wife PHEBE - my freehold land, house, farm tools, shop tools
Son MORDECAI - 68 ac off west end of my tract
Son SETH - 66 ac next to MORDECAI
Son ENOS - 66 ac next to SETH
Daus MARY, JANE, RUTH, PHEBE, BEULAH, & ASENATH - household furniture at decease of wife
Exr: Wife PHEBE MENDENHALL
Wits: Moses Mendenhall, Isaac Mendenhall, John Mendenhall

A:0238 - WILLIAM MARONEY - 14 Dec 1786
Son JOHN - 225 ac on east side of Rock Branch
Wife RUTH - my cleared land & may clear 30 ac more dw
Son ISAAC - to live with JOHN & be schooled, 20 pounds
Daus RACHEL, ELIZABETH, LYDIA - each a bed & furniture, cow at 16
George Hampton - to have cow at age 21
Son NATHAN - five shillings

Exr: Son JOHN MARONEY. Wits: John Ross, Mary Ross
"For probate, see Minute Docket No. 1, p. 3."

A:0239 - THOMAS MAJORS of Alamance Congregation, Planter - 10 Jan 1784 - "For probate see Minute Docket No. 2, p 26."
Wife MARGARET - my mare & saddle, household furniture, 2 cows
Gr son THOMAS PEASLEY - ten pounds
Gr dau ELENOR JOHNSON - twenty pounds
Exrs: Sons by law ROBERT PEASLEY, GEORGE STUART, Col JOHN PEASLEY, MARSHALL MCLEAN
Wits: Isish McBride, Thomas McLean

A:0240 - MATTHEW MACY - 24 May 1804 - Prb Aug 1809
Wife ABIGAIL - use & profits of plantation during widowhood
Daus SARAH SPRINGER, ABIGAIL COFFIN, ELIZABETH COFFIN - residue
Exrs: Zacheus Macy, Paul Macy, Jr.
Wits: Paul Macy, Nathaniel Macy

A:0241 - JOHN MENDENHALL - 20 Mar 1794 - Prb Feb 1800
Wife MARY - 1/3 of profits, furniture she had at marriage
Son MOSES - interest on bond of 24 pds 16 sh I have on home
Zachariah Stanley - 5 sh. Son-in-law NICHOLAS ROBINSON - 10 pds
Dau MIRIAM MENDENHALL - Bible, Fox's, Chalkey's Journals, Isaac Pennington's works, remainder of household goods, etc
Exr: Dau MIRIAM MENDENHALL
Wits: John Howell, Joseph Iddings, Stephano Haworth

A:0242 - EDWARD MULLOY - 27 May 1796 - Prb May 1801
Wife RUTH - share with children after obligations are met
Ch: JAMES, JANE, EDWARD, & DANIEL - all minors
Nephews JEREMIAH MULLOY, JAMES MULLOY (minors), children of my brother JAMES MULLOY late of Rockingham Co., N.C.
Abel & Thomas Edwards, orphan children of Thomas Edwards of Chatham County, N. C., deceased
Exr: Wife RUTH MULLOY
Wits: John Morris, Levi Coffin, Phebe Anthony

A:0243 - WALTER MILEHAM - 1 Sept 1798 - Prb Nov 1798
Wife ANN - third of land & moveable property, bed & furniture
Son WALTER - 2/3 of land, horse named Brock, bed & furniture
Dau SARAH MILEHAM - her mother's share of moveables, bed, etc
Dau CATHERINE WILLIAMS - five shillings
Sons VALENTINE & JOSEPH - land in Delewer State, five sh
Gr ch: SUSANNAH ROSS, TRAINAI ROSS, LEVI ROSS - 10 pds each
Heir of my son SAMUEL - five shillings
Exrs: Wife ANN MILEHAM, son VALENTINE MILEHAM
Wits: Ezekiel Dewiss, Nathaniel Simpson, John Tomlinson

A:0244 - MORDECAI MENDENHALL - 9 Jan 1796 - Prb Nov 1805
Wife CHARITY - my plantation and personal estate
Heirs of son RICHARD, heirs of son THOMAS, heirs of son AARON, and dau CHARITY MILLS - five shillings
Son ISAAC - 300 ac at death of wife, my smith tools
Sons MOSES, STEPHEN, MORDECAI, & ISAAC - money & residue
Exrs: Sons STEPHEN & ISAAC MENDENHALL
Wits: Matthew Coffin, Gallant Ayers, Hannah Coffin

A:0245 - ENOCH MACY - 22 July 1805 - Prb May 1806
Wife ANNA - real & personal estate; if she remarries: horse, saddle, bed & furniture, cow & calf
Son HENRY - 150 ac off south end, 50 ac bought of Henry Gravely
Sons THADEUS & STEPHEN - 140 ac off north end of tract
Daus DINAH, MIRIAM, & SARAH MACY - remainder of household goods
Exrs: Sons THADDEUS, HENRY & STEPHEN MACY
Wits: Isaac Gardner, Bethuel Coffin

A:0246 - WILLIAM MILLS - 17 May 1804 - Prb May 1804
Mother CATHERINE MILLS - $400 if she is living when I die
Polly Price, w/o David Price - $50 for her kindness
Sisters ANNE LACY, MARY MORRISON, MARGRET - proceeds of sale
Exrs: Friends Hance McCain, John Moore
Wits: Obadiah Dick, William Tease

A:0247 - GEORGE MENDENHALL - 3 Oct 1805 - Prb Nov 1805
Wife - use of plantation, featherbed & furniture, stock
Sons NATHAN & RICHARD - 5 pds off last payment of their land
Oldest dau JEMIMA - part of land bought of William Lane & John Sweet, bed & furniture, sorrel colt
Son JAMES - land bought of Isaac Beeson, southern edge of Federal Street, house he lives in, ac on each side
Son WILLIAM - mill seat bought of Samuel Lamb, lot in Jamestown
Dau HANNAH - 75 ac bought of John Talbert, cow, bed & furniture
Dau JUDITH - land adjoining Jamimas, feather bed & furniture
Dau MARY - 75 ac off tract bought of David Hogatt, bed, etc
Dau ABIGAIL - balance of land adj William & Mary, bed, etc
Son GEORGE, at 21 - land Bryan Smith lives on, mills & home plantation, to keep mills repaired and give his mother 1/3
Nathan, Jamima, Hannah, Judith, Mary, Abigail & Judith - each a lot in Jamestown. Mentions Whetstone Quarry in Randolph Co.
Exrs: Sons NATHAN & RICHARD MENDENHALL
Wits: Matthew Coffin, Thomas Moore, James Coffin, John Macy

A:0248 - MOSES MENDENHALL - 2 Sept 1804 - Prb Aug 1805
Wife BETTY - estate to support children; third if she marries
Exr: Father MOSES MENDENHALL
Wits: Moses Mendenhall, Sr., Richard Mendenhall, the 2nd

A:0249 - ABRAHAM MASON - 24 Sept 1814 - Prb Aug (No year)
Wife RACHEL - home plantation adj William Raper; 1/5 remainder
Anny Payne - $20. Dau SARAH STANLEY & THOM STANLEY - 10 sh
Ch: REUBEN, RODA PAYNE, LYDIA SMITH, ORY JONY - remaining 4/5
Exrs: Wife RACHEL MASON, William Raper
Wits: Soloman Raper, Benjamin Payne

A:0250 - JAMES MENDENHALL - 21 Sept 1811 - Prb Nov 1811
Wife - use of home plantation & mills to raise my children
Sons JOHN & AARON - land divided at age of 21
Daus MIRIAM, ANN, MARY, & SUSANNAH - each cow & calf, side saddle, share in proceeds of my riding chair, cotton machine
Exrs: Friends James Thornburgh, Harrison Edwards
Wits: Moses Mendenhall, Thomas Thornburgh

A:0251 - WILLIAM MONTGOMERY - 9 June 1806 - Prb Feb 1811

Wife REBECKAH - profits of estate dw, personal estate, horse
Dau RUTH HODSON - one dollar
Son WILLIAM - tract of land adj Williams' corner, Gardner
Son IRVIN - William to pay him third of worth of his land
Son SAMUEL - 50 ac adj Williams' corner, Caldwell's line
Dau MARY MONTGOMERY - bed & furniture, one dollar
Dau REBECKAH MONTGOMERY - side saddle, bed & furniture, 10 pds
Younger sons JAMES, GEORGE, & LEVI - remainder of plantation
Ch: ROBERT, WILLIAM, RUTH HODSON, SAMUEL, REBEKAH, IRVIN, JAMES, GEORGE, & LEVI - remainder of property
Exrs: Wife REBECKAH MONTGOMERY, son ROBERT MONTGOMERY
Wits: Jonathan Parker, William Beeson, James Leonard

A:0252 - HUBIKKUK MORGAN - 13 Feb 1816 - Prb Feb 1816
Wife NANCY - sole use & management of my estate
Stepson SAMUEL HUNTER - remainder of estate after wife's death
Brother JAMES - ten shillings
Sisters CHARLOTTY HEATH - $50; DEBORHA RIGHT - ten shillings
Larkin More Causey - $50. Smith tools & plantation, formerly the property of John Morgan to be sold; money to NANCY
Exrs: Wife NANCY MORGAN, Jeremiah Forbis
Wits: James Bright, Margret Bright

A:0253 - JOHN MCKNIGHT of the Province of North Carolina and County of Rowan - 12 Aug 1770 - Prb May 1771
Sons ROBERT & WILLIAM - my land, but if the child my wife is with is a boy, land to be divided three ways
Wife CATRINE - two work horses, plow, plow irons, plow harying, use of land until youngest son be of age, four cows
Ch: ELIZABETH, ROBERT, WILLIAM, & CATRINE - to be educated
Exrs: Wife CATRINE MCKNIGHT, Alexander McKnight, Thomas Donnel
Wits: Robert Rankin, James Denny

A:0254 - WILLIAM MCKNIGHT - 24 Nov 1771 - Prb Feb 1772
Brother HUGH MCKNIGHT - remainder of estate after debts paid
Exrs: Matthew Scott, William Scott
Wits: Gabriel Scott, Matthew Scott, Thomas Scott, Wm. Scott

A:0255 - TIMOTHY MCCALL - 25 Oct 1774 - Prb Nov 1774
Fill Putale - 50 pds if found; otherwise to Exr's sick wife
Samuel Morrow - suit of clothes, white shirt
Exrs: Alexander Mood, Thomas Clos
Wits: Henry Colston, James Alton, Samuel Morrow

A:0256 - ALEXANDER MCKNIGHT - 26 July 1774 - Prb May 1775
Son ROBERT - all my land
Wife HANNAH - land until ROBERT is of age dw, bed & furniture
Dau JEAN - 2/3 of moveables when of age, chest of drawers
Exrs: Alexander Caldwell, James Donnell
Wits: Robert Donnell, Moses McClean, Mary McClean

A:0257 - JOHN MCMURRY - 24 Dec 1789 - Prb 1791
Wife - mare & saddle, cow, maintenance by son WILLIAM
Son JAMES, daus BETSEY CARR & MARGARET BROWN - twenty shillings
Son JOHN - 20 shillings & 30 ac adj his own land
Son WILLIAM - home plantation & necessary utensils

Dau JEAN MCMURRY - roan horse & saddle, bed & furniture, cow
Son ROBERT - 100 pds, stallion colt, his boarding fee while he is under the tuition of Rev'd David Caldwell
Exrs: Friends William Gowdy, Henry Ross
Wits: William McAden, William Gowdy, Henry Ross

A:0258 - JOHN MCCALL of York Co., Pennsylvania - 1 May 1780 - Prb Feb 1796. Brother MATTHEW - five pounds
Cousins ELIZABETH WALKER & MARTHA COCKRAIN - 500 pounds
Cousin SAMUEL MCCLELLAND - 300 pds & his two sisters - 100 pds
My cousin, wife of James Hall - 100 pounds
Friend John Lindsay, Senr - 100 pds
Cousins MARY WILSON - 100 pds; AGNES CARSON - 500 pds, JENNE MAYER - 100 pds; any cousins, 1st or 2nd, that come from Ireland - 100 pds; also I bequeath 100 pds for relief of poor
Cousin ROBERT LINDSAY - my land & adj ferry in York & Lancaster Counties, known as Nelsons Ferry in deed from my brother MATHY MCCALL
Exrs: Robert Lindsay, Robert Cockrain
Wits: Jonas Littell, Daniel Baldwin, James Hellan

A:0259 - MARY MCCONNELL - 21 Nov 1794 - Prb Nov 1796
Sons living in Pa.: JOHN MCCONNEL, WM MCCONNEL - each 5 sh
Dau MARY BLAYR - gown, petticote, cloke, pair of bed blankets
Dau MARTHA LACKY - petticote, bed curtains
Son-in-law ADAM LACKY - no charge for his losing my mare
Younger dau LINVILL MCBRIDE - one of my gowns
Margrett McBride, d/o Francis McBride - my corded poplin gown
Martha McBride, d/o Francis McBride - my bed, red quilt, blanket
Samuel, s/o Francis McBride - my shoe buckles
Agnes Blayr, d/o James Blayr - my bonnett
Exr: Adam Lackey
Wits: Jean Elder, Harry Porter, Ralph Gorrell

A:0260 - JOSEPH MCDOWELL - 3 Apr 1797 - Prb May 1797
Wife - half of mansion house, bed & furniture, spinning wheel
Son JOSEPH, daus ELIZABETH DUFF & HANNAH FERGUSON - five sh
Dau MARY MCDOWELL - her bed & bed cloths that she used at Mr. Caldwels & her saddle & bridle, Bible, half the mansion house
Son JAMES (if alive) - all my late son JOHN'S clothes, half the land; if he doesn't return, land goes to dau MARY
Exrs: Son JOSEPH MCDOWELL, Hance McKean
Wits: William Scott, Robert McCuiston, Hugh Shaw

A:0261 - JOHN MCMURRY - 27 Feb 1798 - Prb May 1798
Wife MARY - negro woman Violet & her ch: Sall, Tom, Peter land with every privilege during widowhood
Nephews JOHN, s/o JAMES MCMURRY, & JOHN MCMURRY, s/o ROBERT MCMURRY, dec'd - land after death of wife
Brother-in-law JOHN MITCHELL - my negro Will
Exrs: Wife MARY MCMURRY, James McMurry
Wits: James McMurry, Robert Johnson, Henry Ross

A:0262 - CHARLES MCDARMOND - 15 Aug 1799 - Prb Nov 1799
Wife HANNAH - estate, stock, one still during widowhood
Son JAMES - to inherit from his mother

Exrs: Isack Gray, Williamson Brown
Wits: Michel McDarmon, William Gray, Robert Bell

A:0263 - JAMES MCADOW - 23 Sept 1799 - Prb Feb 1800
Wife MARGARET - land to be sold to buy land in State of Canituck, household furniture until daus come of age
Daus MARY SARAH, DORCAS, & MARTHA
Oldest sons WILLIAM & DAVID - to be bound out to learn a trade
Sons EZRAH - negro Dick; JOHN - my best saddle
Exrs: Wife MARGARET MCADOW, John Houston, Levenus Huston
Wits: William McAdow, William Ryan, Robert Ryan

A:0264 - MOSES MCCUISTON - 5 Dec 1799 - Prb Feb 1800
Wife ELIZABETH - sole of my estate during widowhood
Each of daus at time of marriage - saddle & household furniture
Sons ROBERT, JOHN, WILLIAM - land at age of maturity
"Children to be schooled at expense of ye perishable part of my estate." Exrs: Wife ELIZABETH MCCUISTON, Robert Thompson
Wits: John Cummings, Thomas Blair

A:0265 - JAMES MCGREADY - 20 Sept 1800 - Prb Nov 1800
Son SAMUEL R. - 100 ac on south & east of plantation
Wife JEAN - house, third of moveables, maintenance by SAMUEL R.
Sons JUDAH & AARON - 133 ac of land, mare, colt
Sons JAMES - $10, 133 ac; DAVID - $1; ISRAEL - $40
Exrs: Sons MOSES MCGREADY, Samuel Rutherford McGready
Wits: Isaac Perkins, Pherinah Perkins, Jonathan Hodgson

A:0266 - PATRICK MCGIBBONY - 12 Jan 1804 - Prb May 1804
Son DAVID - negro Jim, horse, farm to be laid off by John Cunningham & Wm. Armfield on waters of South Buffaloe
Dau MARGRET GILLASPIE - negro girl Patience, interest off 100 pds
Dau ISABEL MCGIBONEY - negro Hannah, saddle
Dau MARTHA MCGIBBONY - one bond on Wm. Mills, Jr., Hamilton Nance McCain, & Abner Weatherley
Friend Col Daniel Gillaspie - use of negro Isaac for life
My four youngest daus & dau MARGARET GILLASPIE'S 2nd child that have brown hair - my land in Tennessee
Dau JEAN MCGIBONEY - one negro boy; Guardian: James Denny
Exr: John Cunningham
Wits: William Armfield, Thomas Cummins

A:0267 - JAMES MCMURRY - 23 Mar 1804 - Prb Feb 1805
Son JOHN - proceeds from land to replace the $150 left to him by his uncles at 21, colt
Wife ELIZABETH - horse & saddle, negroes Mary Ails, Will Choice of stock, furniture, certain lands
Daus JEAN (my chest), UPHIAH & HANNAH - bed & furniture each
Exrs: William Smith, John Closs
Wits: Joseph Closs, John Smith

A:0268 - JAMES MCADOW - 8 May 1800 - Prb Nov 1805
Wife - negro woman Silve, bed, 2 cows, her large seal skin trunk, spinning wheel, firewood, half acre of flax grown for her, garden & cotton patch to herself, third of my books, etc
Sons SAMUEL & DAVID - land, negroes George, Jerry, Dinah, Nat, Heber, Jacob, Gilph, Peter, Anne, Nancy, & Judith

Sons JAMES & WILLIAM MCADOW - land whereon they live
Daus MARGARET & JEAN - five shillings each
Gr dau ANN BOYD - horse & saddle, bed & furniture, 2 cows
Exrs: Sons JAMES & WILLIAM MCADOW
Wits: James McAdow, William McAdow

A:0269 - JOHN MCBRIDE - 25 Jan 1806 - Prb May 1806
Unmarried ch: JAMES, ELIZABETH, JEAN & SARAH - all my estate
Son JOHN - $100. Dau MARGARET MCGANPY'S two sons: DAVID & JAMES MCGANPHY - $30 each when they come of age
Gr son JOHN MCBRIDE - $100, one middle rated horse & saddle
"In consideration of the distance of place of residence of my heirs, they are forbidden to sell anything until all agree."
Exrs: Son JAMES MCBRIDE, Samuel Allison
Wit: Samuel McDill

A:0270 - JOHN MCCLINTOCK - 29 Dec 1806 - Prb Aug 1807
Wife ISABELLA - plantation & all my lands, houses, negroes, stock
Sons JOHN, WILLIAM, SAMUEL & ROBERT - inheritance from wife
Daus ISABELLA DICK & NANCY BALLENGER - each $1
Exrs: Wife ISABELLA MACCLINTOCK, John Gilchrist
Wits: John Gilchrist, Moses Gilchrist

A:0271 - JOHN MCLEAN - 15 June 1804 - Prb Aug 1807
Sons JOSEPH, THOMAS, ROBERT & MARSHAL - each $20
Daus NELLY, MARGARET, JEAN, & POLLY - each $20
Son JOHN'S son JOHN & POLLY'S son JOHN - $10
Son ROBERT - land on Alamance Cr adj James Dick, Dorcas McClean
Son MARSHAL (remainder of land) & his dau JEAN - my chest
Dau JEAN - my bed stead, bed & furniture
Daus NANCY & ELIZABETH - each $125, free use of dwelling house to be allowed a half acre of good ground for flax, large Bible
Exrs: Joseph McClean, Senr., Isaiah McBride, Marshal McClean
Wits: Thomas Greer(?), Joseph McGakey

A:0272 - GIDEON MCKENNA - 30 Jan 1809 - Prb Aug 1809
Daus MARY BISHOP & ELIZABETH HARDIN - each five shillings
Sons WILLIAM - 85 ac of land; SHADRACK & JAMES - each 30 ac
Wife CHARITY - stock, furniture, farming utensils during wid.
Exrs: Wife CHARITY MCKENNA, James Wiley
Wits: James Frazier, John McKaige

A:0273 - SAMUEL MCDILL - 19 May 1811 - Prb Aug 1811
Wife JEAN - use of half of plantation & negro Charles dw
Son ZEAK - 215 ac embracing the home place
Dau BETSEY - $100, bed & furniture, horse & saddle, 2 cows
Exrs: Sons ZEAK MCDILL, THOMAS MCCANN
Wits: W. Corsbee, David Matthews

A:0274 - GEORGE MCKENEY - 17 Mar 1801 - Prb May 1801
Son GEORGE & daus JENNY STANFORD, LETITIA MCKENEY - five sh
Wife ELISEBETH - negro Billy, all of estate during widowhood to raise 3 younger children: son DEMSEY, daus POLLY & FANNY
Ch of son JARRAT & dau FANNY MCKENEY's dau CATEY - five sh each
Exrs: Wife ELISEBETH MCKENY, son DEMSEY MCKENEY
Wits: Justain Knott, John Medearis, Patsey Pegram

A:0275 - THOMAS MORELAND - 31 Aug 1792 - Prb Feb 1793
Wife JANE - plantation, negroes Sam, Sue, & Hannah
Son WILLIAM - plantation at wife's death, "one negro man Peter Arney Ellis George Elick & Lucy"
Son FRANCIS - "one negro man Joe Phib Tappley Silvey"
Dau ELIZABETH (left blank) - one negro girl Patt
Dau MARY ASHLEY - one negro man Toney Kett
To Joseph Pangh (?) - that part of land south of the creek
Exrs: Son WILLIAM MORELAND, Hezekiah Bevill
Wits: Thomas Reaves, William Williams, William Simpson

A:0276 - JOHN NATION - 15 Dec 1772 - Prb May 1772
Son JOSEPH - plantation whereon I live
Wife BITHIAH - all moveable property during widowhood
Other ch: CHRISTOPHER, ELIZABETH VICKREY, ANNA BULLAR, BITHIAH ROBINS, FRANCES ROBINS - each one shilling
Exrs: Wife BITHIAH NATION, son JOSEPH NATION
Wits: Benjamin Beeson, Richard Beeson, Isaac Beeson

A:0277 - JOHN NOTS (NOTZ) - 15 Sept 1775 - Prb Nov 1775
Wife IDA(?) - part of mufabels, cow,"five pounds of my land"
Oldest dau CATRENA - 80 ac whereon I live
Youngest dau BARBRA - other 84 ac of my land
Exrs: Mulkia Fogelman, Jacob Greeson
Wits: George Cortner, George Fogleman

A:0278 - ROBERT NEELEY - 6 July 1787 - Prb Nov 1787
Headstones for my father & mother who are buried at Allimance Meeting House
Wife MARTHA - use of plantation, stock, farming equipment dw
Dau ELIZABETH NEELLEY - 100 ac adj John Coe, pewter plates, etc
Son JAMES - 320 ac on head waters of the Alamance, desk, etc
Exrs: Wife MARTHA NEELEY, William Dickey, Thomas Jones
Wits: John Coe, William Dobson, Sarah Coe

A:0279 - ALEXANDER NELSON - 24 Oct 1799 - Prb Nov 1799
Wife JEAN - all my land during widowhood
Sons JAMES & ROBERT - to inherit from their mother
Daus ELISEBETH, RUTH, & EZEBELL NELSON - one cow & calf each
Exrs: Wife JEAN NELSON, Justain Knott
Wits: John Bevill, Abraham Endsley, William Bevill

A:0280 - MARY NEWMAN - 7 May 1810 - Verbal will taken by Robert Bell, J.P., on day of her death
Son EDWARD - one sorrel mare; dau SARAH - one sorrel colt
Dau ANN - pewter dish & bason, plates, forks
Son BENJAMIN - feather bed & furniture, cow
Wits: Proved on date written by Ruth Clark & Elizabeth Tharp

A:0281 - GEORGE NELSON, Sr. - 21 Jan 1801 - Prb Aug 1802
Wife SUSANNA - use of everything not mentioned as belonging to George, until 1813, dw, children to be educated
Sons GEORGE, JESSEY, JOSEPH, & ALEXANDER - each 75 ac
Ch: GEORGE, JESSEY, MARGRET, PRUDENCE, SALLEY, OLLEYFAN, BETSEY, JOSEPH, ALEXANDER, & NANCY NELSON - daus to receive each one feather bed & cow at marriage

Exrs: Drury Peeples, Jeremiah Cunningham
Wits: Joel Harris, Frederich Peeples

A:0282 - SAMUEL OWEN - 19 May 1805 - Prb Aug 1808
Wife JUDITH - bag of feathers, 2 sheets, coverlaid, dresser, etc
Dau MARY at age 18 - bed, coverlaid, 3 sheets, dish & plates
Exr: Harman Howlet
Wits: Jacob Brazell, Ann Howlet, J. H. Howlet

A:0283 - EPHRAIM POTTER - 28 Feb 1774 - Prb Nov 1775
Sons JOSEPH & ABRAHAM - my land on Piney Fork of Town Creek
Daus AILCE, MARTHA, & SARAH POTTER - 1/6 part personal prop.
Wife SARAH - to share personal property with children
Son JOHN - five shillings starling
Exrs: William Garrott, Edward Stubblefield
Wits: Isham Browder, Thomas Norris

A:0284 - JAMES PORTER - 6 Dec 1777 - Prb May 1778
Wife ANN - half of land & moveables
Dau VILET PORTER - to inherit from her mother
Son JAMES - one sorrel mare
Exrs: Wife ANN PORTER, Joseph Brown
Wits: Hugh Porter, John Hodge

A:0285 - DAVID PHILPOTT - 28 Feb 1781 - Prb Aug 1781
Wife MARY ANN - 233 ac on S side Hogans Cr, negroes Nathan, Mall
Son CHARLES - 100 ac bought of Capt John Cook in Caswell Co adj
John McCollum, Major Dixon when he becomes 21
Dau ELIZABETH, at 16 - negro girl Easter, cow & calf
Son EDWARD - 86 ac on N side of Hogans Cr, negro boy Henry
Exrs: Wife MARY ANN PHILPOTT, Brother JOHN PHILPOTT
Witts: T. G. Turner(?), Thomas Weatherly, John McCollum

A:0286 - CALEB PERKINS - 1788 - "See min Doc No 2, p. 25"
Brother JOSEPH, Jr. - my saddle, two bushels of corn
Bro & sister ISAAC & MARY PERKINS - each a cow
Brother JOHN - fifty bushels of corn
Younger bros THOMAS & JARED at 21 - my house, rest of property
Exrs: Brothers JOHN & ISAAC PERKINS
Wits: Joseph Perkins, John Thomas, Aaron Mendenhall

A:0287 - WILLIAM PARKHILL - 26 Aug 1789
Wife NANCY - her bed, my books, 1/2 proceeds of sale of estate
Brother JOHN & sisters MARTHA & MERYANN, and JOHN THOMAS (son
of MERYANN) - other half of proceeds of sale of estate
Exrs: William Eken, William Bready
Wits: William Eken, Jeremiah Shelly
"For probate, see Minute Docket No 2, p 82"

A:0288 - EZEKIEL PRITCHETT - 20 July 1796 - Prb Aug 1796
Sons ZACHARIAH & EZEKIEL - each one shilling & no more
Daus ELIZABETH PRITCHETT & UNITY PRITCHETT - each one shilling
Son ISAAC - home plantation, mare, heifer, 6 pewter plates
Ezekel Gullet - 100 ac on which George Forbis lived
Zebulon Gullett - 100 ac on which John Hood lived
Ch JOHN ZEBLON, ISAAC, HESSIE & SARAH - remainder of estate

Exr: Son ZEBULON PRITCHETT
Wits: Robert Paisley, James Mills, William Paisley

A:0289 - CATHERINE PLUNKET - 1 June 1801 - Prb Nov 1801
Bro THOMAS PLUNKET - my part of my father's estate that has not been yet divided
Exrs: Brother THOMAS PLUNKET, James O'Neal
Wits: William Rose, George Shafnor

A:0290 - WILLIAM PLUNKET - Noncupative will proved in Court Aug Term 1801 by James O'Neal & Samuel Lindsay
Caty - all the moveables, as much of the fruit every year that she wants, one end of the house, firewood, liberty to keep a cow and a horse beast, garden spot and cotton patch
Son IS. - the remainder of my property

A:0291 - EDWARD PEGRAM - 21 Feb 1802 - Prb May 1802
Wife PATTY - third of land during widowhood, all my land until the youngest child becomes of age, negro Fanny & negro girls China, Sucky, & Martha
Exrs: Wife PATTY PEGRAM, William Jean
Wits: Travis Jones, John Medearis, Massey Medearis

A:0292 - ELEANOR PRIOR - 4 Nov 1804 - Prb Nov 1804
Sons EMMERY & PASCHAL BRINNAJIM PRIOR - proceeds of sale, beds
Exr: John Moore
Wits: James Johnson, William Moore, Arno Moore

A:0293 - SAMUEL PORTER - 20 Oct 1806 - Prb Nov 1806
My father - $100. Brother JOHN & wife - $10
Sister MARGARET $500. Cathren Quener - $100
Isaiah McBride - $100 if Cathren Quener should die
William Finley who lives in State of Caintucke - $200
Allimance Congregation - $100. Allimance Settlement & Allimance Congregation - $200 for purchasing books under committee of 7, including Jedediah Cusick and executors
Exrs: John Porter, Isaiah McBride, Walter McCarrel
Wits: Margaret McBride, William McBride

A:0294 - JOSEPH PERKINS - 1 Dec 1806 - Prb Feb 1807
Wife ANN - best bed & furniture, mare, colt, heifer, third
Son JAREA - 2 pair drawing chains, handsaw, frow chisels, augre
Sons JOSEPH, JOHN, ISAAC, & THOMAS - each one dollar
Grandson JOSEPH, son of JOSEPH - $20
Daus MARY & BETTY - each a third of proceeds from sale
Exr: Moses Mendenhall
Wits: Moses Mendenhall, Mary Mendenhall, Charity Mendenhall

A:0295 - JOHN PAISLEY - 25 July 1811 - Prb Nov 1811
Wife MARY ANN - all my estate during her natural life
Son WILLIAM - two negroes Milly & Aaron
Son JAMES - two negroes Gilbert & James
Dau NANCY HANNAH - negroes Sophia & Teny, land whereon I live north of the present Great Road & east of Burch Creek
Son JOHN - negroes Peter, Cate & Dick, home plantation
Son GEORGE - negroes Emmy & Isaac

Dau ELIZABETH GIBSON - negroes Rose & Mary
Dau MARY ANN PAISLEY - negroes Jenny & Moses, enough other property to make her equal what ELIZABETH has received
Exrs: Son JOHN PAISLEY, Moses Gibson
Wits: William Paisley, George Paisley

A:0296 - JAMES POE - 9 Feb 1812 - Prb Feb 1812
Wife SARAH - estate as long as she remains my widow
All my ch: GABRIL, NANCY, METILDY, BETSEY, SANDY, WILLIAM, RENEY, HANNAH, JAMES, POLLY, & JOHN
Exrs: William Poe, Josiah Unthank
Wits: Bethuel Coffin, John Unthank, David McGready

A:0297 - JAMES PORTER - 24 Feb 1812 - Prb Aug 1812
Son JOHN - 360 ac plantation I now live on
Dau MARGARET WILEY - $300, cow, tea table, half the pewter
Exr: Son JOHN PORTER. Wits: W. McConnel, Joseph Hanner

A:0298 - JEHU PEEPLES, Planter - 23 Apr 1813 - Prb Aug 1813
Wife CATY - that part of plantation whereon I live, seven slaves
Children - all stock, tools & furniture my wife doesn't need
Son WYATT - to inherit plantation from his mother, 68 ac of the tract where George McKinney formerly lived
Son HARBERT - 150 ac purchased from Hugh Cummings
Dau SALLY JEAN - $120
Sons DRURY, HERBERT, NATHANIEL & WYATT and daus SALLIE JEAN and NANCY MCKINNEY - to divide slaves
Wife of deceased son SETH PEEPLES - to receive no share
Exrs: Caty Peeples, sons DRURY & WYATT PEEPLES
Wits: Christian Wagoman, T. Bagge

A:0299 - WILLIAM PARSONS - Noncupative will - Sworn to by George Parsons and John Parker before Jonathan Parker, JP on 13 May 1814. Son GEORGE - smith tools
Sons JAMES & JOHN at 21 - property divided equally
Wife ELEANOR - to have peaceful life off of the place
Dau MARY - $5 worth of property
Daus KATHERINE, RUTH, PATIENCE, CHARITY & ELEANOR - remainder

A:0300 - HENRY PORTER - 6 Oct 1813 - Prb Feb 1816
George Griffin's ch - use of plantation for term of four years; then to be sold & proceeds to benefit orphan children
Society Library, if one has been instituted in 4 yrs - my books
Henry Porter Griffin - my Bible at the age of 21
Exrs: Levi Huston, John Finley
Wits: Eliza Finley, William McCaney

A:0301 - WILLIAM QUAIL - 25 July 1803 - Prb May 1805
Wife ELIZABETH - plantation during widowhood
Son SAMUEL - to inherit plantation
Son JAMES - colt bought of Nelly Kirkman, 100 ac on S side
Son ROBERT - 100 ac on E side original tract adj Robert Hannah
Dau ISBEL QUAIL - gray mare, colt, bed, walnut chest, 6 forks
Dau MARGARET QUAIL - heifer, cloke over what she has received
Ch: WILLIAM, AGNES MUEHAED (MOREHEAD?), MARY RIDDLE, DAVID - each ten shillings over what each has received

Gr dau ANN QUAIL MOREHEAD, dau of AGNES - 10 pds hard money
Exrs: Wife ELIZABETH QUAIL, Daniel Gillaspie
Wits: Thomas Landreth, James Hannah

A:0302 - JAMES REEVES - No date. - Prb Aug 1781
Wife MILISENT - plantation, furniture, third of stock, geese
Son MALACHIA - cow & calf. Son JEREMIAH - two yews & a lamb
Son WILLIAM - plantation at wife's death
Dau ELIZABETH HOLMES - two yews & lamb
Daus JUDITH MOORE & DELILAH RUSSEL - each one heifer
Dau RHODA PARKER - one lamb
Gr son JAMES REEVES - my roan horse & saddle & bridle
Exrs: Wife MILISENT REEVES, son WILLIAM REEVES
Wits: John Campbell, Michel Reeves, Jeremiah Reeves

A:0303 - WILLIAM REA - 23 Feb 1789 - Prb May 1789
Wife MARGARET - 50 pds, use of land rented from Jean Blair
My sons & daus as they come of age - land on the western waters of this state, also land on the Cumberland River, after satisfying the Power of Attorney given to James Billingsley
Exrs: Henry Ross, William Gowdy
Wits: James Billingsly, William Gowdy, Henry Ross

A:0304 - HENRY REED - 13 Apr 1789 - Prb Aug 1789
Wife AGNESS - child's part dw to raise & school my children, negro wench to help raise children
Exrs: William Gowdy, William Scott
Wits: William Graham, Moses McCuiston, William Reed

A:0305 - JOHN RUDDUCK - 7 Oct 1787 - Prb Feb 1790
Wife JANE - use of dwelling house & half of plantation
Ch: DINAH MENDENHALL, PHEBE MENDENHALL, JOHN, Jr., JEMIMA PENDY, JANE, RUTH, WILLIAM (plantation), & SARAH SANDERS - each 20 shillings, divide furniture at decease of wife
Exrs: Sons JOHN & WILLIAM RUDDUCK, William Tomlinson
Wits: Jno. Talbert, Samuel Pidgeon, Thos. Thornburgh

A:0306 - JOHN ROSS - 19 Apr 1791 - Prb May 1791
Daus REBECKER, NANCY, MARGRET - horse valued at 12 pds, saddle & bridle, two cows, bed & furniture, each
Youngest daus MARY & JEAN - same as their sisters when of age
Son THOMAS - 200 ac west of John Tomlinson, horse & saddle, 2 cows & calves, plough, plough irons & other tacklins thereof
Son JOHN - 22 ac, reserving the privilege of my wife living in the house & her maintenance
Sons JAMES & ANDREW - 350 ac divided
Wife MARY - her horse & saddle, bed & furniture, household furn
Exrs: Wife MARY ROSS, son THOMAS ROSS, Walter Denny
Wits: John Starrat, Edward Green, Jean Flack

A:0307 - JOHN RHODES of Rockingham Co. - 5 Oct 1791 - Nov 1792
Wife FORTUNE - all effects & land she bought at the vendue (sale) of the effects that did belong to the estate of her former husband Malichia Reeves
Heirs of my first born, Hezikiah - one French crown
Son JOSEPH - one French crown to his use

Dau SARAH - negro named Chib, feather bed & furniture
Son SAMUEL - negro named Chance, 1/2 remainder of estate
Son ABSOLOM - negro named Bob, 1/2 remainder of estate
Exrs: John Rhodes, son-in-law William Reeves
Wits: Henry Work, Samuel Rhodes

A:0308 - ADAM REITZEL - 3 June 1792 - Prb Nov 1792
Wife - all estate for support & education of children; at her decease, inventory to be taken by John Long & John Moore and divided equally between my children
Ch: HENRY, CHRISTOPHER, ADAM, JOHN, MARGRET, MIKE, & GEORGE
Exr: Wife. Wits: John Long, Phillip Kime

A:0309 - JOHN RYAN - 11 Oct 1794 - Prb Nov 1794
Wife MARGARET - third of moveable property, plantation until children come of age, negroes Sall & Press
Daus ELLENOR, MARGARET, & GINNIA - each one cow
Sons ROBERT, JOHN & WILLIAM - share 300 ac of land
Exrs: Sons ROBERT, JOHN, & WILLIAM RYAN
Wits: William Sullaven, Elenar Sullivan

A:0310 - WILLIAM RAPER - 16 July 1794 - Prb Feb 1795
Wife ELIZABETH - use of my house, orchard, garden, corn cribs
Son WILLIAM - plantation whereon I live
Ch of dau CHRISTIAN, dec'd, who married RICHARD GLOVYER - 15 shillings with what I have already given them
Son THOMAS - 10 pds & what he has already received
Sons JACOB & WILLIAM, daus ELIZABETH (wife of JAMES GRAY), & LYDIA (wife of DAVID KILLEY) - remainder of estate
Exrs: Sons JACOB & WILLIAM RAPER
Wits: Nathaniel Moore, Stephen Ruke, Henry Davis

A:0311 - WILLIAM RUSSELL - 19 June 1792 - Prb May 1795
Wife ELINOR - all land & property she had when I married her to dispose of to her children according to agreement; also a cow & calf & her spinning wheel as her portion of my estate
Son ROBERT - land where he lives, east of the still house
Sons WILLIAM, JOHN, DAVID, JAMES, & ALEXANDER - rest of estate
Daus ELISABETH DOWNEY & MARTHA MAXWELL - household furniture
Exrs: Son-in-law JAMES MAXWELL, John Gilchrist
Wits: Valentine Mileham, William Fleming, Berry Daugherty

A:0312 - ROBERT RANKIN - 30 May 1795 - Prb Nov 1795
Son GEORGE - 1,000 ac entered by James Maloy on Buffaloe Cr and land on Duck River, desk, carpenter tools
Gr sons WILLIAM RANKIN WILSON, ANDREW WILSON, MAXWELL WILSON (minors) sons of dau MARY WILSON - remainder of land
Dau ISABEL - negro Rhoda & her bed clothes
my daus - fifth part of moveables with GEORGE a fifth
Andrew Wilson, formerly my son-in-law, to be guardian for gr ch
Exrs: John Dowell, William Scott
Wits: William Scott, Walter Mileham, John Rees

A:0313 - ROBERT RAMSEY - 15 Oct 1799 - Noncupative Will Prb Nov 1799. Wishes his horse to be sold to pay expenses to Thomas McCulloch; Charles Harden to have his shoe boots

A:0314 - JOHN ROSS - 4 Dec 1801 - Prb Feb 1802
Wife MARY - her living off the land as long as she remains unmarried, her bed, saddle, etc; child's part if she remarries
Exrs: Wife MARY ROSS, brother THOMAS ROSS
Wits: John Wollun, James Ross

A:0315 - WILLIAM RANKIN - 5 Dec 1803 - Prb Feb 1804
Wife JENNIE - home plantation, stock, utensils, negro Leven to raise and school my family
Sons THOMAS, ROBERT, & WILLIAM - at 21 have the land at convenience of wife - 200 ac on Reedy Fork adj William Denny & my father-in-law JOHN CHABERS
Son THOMAS - 225 ac on Reedy Br adj William Donnel
Oldest daus ELISABETH, AGNESS & SARAH - 1 pound
Youngest daus ANA & JENCY - each a horse & saddle, 2 cows, bed
Exrs: Wife JENNY RANKIN, son JOHN RANKIN
Wits: John Rankin, Senr., Joseph Rankin, Robert Rankin

A:0316 - WILLIAM RUDDUCK - 17 July 1797 - Prb Feb 1804
Wife MARY - half of plantation & moveable property
Dau JANE - half of estate; all if her mother remarries
Exrs: Wife MARY RUDDUCK, Isaac Mendenhall

A:0317 - ROBERT RUSSELL - 12 Mar 1804 - Prb May 1804
Wife SUSANNA - whole & sole of my estate; third if she marries
Negro Woman Circy & her son Jeffery - their freedom
John Donelson - $50
Robert & Alexander Russell, sons of Robert Russel, dec'd - $50
William Russell (s/o bro WM.), Thomas & Robert Washington Russel (sons of bro DAVID) - remainder of estate
Exrs: Wife SUSANNA RUDDUCK, Robert Thompson, John Gullett
Wits: Edward Weatherly, Martin Weatherly, William Weatherly

A:0318 - ANANIAS RECORDS - 8 June 1806 - Prb Feb 1807
Wife MARY - sole use of plantation during widowhood
Wife MARY'S grandchild, ELIJAH LEWARK - to inherit plantation
Elijah Lewark & Joseph Lewark - moveable property from wife
Exrs: Wife MARY RECORDS, Jeremy Forbis
Wits: Nehemiah Causy

A:0319 - WILLIAM RUSSELL - 21 Aug 1810 - Prb Nov 1810
Wife MARGARET - 50 ac of land & dwelling house during widowhood
Daus SUSANNA ROSS, SARAH CHILCUTT, MARGARET DILWORTH, MARTHA DONNELL - each five shillings North Carolina currency
Daus LUCRETIA & NANCY - each bed & furniture, etc
Sons ROBERT, WILLIAM, & JESSE - divide my lands
Exrs: Wife MARGARET RUSSELL, Thomas Ross
Wits: Howel Parker, James Ross

A:0320 - JAMES RUSSELL - 10 Apr 1811 - Prb May 1812
Sons WILLIAM & ROBERT - each five shillings starling
Son DAVID - 50 ac adj Sampson Stewart, Luke Dier
Son ALEXANDER - 150 ac, moveable property, & DAVID'S 50 ac if he "don't come in six years"
Gr son JAMES RUSSELL, oldest son of ALEXANDER - to inherit land from his father
Dau MARTHA - five shillings starling

Exrs: William Vowell, Alexander Russell
Wits: William Vowell, Wiley Stewart

A:0321 - JOHN RANKIN - 17 July 1812 - Prb May 1814
Wife HANNAH, third of plantation, home, horse & saddle, etc
Youngest son ROBERT - all the land, wagon & gears, farming tools
Daus POLLY & ANN - each a bed & furniture, their loom & gears
My married children - five shillings & what they have received
Exrs: Oldest sons SAMUEL & JOSEPH RANKIN
Wits: James Gray, Robert Rankin, William Rankin

A:0322 - HANNAH RANKIN - 30 Apr 1814 - Prb Aug 1814
Sons JOSEPH & ROBERT - my two sheep, cow & little pot
Daus POLLY & ANN - balance of estate
All my children - to divide my books
Exrs: Oldest sons SAMUEL & JOSEPH RANKIN
Wits: James Gray, Robert Gray

A:0323 - DAVID REYNOLDS - 7 Nov 1812 - Prb Aug 1815
Gr son DAVID BENBO - $100 note I have on Wm. Dun & David Worth
Dau LYDIA BENBO - $100 note on each from Wm Dun & David Worth
Son-in-law BENJAMIN BENBO - $40 for my use of black Bill
Daus ELIXABETH DAVIS & LYDIA BENBO & niece SUSANNAH REYNOLDS
(dau of bro JEREMIAH REYNOLDS) - remainder of my estate
Exrs: Jonathan Parker, Nephew DAVID REYNOLDS
Wits: John Reynolds, Rezin Reynolds

A:0324 - SUCA ROBERTSON - 15 Dec 1796 - Prb Aug 1797
Bro JAMES - my bed I now lie in & furniture, horse colt
Bro NATHANIEL - my cow
Nancy J. Rose - my hunting saddle and cardriel at mother's dec.
Exr: Brother JAMES ROBERTSON
Wits: William Rose, Nathaniel Robertson

A:0325 - JOSEPH RUCKMAN - 13 Apr 1792 - Prb Nov 1792
Wife SARAH - interest on proceeds of sale of free estate, cow, etc
New Garden Meeting - fourth of my free estate
Ch: HANNAH DILLON, ISAIAH, SARAH LEWIS - remainder of free est
Exrs: Enoch Macy & Jesse Williams
Wits: William Armfield, Edward Thornburth

A:0326 - WILLIAM BYFORD - 8 July 1795 - Prb Aug 1796
Wife TABITHA - all my lands, goods, debts, & moveable affects
Exr: TABITHA'S father SMITH HEATH
Wits: Hezekiah Wheeler, Mary Heath

A:0327 - SHUBAL STEARNS - 24 Oct 1771 - Prb Feb 1772
Bro ISAAC STEARNS - my wearing clothes, inside and out
Wife SARAH - all my estate during her life
Bros & sisters: PETER STARNS, ISAAC STARNS, EBENEZER STARNS,
REBECCAH POLK, ELISABETH TIMSON, & MARTHA MARSHALL - estate
after death of wife
Exrs: Seymore York, Tidmore Lane
Wits: Thomas Swift, Jeremiah York, Sarah Cunerod

A:0328 - ENOCH SPINKS - 20 Mar 1772 - Prb May 1772

Wife AMY - negro Samson, her horse & saddle, bed & furniture
Son JOHN - 150 ac on Deep River, negro Adam
Dau MARTHA SPINKS - land incl storehouse that Southerland has
Son ENOCH - land on Fork Cr. crossing at old mill
Son LEWIS - home plantation
Son BOWLEY - 70 gallon still with all the conveniences thereto
Son GARRETT - forty pounds
Dau SARAH SPINKS - eight pounds, bed & furniture
Exrs: Wife AMY SPINKS, John Laurance, John Needham
Wits: John Laurence, William Comb, Junr., Windsor Pearce

A:0329 - JOHN SCOTT - 5 Oct 1774 - Prb Nov 1774
Son THOMAS - part of plantation on north side of Haw River
Wife MARGARET - maintence, 6 bu of corn, half barrel wheat yearly
Dau JINET - her living while single; at marriage her mother's 6 cows, bed & furniture, saddle & bridle
Son SAMUEL - that part of plantation on south side of Haw River
Dau NANCY - privilege of the house & firewood while single
Son WILLIAM - my great coat, one English shilling
Dau MARTHA - one English crown
Exrs: Son THOMAS SCOTT, Gabriel Scott
Wits: Nancy Scott, Tenny Scott

A:0330 - WILLIAM SEARCY - 4 Feb 1776 - Prb May 1776
Wife KERIZIA - her living out of my estate
Son WILLIAM - all lands & livings at death of my wife
Dau KERON SEARCY - neck of land called Mogans Neck, 4 cows, feather bed & furniture, third of pewter & delph ware
Dau MARY PEARCE - 1 shilling. Gr dau MARY PEARCE - 1 heifer
Exr: Son WILLIAM SEARCY
Wits: Arthur Smith, James Whittel, Adam Womack?

A:0331 - BENJAMIN STARRATT - 15 Nov 1776 - Prb May 1778
Son JOHN TOBIAS, son WILLIAM FLEMEN, son JAMES STARRATT - 5 sh
Daus MARY & JOANNA - each hors worth 15 pds, saddle, bed, cow
Gr ____ (not filled in) STARRETT DOBINS - 16 pounds
Ch BENJAMIN (land), HANNA & HESTER - remainder of estate
Exr: Ralph Gorrell. Wit: James McAdow

A:0332 - JOHN SHARP - 6 Mar 1778 - Prb May 1778
Wife CATHREN - plantation, negroes Quash, Tom, Bob & woman Hagoe, stock, household furniture
Sons RICHARD & JAMES - to inherit from their mother
Ch: RICHARD, SAMUEL, ELIZABETH, MARY, SARY, ISHAM, SUSANNAH, & AGNES - remainder of estate
Exr: Not named. Wits: John Reagon, James Pratt

A:0333 - ROBERT SMITH - 27 Nov 1772 - Prb May 1778
Son ROBERT - tract of land on North Buffalow
Sons SAMUEL & ROBERT - all the chattles & moveables
Sons WILLIAM SMITH, THOMAS TULFORD, & HUGH NEELY - each 10 sh
Exrs: Sons WILLIAM & THOMAS TULFORD
Wits: Robert Breden, Edward Gilbert

A:0334 - JOSEPH SCALES, Planter - 17 Sept 1773 - Prb May 1774
Wife MARY - 200 ac plantation, negroes Samson & Nell, grey mare

gelding named Black Jack, saddle, beds, 6 cows & calves, still
Ch: HENRY SCALES (alias HENRY GIBSON), JOSEPH, JAMES, NATHANIEL, AGNESS, BETSY SCALES, SARAH DAVIS, & HANNAH OWINGS - divide proceeds of sale after death or remarriage of wife
Son HENRY - negro man Sciaro, woman Manna, bond on John Glenn
Son JOSEPH - 775 ac, part of tract of 1,075 ac on the great br of Cascade Cr in Pittsylvania Co., Va., negro woman Bett
Son NATHANIEL - to inherit the home plantation, negro Jacob
Son ROBERT - 100 ac of the land in Pittsylvania Co., negro Harry
Son-in-law JOHN DAVIS - rest of 693 ac on Beaver Island Cr
Dau SARAH DAVIS - negro woman Silvis
Dau HANNAH OWINGS - negro woman Sall, one side saddle
Dau AGNESS SCALES - negro woman Jude, feather bed & furniture
Dau BETSEY SCALES - negro Isaac, girl Lett, bed & furniture
Ch: JOHN & THOMAS, ANN HILL, MARY RICE, DAVID - each 5 shillings
Exrs: Sons HENRY SCALES (alias HENRY GIBSON), JOSEPH & JAMES SCALES and Philemon Deatherage. They are to sell my tobacco to pay my debts
Wits: John Morgan, Thomas Walker, Henry Jester

A:0335 - JOHN SMITH - 7 Nov 1776 - Prb Feb 1777
Sarah Powell - plantation, stock, household goods, & debts
Son CHARLES - a carpenters tenant saw
Sons JOSHUA, JOHN, ABRAHAM & dau RACHEL GOACHEN - each 5 sh
Exr: Sarah Powell
Trustees: Friends Alexander Joyce, John Pratt, Philemon Deatherage
Wits: William Watson, Sarah Watson, John Fields, Ansyl Fields

A:0336 - JOHN SHELLY - 17 Sept 1788 - "For probate see Minute Docket No 2, p 17." Wife - one cow
Son JAMES - 500 ac of land, provided he pay: sons JEREMIAH (10 sh), NATHAN (50 pds), and dau MARY - 10 sh
Son JOHN'S three children as they come of age - 75 pounds
Gr son JESY - my bed
Exr: Son JAMES SHELLY. Wit: John Ryan

A:0337 - ROBERT SCOTT - 24 Apr 1791 - Prb May 1791
Wife MARY - house & lot whereon I live in Martinsville, negro girl Patience, providing she doesn't marry for two years
Bro THOMAS - 150 ac in Rockingham Co where he lives, horse
Sister MARGARET GOODING - 50 pds
Half sister HANNAH SCOTT - 10 pds
Thomas Moody - 10 pds, my saddle & bridle. All cash on hand to go to Petersburg on my account with Donaldson & Stoe
Exrs: James McMurry, Thomas Scott
Wits: Rev'd David Barr, James McMurry, James Hamilton

A:0338 - MATTHEW STEPHENSON - 1 Mar 1788 - "For probate, see Minute Docket No 2, p. 142."
Wife ANN - one gray mare, best of cows, household furniture
Ann Stephenson, Junior (dau of John) - gray mare at wife's death
John Stephenson, Junior (son of John) - colt or gray mare
Sons HUGH, WILLIAM, ALEXANDER, & MATTHEW - 20 shillings each
Son JOHN - plantation on waters of Alamance, remainder of estate providing he furnish his mother with provisions and firewood

Exrs: Son JOHN STEPHENSON, William Dicky
Wits: Soloman Shannon, George Johnson, William Shannon

A:0339 - LUDWICK SWING, Planter - 16 Oct 1790 - "For probate see Minute Docket No. 2, p. 142."
Wife - plantation during widowhood
Son GEORGE - to inherit plantation from his mother
Remaining sons & daus - to inherit my moveables
Gr son LUDWICK SWING - 50 ac adj son GEORGE & ANTHONY COBLE, part of a plat surveyed 3 Sept 1790
Son JOHN - 50 ac on north side of tract
Son MATTHEW - 50 ac on south side of tract
Exrs: Wife & David May
Wits: George Cortner, Mathew Swing, George Swing

A:0340 - ELIJAH STACK - 17 Sept 1791 - Prb Nov 1791
Wife - plantation dw or until my children come of age
Sons THOMAS, DAVID, & ELIJAH - plantation
Dau RACHEL - five pounds
Child my wife is with - 5 pds if a girl; land, if a boy
All my children - share in residue of estate
Exrs: John Ryan, William Sillivan
Wits: George Pope, J. McBride, Levi Sillivan

A:0341 - JOHN SANDERS - 4 Mar 1790 - Prb May 1793
Wife - all that I possess
Son JOEL - to inherit plantation from wife
All my children - moveables equally divided
Philip Ham's ch - the share of their deceased mother
Exrs: Sons JOHN & JOEL SANDERS
Wits: Matthew Macy, Amos Mills

A:0342 - WILLIAM SHAW - 9 Sept 1793 - Prb Nov 1793
Bros JOSEPH ROSS & BENJAMIN - all my clothes
My mother & two young sisters JEAN ROSS & SUSANA - 3 pounds
Two older sisters SARAH SHAW & GRIZZALD & GRIZZALD'S youngest son, THOMAS ROSS - remainder of my estate
Exrs: Thomas Wiley & Robert Shaw. Wit: William Matthews

A:0343 - SHADRACK STANLEY - 1 Aug 1792 - Prb Nov 1793
Son ROBERT - land adj mine bought of John Rankin
Son JESSA - use of estate till all my children come of age
Sons JESSA, EDWARD, RICHARD, HENRY - to divide land
Daus MARY, JUDITH, ELIZABETH, & AGNESS - personal estate
Son JESSA - a debt to me from William Duvan of Virginia
Exrs: Son JESSA STANLEY, Joel Sanders
Wits: Hezekiah Starbuck, Elazer Hunt, Phebe Stanley

A:0344 - RICHARD SIMPSON - 24 Dec 1793 - Prb May 1795
Son THOMAS - one breeding saw and a chair
Son RICHARD - land on which I live, 20 ac on which Elizabeth Carrol lives, & land on which he lives
Son NATHANIEL - a white mare
Daus ELIZABETH KNIGHT & JANE MARCELLIOTT - feather bed & what feathers I have, trunk, chair, basons
Dau ELEANOR HICKS - pewter basin & my stone quart mug

Step dau ELIZABETH CARROL - spinning wheel, basin, bed, tub
Gr dau ELIZABETH REES HICKS - 3 yr old heifer
Gr dau ELIZABETH SIMPSON, d/o THOMAS - my chest
Gr son NATHANIEL SIMPSON, s/o THOMAS - young cow named Rock
Gr sons RICHARD SIMPSON (s/o THOMAS), PETER RYAN SIMPSON, WILLIAM SIMPSON & RICHARD SIMPSON (sons of RICHARD) - proceeds from sale of remainder of property
Exrs: Sons THOMAS & RICHARD SIMPSON
Wits: John Campbell, Mary Campbell, Edward Edwards

A:0345 - ANN STEVENSON - 3 Oct 1796 - Prb Feb 1797
Gr dau ANN STEVENSON - all goods, chattels, money, debts
Exr: William Dickey Wits: John Coe, John Stevenson

A:0346 - JAMES SHELLY - 21 Sept 1798 - Prb Nov 1798
Wife MARY - plantation, bed, cow, horse & saddle during widowhood
Daus ELINNOR, BETSY, & MARY - to inherit the above
Sons JOHN, FRANCIS, & WILLIAM - proceeds of sale of property
Exrs: Wife MARY SHELLY, William Ryan
Wits: J. Henley?, William Stanfield, Margaret Ryan

A:0347 - GEORGE STALKER - 19 Aug 1797 - Prb May 1798
Wife RACHEL - a comfortable and peaceable living for her and our children under age during her widowhood
Dau ALICE DAVIS - 5 shilling, she having been given her part
Son THOMAS, dau RACHEL STANFIELD, dau GRACE STANFIELD - ea 5 sh
Dau REBECKAH STALKER - cow, 3 sheep & what she has received
Wife's dau SARAH BRADLEY - one cow & 3 sheep
Son JONATHAN - 124 ac called the school house tract
Son JOHN - 100 ac of a tract on waters of Back Cr in Randolph Co
Son GEORGE - 100 ac being the improvement part of the tract
Under aged ch: LYDIA, HANNAH, ELIZABETH, GEORGE, & DEBORAH
Exrs: Wife RACHEL STALKER, son JONATHAN STALKER
Wits: William Gifford, James Caldwell

A:0348 - JOSEPH SHARBROUGH - No date - Prb May 1799
Son MALAKIA - 20 sh. Sister BARBRA SMITHSON - 25 pds
Wife PERTHENIA - all the remainder of my estate
Exrs: Wife PERTHENIA SHARBROUGH, friend John McDaniel
Wits: John Rudduck, Nancy Jennings, Miriam Jennings

A:0349 - WILLIAM SCOTT - 8 Nov 1798 - Prb Feb 1801
Wife REBECKAH - furniture she got by her mother's will, horse & saddle, 2 cows & calves, sheep, half bu of flax to be sown for her yearly, use of mansion house, springs house, smoak house
Son SAMUEL - 30 pds of the money son ADAM owes to me
Son WILLIAM - tract adj mine & Joseph McDowll's, Andrew Wilson, son ADAM on Reedy Fork and the Court House Road
Son THOMAS - my mill place & mills on each side Reedy Fork
Daus MARY, MARGARET, REBEKAH, & NANSEY - 50 pds hard money, horse, saddle & bridle, bed & furniture, cow & calf to each
Exrs: Wife REBECKAH SCOTT, Hanse McKain, Esqr.
Wits: John Gilchrist, John Reece

A:0350 - JACOB SUTZ - 7 May 1793 - Prb Aug 1800
Sons CHRISTIAN, ADAM, & FREDERICH - each 1 English shilling

Dau MARGARET SUTZ - 100 ac on waters of Alamance, adj son JACOB
Son TOBIAS - my carpenter's tools, 200 ac adj son JACOB
Wife MARY - 100 ac adj son JACOB on south side & Jacob Class, John Swing on the north west side
Youngest dau MARY - one shilling
Exr: None named. Wits: George Cortner, Jacob Sutz

A:0351 - WILLIAM SHAVER - 17 July 1801 - Prb Nov 1801
Wife CATHERINE - privilege of living in the home, third of furniture, two cows & calves, horse, saddle & bridle
Sons JACOB & WILLIAM - tract purchased of Adam Larance
Son CONRAD - 160 ac on which he lives
Youngest son LAISH? - residue of land
Dau ELIZABETH SHAVER - $150, stock, furniture
Oldest dau CATHERINE LONG - $3, she having received her share
Exrs: Son JACOB SHAVER, Wife CATHERINE SHAVER
Wits: William Patterson, Ralph Gorrell

A:0352 - PATRICK SHAW - 1 Jan 1802 - Prb Feb 1802
Oldest sons JOHN, WILLIAM, & HUGH - five shillings
Wife NANCY & daus BETSEY SHAW, POLLY AYDLETT, NANCY SHAW - residue of estate
Exrs: Wife NANCY SHAW, James S. Gillaspie
Wits: David Price, James Holland

A:0353 - HENERICH SIGFRIED - 22 Apr 1801 - Prb Feb 1802
My daus CATHERINE, MARY, NEOMI - my moveables
Son JOHN - my land along his line
Exrs: William & John Hodgson
Wits: Isaac Frazer, Rebeckah Frazer

A:0354 - WILLIAM SMITH - 15 June 1801 - Prb Nov 1802
Wife ELIZABETH - home plantation, negroes Dick & Sall
Sons JOSEPH, WILLIAM & ROBERT - to inherit from wife, other tracts, negroes Eley, Richard, Andrew, George, John, Tom, & Nance
Exrs: Sons JOSEPH & WILLIAM SMITH. Proven by John Nelson

A:0355 - JAMES STARRAT - 30 Aug 1803 - Prb Aug 1804
Gr son WILLIAM - half of horned cattle, hogs, household furniture, 250 ac already given him, money lent to James Hall Starrat, half of farming tools
Son JOHN - other half of stock, furniture, tools, 100 ac already given him, 100 ac on west branch of Buckham
Daus MARY HALL & ISABELL TELFORD - five pounds
Exr: Son JOHN STARRATT
Wits: Edward Green, Benjamin Wilson

A:0356 - REBECCA SCOTT - 1 Jan 1806 - Prb May 1806
Dau NANCY SCOTT - one heifer, besides the cattle willed to her by her father, $10 to make her an equal share with my daus MARY & MARGARET RANKIN
Son THOMAS - his bed & furniture, a stand of curtains
Gr dau HANNAH RANKIN - my bed tick & curtains
Elizabeth Henderson, now living with me - one heifer I got from James Russell

Gr dau REBECCAH MECK SCOTT, dau of son SAMUEL living in Tenn - share in remainder of estate
Exrs: Son-in-law SAMUEL RANKIN, Hanse McCain
Wits: Asa Brasher, Junior, John Rankin

A:0357 - WILLIAM SHANNON, Planter - 12 Aug 1803 - "For probate, see Minute Docket No. 3, p. 436."
Dau MARGARET GOSSIT, gr daus ANN & ISABELLA SHANNON, dau ANN WILEY, dau JANE WILSON, dau ISABELLA WILSON - each a fifth
Exrs: Daniel Sherwood, George Johnson
Wits: John Stephenson, Junr., John Stephenson

A:0358 - WILLIAM SPRUCE - 10 Aug 1808 - Prb Nov 1808
Wife SARAH - personal estate; if she marries, third of land
Son GEORGE - 2 ac of land to be laid off
Dau ELIZABETH SPRUCE - one horse called Copper
Ch: JOHN, WILLIAM, QUINTON, JOSEPH, & SARAH SWAIN - ten sh each
Son THOMAS - to inherit from his mother, one colt
Exrs: Wife SARAH SPRUCE, George Nicks, Senr
Wits: James Denny, Robert Hatrick, George Dowell

A:0359 - FINLEY STEWART - 12 June 1807 - Prb Feb 1809
Wife PRUDENCE - negroes Jean & Rose, mare named Phenix, land
Son JOHN - negroes Will & Abel - remainder of estate
Son ROBERT - $50. Gr son FINLEY STEWART - $50
Son JAMES - $5. Gr son FINLEY G. STEWART - $50
Dau SUSANNA - $100
Dau JENNET - $50, negro girl named Becky
Gr son FINLEY SHAW FORBIS - $50, negro named Hanna
Dau EAPHARUS? - $100, negro named George
Gr dau SARAH HANNAH (alias MCADOO) - negro boy named Billy
Exrs: Son JOHN STEWART, son-in-law DAVID GORRELL
Wits: Roddy Hannah, Esqr., Isaiah McBride

A:0360 - JOHN SANDERS - 8 Apr 1809 - Prb May 1809
Heirs of son JESSE, dec'd: FORREST, JEMIMA, JOHN, JANE, SUSANNAH, & JESSE - fourth of proceeds of sale of estate
Daus of dau MARTHA HUBBARD, dec'd: SUSANNA, ELIZABETH, JANE, MARTHA, JUDITH & SARAH - fourth of proceeds of sale
Son JAMES - fourth of proceeds
Son JOSEPH - fourth part, provided he pay $60 to children of his brothers, namely JESSE & JAMES SANDERS
Exrs: Barnabas Coffin, Son JOSEPH SANDERS
Wits: Divid Sanders, Valentine Pegg, Charles Gordon

A:0361 - JOHN SULLEN, Planter, "somewhat troubled with the infirmities of old age" - 8 Mar 1802 - Prb Aug 1809
Wife BARBARY - whole of my estate both real & personal
Ch: ELIZABETH (w/o WILLIAM SPIKEMAN), CATHERINE (w/o JAMES SULGRAVE), MARY (widow of ANDREW LOWERY), ANN or NANCY, MARGARET
Son JOHN - estate after wife's decease if he give a reasonable maintenance to my son JACOB
Exrs: James Mendenhall, Son JOHN SULLEN
Wits: David Mendenhall, Enos Hiatt, Isaac Hiatt, James Salgrave

A:0362 - DANIEL SULLIVAN (Sillivan) - 1 Feb 1805 - Prb Nov 1809

Ch: WILLIAM, MARY ANN, SARAH SHEPARD, DAVID, EDWARD, heirs of son FLORENCE, & CALEB - one shilling starling
Son JOHN - one horse beast by name of Kill Devil
Daus NANCY & HENNEY SILLEVAN - bed & furniture, cow, loom ea
Son JOEL - to inherit at his mother's decease or marriage
Wife MARGARET - land, remainder of stock, furniture, tools
Exrs: Andrew Williams, Andrew Russel
Wits: Obed Aydelett, John Oament, Winsmore Howren

A:0363 - ROBERT SAPP - 28 Dec 1809 - Prb May 1810
Wife SARAH - whole of my estate during widowhood
Sons SAMUEL & JAMES - to inherit from my wife
Dau DOROTHY SAPP - cow & calf, saddle, feather bed & furniture
Sons ROBERT & BENJAMIN - each ten shillings
Exrs: Wife SARAH SAPP, son SAMUEL SAPP
Wits: Ammel? Edwards, Joshua Edwards

A:0364 - JOHN STONE - 7 June 1808 - Prb Feb 1812
Only son SALLATHIEL - my carpenter's tools & wearing apparel
Gr son SALLATHIEL STONE - land on east side of Polecat Creek
My three ch: SALLATHIEL STONE, HULDA PHILLIPS, CHRISTIAN RUSSELL - residue of my estate
Exrs: Son SALLATHIEL STONE, David Worth
Wits: William Dicks, Job Worth

A:0365 - SUSANNAH SHOEMAKER - 15 Oct 1808 - Prb Feb 1813
Daus BARBARA & ELIZABETH - negro woman Charlot, negro boy Abner, all my horse critters, furniture, iron pot, Dutch oven, etc
Daus CATY, SUSANNA, & MARRY - each fifty silver dollars
Sons GEORGE, JACOB, CEMRATT?, ADAM, JOHN & CHRISTIAN - have already received $100, share with daus residue of estate
Exrs: John Coble & John Crissman. Wit: Caty Coble

A:0366 - JOSEPH SMITH - 5 Feb 1813 - Prb Feb 1813
Dau SALLY - negro Jane & her children which she has now
Son NATHANIEL - 176 ac on Ritchland where he lives, negro boy Jim & girl Edel
Son LARKIN - negro girl Lile & negro boy Peter, bed & furniture
Son JOHN - land on which he lives, negro girl Nan?, boy Howard
Mrs. Polly Banner - my negro man Pompy, during her widowhood
Exrs: George Nix, Jr., John Smith
Wits: Robert Lindsay, Joseph Johnson

A:0367 - PETER SMITH - 11 Sept 1813 - Prb Nov 1813
Sons NICHOLAS & ADAM - 500 ac on Pleasant Mountain Cr bought of Nathan Aldridge and valued at $542
Son JOHN - 172 ac bought of Nicholas Smith, rated at $387
Son DAVID - 100 ac where he lives bought of James Wire rated at $350, also off the tract I live on, west side of Fayetteville Road, valued at $2 per ac
Son JACOB - 150 ac adj sons JOHN & DAVID, rated at $290
Son PHILIP - remainder of tract I live on, rated at $500
Dau MOLLY - my dwelling house on Philip's place, half the garden, firewood, fruit privileges, $60 for tending me
Exrs: Henry Wrightsel, Jonathan Hadley - to sell my share of bro ADAM'S land. Wits: George Coble, Philip Kime

A:0368 - GAYER STARBUCK - 5 Mar 1813 - Prb May 1814
Wife RACHEL - profit and income from estate during widowhood
Dau EUNICE STARBUCK - comfortable living at home while single, clock, walnut table, loom, pewter basin, knives & forks, etc
Son REUBEN - to inherit plantation with all buildings, farming tools, also my large chest that was my sea chest
Gr son DANIEL STARBUCK, son of PETER, dec'd - horse & saddle
Ch: PAMELY, ELIZABETH, RACHEL, THOMAS, RUTH, LYDIA, DORCAS, REUBIN, EUNICE & gr son DANIEL - residue of estate
Exrs: Brother HEZEKIAH STARBUCK, son THOMAS STARBUCK
Wits: Paul Macy, Lathum Starbuck, Jemima Macy

A:0369 - JOEL SANDERS - 2 Mar 1814 - Prb May 1814
Wife MARY & son JESSE - use & profits of my mills & land on S side Mill Pond Cr, fields adj Charles Bembo, Soloman Dean
My coloured man Tony - land bought of Jesse Dillon
Dau PRISCILLA BEASON - third of meadow ground bought of Edward Bullock's estate on Haw River
Son JOEL - third of meadow on Bold Branch adj Archalos Bowman
Son THOMAS - balance of Bullock tract, 110 ac on Deep River adj Hezekiah Hanna and John Goardin
Son JOHN - tract whereon he lives
Son HEZEKIAH - tract on north side of Reedy Fork adj land where William Bunck lived, land he bought of William Ogburn
Dau MARY BEMBO - half of meadow ground, third of household furn
Daus PRISCILLA & JEAN - remainder of household furniture
Gr dau MARTHA SMITH SANDERS - $100, horse & saddle, cow, bed
My five sons & three daus: JESSE, JOHN, HEZEKIAH, THOMAS, JOEL PRISCILLA BEASON, JEAN GROOSE, & MARY BEMBOW - residue
Exrs: Sons JOHN & JESSE SANDERS
Wits: Barnabas Coffin, John Hubbard, John Stewart

A:0370 - MATTHEW STARBUCK - 14 Jan 1815 - Prb Feb 1816
Wife DINAH - use of third of plantation, house during widowhood
Son REUBEN - $20 with what I have already given him
Sons JOHN, GEORGE, CHARLES & BENJAMIN - all land in Guilford Co.
Dau EUNICE GARDNER - 5 shillings with what I have given her
Daus MARY STARBUCK, SALLEY COFFIN, LYDIA WHEELER - each $50
Dau AVICE STARBUCK - $50, bed quilt I bought at Nantucket
Son SETH - to share farming utensils with brothers
Dau ELIZABETH - to share in residue of personal estate
Exrs: Sons SETH & GEORGE STARBUCK
Wits: Barnabas Coffin, William Starbuck, Paul Starbuck

A:0371 - HEZEKIAH SANDERS - 13 May 1789 - Prb Aug 1789
Wife MARTHA & six daus: MARY, ELIZABETH, MARTHA, SARAH, REBECKAH, & JEMIMA - full use of plantation until my wife remarries & my daus marry; if wife marries, she is to have the legacy of her father in Virginia
Son JOHN - plantation on which he lives, carpenters tools, horse
Son DAVID - plantation on which he lives, grist mill
Exrs: Brothers JOHN & JOEL SANDERS
Wits: Barnabas Coffin, Samuel Coffin, Matthew Macy

A:0372 - RICHARD SIMPSON, Senr - 20 Nov 1802 - Prb Feb 1804
Wife SELAH - third of my estate for her lifetime

Son WILLIAM - 50 ac near where my bro THOMAS did live and remainder of my land
Sons PETER, RICHARD, & JAMES - Selah's land at her decease
Nephew THOMAS KNIGHT - my young sorrel mare
All my children: PETER, PHARBY, WILLIAM, RICHARD, ELLENER, ANNA, & JAMES - remainder of estate at Selah's decease
Exrs: Eldest sons PETER & WILLIAM SIMPSON
Wits: Thomas Kirkman, Richard Simpson

A:0373 - HENRY THOMPSON of Second Creek - 22 July 1771 - Nov 1771
Wife - all my household goods & personal estate; if she remarries, two thirds to be used for the children
Exrs: Wife, brother JOHN THOMPSON
Wits: Thomas Millsap, William Draper

A:0374 - SIMEON TAYLOR - 12 July 1773 - Prb May 1774
Wife - to have maintenance from my estate
Ch: THOMAS, RACHEL LAMB, CATHRAN ELDRIDGE, ANN HENRY, & JOHN - to divide estate at wife's decease
Exrs: Son-in-law ROBERT LAMB, brother-in-law ZACHARIAH DICKS
Wits: William Williams, Jane Williams

A:0375 - THOMAS THORNBURGH - 21 Apr 1796 - Prb May 1797
Son-in-law JOHN FARRINGTON - 32 ac of land on McGradys Branch
Wife MARTHA - use of dwelling house, garden, & pasture, third of orchard, my horse cart & horse, cow & calf, during widowhood
Dau PRUDENCE HUNT - bed & furniture
Dau-in-law MARY THORNBURGH - my Sewel's History
Son JAMES - remainder of plantation from wife, carpenters tools
Son JOSEPH - my new cloath coat
Daus ELIZABETH FARRINGTON (cow & $5); SUSANNA STERT and JUDITH HORNE - each $1
Exrs: Son JAMES THORNBURGH, William Starbuck
Wits: Strangeman Stanley, Micajah Stanley, Temple Stuart

A:0376 - THOMAS THORNBURGH, Junr - 1 Sept 1787 - "For probate see Minute Docket No. 1, p. 316."
Wife MARTHA - use & profits of plantation dw or until youngest son WILLIAM comes of age; after that a third, riding mare, saddle, my share of saw mill on land of John Thomas
Son THOMAS - 50 ac bought from my bro JOSEPH, horse, Bible
Sons HENRY & WILLIAM - remainder of estate
Sophiah Ballenger - feather bed & furniture, one cow, ewe sheep
Daus RUTH, HANNAH, & MARY THORNBURGH - each a feather bed & furniture, one cow & one ewe sheep
Exrs: Son THOMAS THORNBURGH, Jacob Hunt
Wits: Jesse Williams, Hannah Ballenger, Jemima Stanley

A:0377 - JAMES THOMAS - 16 Sept 1788 - "For probate, see Minute Docket No. 2, p. 16."
Wife MILLY - house & plantation, horse, stock, during widowhood
Son BENJAMIN - the land after decease of wife
Son JOHN - tract on Bare Creek in Richmond Co., N.C., horse
Ch of JOHN THOMAS: ELIJAH, STEPHEN & FRANCIS - to inherit land should both of my sons die young
Exrs: JOHN THOMAS and ISAAC, his son

Wits: Aaron Mendenhall, Laban Tharp, Thomas Willents

A:0378 - JOHN THOMPSON - 28 Nov 1793 - Prb Feb 1794
An oral will taken by Col John Gillaspie, JP
Sons WILLIAM F. THOMPSON & younger sons JAMES & JOHN - his estate
Exrs: Col John Gillaspie, James Thompson
Wit: Ralph Gorrell, JP

A:0379 - NICHOLAS TALLEY - 7 Mar 1795 - Prb May 1795
Wife MARY - all my estate; at her decease, divided as follows:
Son JOHN - 200 ac & dwelling house where I live
Gr son NICHOLAS (son of JOHN) - 100 ac convenient to Rock Spring
My eight children - personal estate, sale of Aggie & her children
Exrs: Wife MARY TALLEY, Josua Haines
Wits: Phebe Rich, Joseph Haines

A:0380 - JOSEPH THORNBURGH - 27 Jan 1793 - Prb Aug 1800
Wife ANN - mare, 2 cows, furniture, maintenance during widowhood
Son JOSEPH - 100 ac where he lives
Sons EDWARD & ISAAC - remainder of land
Daus ANN HOGGATT, MARY HODGSON, MARGARET HOGGATT, & ELIZABETH HODGSON - each five shillings
Exrs: Sons EDWARD & JOSEPH THORNBURGH
Wits: William Armfield, Esqr., Joseph Thornburgh

A:0381 - GEORGE TILLEY - 28 July 1801 - Prb Aug 1801
Noncupative will committed to memory by John Guin & Joseph Guin as George Tilley lay sick at the home of Soloman Jones where he resided
Dau NANCY - $30. Dau BETSY JONES - remainder of his money
Soloman Jones - his working tools

A:0382 - THOMAS TAYLOR - 6 July 1802 - Prb Aug 1802
Wife MARY - use, profit & income from estate during widowhood
Sons THOMAS & ALEXANDER - all my land, provided they pay their brothers & sisters five shillings
Exrs: Son-in-law WILLIAM STARBUCK, Hezekiah Starbuck
Wits: Hezekiah Starbuck, Thomas Benjamin, John Kellam

A:0383 - MARY TAYLOR - 21 Feb 1806 - Prb May 1806
Sons NATHAN, SIMEON, THOMAS, ALEXANDER, & JOHN - five shillings
Daus RUTH & LYDIA - five shillings
Daus JEAN STARBUCK, PHEBE FULPS, ESTER BENJAMIN, & ANNA FARRINGER - remainder of my estate
Exrs: Son-in-law WILLIAM STARBUCK, Hezekiah Starbuck
Wits: Zacharias Coffin, Hannah Dillon, William Starbuck

A:0384 - EDWARD TATUM - 24 Sept 1805 - Prb Feb 1811
Wife SUCKY - personal estate, incl slaves Suck, Beck, & Sarah?
Son HARBERT - $70, pewter dish & what he has already received
Son SIHON - land & improvements where John Pyatt lived & that part of the tract bought from his heirs on upper side of Pyatt's Branch, $40, dish, 6 plates
Son EDWARD - land between HARBERT & SIHON, $40, dish, plates
Son HENRY - land whereon I live, pewter dish, plates, bason
Dau BETSEY - $25 in addition to what I have heretofore given her

Exrs: Wife SUCKY TATUM, sons HARBERT & SIHON TATUM
Wits: William Ogburn, Kinchin Vaughan, Tabitha Vaughan, Charles Bruce

A:0385 - JAMES THORNBURGH - 18 Apr 1810 - Prb Aug 1814
Wife MARY - use & profits of plantation dw, sorrel mare, cow, choice of featherbeds, half of kitchen furniture
Sons THOMAS & RICHARD - each ten shillings
Son BENJAMIN - 50 ac off the southwest corner of this tract
Daus RACHEL MENDENHALL, SUSANNAH RAYE, ABIGAIL STANLEY, ANN JACKSON, MARY CLARK - each ten shillings
Dau MARTHA THORNBURGH - remainder of household furniture, cow
Son-in-law EDWARD STANLEY - that tract on Brush Cr that was formerly my father's, provided he supply my step-mother, MARTHA THORNBURGH with a comfortable living while she is a widow
Exrs: Son THOMAS THORNBURGH, Bethuel Coffin
Wits: Hannah Coffin, Paul Macy, Ester Connly?

A:0386 - JAMES TOUCHSTONE - 23 Mar 1815 - "For probate & C & C, see Minute Docket No. 4, p. 418."
Wife SARAH - as much land as she thinks proper to cultivate, dwelling house, 2 horses, 2 cows, hogs, 2 beds & furniture
Dau JEAN DELAY - 200 ac on Haw River adj Asa Brasher's corner, Jesse Brasher's line, James Hays, dec'd, Jacob Walker's corner, William McKinseys, Casper Suits line
Dau MARY ROSS - balance of land estate, mare, cow, bed & furn
Gr son JONAS ROSS - $100 to be put on interest until he comes of age; interest to be used for a liberal education
Exrs: Thomas McCuiston of Buffaloe, Samuel Hunter
Wits: Z. D. Brasher, Thomas McMicheal, Noel Parrish

A:0387 - SAMUEL THOMPSON - 29 June 1801 - Prb Aug 1801
Son JOHN - sorrel colt named Flincho, $500
Brother ROBERT THOMPSON - 10 ac island in Reedy Fork
Remainder of estate to be appraised by William McAlkalton, James Finley, & Thomas Dick
Wife MARGARET, son JOHN, and my six daus: LETICE, ISABEL, REBECCA, MARGARITT, LEVINS, & NANCY - remainder of my estate
Exrs: Wife MARGARITT THOMPSON, son JOHN THOMPSON to take over estate and raise and educate my children from the interest and give each a share when they come of age
Wits: Alexander Pritchett, Henery Hullum, Thomas Dick

A:0388 - LEVI TUCKER - 4 Mar 1816 - Prb May 1816
Wife PEGGY - land south of Fayetteville Road dw, bed, cows, etc
Son ZODAC - to inherit land from his mother, still house, clock
Son ANDERSON - 150 ac where he now lives
Son JOHN - 200 ac whereon he lives called the Neely tract
Dau MARY - $100, bed & furniture, horse beast, side saddle, cow
Son ABBIT - tract north of Fayetteville Road adj corner once belonging to Andrew Gamble, Frederich Tyer's line, Zadoc
Dau NANCY, wife of CHARLES CAUSEY - $100
Dau DIANA - $200, feather bed & furniture, cow & calf
Dau LEAH TUCKER - $250, interest until 18, feather bed, cow
Youngest daus SARAH & ELIZABETH TUCKER - each $300, interest until 18; money to be raised from sale of my western lands

Anderson Tucker's dau Patty - 30 ac adj her father when 18
Exrs: Wife PEGGY TUCKER, Anderson Tucker, Zadoc Tucker
Wits: Thomas McCullock, Frederich Tyer, Thomas Turner

A:0389 - JOSEPH UNTHANK, Yoeman - 5 Apr 1780 - Prb Apr 1782
Son JOSIAH - tract whereon I live (except 17 ac), 300 ac adj the meadow over the creek--part of 900 ac tract bought of John Whittly, near Robert Lindsay
Son JOHN - 1/2 remainder of the 900 ac tract on Brush Cr & Horspen (Creek), third of books, etc
Son ALLEN - 1/2 remainder of 900 ac tract, 17 ac home place, books
Gr son JOSEPH UNTHANK - gun, bay horse, my best breeches, etc
Gr son JONATHAN UNTHANK - gun that was in hands of William White, young mare
Wife JUDITH - use of plantation whereon I live, third of personal estate, maintenance of son JOSIAH until he is 18
Exrs: Sons JOHN & ALLEN UNTHANK
Wits: Thomas Thornburgh, William Coffin, Richard Williams

A:0390 - JOHN UNTHANK - 8 Oct 1780 - Prb Aug 1782
Bro ALLEN - a small tract of land adj his land
Bro-in-law JACOB HUNT - 30 ac bought of Hugh Foster adj his land
Bro-in-law WILLIAM HUNT - 100 ac of best part of rest of tract
Daus MARY & HANNAH - 100 ac adj John Hussey near Salisbury Road
Wife SARAH - use of plantation dw until son JOSEPH becomes 21
Sons JOSEPH & JOHN - residue of estate
Exrs: Bro ALLEN UNTHANK, bro-in-law WILLIAM ROBINSON
Wits: William Coffin, David Brooks, Strangeman Stanly

A:0391 - MICHAEL WITT - 26 Mar 1790 - Prb Nov 1795
Wife MARY - third of all my estate; at her death it to be divided equally among the children
Dau MARY - 12 pds in money, one cow, (third article left blank)
Daus ELIZABETH, ESTHER, JEAN, MARGARET, ROSANAH, RACHEL - each 12 pds, one cow. Son JOHN - all my plantation
Child my wife is big with - share of land if a boy, same as other daus if a girl
Exr: Wife MARY WITT Wits: Andrew Smith, Jacob B______?

A:0392 - THOMAS WELBORN - 2 Apr 1778 - Prb May 1778
Wife - privilege to live on plantation, stock, horse & saddle, negro Dinah dw to raise the children until they come of age; then 2/3 to be sold & divided among my children
Eldest son JOHN - 50 pounds
Dau RUTH - choice of young mares, saddle & bridle, bed & furniture, cow & calf as soon as she is married
Son JOSHUA - his horse & saddle & wearing clothes
Rest of ch: CALEB, THOMAS, EPHRAIME, ELIJAH, EZEKIEL, WILLIAM, & AMY, as they come of age - horse & saddle, suit of clothing
Exrs: Wife, son JOSHUA WELBORN
Wits: James Hunter, Semore York, Sarah Engleson

A:0393 - JOHN WRIGHT - 19 Feb 1783 - Prb Aug 1784
Son JAMES - my land, 3 cows, 4 sheep, 4 horses, negro wench Eala?, child Fan
Son JOHN - negro Tom, half of moveables, 26 ac of land
Exr: Son JAMES WRIGHT. Wits: Robert Wright, William McMurry

A:0394 - JAMES WRIGHT, Jr - 28 June 1794 - Prb May 1785
Wife PRUDENCE - 100 ac whereon I live, part of moveables, two work creatures, etc for her & her family's sustenance
My seven children: ALEXANDER, ELIJAH, WILLIAM, MICAJAH, DIANNA, JANE, & LYDA WRIGHT - remainder of estate & land my father, JAMES WRIGHT Sr. lives on at death of him & mother
Exr: Wife PRUDENCE WRIGHT
Wits: Michael Henderson, Lucy Wright, James Reagon

A:0395 - JOHN WHITE - 5 Feb 1787 - Prb May 1787
Wife JEAN - third of my lands to be enjoyed forever, third of money, house, barn, firewood to be hauled to her door, etc
Son-in-law JOSEPH MCDOWELL - 2/3 of land, remaining personal
Exrs: Wife JEAN WHITE, Joseph McDowell, Jr., Robert Peasley
Wits: W. Gowdy, Steven Goff, Robert McCain

A:0396 - ALSE WALTON - 30 June 1791 - Prb Aug 1791
Youngest son NATHANIEL - 240 ac on which he lives
Wit: John Walton

A:0397 - ALLEN WILSON, Planter - 9 Apr 1792 - Prb May 1792
Cousin ALLEN WILSON, son of JAMES & JANE WILSON - all my rail & personal estate. Exr: James Wilson
Wits: John Canady, John Wilson

A:0398 - EDWARD W. WILLEY of Dorchester Co., Md. - 5 July 1793 Prb Aug 1793
Bros JOHN & THOMAS W. WILLEY - all my right & claim to the land willed me by my father PRICHARD WILLEY, dec'd, near the town of Cunna? on the Eastern Shore of Maryland
Sister EMELIA WILLEY - money remaining after debts, given to her at discretion of Aunt Sarah White residing on Great Choptank River.
Wits: Richard Sanford, John Van Storre, Cathren Van Storre

A:0399 - JAMES WADDELL - 2 June 1786 - Prb Nov 1796
Wife ELIZABETH - all I have & possess during widowhood
All my children - to inherit from their mother when of age
Exr: Levin Minor
Wits: Levin Minor, Joshua Holland

A:0400 - JOHN WOODSIDE - 24 Feb 1796 - Prb Nov 1801
Wife HANNAH - third or child's part during natural life
Sons WILLIAM, SAMUEL, JOHN, JAMES, & ROBERT - my lands divided
All my ch - personal estate divided equally
Exrs: Charles Bruce, Son WILLIAM WOODSIDE
Wits: John Endsley, Alexander Nelson, Jane Nelson

A:0401 - RICHARD WALKER - 16 Apr 1802 - Prb May 1802
Wife ELINER - all my estate during widowhood
Son JAMES - to inherit all of estate from wife
Son JOHN - all my wearing apparel
Exrs: Wife ELINER WALKER, son JAMES WALKER

A:0402 - JOHN WORK - 2 Aug 1781 - "See Min. Doc. No.3,p 214"
Wife MARGARET - to have charge of estate during widowhood; child's part when children come of age

My three ch: JEAN, SARAH, & ELIZABETH WORK
Child yet unborn - land if a boy, if a girl same as other girls
Exrs: John Cunningham, Henry Work, their uncle; wife MARGARET
Wits: Henry Work, Francis McBride

A:0403 - JONATHAN WILSON - 13 May 1805 - Prb May 1805
My three sons: JONATHAN, WILLIAM, & ROBERT - to inherit land when of age - JONATHAN to study trade of blacksmith; WILLIAM, a joiner; ROBERT, a tailor
My six daus, all under age except NANCY - to live on interest of proceeds of sale of personal property
Exrs: Matthew Coffin, James Dunning
Wits: Silas Peace, Edward Ricks

A:0404 - WILLIAM WEATHERLY - 16 Sept 1805 - Prb Nov 1805
Wife ELIZABETH - 133 ac bought of Jeremiah Pritchard on Haw River
Son LEVI - to inherit from his mother, to have use of all land
Gr son NOAH WEATHERLY when he comes of age - horse, $40, clothes
Dau MARY WEATHERLY, mother of NOAH - cow, pewter dish & plates
Exrs: William Brown, son LEVI WEATHERLY
Wits: John Coe, William King

A:0405 - WILLIAM WHITE - 29 Mar 1806 - Prb Nov 1806
Wife SUSANNA - estate during lifetime; then sold and divided
Sons THOMAS, JOHN, WILLIAM, JAMES, JOEL, & ISAAC WHITE (whom I have already provided for) - each one dollar
Susanna Sanders who I have already provided for - one dollar
Daus ELIZABETH THORNBURGH, HANNAH WALKER, MARY CARNEY, ALICE GOSSET, & SARAH WALKER - remainder of estate
Exrs: Sons THOMAS & JOSEPH WHITE
Wits: John Underhill, Leonard Marsh

A:0406 - FRANCIS WORTH - 5 June 1804 - Prb Aug 1807
Wife MARY - all my estate for life; then divided thusly:
Dau PHEBE WOOTEN - five pounds
Dau MARY WORTH - 50 ac where she chooses, half of household furn
Dau ANN DAVIS - half of household furniture
Son WILLIAM - remainder of estate
Exr: William Starbuck
Wits: George Rayl, Junr.; George Hubbard

A:0407 - WILLIAM WOODBURN, Blacksmith - 18 Oct 1806 - Prb Nov 1806
Wife THANKFUL - land during widowhood, black horse, 2 cows, etc
Dau ANN WOODBURN - black colt, bed & furniture, half of money
Bryan Pierce, my apprentice - half money after debts are paid
Exrs: Bros JEDIDIAH CUSICK, ARTHUR WOODBURN
Wits: James Denny, Sr., James Denny, Jr.

A:0408 - EDWARD WEATHERLY - 12 Sept 1810 - Prb Nov 1810
Wife HENRIETTA - that part of plantation where I live dw; to exchange negro Carter with Thomas Bevill for one of his as his wife belongs to Bevill
Sons MARK & EDWARD - land whereon they live
Son WILLIAM - $50, land where he lives, to inherit from his mother. Son MARTIN - $40
Dau MARY WEATHERLY - negro Abraham at mother's dec, horse, bed

Daus SALLY MCCLINTOCK, ELIZABETH FULTON, HENRIETTA STAFFORD, DEBORAH SHILCOTT - one dollar
Exrs: Sons MARK & EDWARD WEATHERLY

A:0409 - ISAAC WHITE - 16 Sept 1803 - Prb Nov 1811
Son STANTON - land whereon he lives with farming utensils
My seven daus - my moveable property
My sons & daus - the money remaining
Exrs: Thomas White, Stanton White
Wits: Richard Williams, Ruth Stanton

A:0410 - THOMAS WILEY - 31 May 1812 - Prb Aug 1812
Sons DAVID & ELY - my land divided equally
Dau ANN - the house & 3 ac while unmarried, 2 horses, 2 cows, third of sheep, books to be divided
Gr dau MARY MATTHEWS - the other horse, cow, third of sheep
Ch: WILLIAM (my wearing clothes), JOHN, ELIZABETH FORBIS, MARY MATTHEW & HUGH MATTHEW - one dollar each
Son HUGH WILEY - one dollar & if he is living in this county, he is to pay $50 to the four at home
Exrs: Sons DAVID & ELY WILEY
Wits: Robert Wiley, James Wiley

A:0411 - JOHN WHITE - 10 Aug 1812 - Prb Aug 1812
Nephews JOHN & BENJAMIN WHITE - all my estate
Exrs: Abraham Cook, Benejah Hiatt
Wits: Joel Willis, William Hiatt

A:0412 - WATSON WHARTON - 6 Dec 1812 - Prb Nov 1813
Sons ELAM, ELISHA, JOHN, & GIDEON - already have deeds & money
Dau TABITHA RANKIN - negro Steven & wife Susie, boy Noah, girls Abigail & Hanay, my clock and case
Dau MARTHA WOODBURN - $500, negro girls Sall & Ruth, book case
Sons EVANS & wife ANGALATTA - plantation if they do well and abide by the will; otherwise, my seven children (EVANS included) to divide proceeds of sale
Wife ANGALATTA - one reasonable bed & furniture, chest, etc
Negro woman Abigail to have her choice of the one she wants to live with of my wife and children
Exrs: Sons ELAM & ELISHA WHARTON
Wits: Robert Rankin, Margaret Rankin

A:0413 - JOHN WORK - 25 Dec 1801 - Prb Aug 1802
Wife POLLEY - negro girl Jude, negroes Abb, Ned, Isaac, Dick & Jin, plantation, household furniture during widowhood
My wife being with child - if a dau, the negroes; if a boy, land
John Massey, son of Nathan - plantation if my wife has a dau; everything if there is no heir
Thomas & John Massey, sons of Nathan - each $20
Exrs: John Cunningham, Abraham Peeples
Wits: Hubbard Peeples, John Work, James David

A:0414 - DAVID WILEY, Senr. - 9 Mar 1816 - Prb May 1816
Wife PEGGY - 100 pds in cash, command of the house, negro woman Sall, clothing she brought here, 2 cows, 2 sheep, horse, saddle
Son-in-law ROBERT MCKNIGHT - negro named Easter, provided he pay
Son-in-law WILLIAM THOM (or THORN) - half value of negro Easter

Son THOMAS - $100.   Son JAMES - negro girl Beck
Son HUGH - negro girl Dice now in his possession
Son DAVID - 378 tract whereon I live, negro Isaac
Son-in-law HARPER TORNE - $100; POLLY PORTER TORNE - cabinet
Daniel Torne, son of Harper & Cathren Torne, $25 when of age
My ch: MARY MCKNIGHT, NANCY TORNE, THOMAS, JAMES, HUGH, DAVID, CATREN TORNE - residue of estate
Exrs: Wife PEGGY WILEY, son DAVID WILEY, William Torne
Wits: Andrew McGee, Eli Wiley

A:0415 - THOMAS WRIGHT - 15 Apr 1816 - Prb May 1816
Wife REBECKAH - use & profits of my estate during widowhood except my black people: negro woman Peg, negro woman Lot, young man Jim, boy Sam, girl Hannah, child Daniel
New Garden Meeting - proceeds of sale of my black people
"Sopossed" son WHILEY - ten shillings; his son THOMAS - $50
Exrs: Bethuel Coffin, Joshua Dicks, William Hunt
Wits: Seth Dicks, Ann Dicks, Deborah Evans

A:0416 - ARTHUR WOODBURN - 26 Apr 1816 - Prb May 1816
Wife PATSY - profits of my two plantations until ch come of age
Sons WATSON & WILLIAM - my Buffalow plantation
Sons ELAMANUEL, EMSLEY - plantation whereon I live
Dau TABITHA E. WOODBURN - $150
Jonathan Wilson - $50 to keep & care for my stud horse
Exr: Wife PATSEY WOODBURN
Wits: Obed Aydelette, John Landreth

A:0417 - GEORGE ZIMMERMAN - 10 Oct 1800 - Prb Aug 1812
Son GEORGE - the plantation
Daus MARY MARGARET, HANNA, MARY DOROTHY - each $25
Wife MARY MARGARET - maintenance by GEORGE, divide moveables with my four children
Exrs: Son GEORGE ZIMMERMAN, John Boon, Senior
Wits: John Boon, George Shoemaker

A:0418 - ROBERT LINDSAY - 5 Feb 1801 - Prb May 1801
Wife NANCY - $1,000 use of house, my horses, cattle, hogs, sheep, & untensils of husbandry, household furniture, 5 beds, etc
Son SAMUEL - ________ (left blank) & $50
Son ROBERT - $250, Tract #4 of division as described on another page. Son WILLIAM - $2,000 & Tract #3
Son ANDREW - $1,500, Tract #5
Daus JENNA & ELIZABETH - each $2,000, Tracts #2 & #6
Dau SUSANNAH - $2,400
Exr: Wife NANCY LINDSAY
Wits: Jane Lindsay, Elizabeth Lindsay
Handwriting proved by Samuel Hargroves, Paris Chipman, & Moses McGrady

END OF WILL BOOK A

B:0419 - CALEB BUNDAY - 9 Apr 1813 - Prb Aug 1816
Wife SARAH - land whereon I live bought of Joseph & Silas Peace, gristmill & 25 rods wide on north side of 100 ac bought of John Clark on Richland Creek adj Jonas Ricks
Son NATHAN - to inherit from his mother
Dau MARY, w/O WILLIAM SMITH - balance of 100 ac bought of John Clark whereon she lives and then to be divided between her children SARAH & WILLIAM SMITH
Gr son ALFRED BUNDAY, s/o NATHAN - $100 on interest until of age
Exr: Son NATHAN BUNDAY
Wits: James Boyd, Isaac Odell

B:0420 - SARAH BUNDAY - 25 May 1816 - Prb Aug 1816
Dau MARY SMITH - ten shillings
Son NATHAN - clock & case, 2 beds & furniture, cow, 3 sheep
Gr daus SARAH & MARY SMITH - one feather bed and furniture
Gr son ERI SMITH - bed & furniture, chest of drawers, $100, etc
Exrs: John Bell, Phinebas Albertson
Wits: Ebenezer Horneby, Joseph Riley

B:0421 - GEORGE COBLE - 26 Apr 1816 - Prb Aug 1816
Sons PHILIP, PAUL, JACOB, PETER, FREDERICH & NICHOLAS - certain lands specified by me in bonds
Dau MARY COBLE - remaining 125 ac, use of half the barn, furn
Exrs: Son PHILIP COBLE, William Coosbee
Wit: Frederich Coble

B:0422 - PETER FIELD - 19 Nov 1809 - Prb Aug 1816
Wife CHARLOTTE - part of estate sufficient to support her and her children dw, negro girl Beck
My six daus: HANNAH, LYDIA, CHARLOTTE, RUHAMA, JERETER, & POLLY - to be raised & schooled, all daus to match the $150 that HANNAH has received. If not enough money, they may hire out negro Bob until POLLY is 10; then set him free
Son CHRISTOPHER - tract purchased of Robert Deen & 21 ac bought of James Alexander making 214 ac when of age or married
Sons JEREMIAH & ABSOLEM - 440 ac: home place with mother for ABSOLAM, adj place called "Oatwell" for JEREMIAH, each a horse
Exrs: Wife CHARLOTTE FIELD, Jeremiah Field, s/o William, dec'd & Christopher Vickery
Wits: William Swaim, Daniel Swaim

B:0423 - WILLIAM GORRELL - 27 May 1816 - Prb Aug 1816
Son-in-law ALEXANDER BEVILL - land given to my dau AGNES CUNNINGHAM GORRELL, his wife & whatever may be coming from my Aunt AGNES GORRELL, widow in Stanton, County of Augusta, Va
Ch of dau AGNES - $10 each, coming out of my part of my father & mother's estate
Son RALPH - land on which I live, agreeable to the will of his gr father, RALPH GORRELL, dec'd; also his stock of horses which were a present from his grandfather
Daus CATHERINE, JENNEY, MARY ANN - $100 from estate of my mother & father
Exrs: Samuel Stuart, James Maxwell (Both renounced right during Feb Court 1818 and Robert Donnell was appointed Adm.)
Wits: Howell Parker, Thomas McNeely

B:0424 - ELEAZER KERSEY - 29 May 1816 - Prb Aug 1816
Wife ELIZABETH - moveable effects, house, maintenance dw
Dau ELIZABETH KERSEY - remainder of moveables, bed & furniture
Sons STEPHEN & WILLIAM - land bought of William Beals
Sons ENOCH, JESSE, ELEAZER, & MOSES - land whereon I live
Exrs: Brother-in-law STEPHEN HARTIN, wife ELIZABETH KERSEY
Wits: Amos Kersey, William Kersey, Elizabeth Kersey

B:0425 - MEARES MINER - 7 June 1816 - Prb Aug 1816
Wife ELIZABETH - real & personal estate, horse beast, stock, etc
My children - to be schooled, plantation when old enough
Exr: Wife ELIZABETH MINER
Wits: William Kerr, Thomas Bevill, Alise Kerr

B:0426 - JACOB ROGERS - 12 July 1816 - Prb Aug 1816
Wife ANN - dwelling house & maintenance; if she marry, feather bed & furniture. Son JACOB - plantation on which I live
Daus ELIZABETH, JAMIMAH, & RACHEL ROGERS - maintenance while single, young mare, residue of estate
Exrs: John Caldwell, Henry Macy
Wits: Joshua Dicks, Isaac Harvey, Thomas Hunt

B:0427 - JAMES STAFFORD - 3 Feb 1812 - Prb Aug 1816
Wife SARAH - house & plantation, negro woman & her children
Oldest son GEORGE - his plantation bought of John Dinkins
Son ANDERSON? - his plantation bought of Edward McGlamere
Daus POLLY & SARAH STAFFORD - horse & saddle, bed & furniture, etc
Sons JAMES & JOHN - plantation at decease of their mother, horse & saddle, bed & furniture, cow & calf each, wagon & gears, etc
Eldest dau RHODA WEATHERLY & dau ANN MCCLINTOCK - each $1
Exrs: Sons GEORGE & ANDERSON STAFFORD
Wits: John Gilchrist, Adw. (Edward?) Scott, John Cathey

B:0428 - JAMES WEATHERLY - 24 Mar 1816 - Prb Aug 1816
Wife MARY - all my estate during widowhood; then to be sold and divided among ALL MY CHILDREN
Son JAMES - horse & saddle that was Jessie's
Exrs: Wife MARY WEATHERLY, James Mills, Jehu Hancock
Wits: Mars Miner, John Craft

B:0429 - ANCEL VALLIENT - 7 June 1816 - Prb Aug 1816
Wife JINNCY - third of 100 ac
Neely Cox, gr dau of my first wife - bed & furniture, chest, etc
Stephen Hester, Elizabeth Hester, Ann Hester & Patsy Hester; also 3 ch of Jincy Cox: Neely Cox, Burnetty Cox, & Mary Cox - residue of my estate
Exrs: Wife JINNCY VALLIENT, Daniel Hobby
Wits: John McBride, Isaac Coleman

B:0430 - JACOB COBLE - 26 Oct 1816 - Prb Nov 1816
Daus EVE LOWE, MARY ROSE, CATHERINE BURROW, JULIANNA? HARRISON, MOLLIANNA GREESON, & DOLLY COLLINS - $100
All my children - proceeds from sale of property
Exrs: Son NICHOLAS COBLE, Jonathan Hadley
Wits: George Shatterly, David Glass, James O'Neal

B:0431 - PALL GLASS - 8 Aug 1816 - Prb Nov 1816
Wife EVE - third of plantation, barns, mare, furniture, stock
Son DAVID - remainder of plantation, mother's part at her death
Sons JOHN & ADAM - land from two deeds by William Jones & Jacob Marshal
My five daus: DOLLY KIMES, MARY GLASS, MOLLY GLASS, EVE GLASS, & CATHERINE AMECK - each $100, extra $10 for MARY, MOLLY & EVE
Land covered by deed from Philip Amick to be sold
Exrs: William Corsbie, Nicholas Coble
Wits: Christian Farmer, Henry Shoe

B:0432 - JOHN JOHNSON - 22 Dec 1808 - Prb Nov 1816
Ch of my bros and sisters - proceeds of sale of my estate
Exrs: Alexander Johnson, William Johnson
Wits: Daniel Sherwood, George Johnson

B:0433 - ALEXANDER JOHNSON - 17 Oct 1816 - Prb Nov 1816
Wife NELLY - third of plantation, horse creature, cow & calf
Daus ABIGAIL, CATY, & NELLY - land called Hickman's place
Wife & Children - proceeds from sale of stock
Exrs: Brother WILLIAM JOHNSON, son JAMES JOHNSON
Wits: David Worth, William Dickey

B:0434 - WILLIAM DICKSON - No date - Prb Feb 1817
Wife NANCY - ten shillings
Youngest son JOHN - 100 ac N of my tract from William Dickson's line to Samuel Goff's line, half benefit of orchard, bed
Gr son WILLIAM DICKSON, son of ROBERT - 100 ac, house & orchard
Son ROBERT - lifetime interest in his son WILLIAM'S place
Gr son JAMES PIRCHESON (sic) - remaining land
My three sons - carpentry tools, farming tools
My children - my books to be equally divided
Daus NANCY PILKONTON, MARTHA IDELOT
Exrs: William McMurry, Thomas McMicheal (Thomas McMicheal relinquished his right and Adm was granted to David Aidelett and Larkin Pilkinton).
Wits: James Tomlinson, Elender Goff, Polly Tomlinson

B:0435 - WILLIAM CUSICK (written as WILLIAM BUSICK in probate)
4 May 1816 - Prb May 1817
Wife - estate, money & notes dw for her comfort & maintenance
My negro Will & his wife Candy - to be freed after decease of wife & have farming untensils, stock & necessary comforts
Ch of Robert Rankin, Sr. and deceased dau POLLY: LYDIA, ISBEL, & THANKFUL - negro woman Jean & their mother's share of est
Dau THANKFUL - use of negro boy Joe during her widowhood if she lives where she now lives now (my desire) or if she moves to her place on North Buffaloe
My ch - all deeds & bills of sale of negroes are valid
Exrs: William Mabane, Jedediah Cusick
Wits: William Matthews, William Fluke

B:0436 - RICHARD BURTON - 22 Feb 1817 - Prb May 1817
Wife ELIZABETH - land & personal estate during widowhood
Sons JOHN, RICHARD, & WILLIAM - division of land on death of wife
Daus - to inherit personal property from wife

Exrs: William Winchester, Levin Coosy
Wits: Sarah Covey, William Wofford

B:0437 - SARAH BURTON - 21 July 1814 - Prb May 1817
Dau ELIZABETH BURTON, w/o RICHARD BURTON - bedstead, flax wheel
Dau NANCY CLARK - chest, 2 chairs, cotton wheel, looking glass
Gr daus PATSY MOORE, BETSY STAFFORD & SALLY CLARK - feather bed
Gr daus SALLY WAFFORD & LEVINA WAFFORD - each one cow
Dau SARAH WAFFORD - the small balance of property
Exr: Son-in-law WILLIAM WAFFORD. Wit: James Johnson

B:0438 - JOHN W. JONES - 1 Mar 1817 - Prb May 1817
Wife DEBORAH - all lands, tenements, dwelling house, furniture during life; to care for old negro Lucy & support her for life
Sons-in-law RICHARD LANHAM HUMPHREYS & VINCENT SIMPSON - ea 50¢
Son JUDSON JONES - $100
Youngest sons ELICHOUS, RICHARD, ROBERT, JOHN M. - inherit lands
Exr: William Walker
Wits: George Harbin, Hugh Watt, Joseph McCain

B:0439 - RICHARD OZMENT - 9 June 1809 - Prb May 1817
Gr sons RICHARD & PRICE (sons of THOMAS) - land whereon I live
Ch: SAMUEL, RICHARD, BETSY, JOHN, NELLY, JAMES, SARAH, & THOMAS - remainder of estate & negroes Sam & Vilet
Gr ch NANCY & JINCY OZMENT & JOSEPH RICHFIELD OZMENT (ch of THOMAS) - $300 divided, THOMAS to have blacksmith tools
Exr: Son THOMAS OZMENT
Wits: William Ryan, Levi Huston, John McAs_?___

B:0440 - GEORGE PATTERSON - 17 Feb 1817 - Prb May 1817
Bro ROBERT - $30 note on Andrew Patterson, brand new cloth
Father MICHAEL - my saddle
Mother & sisters MOLLY & MATTY PATTERSON - my cow, dutch oven, frying pan; my fur hat for my mother
Brother ANDREW - my great coat
Nephew JOHN G. PATTERSON & niece MARTHY PATTERSON - each $1
Sister REBECKAH PATTERSON - $1 owed by ANDREW
Exr: Brother ROBERT PATTERSON who receives residue of estate
Wits: Robert Mayben, William Thom

B:0441 - EDWARD MILLIS - 18 June 1817 - Prb Aug 1817
Wife RACHEL - all profits from plantation during widowhood
Dau ELIZABETH JACKSON - feather bed & furniture
Son NICHOSON - divide land with ELIZABETH at wife's decease
All my children - proceeds from sale of some items
Exr: James Millis. Wits: Thomas Swain, Richard Wheeler

B:0442 - WILLIAM WHEELER - No date - Prb Aug 1817
Wife LYDIA - benefits of estate to raise & school my children, choice of stock, furniture that she brought from her father
Exrs: Wife LYDIA WHEELER, father JOHN WHEELER, Nathan Mendenhall. Wits: Joshua Johnson, Esther Stevens?

B:0443 - WILLIAM BROWN - 17 Sept 1817 - Prb Nov 1817
Wife JANE & my five children as the children come of age
Exrs: Benjamin Brown, Elisha Wharton

Wits: Thomas Flack, Sally Brown

B:0444 - DANIEL MENDENHALL, Planter - 22 Aug 1817 - Prb Nov 1817
Wife DEBORAH - use of plantation dw to raise & school my 8 ch
Sons ELIJAH - $150 & William - $200 & a horse worth $60 when he comes of age
Rest of ch: JONATHAN, PARIS, JAMES, DAVID, LYDIA, MARY, DEBORAH, & ESTHER MENDENHALL - divide rest of estate at wife's decease
Exrs: James Mendenhall, Isaiah Mendenhall, Deborah Mendenhall
Wits: John Stuart, Robert Stewart

B:0445 - JAMES FRAZIER - 24 Oct 1811 - Prb Nov 1817
Wife MARTHA - land whereon I live for her maintenance dw
Ch: SOLOMAN, WILLIAM, JANE COALTRAIN, ISAAC, ABNER, SARAH COLTRAIN - each one dollar
Dau MARGRET CUMMINS - my watch
Sons ENOS & JAMES - 300 ac tract whereon I live
Exrs: Wife MARTHA FRAZIER, Levi Huston
Wits: John Finley, William Harvey

B:0446 - JOHN PORTER - 21 June 1817 - Prb Nov 1817
Wife MARTHA - land whereon I live during widowhood
Matthew Young - my land at decease of my wife
Sister MARGARET WILEY - $10
Exrs: Wife MARTHA PORTER, Matthew Young
Wits: Joseph Hanner, Sampson Stewart

B:0447 - ISABEL WILEY - 24 Sept 1817 - Prb Nov 1817
Dau RUTH - my two beds, 4 sheets, 2 coverlids, rug, quilt, stand of curtains, chest, Bible, pewter plates, spinning wheel, part of my father's estate that is coming to me
Sister-in-law POLLY WILEY - $10
Mother - one big coat & flaming shift
Exrs: Bro DAVID WILEY, Robert S. Gilmore
Wits: Hannah Wiley, Anne Wiley

B:0448 - WILLIAM GARDNER - 1813 - Prob Nov 1817
Wife DEBORAH - a comfortable living in East room of my dwelling house with no contradiction from my heirs
Son JESSE - homeplace if he maintains my wife, smith tools, etc
Sons THADDEUS & JAMES - land I bought with bro STEPHEN adj Nathan Mendenhall
Son OBED - 140 ac on north side of tract
Son WILLIAM - to divide moveable property with Jesse
My 7 daus: SUSANNAH, RACHEL, ELIZABETH, MARY, ANNE, JUDITH, & JEMIMA - the Nantucket land left to my first wife SUSANNAH by her father James Gardner
Bros STEPHEN, ISAAC & I being sued by George Levens? over his share of his grand father's estate
Wits: Barzella Gardner, Stephen Gardner

B:0449 - MARTHA SAUNDERS - 16 July 1816 - Prb Nov 1817
Dau MARY CLARK - one sixth part of my estate
Hezekiah Chipman, Paris Chipman, Joel Chipman, Mary Chipman, Hannah Chipman, Martha Chipman, Elizabeth Chipman - sixth part

Hezekiah Henley, Mary Henley, John Henley, Joseph Henley, Rebecca Henley & Henry Henley - one sixth part
Dau SARAH JOHNSON & her heirs - one sixth part
Sarah Sanders, Mary Sanders, Patrick H. Sanders, & Jemima F. Sanders - one sixth part
Dau JEMIMA SANDERS - one sixth part
Son DAVID - my part of the wagon
Daus ELIZABETH STEWART & MARTHA TINLEY (FINLEY?) - 5 shillings
Louisa Brisendren - bed & furniture I have given her
Exrs: David Sanders, John Stuart
Wits: Jane Sanders, Louisa Brandren

B:0450 - HEZEKIAH HIGHFILL - 5 Jan 1818 - Prb Feb 1818
Wife DELLY - use & benefit of all my estate dw for maintenance of as many of my children that may be with her; children under age to be educated
Son HEZEKIAH - tract on north side Haw River, part of tract on which David Mortimer settled
Sons WILLIAM & JOHN - home plantation at marriage or death of wife
My daus - residue of personal estate
Exrs: Samuel Hunter, Henry Tatum
Wits: James Tharp, Jacob Walker, William McGee

B:0451 - LUCY HAYNES - 12 Mar 1816 - Prb Feb 1818
Dau MARY BARROW - negro Chancy & her children: Ben, Suzy & Amy
Gr gr ch: ELIZABETH NOBLIN, HARRIET NOBLIN, LUCY NOBLIN, & MARY NOBLIN (ch of gr son CHRISTOPHER NOBLIN & wife LITHA) - negro woman Nancy, furniture
Gr gr dau LUCY HANES NOBLIN (d/o gr son WILLIAM NOBLIN & wife SUSANNAH) - slaves Milly & James
Gr son GEORGE NORTHUM, gr dau MELA NORTHUM - each 10 shillings
Exrs: Edward Green, Joseph Denny
Wits: James Green, Robert Wilson

B:0452 - JOHN MORRIS - 12 Oct 1817 - Prb Feb 1818
Son SILAS - third of moveable property, my best hat
Son AARON - plantation, farming tools, third of moveables, Bible
Gr dau JANE MORRIS - proceeds from sale of my desk
Gr son JOHN MORRIS - third of moveables
Dau HANNAH MILLS & gr dau JANE HODSON - ten shillings
Exr: Bethuel Coffin. Wit: Hannah Coffin

B:0453 - FREDERICH TROLLINGER - 26 June 1817 - Prb Feb 1818
All my children - division of property after debts are paid
Exrs: Joseph Gibson, Esqr; George Christman (Barbara Trollinger was granted Administration by the Court.)
Wits: Joseph Gibson, Adam Strader

B:0454 - DEMENY JENKINS - 2 Dec 1817 - Prb May 1818
Dau JENNY RICKS - $280, tract purchased from Orten Newell
Son PETER - plantation, stock, negroes Hannah & Flora, bond on Samuel Webb. Dau POLLY PARKER - 20 shillings
Exrs: Son PETER JENKINS, Andrew Flack
Wits: William Weatherly, George Lowery

B:0455 - ISAAC LINEGAR - 18 May 1818 - Prb May 1818

Wife ROSANNAH - all my chattel property, rent of land
Exrs: Joseph Hunt, Phineas Albertson
Wits: Isaac Odell, Meredith Price, Thomas Hodson

B:0456 - HENRY ANTHONY - 20 May 1818 - Prb Aug 1818
Sister SINTHY ANTHONY - proceeds from sale of property
Bros WILLIAM & JAMES - my wearing clothes
Exr: Soloman Warren. Wits: John Medearis, Wyatt Peeples

B:0457 - JAMES BROWN, Senr. - 4 Feb 1818 - Prb Aug 1818
Son JAMES - my whole estate
Exr: Son JAMES BROWN
Wits: Jeremiah Hubbard, Rebecca Brown

B:0458 - PETER COFFIN - 29 Apr 1812 - Prob Aug 1818
Son JOSEPH - 80 ac on east side of my tract
Wife MIRIAM - use & profit of remaining estate during widowhood
Daus SARAH BROWN (10 ac) & ANNA COFFIN (20 ac)
Gr son EZECIL - 20 ac
Dau PRISCILLA BALLARD'S three children - each five shillings
Gr dau PRISCILLA WHEELER and dau ELIZABETH GARDNER - each 5 sh
Son JOSEPH, daus SARAH BROWN & ANNE COFFIN - residue of estate
Exr: Son JOSEPH COFFIN
Wits: Paul Macy, Nathaniel Macy, Lebni Barnard

B:0459 - ABEL FRAZIER - 7 June 1818 - Prb Aug 1818
Wife REBECCA - use & profits of plantation during widowhood
My five ch: RACHEL, JOHN, SARAH, MARTHA, & MARY FRAZIER - division of estate after marriage or decease of wife
Exrs: Caleb Beals, Wife REBECCA FRAZIER
Wits: Jesse Hodson, John Beal, William Kersey

B:0460 - RICHARD GARDNER - 4 Jan 1818 - Prb Aug 1818
Wife ELIZABETH - whole of my estate during widowhood
Bro HEZEKIAH'S ch - estate after widowhood of wife
Exrs: Bro JONATHAN GARDNER, Joseph Coffin
Wits: Paul Macy, Deborah Macy, William Shaw

B:0461 - TIMOTHY MORGAN - 28 May 1818 - Prb Aug 1818
Wife MARY - use & profit of land, negro Joc, furniture, horse
Daus LUCY BOCKIN & MARY MATTHEWS - each five shillings
Son ELIAS - 30 ac off SW corner that joins his line
Dau SELAH MILLS, son THOMAS, dau MARTHA MORGAN, & son KERSHEW - each five shillings
Son GREEN - to inherit land from his mother, blacksmith tools
Gr son ENOS MORGAN - tract John Ham bought of Isaiah Stanley
Exrs: Son ELIAS MORGAN, Abel Coffin
Wits: Hezekiah S. Clark, Wenny Bird

B:0462 - ROBERT LINDSAY - 16 July 1818 - Prb Nov 1818
Wife LETTY - $10,000, home plantation called "Old Town Tract", interest from 40 shares of State Bank of N. C., tract bought from William Dick, negroes Charles, Mary, Chaney & Fan
Son ROBERT - to inherit from his mother
Son A. T. HARPER LINDSAY - $12,000, land adj Town of Greensboro, Lot #1 in Greensboro, negro Jake

Son JESSE H. - $12,000, tract on Deep River left to me by my father, tract west & north of Greensboro, 2 lots in Greensboro: one adj #1 & R. Donnell; other adj Joseph Davis; 14 shares in Cape Fear Bank, negro boy James
Son ROBERT - $12,000, land on Alimance purchased from Stephen Holland, land purchased from Levin Caulk adj the Martinsville Lindsay's, negro Frank
Dau ANN E. LINDSAY - $11,000 in cash, 218 ac purchased from John Moore and Daniel Black adj Wm. McCain
Dau MARY LINDSAY - $11,000 in cash, 100 ac near Jamestown
Exrs: Jesse Harper Lindsay, Absolom T. Harper Lindsay, Andrew Lindsay
Wits: John Thompson, Robert Johnson, Hance McCain, James Cole

B:0463 - JOHN MAXWELL - 12 July 1817 - Prb Nov 1818
John Maxwell, son of James - 160 ac whereon I live
Nancy Maxwell, dau of William - one cow first choice
Brothers WILLIAM & JAMES - my clothes & my negroes
Haw River Meeting House - $25 for repairs
Exrs: Thomas Webb, William Maxwell
Wits: Matthew Brown, Alexander Fulton, John Walker

B:0464 - WILLIAM CRISWELL - 12 Apr 1816 - Prb Feb 1819
Bro JAMES & sister MARY CRISWELL - whole estate, incl negroes
Exrs: Bro JAMES CRISWELL, Daniel Donnell
Wits: John Gilchrist, Andrew Donnell

B:0465 - ABIGAIL CANNADY - 13 Jan 1807 - Prb Feb 1819
Son NATHAN CANADY - cow & calf, 2 hogs, 2 ewes
Son JOHN - black walnut chest, iron pot, feather bed & furniture
Son WILLIAM - 2 beds & furniture, remainder of stock
Daus MARGERY HARRIS, HESTER KELHAM, MARY CLARK, MARGRET HARNER, HANNAH RAIL, DINNAH KELHAM, ABIGAIL NEWNAM - ten shillings
Exr: Nathan Canady
Wits: Drury Peeples, Charles C. Kelham

B:0466 - ELIZABETH CARTER - 5 Feb 1819 - Prb Nov 1819
Dau CLOE WALKER - one dollar
Son MIAL - remainder of estate, furniture, stock
Exr: Henry Tatum
Wits: Sebon Tatum, Garrison Justice, Harbart Tatum

B:0467 - SARAH SPRUCE - 22 Nov 1818 - Prb Feb 1819
Sons JOHN H., WILLIAM, JOSEPH, QUINTON, THOMAS, & dau SARAH STRAIN - each five shillings
Son GEORGE - negro girl Sally, feather bed & furniture, & discharge him from debts due me
Dau BETSY - negro girl Cate, remaining beds & furniture, stock
Exr: Son GEORGE SPRUCE
Wits: Simpson Spruce; proved by George Nicks

B:0468 - ALEXANDER FERGUSON - 5 Feb 1819 - Prb May 1819
Wife SARAH - ten shillings
Son SAMUEL - all my lands, stock, household property, tools
Exr: Son SAMUEL FERGUSON. Wit: Mary Talbert
In court, Samuel Sapp attested to the signature of Mary Tal-

bert, dec'd. Also the executor (and son), Samuel Ferguson, had deceased and the court appointed Jeffery Horney as Adm with Philip Horney as Security.

B:0469 - MARTHA CLARK - 24 Aug 1818 - Prb May 1819
Dau MARY HUSSEY - $40 owed by Will Jessop that Thomas Hunt is to collect, $45 from Benjamin Clark for 100 bu of corn, chest
Dau SOPHIA GIBBONS - my saddle, cloak, pewter bason
Gr son WILLIAM THORNBURGH - my little oven
Gr dau LIDDY JESOP - my bed sheets, bed, bed quilt, 2 pillows
Sons-in-law WILLIAM JESSOP & PATRICK GIBBONS - each 5 shillings
Exrs: Mary Hussey, Josiah Unthank
Wits: Anna Unthank

B:0470 - ROBERT HANNAH - 14 July 1818 - Prb May 1819
Sons ROBERT, JOHN, JAMES, JOSEPH, & ABNER - each $10 with what they have already received
Son JESSE - $200 and his Book Account to be erased
Dau NANCY GILLASPIE - $10 with what she has received
Sons ALEXANDER & WILLIAM - plantation, waggon, farming tools negro man Bob, negro boys Isaac & Ned, still & still vessels
Gr daus IBBY (dau of ROBT), MELINDA (dau of JOHN), IBBY (dau of JOSEPH) - each one feather bed & furniture
Balance of my gr daus named IBBY - $25
Gr son ROBERT, son of JOSEPH - his father's land when he comes of age, my saddle
Gr son ROBERT GILLASPIE, son of ROBERT GILLASPIE - negro girl
Exrs: James Hannah, John Landreth
Wits: John Coe, William Doak

B:0471 - EPHRAIM TROTTER - 20 Mar 1819 - Prb May 1819
Wife - all lands & property during widowhood
Edward Oalddom Trotter - to inherit land where I live
Son EPHRAIM - shall live on the place he settled until my youngest child comes of age
Sons SHADRACK, JAMES, EPHRAIM, RUBIN, BENNET, & HARDIN - proceeds of sale from 100 ac of land
My four daus - balance of my personal property
Wits: David Armfield, John Wheat
Adm granted by court to Polly Trotter & Shadrack Trotter

B:0472 - SAMUEL OZMENT - 9 Apr 1819 - Prb May 1819
Wife - home & land & all I possess during life
Ch: JONATHAN, CATY WEATHERLY, MARY CLOMENS?, DORKAS OZMENT, DAVID, SARAH STACK, WILLIAM, CHARLES, LEAH RUSSELL, RICHARD - each five shillings
Sons SAMUEL & JOHN - land after decease of my wife
Exrs: Charles Ozment, William Mayben
Wits: Richard Ozment, John Carter

B:0473 - HEZEKIAH GARDNER - 31 Jan 1819 - Prb Aug 1819
Step dau HANNAH HILTON - bed & furniture
Step sons SAMUEL & ALEXANDER HILTON & step dau MARY IRWIN - what has been advanced before
Wife JANE - remainder of estate during widowhood
My seven ch: SARAH GARDNER, HEZEKIAH, LYDIA GARDNER, OBED,

THOMAS CLARK GARDNER, NANCY GARDNER, & RICHARD - proceeds of sale of estate at marriage or decease of wife
Exrs: Brothers SILVANUS GARDNER & JONATHAN GARDNER
Wits: George Gardner, David Armfield, Stephen Gardner

B:0474 - MICAJAH STANLEY - 5 Feb 1819 - Prb Aug 1819
Dau CATHERINE STANLEY - use of house, 40 ac while single, maintenance, horse, cow, household furniture
Son ISAAC - remaining lands, horses, cattle, sheep, & hogs & carpenter tools. Son ANTHONY - $52.50
Sons MAHLON & JAMES & dau SARAH WHITE - 50¢ each
Exrs: Micheal & Jesse Stanley, sons of Strangeman Stanley
Wit: William Stanley

B:0475 - RICHARD LINTHICUM - 21 Sept 1819 - Prb Nov 1819
Wife SARAH & her son - plantation for all their lives, 1 feather bed, 1 chaff bed, all their furniture, stock, etc
All my children - residue of estate
Wits: Micheal Wilson & Soloman Hodson testified in Court that the deceased was too weak to sign his name to the will; the Court appointed Micheal Wilson as Adm.

B:0476 - ROBERT WILEY - 12 Oct 1819 - Prb Nov 1819
Son JAMES - $1. Dau REBECCA WILEY - one cow
Five daus now living at home - a home until death or marriage
Son ROBERT - most of land, black boy Peter, still, brandy, corn
Sons MATTHEW & DAVID - 100 ac or price thereof from Robert
Dau JEAN - black girl Amy, my two old black ones Peter & Caty provided she pay $50 each to Esther, Abby, and Anna Wiley
Exrs: John Wiley, Robert Wiley
Wits: John H. Thom, William Matthews

B:0477 - WILLIAM C. CHAPMAN - 5 Feb 1819 - Prb Feb 1820
Wife JANE, daus MATILDA HANNA, ELIZA JEAN, & REBECCA GOODRICH - to divide estate. My three daus above named to divide estate coming to me from my father in Virginia
Exrs: Henry Humphreys, John Hanner
Wits: Abraham Gwin, John Scott

B:0478 - NATHAN DILLON - 20 Oct 1818 - Prb Feb 1820
Wife SARAH - all of estate, negroes Rhoda & Tom
Son PETER - after his mother's decease a tract on Haw River where Andrew Cain, dec'd, formerly lived, being balance of tract I gave Rachel Dillon
Gr son Jake Dillon - tract on Beever Creek adj Sanders, Bembo, & Medearis where Joseph Patterson lives
All my daus - have already received their share of estate
Wits: John Pegg, George Middleton

B:0479 - HEBERT PEEBLES - 24 May 1819 - Prb May 1820
Negroes Lewis & Edmund to be sold to satisfy debts
Wife SALLY may keep Edmund if debts paid, negro Anny, Isaac, choice of stock, home plantation, the following negroes for ten years: Jerry, Ruebin, Nathan, Polly (& her two children Abram & Wiley), Hannah
My ten ch (all minors): JOEL W., ROBERT G., WYATT M., SALLY W.,

HERBERT J. PEEBLES, CATHERINE S., JOHN R., DRURY W., URIAH, & MARTHA ANN PEEBLES
SALLY & CATHERINE - negroes Dorcas & Anne
Joel - to be overseer of farm & have horse that did belong to Hugh Cummings, continue oversight of farm when he marries
ROBERT G. & WYATT M. to have woodland S of Haw River when they marry. Land & slave divided equally after decease of wife
Exrs: John Moore, Travis Jones who refused and Sally Peebles & Reuben Folger were appointed by the Court
Wits: Demsey McKinney, John Jones

B:0480 - TIMOTHY RUSSELL - 12 Feb 1818 - Prb May 1820
Wife JUDITH - what household stuff that she brought into my house that is remaining, use & profit of plantation dw
Dau SARAH RUSSELL - my southern most house at death or remarriage of my wife, desk, bookcase, half of furniture
Dau MIRIAM SWAIN - walnut table
Dau HEPHZEBAH STARBUCK - half of household furniture
Dau MARY JESOP - one feather bed
Sons WILLIAM & GEORGE - ten shillings
Son-in-law REED SWAIN & his wife and dau SARAH RUSSELL - tract I live on provided they have care & support of son DAVID during his natural life
Exrs: Son-in-law REED SWAIN, dau SARAH RUSSELL
Wits: Levi Coffin, Libni Barnard

B:0481 - JOHN BEESON - 27 Apr 1820 - Prb Aug 1820
Wife PRISCILLA - plantation, use of all estate dw to raise & educate the children, negro woman Mariah
Son JOHN A. - plantation at death or remarriage of my widow
Sons JESSE, JOEL, & HASTEN W. - my Bullock tract, also meadow adj Thomas Sanders
Daus JANE & LEUTISHA - $400 each when they come of age
Exrs: Wife PRISCILLA BEESON, Thomas Sanders
Wits: Jesse Sanders, Jesse Stanley

B:0482 - SAMUEL IRWIN - 24 Dec 1815 - Prb Aug 1820
Wife ELIZABETH - plantation, household furniture dw
Dau NANCY IRWIN - feather bed, cow
Daus POLLY HELLIT & RUTH LOW - ten dollars
Son GEORGE - my rifle gun
My six sons: ABEL, SAMUEL, GEORGE, JOHN, ROBERT, & JAMES - all my lands equally divided
Exrs: Sons ABEL & JOHN IRWIN
Wits: Nicholas Millis, James Millis

B:0483 - SAMUEL ALLISON - 9 April 1816 - Prb Nov 1820
Wife ELIZABETH - horse & saddle, stock, household furniture dw
Dau SALLY WEATHERLY - $10; her son BILLY - $5
Ann McKnight - $10; her dau Betsy - $5
Becky Finley - $10; her dau Betsy -$5
Sons JOHN & ARTHUR - $100 for good brood mare, mill & plantation, negro Sam
Wits: Robert Mayben, John W. Caldwell

B:0484 - PHILLIP HORNEY - 11 Sept 1820 - Prb Nov 1820

Wife NANCY - all of my land on east side of Bull Run, wagon, gray mare, slave Grace; slave George to remain & work for support of my wife
Son JOHN C. - two thirds of land when he comes of age & other third at decease of wife, slave called Mingo
Oldest son MANLOVE - slave woman Juda
Sons JEFFERY, SAMUEL & PHILLIP - woman slave Miriam
Daus PERMILLA, SALLY, ANNE & TERRESSA - land west of Bull Run
Oldest dau PERMILA - woman slave called "Lydia the younger", cow & calf, feather bed & furniture worth $30
Dau SALLY - slave Alice, cow & calf, feather bed, horse worth $70
Dau ANNE - slave Salmice, cow & calf, feather bed, horse
Dau TERRISSA - yellow slave (dau of Miz) named Sarah, cow, etc
All my children: MANLOVE, JEFFERY, SAMUEL, PHILLIP, PAMELA, JOHN C., SALLY, ANNA, & TERRESA - residue of estate
Exrs: Son JEFFERY HORNEY, dau PAMELA HORNEY
Wits: Robert Campbell, James Mendenhall, Mary T. Mendenhall, Richard Mendenhall

B:0485 - MARTHA LACKEY - 30 Aug 1816 - Prb Nov 1820
Nephew Col WALTER MCCONNELL - bed & furniture, desk, bookcase, choice of two tables and two heads of cattle, books, etc
Margaret Stewart - bed with all its furniture, books
Adam Lackey Stewart - bed & furniture, horse or $60 for a horse, his uncle's walnut chest, negro girl Gincey, books
Finley Stewart - one two year old heifer
Martha Stewart - one three year old cow
Prudence Stewart - my large walnut table
Martha Lemons, w/o John Lemons - $20
Martha Lackey McBride, d/o Samuel McBride, now both living in Tennessee - $20
Exrs: Daniel Gillaspie, Walter McConnell
Wits: Walter McConnel, Robert Hanner

B:0486 - WILLIAM PATTERSON - 31 July 1817 - Prb Nov 1820
Dau MARGARET - horse & saddle, cow, bed & furniture, her flax & cotton wheels, two sheep, her flax & cotton supplied
Dau NANCY - has already received her share
Dau CATY - horse & saddle, cow, bed & furniture, sheep, etc
Sons WILLIAM H. & NATHANIEL B. - remainder of estate; NATHANIEL to be schooled till he understands the Rules of Three
Exrs: John S. Gillaspie, William H. Patterson
Wits: Joseph Ross, John McMurry

B:0487 - WILLIAM WEDDOP (or WEDDOSS?) - 21 Jan 1819 - Nov 1820
Dau ELIZABETH CONNER, dau PEGGY WEDDOP, son THOMAS, son WILLIAM - ten shillings
Son CHARLES - my tract of land, stock, & other property
Wife WINNY - care of my land until CHARLES becomes of age; then support for her & dau POLLY WEDDOP by CHARLES
Betsey Conner - 4 ac tract to build a home during widowhood
Exr: Ithamar Hunt. Wits: Elizabeth Conner, Peggy Weddop

B:0488 - THOMAS DICK - 12 Dec 1820 - Prb Feb 1821
Son JOHN W. - 1,000 ac whereon I live, mills, negroes Jim, Harry, & wife Jennie, Library of books, good horse & saddle, bed

Dau MARTHA W. DICK - negro girl Looey, horse & saddle, bed, etc
Son THOMAS J. - my upper mills & plantation, negro Abram, boy Masdey, man Frank, good horse & saddle, bed & furniture
Dau JANE E. DICK - horse & saddle, bed & furniture when 18
Thomas Lindsay (son of Andrew Lindsay) - negro boy Manuel
Three youngest ch - educated from proceeds of sale of remaining property that is to be put on interest
Exr: John W. Dick
Wits: Josiah Jessop, Mark W. Killingsworth

B:0489 - BENJAMIN BISWELL - 21 Apr 1819 - Prb Feb 1821
Mary Ann Biswell, Elizabeth Biswell & Susannah Biswell - negro man Abraham, 18 hogs, all my corn & bacon
Sister MARTHA BOOKER - five shillings
Exr: Martin Wright
Wits: William Weatherly, Thomas Moore

B:0490 - WILLIAM BALLARD - 5 Sept 1818 - Prb Feb 1821
Son WILLIAM - 90 ac whereon I live and all the privileges thereto
Son THOMAS - 120 ac whereon he lives
Dau MARY BALLARD - dwelling house, 26 ac, half the orchard, cow
Son NATHAN - residue of estate
Daus SUSANA LAND (or SAND), ELIZABETH GRAY, SARAH GRAY & ANNE FISHER - each five shillings
Exrs: James Chipman, Nathan Cook
Wits: Nathan Cook, Charles Starbuck, William Whicker

B:0491 - JOHN CUNNINGHAM - 15 Jan 1820 - Prb Feb 1821
Wife MARY - home plantation including garden, mansion house, kitchen & all necessary out houses, all land south of the Great Road during widowhood, $400, horse & saddle, furniture
Son MITCHELL - that tract on which he has made a crop, rifle, negro Tom, wagon, sorrell mare, heifer, steer, hogs, etc
Son JOSEPH - tract conveyed by James Ward, $1,300, negro Abram
Dau POLLY CUNNINGHAM - negro Mimi & child, bay horse, side saddle, wheel, table, chest, cupboard, $100, bed & furniture
Son WILLIAM - home plantation at death or marriage of wife, negro Nathan who is to be put to the use of clothing and schooling son William
Son ANDREW - plantation where James Cunningham did live adj William Montgomery, also tract where David Brown did live, negro Willis, the hire of Willis to be used for clothing & schooling son Andrew
Two little daus ELIZABETH - negro boy Jacob, girl Looce, bed & furniture; NANCY - $800 on interest
Dau HANNAH DONNELL, w/o ERWIN DONNELL - negroes Beck & Barbara and other property she has been given, $35
Gr sons RUFUS SIMS, MILTON CUNNINGHAM, JAMES CUNNINGHAM - ea $5
Exrs: Son JAMES CUNNINGHAM, son-in-law ERWIN DONNELL
Wits: John W. Dick, Mark W. Killingsworth, William Gilchrist

B:0492 - DAVID MAYBEN - 10 Oct 1814 - Prb Feb 1821
Wife ANNE - plantation dw, choice of horses, beds, spinning wheel, side saddle, $100, negro man Ned
Three youngest ch: CUMMINS, NELSON & RUHAMA - proceeds of sale of items to be put on interest

Eldest dau ELIZABETH - 10 shillings, interest on $250 for use of her youngest child
Dau POLLY MAYBEN - $300, 6 months schooling, cow & calf, bed
3rd dau CATY MAYBEN - $300, 9 mos schooling, cow & cald, bed, etc
Eldest son CUMMINS - plantation at death or remarriage of wife, silver watch, 2 years schooling
2nd son WILLIAM N. - tract purchased of David Caldwell, $250, my gun & shot bag, 5 volumes of Hinay's Works, 2 yrs schooling
Son NELSON - to go to Tanners Trade at 18, silver knee buckles, lot in Greensboro adj Henry Humphreys
Youngest dau RUHAMER - negro boy Matt?, $300, bed & furniture
Exr: Friend Robert Mayben
Wits: William Mayben, James Silavan

B:0493 - GEORGE TROTTER - 18 Apr 1819 - Prb Feb 1821
Wife - all my lands during widowhood
My four daus - proceeds from sale of land after death of wife; girls to pay John Trotter ten shillings
Exrs: John Trotter and his Mother, Sarah Trotter
Wit: John Hunt

B:0494 - RICHARD WHEELER - 1 Aug 1817 - Prb Feb 1821
Wife MARY - all my lands during widowhood
Sons RICHARD & AMOS - to inherit from my wife
Daus NANCY JENKINS, SARAH CHAPPLE, ELIZABETH MASSEY - furniture
Exr: John Beard
Wits: Nicholas Millis, Ambrose Chapple

B:0495 - EZEKIAL DEWISE - 11 Apr 1820 - Prb May 1821
Wife SARAH - 175 ac plantation, house, household furniture
Son CALEB - to inherit plantation from wife
Heirs of dau MARY SIMPSON - $50. Dau SARAH DILWORTH - $50
Gr son ABSOLEM DILWORTH - $12.50
Gr daus JANE, MARY & ANN DILWORTH - each $12.50
Sons JOSEPH, EZEKIAL, & ELIJAH - ten shillings each
Exrs: Son ELIJAH DEWISE, Abraham Peeples
Wits: Jeremiah Crowder, Elizabeth Dewise

B:0496 - JEREMIAH FIELD, Senr. - 19 Dec 1818 - Prb May 1821
Wife - plantation during widowhood, negro Dinah, horse, furniture
Sons JOSEPH, BENJAMIN, & JOHN - each $5
Eldest daus: RUTH, JANE & MARY - each $50
Youngest daus: ELIZABETH, RACHEL & TABITHA - each $1
Son JEREMIAH'S widow POLLY FIELDS - all demands against her & 50¢ and her son ELOTT - $20 for schooling
Son WILLIAM'S widow, NANCY FIELDS - 50¢
My ch: RUTH, JOSEPH, BENJAMIN, MARY, JANE, ELIZABETH, TABITHA, RACHEL & JOHN - residue of estate; if JOHN does not return within 12 years, his part to be divided between the rest
Exrs: Son-in-law NATHAN ARMFIELD, Samuel Hempbell, Senr.
Wits: William Dicky, Robert Ryann

B:0497 - DANIEL GREESON - 11 Mar 1821 - Prb May 1821
Ch: MILLEY, RACHEL & GUIDEON - plantation when GUIDEON is 21
Exr: Christian Clapp
Wits: Jacob Greeson, Barnay Clapp

B:0498 - JEFFERY HORNEY - 19 Apr 1821 - Prb May 1821
Wife - black girl Cinda, home & plantation during widowhood
Dau SARAH - cow & calf, feather bed & furniture
Daus NANCY & KERSIAH - each $30
Sons JARED & JASON - slave George; Meddola & Perry to be sold
Exrs: Kisiah Horney, Philip Horney
Wits: Wm. Manlove, Manlove Horney, Reuben Swain, James Gordon, Jonathan Manlove, Phillip Horney, Jr.

B:0499 - PRUDENCE STEWART - 15 May 1819 - Prb May 1821
Son ROBERT - negro girl Ruth, chest of drawers, half Bible
Son JOHN - half of three volumes Scots family Bible
Dau SUSAN CLOUD - negro girl named Nora; negro woman Jane & her 6 mo old boy Andy, this for taking care of negro woman Hopperlong in her old age
Dau UPHANE GORRELL - horse, 2nd volume of Scott's family Bible
Heirs of son JAMES, dec'd - $205
Gr dau SARAH HANNER - negro girl Jincy, corner cupboard
Gr children (children of Judith McAdow) - each $5
Gr sons FINLEY WASHINGTON GORRELL & FINLEY A. STEWART CLORO? - proceeds of $100 note on Joseph Cloro
Gr sons ROBERT SHAW STEWART (s/o ROBERT STEWART), ROBERT SHAW STEWART (s/o JAMES), and JAMES ADDISON STEWART (s/o JOHN) - each $50
Dau JANE FORBIS - my bed & its whole furniture
Negro woman Rose - her spinning wheel, chest & bed
Exrs: Sons ROBERT STEWART, JOHN STEWART, son-in-law DAVID GORREL. Wits: William Causbie, Daniel Albright

B:0500 - WILLIAM BEVILL - 1 Aug 1821 - Prb Aug 1821
Wife LUCY A. - part of tract whereon I live adj Cole plantation and Archibald Whiteworth during widowhood, negro woman Luce
Sons VIVANT & JOEL T. - to inherit from my wife
Son VIVANT - half the rest of land, negro boy called Bedford
Dau ALIS BEVILL - negro girl Sarry, bed & furniture
Son JOEL T. - balance of land, horse when he is 21; he is to be bound out to Alexander Bevill at my death who is to give him a set of black smith tools at 21
Dau ELIZABETH BEVILL - negro girl called Peg, bed & furniture, horse, $30 for schooling
Exrs: John Tomlinson, Alexander Bevill
Wits: James Tomlinson, Sally Bevill, Mary Tharp

B:0501 - JAMES CUNNINGHAM - 27 Apr 1821 - Prb Aug 1821
Wife MARY - negro woman Phillis, boy Jack, girl Sally, sorrell horse, mare, 3 featherbeds, half of cupboard ware, looking glass, choice of stock, third of books, loom, plantation
Son JOHN W. - half of another tract when he becomes 21, negro girl Thamar, negro boy Jo, negro fellow Peter
Dau NANCY W. CUNNINGHAM - negro boy Rawley, negro girl Caty, boy Nathaniel, girl Minerva, my Rockingham Co. tract of land
Ch of my sister ISABELL SIMS - fourth of my estate
Mitchell Cunningham, Hannah Donnell, Joseph Cunningham & Polly Cunningham - fourth of my estate divided between them

B:0502 - DAVID HARRELL - 27 Mar 1821 - Prb Aug 1821

Wife ELIZABETH - 200 ac of land, negroes Bob & Amey, 2 horses, choice of stock, household & kitchen furniture, etc
Son JOSEPH - 200 ac I lend to my wife, negro York, horse, bed
Son STEPHEN - 100 ac where he lives & what he has received
Son HENRY - $330 I have settled on him, gray mare, bed & furn
Son DAVID - 100 ac on east side of Dicks Road, horse, cow, bed
Dau ELIZABETH UNDERWOOD - negro Jinny, property received
Dau SARAH ATKINS - negro girl Fillis, property already received
Dau RACHEL HARRELL - $100, negro boy Caleb, bed & furniture, cow
Dau ABIGAIL HARRELL - negro girl Dinah, bed & furniture, cow
Dau MARTHA COALMAN - $300
Son JOHN - 100 ac on west side of Dicks Road where Henry Harrel did live, bed & furniture, cow & calf, horse, sow & pigs
Son JAMES - negro Sam, horse saddle, bed & furniture, cow & calf
Exrs: Wife ELIZABETH HARRELL, Abraham Peoples
Wit: William King

B:0503 - JOHN HORNEY - 29 May 1821 - Prb Aug 1821
Wife MARY - 100 ac, $300, horse & saddle, furniture, cow & calf
Dau SARAH - to have home with her mother while single
Son JEFFERY - $100 note I have against him
Son PHILIP - remainder of land he did not sell to Jeffery Horney and Joshua Chadwick
Ch: JOHN - $2; ELIZABETH PEGG - $5; SOLOMAN - $2; JONATHAN - $100 note I have against him; JAMES - $37; ESTHER MENDENHALL - $175; STEPHEN - $15
Gr son DAVIS HORNEY - $50
Dau SARAH & son PARIS - remainder of land & estate, their mother's part at her death
Exrs: Dau SARAH HORNEY, son PARIS HORNEY
Wits: John Stuart, Elizabeth Stuart

B:0504 - TARLTON JOHNSON - 19 Apr 1820 - Prb Aug 1821
Wife SARAH - privilege of plantation during life
Son NATHAN - 200 ac whereon I live, proceeds from sale of 100 ac
Son CHARLES - 188 ac tract north of my plantation
Daus HANNAH, SARAH, MIRIAM, MARGARET, MARY, REBECKAH - each 50¢
Heirs of son JOSHUA - 50¢; also gr dau ELVIRAH - 50¢
Dau RACHEL BALES - to inherit land from my wife
Exrs: Samuel Carter, Eleazer Beals
Wits: Mordecai Mendenhall, Joshua Moore

B:0505 - ROSANNAH LINIGAR - 20 June 1821 - Prb Aug 1821
Sister-in-law ELIZABETH LINIGAR, Elizabeth Kersey, & Eleazer Kersey's widow - each $50
Caleb Beals - remainder of estate & household furniture
Exrs: John Beals, Samuel Beeson appointed by court
Wits: Isabel Beeson, Anna Beals

B:0506 - MARGARET NELSON - 12 June 1820 - Prb Aug 1821
My five ch: SAMUEL NELSON, MARY NELSON, ANNA NELSON, BELINDA NELSON, & WILLIAM KERSON NELSON - division of estate except two youngest, BELINDA & WILLIAM K., have $50 more
Exrs: Bro JOSEPH RANKIN, Joseph McCain
Wits: John A. Foulkes, Alfred Scales, Robert Rankin, Joseph Hanner

B:0507 - JAMES RICKS, Farmer - 2 Apr 1806 - Prb Aug 1821
Wife GWINN - interest on money, room with a fire place at east end of mansion house
Daus HANNAH, NANCY, BETSY, GWINN - household furniture
Son EDWARD - has his part by deed conveyance
Son THOMAS - 100 ac on north end of tract
Son JONAS - 140 ac whereon I live, anvil & vice
Exrs: Son EDWARD RICKS, William Tomlinson
Wits: Jesse Hoggat, Thomas Kersey

B:0508 - ELIZABETH SPRUCE - 7 Aug 1821 - Prb Aug 1821
Niece SALLY FREEMAN SPRUCE - feather bed & furniture, saddle
Bro GEORGE SPRUCE - negro girl Cate, balance of property
Exr: George Spruce
Wits: George Nicks, Jr., John Karr

B:0509 - SOLOMAN SILLIVAN - 22 Feb 1821 - Prb Aug 1821
Wife SARAH - all my goods & chattles for life and then:
Son JAMES - bed & furniture, one sow, 2 chairs, half the pewter
Daus RACHEL RUSSOM, MARY SILLIVAN - ten shillings
Gr dau LEVICY SILLIVAN - one red heifer
Son SOLOMAN - bed & furniture, 2 heads of cattle, 5 hogs, remainder of household furniture
Gr son JOSEPH SILLEVAN - one ewe
Exr: Son SOLOMAN SILLIVAN. Wit: James Millis, Esqr.

B:0510 - JONATHAN TWIFORD - 11 June 1821 - Prb Aug 1821
Bro EDWARD W. - black woman Candice at my mother's death, residue
Sister ELIZABETH TWIFORD - $45 owed me by my brother ROBERT
Exr: James Polk, Senr. Wit: Jonathan Parker

B:0511 - JOSEPH WHITTINGTON - 19 Apr 1821 - Prb Aug 1821
Son THOMAS, dau ELIZABETH GREESUM, son EZEKIAL, dau MARY AYDLETTE, son NEHEMIAH, dau NANCY PARDUE, dau SARAH IRELAND ($10), & dau SEALEY ANDREW - each $1
Wife NANCY & her seven children - remainder of my estate
Exrs: Wife NANCY WHITTINGTON, son THOMAS WHITTINGTON
Wits: Thomas Bevill, Shadrack Andrew

B:0512 - C. B. BARTLETT - "Friday Morning Sept. 7, 1821, Native of Virginia but a sojourner to Lawrence District, S. C. the past 18 years, laboring under the disease I believe about to take me..." Dated 10 Oct 1821 at bottom of will. Prb Nov 1821
Capt M. Young - my shaving glass & tools for himself; sell the silver watch & other property & go to Richmond and distribute proceeds among those he thinks best
Exr: Matthew Young. Wit: Joseph Vance

B:0513 - THOMAS ELLIOTT - 21 Mar 1812 - Prb Nov 1821
Wife MARY - all my worldly goods during widowhood; at her death:
Daus - to inherit all moveable property; sons - all my lands
Exrs: John Wayman, Jesse Burton appointed by the Court
Wits: John James, Isaac Burton, Jesse Burton

B:0514 - SAMUEL FULTON - 22 Apr 1820 - Prb Nov 1821
Wife MARY - home plantation, negro woman Milley

Gr son JAMES CAPPS FULTON - horse, saddle & bridle worth $80
Daus JANE WEATHERLY & MARY WEATHERLY -lands adj plantation
Son ALEXANDER - to inherit negro woman Milley from my wife
Son SAMUEL - negro boy Isaac six years old
Son THOMAS - negro boy Jacob ten years old
Son GEORGE - negro boy Abraham six years old
Exrs: William Weatherly, Alexander Fulton, Andrew Weatherly
Wits: Howell Parker, William Maxwell

B:0515 - MARY HUSSEY - 22 July 1820 - Prb Nov 1821
Gr sons JONATHAN, HENRY & JOSEPH, sons of John Hussey dec'd
- each $500 when they arrive at the age of 21
Son THOMAS - land that has been conveyed to him, half of residue
Gr dau MARY HUNT - one pine chest & one three quart bason
Son STEPHEN - my bed & furniture, set of spools, pair of sheep shears, pewter plates & dish, stock, half of residue
Dau SARAH COFFIN - pewter basin, pewter dish, 3 pewter plates
Gr ch ELIZA & JOHN HUSSEY, ch of JOSEPH of Rowan Co. - each 5 sh
Daus SARAH, LYDIA, REBECKAH & ANN - my wearing clothes
Exrs: Sons THOMAS & STEPHEN HUSSEY
Wits: Abel Knight, 3rd; William Hussey

B:0516 - HUBBARD PEEPLES - 29 Sept 1821 - Prb Nov 1821
Son ABRAHAM - part of my land on Mill Road & Haw River, third of negroes, stock, & household furniture
Dau ELIZABETH FOSTER PEEPLES - third of negroes, stock & furn
Dau POLLY BRASWELL - third of negroes, stock & furniture
Heirs of son EDWARD R. PEEPLES, dec'd - $200, share in land
Heirs of dau FAITHEY PERKINS, dec'd - $200, share in land
Exrs: Son ABRAHAM PEEPLES, son-in-law BLAKE W. BRASWELL
Wits: Howell Parker, John Work, Branch Gordon

B:0517 - HANCE CORSBIE - 10 July 1809 - Prb Feb 1822
Wife ANN - free use of the plantation during widowhood
Son WILLIAM - 200 ac home place at decease or marriage of wife
Dau MARGARET - two cows & one heifer
Exr: Son WILLIAM CORSBIE Wit: Isaiah McDill

B:0518 - MAIKEL JESTER - 2 Jan 1822 - Prb Feb 1822
Wife MARGARET - balance of estate after tracts sold for debts
Sons JOHN, WILLIAM, & MAIKEL - 160 ac at death or marriage of wf
Daus REBECCA & PHEBE JESTER - each bed & furniture, cow & calf
Dau ELIZABETH JESTER - ten shillings with what she has received
My six children: REBECCA, JOHN, MARGARET, WILLIAM, MAIKEL, & PHEBE - residue of estate
Exrs: Wife MARGARET JESTER, Richard Mendenhall
Wits: Samuel Sapp, Caleb Beals, Henry Hayworth

B:0519 - ISAIAH HUNT - 29 Aug 1821 - Prb Feb 1822
Wife MERIAM - 2 beds & furniture, my gray mare, carriage, saddle flax wheel, chest & all the household furniture that she had
Son WILLIAM - five shillings
Daus by my first wife - each five shillings
Son JESSE - half of my wagon
Sons JOEL & ISAIAH - each five shillings
Son THOMAS - home plantation, half my wagon

Dau MERIAM - learning sufficient for a woman, bed, chest, cow
Exr: Abel Knight, Junr.; William Unthank, Esqr.
Wits: Ithamar Hunt, Reuben Wilson

B:0520 - DAVID WANICK - 3 June 1815 - Prb Feb 1822
Wife ELIZABETH - 100 ac choice of my tract, choice of stock, farming tools, household furniture, kitchen furniture
Dau CHARITY - $50, maintenance, home place at death of my wife
All my children except JESSE & POLLY - $5 toward schooling them
Exrs: John Chrisman, Elizabeth Wanick
Wits: David Thomas, Adam Strader

B:0521 - THOMAS WOODBURN - 14 May 1821 - Prb Feb 1822
Ch: JOHN, WILLIAM, DAVID, heirs of son ARTHUR, MARY WHARTON, ANN DONNELL - each $1
Ch of son ROBERT: MARY, ANN, MARGARET, HANNAH, EVELINA & JESSE SWAIN WOODBURN - my land
Exrs: Son DAVID WOODBURN, Jesse McCuiston
Wits: Simon Landreth, John Landreth

B:0522 - JOHN DONNELL - 12 Mar 1822 - Prb May 1822
Wife ELIZABETH - maintenance dw, negro George, stock, furniture
My sons now married & my dau JANE - one dollar
Daus HANNAH, NANCY & MARY - each one dollar
Dau BETSEY DONNELL - $200, negro girl Ayles, book case, bed
Dau SARAH DONNELL - $600, one bed & furniture
Dau RUTH DONNELL - $200, land bought of Daniel Shoemaker, negro girl Charity, bed & furniture, book case
Son LEVI - remainder of lands, negro Bill, stock, horse & saddle; books to be divided among all my children
Son JAMES - my surveying instruments
Exrs: Wife ELIZABETH DONNELL, son JAMES DONNELL
Wits: Robert Donnell, Sr., Robert Donnell, Jr.

B:0523 - ALLEN UNTHANK - 19 June 1820 - Prb Aug 1822
Wife JEMIMA - use & profit of plantation, horse & saddle
Son ALLEN - 200 ac plantation provided he cares for his mother, wagon, harrow & farming tools, writing desk, clock
Dau RUTH UNTHANK - choice of horses, saddle, big Bible, chest
Sons WILLIAM, JOHN & ALLEN - smith tools & jack screw
Ch: RACHEL, JONATHAN, WILLIAM, JOHN, ANNA, RUTH, JEMIMA & ALLEN - residue of estate, my books
Exrs: Son WILLIAM UNTHANK, son-in-law JOSEPH HUNT
Wits: Josiah Unthank, Isaac White, William Armfield

B:0524 - JESSE KERSEY - 6 Nov 1822 - Prb Nov 1822
Wife - reasonable support from my estate during widowhood
My daus - each a bed
My family - each a share in estate
Exrs: William Kersey, Nathan Mendenhall
Wits: Stephen Harlon, Robert Hodson, Marmaduke T. Mendenhall

B:0525 - YOUNG PATTERSON - 29 Apr 1821 - Prb Nov 1822
Wife ELIZABETH - all my personal & real property during life
Son WILSON - estate after decease of his mother
Son THOMAS & dau NANCY WALKER - each five shillings
Exr: Wilson Patterson. Wits: Jonas Case, Charles Case

B:0526 - WILLIAM PAISLEY - 25 Feb 1822 - Prb Nov 1822
Ch: JOHN, WILLIAM'S children, SAMUEL, ROBERT ($50), BETSY FINLEY - each one dollar
Exr: Son PRESTON PAISLEY who inherits land & estate
Wits: John Paisley, William McClain

B:0527 - JOSEPH UNTHANK - 4 Mar 1823 - Prb May 1823
Wife REBECKAH - comfortable support during widowhood, horse creature she usually rides, saddle, bed & furniture, cow & calf
Son ELI - 8 ac that is part of tract bought from my bro JOHN
Sons TEMPLE & WILLIAM - remaining estate to support their mother
Dau BULY WILLIAMS - $100 more than I have given her
Daus MAHALY, BETSY & SALLY UNTHANK - each $150, bed & furniture
"If my wife & children should be agreed to sell and move to the Western Country, it is my will for them to do so."
Exrs: Josiah Unthank, Son TEMPLE UNTHANK
Wits: Bethuel Coffin, Jonathan Clark

B:0528 - WILLIAM DONNELL - 26 Oct 1816 - Prb Feb 1823
Wife NANCY - $200, household furniture, negro woman Biddy & her Ch: Zirza, Retty Lee, Leddy, Calvin & Levenich; stock, tools
Bros JOHN, THOMAS, ANDREW, LATHEM, ROBERT, heirs of JAMES, & heirs of sisters HANNAH & JANE - one dollar each
Nephew GEORGE DENNY, son of GEORGE - Guardian of slaves who are to be freed at wife's decease
North Buffaloe Congregation - $50
Exrs: Wife NANCY DONNELL, brother JOHN DONNELL
Wits: Moses McGready, George Denny

B:0529 - ADAM STARR - 22 May 1819 - Prb Feb 1823
Oldest dau MARY - $50, horse, household furniture
Oldest son DAVID - $50, & deed for 200 ac of land
Dau SUSANNAH - has received negro Pation, bedding & furniture
Son ADAM - I paid $300 for his land and gave him black smith tools
Son PETER - $50 besides $200 & a mare I have given him
Dau CATY - $50 besides negro Rose, bedding & furniture she has
Dau ELIZABETH - have given her $300 with bedding & furniture
Son HENRY - $50, 200 ac tract whereon he lives
Son ABNER - my old plantation adj John Nees, farming & black smith tools, negroes Jim, Charles & Anny, stock
Wife - full support by Abner & full privilege of mansion house
Youngest dau BARBARY - $200, yellow negro girl Nelly, horse worth $65, bed & furniture, cow & calf
Exrs: Joseph Gibson, Esqr., Capt. Ludwick Low
Wits: Henry Barnheart, Senr., William Johnson, Henry Barnheart,Jr

B:0530 - JAMES CRISWELL - 2 Sept 1822 - Prb Aug 1823
Friend John Wilson - my plantation with my smith tools
Nephew MARGARET SHORT - $40, my land on Meyers Fork where she lives. Sister MARY DONNELL - $10
Buffaloe Congregation - $100
Elijah Shoemaker, a crippled boy - $20
Nephew JEAN SHORT - $20, share with MARGARET household furniture
Synthy Ireland - $20
Exrs: Major Robert Donnell, Latham Donnell, Sr., Moses Gilchrist
Wits: John Gilchrist, Sr., John Gilchrist, Jr., Moses Gilchrist

B:0531 - JOHN WALKER - 10 Sept 1822 - Prb Aug 1823
Son LEVIN - two thirds of estate
Gr son JOHN, son of LEVIN - one third of estate
Exr: Son LEVEN WALKER
Wits: George Finley, William Maxwell

B:0532 - JONATHAN WILSON - 8 Oct 1823 - Prb Nov 1823
Wife LUWE - all my property real & personal during widowhood
My four ch: LETHA, NANCY, HENRY & WILL WILSON - estate after decease or marriage of wife
Exrs: Henry Weatherly, Isaac Weatherly
Wits: Levi Huston, John Dilling, David Caldwell

B:0533 - MARY TURNER - 12 June 1823 - Prb Nov 1823
Sister JANE GIBSON - all my property
Exr: Joseph Gibson. Wit: Moses Gibson

B:0534 - JANE WOLFINGTON - 13 Nov 1820 - Prb Nov 1823
Son SAMUEL - all my estate except what is otherwise bequeathed
Son ISAAC - one cow
Dau SARAH LEONARD - bed & furniture, looking glass
Dau REBECCA JACKSON - one little wheel
Gr daus JANE & MALINDA LEONARD - saddle, loom, chests
Son DAVID - my fire tongs
Exr: Son DAVID WOLFINGTON
Wits: William Leonard, Jesse Kersey

B:0535 - MICHAEL WILSON - 5 Nov 1823 - Prb Nov 1823
Wife JEMIMA - benefit of plantation during her lifetime
Dau UNIS - 2 feather beds & furniture when she comes of age, horse & side saddle
Exrs: Wife JEMIMA WILSON, Jonathan Newman
Wits: Nathan Armfield, Rutherford Petty

B:0536 - ANDREW GIBSON - 21 Feb 1823 - Prb Nov 1823
Wife JANE - negroes: Plowman John, Bett, Luca, Jacob, Dave & Mariah - 2 horses & cows, bed & furniture, pleasure carriage
Son JOSEPH - to maintain his mother, plantation, stock, tools, negroes Mary & Dorkas & their increase Sina; Allen & Luce
John F. - $350, tract on which he built & improved, also land on Back Creek called the Indian Field in Orange County, negroes Natting & Dick
Moses Gibson - 350 ac tract he lives on near Hillsboro Road & his bro John, negroes Paddy & Bill, one cow & calf
Heirs of Elizabeth Gibson (but she to have maintenance during her life) - tract near county line on Hillsboro Road, negroes Hannah & Aylse, horse, chest, bed--all of which I loaned her
Heirs of Jane Gibson (though she to have maintenance) - half of tract known as Thompson tract, horse & saddle, bed, etc
Heirs of Nancy Gibson (though she to have maintenance) - half of Thompson tract, negroes Nell, Reuben, Rachel, & Anny, horse, saddle, 2 cows & calves, 2 beds & furniture
My ch - after decease of wife, all my lands in North & South Carolina, Georgia & Tennessee
Exrs: James Gibson, Joseph Gibson
Wits: Morrison Donnell, John Latta, David Low

B:0537 - WILLIAM BARNEY - 4 Oct 1823 - Prb Feb 1824
Wife MARY - household furniture, negro girl Jin, mare, 2 cows
Ch: JOHN, MARY WILEY, SAMUEL, CATHREN OLIFER, ROBERT, ODELL & ADAM - ten shillings above what they have received
Sons DAVID & JOSIAH - plantation whereon I live
Dau SALLY SPENCE - negro girl she now has
Dau PEGGY THOMAS - $100, negro girl
Son JOSIAH - negro boys Jim & Garrison
Dau REBECCA - negro Jin at wife's decease, horn saddle, $50
Exrs: David Thomas & son JONAS BARNEY
Wits: John Apple, John Gormet?

B:0538 - WILLIAM WEATHERLY - 1824 - Prb Feb 1824
Wife JANE - home plantation to raise & educate gr son MILTON as he has no father & mother
Son ABNER F. - to manage the plantation
Philip Eubanks ran off with dau POLLY'S property & left MILTON
George has a father & I have done what I could for him
ABNER'S 3 daus: ELIZA, MARY & FRANKY - proceeds from sale
Exrs: Son A. F. WEATHERLY, wife JANE WEATHERLY
Proved in Court by James Fulton, Esqr., Mark Weatherly

B:0539 - WILLIAM DICKY - 20 Feb 1824 - Prb May 1824
Wife POLLY - $100, third of home tract, household furniture, horse; all my negroes to be hired out until youngest son is 21
Ch: REBECCA, JANE, EDWARD & JOHN - land to be divided among sons, negroes to be divided between all four children
Exr: John Armfield
Wits: Thomas McCulloch, Timothy Could

B:0540 - AMBROSE CHAPPLE - 28 Apr 1819 - Prb May 1824
Wife SARAH - all my estate for the benefit of raising the ch: DELILA CHAPPLE & ELIZABETH WHEELER, my wife's dau
Exr: John Lowder. Wits: Nickleson Millis, Nancy Millis

B:0541 - DAVID HAROLD - 2 Jan 1824 - Prb May 1824
Bro HARVEY HARRILL - 100 ac adj Thomas Ross
Others bros & sisters - proceeds of sale of other land
Exrs: Robert C. Rankin, John Daugherty
Wits: Noah Maronny, Charles W. Daugherty

B:0542: JOHN THOM - 9 June 1821 - Prb May 1824
Dau NELLY - negro Sal, choice of East rooms of my house, mare
Son DANIEL - to furnish provisions from the plantation for Nelly
Son EBENEZER - my desk & folding table
Little gr daus JANE & CATEY? MCLEAN - each a heifer
My married sons - each $2. Dau MARY'S heirs - $6
Dau CATHERINE'S heirs - $8. Dau JANE - $4
Exrs: Sons WILLIAM & DAVID THOM
Wits: John Wiley, John Cooper

B:0543 - DAVID CALDWELL - 14 Mar 1822 - Prb Aug 1824
Wife RACHEL - negro girl Victoria?, a good room & first class furniture for it, maintenance by son ROBERT
Son SAMUEL - negro Bill now in his possession, Hebrew books
Son ANDREW - negro girl Charlotte, bed & furniture, $400 of the $500 note on him

Son DAVID - negro Ally he has, tract of land bought of David and Robert Mabane
Dau PATSEY - to be cared for by son DAVID who receives her share
Son THOMAS - negro Margarett now in his possession, $100
Son JOHN - negro girl Beck, bed & furniture, $100
Sons JOHN H. & ROBERT - charge of sons ALEXANDER & EDMUNDS
John Rankin, George Rankin & Samuel Mitchell - $100 for the foundation of a fund for the support of the Presbyterian Religion of the North Buffaloe Church
My helpless ch: ALEXANDER, EDMUND & PATSEY - $60,000 to be divided between sons DAVID, JOHN, & ROBERT, provided each take charge of one
Son ROBERT - home plantation & adj tract, stock, tools, negroes Sam, Pattie & Washington; Cyclopedia presented me by Gov Martin, and the works called NATURE AND ARTS, money coming to me from Lancaster, Pennsylvania
Exrs: Sons JOHN & ROBERT CALDWELL
Wits: Elias Jessop, John McKnight

B:0544 - WILLIAM LUCAS - 22 Jan 1824 - Prb Aug 1824
Sons JAMES, JOHN & WILKINS - each fourth part of my estate
Gr ch WILLIAM & FRANKY FINDLEY - divide fourth part of estate
Exr: Son WILKINS LUCAS
Wits: Leven Gladson, Mark W. Killingsworth

B:0545 - MESACK COUCH - 19 Aug 1820 - Prb Aug 1824
Wife MARY - use of plantation, home, stock, tools, dw
Son MESHACK - to manage the plantation for half the profits
Dau MARY - feather bed & furniture, chest, cow & calf
Dau PRISCILLA - feather bed & furniture, chest, cow & calf
Sons JOHN, MESHACK & JOSHUA - plantation after decease of wife, to be divided equally by Evan Stephens & Joshua Johnson
Ch: SALLY, SAMUEL, CHARLOTTE, PHEBE, JAMES, JOSEPH, WALTHAM & MARY - one dollar
Exrs: Wife MARY COUCH, son MESHACK COUCH
Wits: Nathan Mendenhall, Judith Mendenhall

B:0546 - JOHN BALDWIN - 20 Sept 1824 - Prb Nov 1824
Dau ELIZABETH - feather bed & furniture, case of drawers, six pewter plates, six delf plates, six spoons, coffee pot, etc
Dau JANE - chest, table, 5 chairs, dutch oven, cow & calf, ewe
Dau SARAH PITTS - the large pot
Wife JEMIMA - use of plantation, moveable property, bed, etc
Son JOHN - tract adj my corner, Robert Stewart, John Stewart
Daus ELIZABETH, JANE GALBREATH, SARAH PITTS - to be paid $100 by JOHN, JESSE & DANIEL
Sons JESSE & DANIEL - middle & north parcels of land
Exrs: Nathan Cook, Abel Coffin

B:0547 - SILVANAS SWAIN - 8 June 1824 - Prb Nov 1824
Wife RHODA - proceeds of plantation dw until youngest child 21
Ch: CYNTHIA, IVEN, NARSISSA, EUNICE & ELISIA - divide proceeds of property with wife after all are 21
Exrs: Jethro Swain, William Worth
Wits: Benjamin Wheeler, John Barnard

B:0548 - GEORGE JOHNSON - 31 Aug 1824 - Prb Nov 1824

Wife SARAH - 150 ac on south side of tract with the house
Sisters ELIZABETH & ISABELL JOHNSON - 150 ac on north side of tract; share use of barn with wife
Bound girl Jane Manship - one bed & wheel, cow
Hugh Steveson & Jahne Dobios - each $10
Exrs: Frederich Finley, David Worth
Wits: Nathan Dicks, Thomas Swain

B:0549 - HANCE MCCAIN - 1 Oct 1824 - Prb Nov 1824
Wife JANE - maintenance, choice of kitchen ware & furniture
Dau MARY - cupboard, her bed & furniture, her saddle, oven & hooks
Sons HUGH & JOHN - my four lots joining each other on Hillsboro Street in Fayetteville
Son HANCE - land east of Phebe? Branch on Hunting Creek, a corner on Schoolhouse Branch adj Daniel Hobbs, James Donnell
Sons GEORGE, FORBIS, GUY & GREEN - balance of home tract, GUY & GREEN to be schooled
Daus LYDIA BARNEY, MARY MCCAIN - my half of a tract that belonged to John Hamilton & Tho. Henderson on Still House Br of Rock House Creek of Dan River in Rockingham County
Sons WILLIAM, HUGH & JOHN - $25 to make them equal
Exrs: Sons WILLIAM & HUGH MCCAIN
Wits: James Donnell, James Hobbs, Joseph T. Coffin

B:0550 - WILLIAM L. WALKER - 7 Sept 1824 - Prb Nov 1824
Daus BETSY & MATILDY - feather bed & furniture
My family - to live together until youngest son SAMUEL is 21
Next youngest son HENDERSON
All my children - proceeds from sale of land when all are 21
Exrs: Henry Taterman, Thomas McCuiston
Wits: Samuel Hunter, James Walker

B:0551 - WILLIAM DENNY - 12 Dec 1824 - Prb Feb 1825
Eldest dau REBECCA BLACK, eldest son JAMES, dau PAMELA WILSON, 2nd son WILLIAM - each one dollar
Dau NANCY DENNY - horse valued at $75, side saddle, 2 cows, bed & furniture, cotton spinning wheel, pair of cotton cards
Youngest dau ISABELL - same as NANCY DENNY, bureaus for both
Gr dau HARRIETT DENNY - bed & furniture to be in care of her mother NANCY DENNY
Youngest son ALLEN - home plantation, part of tract I gave son WILLIAM on Redy Creek
Exrs: Son ALLEN DENNY, bro-in-law GEORGE RANKIN
Wits: George Denny, Joseph A. McCain, Samuel Hatrick

B:0552 - WILLIAM MOORE - 2 Apr 1824 - Prb Feb 1825
Wife HANNAH - all property during life except the following:
Son JULIUS ELMIS MOORE - horse & saddle, negro Edmund about 7 years old, bed & furniture
JOHN MOORE - $1. JAMES MOORE - $100. ELIJA MOORE - $100
Ch of dau NANCY LINVILLE & son-in-law ANDERSON SMITH - to share equally with all my children at decease of wife
Exrs: Sons JOHN & JULIUS ELMIS MOORE
Wits: Richard Bowman, William Bowman

B:0553 - MARY WIRICK - 17 Feb 1825 - Prb Feb 1825

Dau PEGGY - bed & furniture, oven, flaxwheel, notes on William Knight for $25, on Jno King for $5, Andrew Lanier for $7.24
Exr: Friend George Wirick (Wyrick in probate)
Wits: James Fulton, Jesse Smith

B:0554 - ELIZABETH LATRELL - 25 Jan 1825 - Prb Feb 1825
Sarah & Lucy Latrell, daus of Samuel - each feather bed & furniture, cow, pot & hooks, pewter bason
Gr son PRESLEY - cow marked with a swallow fork in right ear and cross of the left ear
Son SAMUEL - balance of estate to be used for his family
Exr: Cornelis Boroughs
Wits: Benjamin Buroughs, John Chatman

B:0555 - REUBEN BENSON - 21 Mar 1825 - Prb May 1825
Son JOHN - my shoemakers tools, ox, 2 hoes, all my estate
Dau ANN - cotton wheel, check reel, iron pot
Dau PHEBE - flax wheel, cotton cards, dutch oven
My three ch - share remaining pension after debts are paid
Exr: Nathan Mendenhall
Wits: George C. Mendenhall, S. G. Mendenhall

B:0556 - THOMAS BENBOW - 19 June 1818 - Prb May 1825
Wife HANNAH - 4 ac with home & share meadow, horse, furniture
Son WILLIAM - my plantation
Son THOMAS - $200, tract on Horsepen Cr, blacksmith tools
Daus SARAH & ANN BENBOW - each $100, bed & furniture
Son CHARLES - $10, having already received his share
Dau ELIZABETH THOMPSON - 10 shillings, having received her share
Sister ELIZABETH CLAYTON - her house and 20 ac
Exrs: Sons CHARLES BENBOW, J. WILLIAM BENBOW
Wits: Hance McCain, John Clayton

B:0557 - THOMAS BLAIR - 6 May 1825 - Prb Aug 1825
Ch: JOHN, JAMES, SAMUEL, RUTH BLAIR, MARTHA BLAIR, THOMAS, SARAH PARMOR - each 20 shillings
Son WILLIAM - whats left of plantation, all other property for providing for me and my old slaves
Exr: Son WILLIAM BLAIR
Wits: D. N. Ogburn, Charles Brown

B:0558 - JOSEPH CHRISTMAN - 7 Nov 1825 - Prb Nov 1825
Wife ELIZABETH - plantation, household furniture, etc for life
Dau ESTHER & her husband, SPENCER A. HOLEMAN - 100 ac tract where they did live. Son JACOB - my wagon
My wife & 2 ch - divide proceeds of sale of certain items
Exrs: Son-in-law SPENCER A. HOLEMAN, son JACOB CHRISTMAN
Wits: Henry Hart, William Thomas, John Christman

B:0559 - ELIAS PETTY - 1 Nov 1825 - Prb Nov 1825
Wife RACHEL - all my estate dw; if she remarries property to be sold & proceeds divided between my five children:
WATSON PETTY, POLLY HODSON, JAMES, SAMUEL & WILLIAM PETTY when all reach full age
Exrs: Friends William Worth, Watson Petty
Wits: David Worth, Eunice Worth

B:0560 - SAMUEL FOUNTAIN - 19 Aug 1824 - Prb Nov 1825
Wife SALLY & son WILLIAM - land west of road from Greensboro to Mendenhall's mill, dwelling house, stock, furniture
Sons ANDREW, JOHN, & ELI - land east of the road, horses, beds
Daus ELIZABETH TROTTER & MARY ANN HARVEY - cows they have
Son-in-law ANSEL LAND - five shillings
Dau SALLY FOUNTAIN - bed & bedding, her saddle, cow & calf
Exr: Son WILLIAM FOUNTAIN
Wits: Robert Moderwell, Benjamin Overman

B:0561 - DAVID CURRY - 25 Aug 1825 - Prb Nov 1825
Daus MILLEA & NANCY - all my estate excepting other bequeaths
Son EDWARD and son DANIEL - half of land where daus of Reuben Benson live adj Edmund's
Exr: Stephen G. Mendenhall
Wits: Nathan Mendenhall, Joseph C. Stafford

B:0562 - WALTER MCCUISTON - 30 June 1822 - Prb Nov 1825
Son THOMAS - tract of land whereon I live, wagon, gears, tools
Son ROBERT - walnut chest, family Bible
Gr dau LEVINA MCCUISTON - my household furniture
Gr dau JANE JOHNSON - one large dutch oven
Gr son WALTER JOHNSON - bay horse colt now two years old
Exrs: Son THOMAS MCCUISTON, William McCuiston
Wits: James McNairy, Edmond Bowman

B:0563 - JOHN GILCHRIST - 15 Aug 1821 - Prb Nov 1825
Son MOSES - all land & estate except other legacies
Son WILLIAM - $1
Dau MARGARET MCGIBONY & her dau MARTHA - $25 allowed by her Aunt Martha, dec'd
Gr son JOHN GILCHRIST, s/o SAMUEL - my rifle gun
Gr son JOHN GILCHRIST, s/o ROBERT - the bed on which I lodge
Gr sons JOHN W. MCGIBBONY, DAVIDSON GILCHRIST, JAMES GILCHRIST - monies on book debts
Exrs: Sons ROBERT & MOSES GILCHRIST
Wits: Samuel McClintock, John W. McClintock, John B. Stafford

B:0564 - THOMAS OZBURN, Yeoman - 15 July 1825 - Prb Nov 1825
Eldest son ELISHA - third of land to be taken off the east side
Sons THOMAS & JOHN - remaining land
Wife REBECCA - peaceable possession of my home and sufficient maintenance during widowhood
Eldest dau SARAH & daus MARY & REBECCA - spinning wheel, cow, bed
Exrs: Wife REBECCA OZBURN, JOHN BEARD
Wits: William Hodson, Soloman Mills, Samuel W. Hodgins

B:0565 - State of Virginia, Logan County - 9 Mar 1824
Present John Cooke, Junior; John Harvey, William Hinchman, John Sparr, Thomas Linvill, Philip Ballard & Francis R. Pinnel all Gentlemen Justices. The last will & testament of ELIZABETH LINEGAR was produced in open court & duly proved by the oath of Francis W. Pinnell & Thomas Bays and ordered to be recorded...the following is a copy, to wit:
ELIZABETH LINEGAR of Giles (now Logan) County, Va - 23 Jan 1823
Proven in Guilford County, North Carolina Nov Term 1825

Son ISAAC LINEGAR - all my estate both real & personal
Exr: Son ISAAC LINEGAR
Wits: Francis W. Pinnell, Thomas Bays, Nancy Bays

B:0566 - GEORGE LIMEBURY? - 29 Nov 1824 - Prb Feb 1826
Wife CATHERAN & dau SUSANNAH - use of my land and sufficient land for SUSANNAH to live on at decease of wife
All my children - proceeds of sale at decease of wife & SUSANNAH with what each has received being deducted
Exrs: Son DANIEL LIMEBURY, son-in-law JOHN EULASS
Wits: Samuel McWhicker, Jonathan Hadley

B:0567 - PHEBE MENDENHALL - 21 July 1816 - Prb Feb 1826
Dau RUTH MENDENHALL - 45 ac of land, it being part of a tract that descended to a friend of my brother, William Ruddock, dec'd, adj dau BEULAH MENDENHALL, ISAAC MENDENHALL
Dau BEULAH MENDENHALL - 35 ac of above tract
Dau PHEBE RICKS - remaining part of above tract
My dec'd daus MARY KISLER & JANE RICKS - received their shares
Sons MORDECAI, SETH & ENOS MENDENHALL - received their shares
Exr: Zebulon Stuart
Wits: Richardson Wright, Martha Hunt

B:0568 - NATHANIEL KERR - 23 Oct 1821 - Prb Feb 1826
Wife MARGARET - the room & fire place in the west of the house, land sufficient to maintain her, two negroes Will & Charlotte, stock, spinning wheel, looking glass, sufficient furniture
Son SAMUEL - my book accounts against him
Dau PEGGY GILBREATH & her children - negro girl Jain, wheel I lent her when she removed from Guilford Co., $100
Son WILLIAM - book accounts against him, negro Bob
Dau POLLY MCLEAN - all the property she now has
Son JAMES - my book accounts against him
Son NATHANIEL - my book accounts against him, $70
Exrs: Elisha Wharton, son SAMUEL KERR
Wits: John Finley, Marshall McLean

B:0569 - SAMUEL CUMMINS - 10 Feb 1826 - Prb Feb 1826
Sons THOMAS, JOHN & WILLIAM - land I have heretofore given them
Sons SAMUEL, ROBERT & JAMES - the other half of my land divided
Dau ISABELL - has already received her inheritance
Daus MARY, JANE, SALLY, & RUTH - each $150, cow, bed & furn
Exrs: Sons THOMAS & SAMUEL CUMMINS
Wits: Joseph Gibson, Robert Law

B:0570 - AMOS MILLS - 24 Jan 1826 - Prb Feb 1826
Wife ELIZABETH - all my lands & tenements during natural life
Son JEREMIAH - to manage plantation and care for his mother
Son NATHAN - my rifle gun
Son JONATHAN - six yards home spun cloth
Daus ELIZABETH COUCH & RACHEL MARIS - each 2 ewe sheep
Gr Dau RACHEL MILLS - 2 year old heifer
Gr dau RUTH MILLS - the first heifer calf
Gr dau BETSY MILLS - the next heifer calf
Exrs: Son JEREMIAH MILLS, John Maris
Wits: George Stephens, Jehu Stephens, Mashack Couch

B:0571 - ZACHEUS SWAIN - 5 Nov 1824 - Prb May 1826
Sisters ELIZABETH RAY & PHEBE MOWERS - tract in Nantucket Co., Mass that was devised to me by my father, CHARLES SWAIN
Greensboro Lodge of Free & Accepted Masons - $100
Wife REBECCA who has long lived separate from me - third part of my North Carolina estate
NANCY SWAIN, alias ANNY MCMURPHY, to whom I have been married and who has lived with me as a faithful wife - rest of estate
Exrs: Wife NANCY SWAIN, Abraham Girm, Esqr.
Wits: Lot? G. Watson, Benjamin Overman, George Swain

B:0572 - RICHARD DAY - 6 Feb 1822 - Prb May 1826
Son RICHARD - half of proceeds from sale of my land
Daus DEBORAH HAYWORTH & MARY ANDERSON - each third of other half
Natural born ch of dau RHODA RENNOLDS - other third
Son WILLIAM - has received his full share
Exrs: Joseph Hunt, Zebulan Hunt
Wits: Thomas T. Hunt, Nathan Hunt

B:0573 - JAMES DICK - 6 Dec 1825 - Prb May 1826
Wife PATSY - $200, bed & furniture, chest, chest of drawers
Son HIRAM CAMPBELL DICK - 165 ac tract whereon I live on north side of Alamance, 23 ac bought of John & Elizabeth McMurry, 30 ac on east side of Rock Creek bought of Andrew Ayners?, 25 ac on south side of Alamance, all of which are worth $2,000, negro boy Jo worth $400, negro girl Eliza worth $225, negro woman Hannah worth $250
Dau JANE M. DICK - $790, negro girl Maria worth $275, negro woman Rachel worth $250, 226 ac known as Crumpton Plantation
Sons REUBEN - negro man Martin; THOMAS - negro boy George; JOHN M. - negro boy Jacob
Son JAMES, dec'd - his land on little Alamance to be sold
Exrs: Sons JOHN M. & REUBEN DICK
Wits: William Denlos, Joseph Clap, J. L. Prather

B:0574 - JONATHAN HADLEY - 22 Feb 1822 - Prb May 1826
Wife ANN - whole of estate for benefit of my children while she remains my widow, until youngest becomes 21
Son ALFRED - to head the house if wife dies before youngest is 21; son JOHN next in line to take place of ALFRED; son DAVID next; HIRAM next. POLLY has received $283 & ALFRED $40
Exrs: Wife ANN HADLEY, son ALFRED HADLEY. No witnesses

B:0575 - JAMES RANKIN - 19 June 1835 - Prb Aug 1826
Sons WILLIAM - tract whereon I live; ROBERT - $200
Gr dau JANE SCHOOLFIELD - bed & furniture, flax & cotton wheel
Daus ELIZABETH WHARTON, SARAH WHARTON, ANNA DONNELL & JANE SMITH - to have choice of slaves: Lindsay, Susie, Levi?, Dick, Irvin & Soloman
Dau AGNESS SCHOOLFIELD'S ten children - to have a slave
Negro girl Hannah - to have her freedom under care of executors
Exrs: Sons JOHN & THOMAS RANKIN
Wits: Robert Rankin, John Schoolfield

B:0576 - JOHN LANE, Senr. - 9 May 1826 - Prb Aug 1826
Son REUBEN - bed & furniture, counterpins, coverlids, pillows

Dau SARY LANE - 100 ac of plantation
Daus ESTHER LANE & NANCY LANE - 150 ac of land
Son JOHN & his wife - tract whereon he lives
Gr son JOHN HOLDER - one great coat
Gr dau NANCY HOLDER - one bed & furniture, kitchen furniture
Ch: REUBEN, SARAH, ESTHER, NANCY & JOHN - divide proceeds of 77 ac tract, but JOHN to have only half as much as the others, land adjoins James Tomlinson & Elijah Dewise
Exr: Son REUBEN LANE
Wits: Aaron Bishop, Lindsay Bishop, John Tomlinson

B:0577 - MARY HACKET - 13 Apr 1826 - Prb Aug 1826
My sister's ch - property after debts & funeral expenses
Exr: William Hodson. Wits: Geo. Hodson, Nathan Armfield

B:0578 - (Signed) Old T. J. PLUNKET - 6 Sept 1823 - Prb Aug 1826
Sons WILLIAM, THOMAS & JOHN - plantation & other land
Dau ROSANNA - $90. Son-in-law DAVID SHOFNER - $1
Gr dau NANCY SHOFNER - bed and all that belongs to it
Mary's children - half of the furniture
Exr: None named. Wits: Jacob Greeson, Henry Albright

B:0579 - WILLIAM BROWN - No date - Prb Aug 1826
COMPANION COMFORT (wife) - mare, household furniture, tools dw
Dau NANCY - to inherit from COMPANION COMFORT BROWN
Son WESTLEY - 44 ac to be taken off the east end of tract
Dau ADETH RUSSELL - 12 ac taken off the west end of tract
Exr: None named. Wits: John Pegg, Thomas Starbuck

B:0580 - CRAFT JACKSON - 9 Apr 1826 - Prb Aug 1826
Wife NANCY - house & plantation dw to raise & school the ch so that WILLIAM shall have as much learning as JOEL
Sons JOEL & WILLIAM - to divide land after wife ceases to be my widow. Daus to be as well schooled as circumstances allow
Exr: Nathan Mendenhall
Wits: George Beard, Joel Jackson

B:0581 - WILLIAM DENNEY - 8 June 1826 - Prb Nov 1826
Wife JANE - house, land, horse, 2 cows, necessary furniture dw
Oldest dau MARY ANN - horse & saddle, 2 beds, clock, 2 cows
Oldest sons ELIJAH & SAMUEL & youngest dau REBECCA - $1 and what they have received
Youngest son WALTER - all my lands at decease of wife
Exr: Walter Denney
Wits: Alexander Gray, Jr., Thomas Gray

B:0582 - MANLOVE WHEELER - 3 Jan 1826 - Prb Nov 1826
Sons JOHN, MANLOVE & JONATHAN - plantation & other lands
Daus KESIA WALKER, CHARITY GORDON & HANNAH THOMAS - 165 ac
All my ch - to share in moveable property
Son HENRY'S ch - to have their father's share of moveables
Exrs: Sons JOHN, MANLOVE & JONATHAN WHEELER
Wits: John Wheeler, Jesse Wheeler

B:0583 - JOHN CLEMER - 18 Sept 1826 - Prb Nov 1826
Wife ELIZABETH - tract of land whereon I live

Sons THOMAS, DUDLEY, heirs of JOHN, heirs of CHARLES, dec'd & WILLIAM - each one dollar
Dau SARAH CLEMER - 25 ac, part of tract where Aaron Clemor lives, firewood for lifetime, feather bed & furniture
Gr son THOMAS CLEMOR - to live with my widow until free, horse
Gr son SETH CLEMOR - to live with my widow until free, horse
Sarah Clemor, Mary Schoolfield, Elizabeth Griffin - residue
Exr: Son AARON CLEMOR
Wits: Jas Chilcutt, Jno Chilcutt

B:0584 - JOHN STUART - 25 Apr 1823 - Prb Aug 1827
Wife SARAH - use of plantation, tools, household goods, stock
Sons AMOS - to inherit plantation at his mother's decease
Daus MERIAM & RACHEL STUART - personal estate at their mother's decease or remarriage
Sons ROBERT, JOHN & JEHU - 5 sh each & what they have received
Daus ELIZABETH MARTIN, SARAH STUART, MARY GAYRE - each 5 sh
Gr sons AMBROSE HEATH? & ROBERT SHARP? - five shillings
Exrs: Wife SARAH STUART, Abel Coffin
Wits: Jonathan Anthony, William Worth

B:0585 - JAMES PETTY - 24 Mar 1827 - Prb Aug 1827
Bros WATSON, SAMUEL & WILLIAM - all my estate
Exr: Watson Petty
Wits: Jonathan Anthony, William Worth

B:0586 - MOSES ELLIOTT - 20 Aug 1825 - Prb Nov 1827
Gr dau VINA ELLIOTT - my looking glass
Son SPENCER - balance of property
Exr: Son SPENCER ELLIOTT. Wits: John Rankin, Isaac Coleman

B:0587 - ELIZABETH GRAY - 25 Oct 1827 - Prb Nov 1827
Sister JENNY DENNY & her dau MARY ANN DENNY - land I live on
Sally Hatten - 30 ac field & my house for her lifetime, rent of my plantation for three years
Niece BETSY ANN STARRATT - case of drawers
Sally Denny, Margret Watson, Anny Starratt - proceeds of sale
Bros JAMES, THOMAS, & ALEXANDER GRAY - each 50¢
Exrs: William Starratt, Alexander Gray, Jr.
Wits: Alexander Gray, Elijah Denny

B:0588 - CHRISTOPHER GRESON - 7 Oct 1827 - Prb Nov 1827
Wife NANCY - all my land during her natural life
Eldest dau SARAH CRAFT, sons JOHN, JAMES, DARRIAS, ARTHUR, daus ANNY WHITTINGTON & ELIZABETH WHITTINGTON - proceeds of sale after decease of my wife
Exrs: Arthur Greesom, Thomas Whittington
Wits: James Denny, Sarah Gresom

B:0589 - WILLIAM HARVEY - 23 Dec 1827 - Prb Feb 1828
Wife ELIZABETH - chest, table, cow & calf, cupboard & all its furniture, bed & furniture, spice mortar, cotton wheel & cards, stock enough to support her one year
William Kirkman, son of Peter Kirkman, dec'd, the child that I raised - all my lands
Gr son WILLIAM KENDLE - $150

Ellender Quart - $10, one heifer, calf she always claimed
George Kirkman, son of William - horse called Brandy
Polly Kirkman - one white faced heifer
Exr: William Kirkman
Wits: N. Millis, John Jackson, Edward Jackson

B:0590 - JAMES OTWELL - 18 June 1827 - Prb Feb 1828
Wife ELLENDER - house & lot where I live, horse, bed, cow, etc
Daus POLLY FRAZIER, NANCY MILLIS - 50¢ each
Dau ANNY JACKSON - $10
Son CURTIS - balance of my land
Dau ELLENDER OTWELL - $20, bed & furniture
Exr: Curtis Otwell, William Millis
Wits: N. Millis, Joseph Jackson

B:0591 - CHRISTIAN ROCHELLE (signed CRISY) - 30 Aug 1827
Prb Feb 1828. Niece REBECCAH WALL - $1
Church friends: Phebe Coffin, Rhoda Gurly, Jane Coffin, Ann Gardner, Sally Dwiggen & Lydia Dean - my wearing apparel & proceeds from sale of remainder of my estate
Exrs: My Church friends Zacharias Coffin, Samuel Dwiggen
Wits: Jesse Stanley, Joseph Reid

B:0592 - LEBNI BARNARD - 7 May 1828 - Prb May 1828
Wife EUNICE - land whereon I live, tools, stock, furniture, dw
Son-in-law ARIND (or ASMA?) COFFIN - shall tend the land with my wife & show her support as long as she lives
Dau MARY PARSONS & son ELIHU - land at decease of wife
Dau MARY - the looking glass that was her mother's
Sons JOHN, GORAM & ELIHU - each one share in the Cape Fear Navigation Company
Son REUBIN - half of tract on Bullrun, blacksmith tools, bed
Exr: Son-in-law JAMES PARSONS, sons JOHN & ELIHU BARNARD
Wits: James Newsom, Johnson Yaks (Yates in probate)

B:0593 - MALCUM MORRISON - 4 Mar 1828 - Prb May 1828
Wife KATHERINE - all my land & possessions during widowhood
Son KENNETH - same at decease or marriage of widow
My ch: DAVID, MARY, KATHERINE, EFFY, ELIZABETH & REBECCA - proceeds of sale
Dau NANCY MYRES - one cloak
Dau MARY MORRISON - feather bed & furniture, spinning wheel
Dau SALLY MINZES? - 50¢
Exr: Nathan Hunt
Wits: Thomas T. Hunt, Daniel D. Stockton, Ed Ricks

B:0594 - MARTHA WINN of Nottoway Co., Va. - 3 Sept 1827 - Prb Nottoway Co 4 Oct 1827. Prb Guilford Co May Term 1828
Niece MARTHA SMITH - negro girl Liddia who is now in N.C.
Bro RICHARD - negro boy Ben who is now in N.C.
Bro PETER - remaining part of my property
Exr: Brother PETER WINN
Wits: Frank Osborn, John D. Royall, Henry C. Robertson

B:0595 - MARY DICKEY - 19 Mar 1821 - Prb Aug 1828
Rebecca Dickey, dau of Wm Dickey - bed & furniture

Jane Dickey, d/o Wm Dickey - bed & furniture, desk, cupboard
Sister REBECCA DICKEY - all my clothes
Exr: William Dickey who inherits balance of estate
Wits: Salathiel Lamb, N. Armfield

B:0596 - ANNY CAPPS - 7 Feb 1827 - Prb Aug 1828
Daus AMY & NANCY - each a cow, bed & furniture, chest, part of household furniture, hogs
Son BENNETT - my plantation, 2 horse beasts, balance of stock
Exrs: Benneyy Capps, John Troxler
Wits: J. Troxler, Eli Troxler

B:0597 - ANDREW RUSSELL - 24 Oct 1828 - Prb Nov 1828
Sons ANDREW & DANIEL - plantations on which they live
Son ELIJAH - 150 ac adj land of Charles Ozment
Wife SARAH - use of plantation, negro Fly, furniture, stock
Son JAMES - $10 at decease of my wife
Daus MARY, ELIZABETH, NANCY, SARAH & ANNA - proceeds of sale
Exr: Sons ANDREW & DANIEL RUSSELL
Wits: James Wilson, Elizabeth Russell, William Armfield

B:0598 - WILLIAM DENTON - 1 Jan 1824 - Prb Nov 1828
Wife POLLY - home plantation, small tract where David Iseley lives, negroes Jack & Emsley, silver watch
My wife & family - proceeds of sale from SE quarter of Section 26 of Township One, file #8937 & other tracts. Two quarter sections of land in Illinois to pay debts - file #3955
Exr: Wife POLLY DENTON, Benjamin Ross
Wits: Oliver Huffman, George Huffman

B:0599 - JOSEPH IDDINGS - 15 Aug 1828 - Prb Nov 1828
Son JONATHAN - 100 ac on west side of plantation
Son MARK - $25, he having received his portion
Son JAMES & children of WILLIAM - plantation whereon I live
Dau MAUDE'S two sons, JOSEPH & ABNER H. OGBURN - land on Salisbury Road when they become 21
Dau HANNAH'S son JOSEPH J. COFFIN - $10, having deeded him land
Dau SARAH HUGHES - $250
William Coffin - 5 sh or 62½¢; Job Ogburn - one dollar
William Idding's children - share in residue of estate
Exr: Jonathan Iddings & Mark Iddings
Wits: Obed Gardner, Joshua Iddings, Edward Kelley

B:0600 - BARNELL INGLE - 29 May 1827 - Prb Nov 1828
Sons DAVID & REUBEN - tract where I live & tract bought of my brother ADAM
Dau CATY - horse & saddle, 2 beds & furniture, 5 heads of cattle such as her sisters got when they left me
Wife - negro boy Peter, dwelling house, maintenance from sons
Dau SALLY ABEGAIL'S children - a share in residue of estate
Exrs: David Ingle, Jacob Wyrick
Wits: Joseph Gibson, David Clapp

B:0601 - ELIZABETH SHAW - 11 Oct 1828 - Prb Nov 1828
Son FINDLEY - one large Bible
Dau JANE HAMILTON - bed & furniture, spinning wheel, clock

Son JOSEPH - all the plows & farming utensils, stock, chest
Son WILLIAM - the wagon jointly with his brother
Daus MARGARET SHAW & ANN - all household furniture, flax, cotton, and all the sheep
Exr: Son FINLEY SHAW
Wits: David Cooper, William Corsbie

B:0602 - JOSHUA MARTIN - 21 Aug 1824 - Prb Nov 1828
Son EZEKIAL WITTY MARTIN - 100 ac tract I live on, horse, stock
Son JOSHUA - $1.25
Exr: Son EZEKIEL WITTY MARTIN
Wits: John Winchester, Enoch Martin

B:0603 - JAMES WILSON - 2 Nov 1828 - Prb Nov 1828
Wife JANE - cow known as Blos, heifer, 2 hogs in the fattening pen, four sheep, 2 beds, desk, furniture, proceeds of sale
Ch: RUTH ELLIOTT, RACHEL THORNBERRY, NANCY LAUGHTON, THOMAS WILSON, JANE WILLIAMS & BETSY MILLIS & ALLEN WILSON - estate at decease of wife
Exrs: Allen Wilson, Joshua Cranor
Wits: William Armfield, Jemima Wilson

B:0604 - MARY ANN BYWELL - 7 Feb 1815 - Prb Feb 1829
My ch now living: MARY ANN BYWILL, ELIZABETH BYWILL, SUSANNAH BYWELL & BENJAMIN BISWELL - each share in the estate
Exrs: Son BENJAMIN BISWELL, Thomas Stokes
Wits: John Stokes, William Brown

B:0605 - BENJAMIN BENBOW - 26 Jan 1829 - Prb Feb 1829
Son BENJAMIN - 184 ac tract whereon I live
Wife LYDIA - $40, support by BENJAMIN, privilege of the house dw
Daus ELIZABETH & ANN - household furniture at decease of wife
Sons JOHN, DAVID & BENJAMIN - residue of estate
Exrs: Sons DAVID & BENJAMIN BENBOW
Wits: Moses Owens, Nicholas Clark, Thomas Lloyd

B:0606 - DANIEL GILLASPIE - 3 Jan 1820 - Prb Feb 1829
Wife PEGGY - $100, support, home, negro woman Rose, horse
Son JOHN - $600; son JAMES - $500
Daus NANCY RANKIN, w/o GEORGE RANKIN & ANN ANDERSON, w/o WM ANDERSON - each $500
Son ROBERT - $500, the plantation, including where he lives
Son PATRICK - $500; dau THANKFUL, w/o WILLIAM DOAK - $500
Son DANIEL'S ch PEGGY & MARY ANN - each $100
My three daus - proceeds of land called the "Patrick Gillaspie Plantation". All my ch: JOHN, JAMES, NANCY RANKIN, ANN ANDERSON, DANIEL, ROBERT, PATRICK & THANKFUL DOAK - divide my negroes
Exrs: George Rankin, William Doak, Robert Gillaspie
Wits: Parabow Boswell, Thomas McCulloch

B:0607 - MICHEAL SHATTERLY - 17 Jan 1826 - Prb May 1829
Son GEORGE - tract whereon I live bought of Matthias Amick
Wife MILLY - maintenance by GEORGE, use of furniture, choice of stock, my gray mare
Dau BARBARA COBLE - my colt two years old last spring

All my daus & ch of dau MOLLY COBLE - proceeds of sale
Exrs: Micheal Holt appointed by Court
Wits: John Shatterly, Frederich Suits

B:0608 - JOSEPH SWAIN - No date - Prb May 1829
Wife - all my estate for her support
My son & daus that yet remain in this country: JETHRO SWAIN, ANNA COFFIN, LYDIA WORTH & SARAH LEMONS - division of estate after decease of wife
Exrs: Son JETHRO SWAIN, son-in-law REUBEN WORTH
Wits: David Worth, Obed Swain

B:0609 - JOHN BRINCEFIELD - 25 Mar 1829 - Prb May 1829
Wife DELITHA - land where I live & where son-in-law ALEXANDER SKEANS lives dw, stock, household furniture
Son THOMAS - to inherit land at decease or marriage of wife
Son-in-law ALEXANDER SKEANS - 50 ac out of the tract where he lives including dwelling house, kitchen & stables
Son CLEMENT & dau ELIZABETH JONES - proceeds of sale of a tract
Dau LILLY UNDERWOOD - $1; son JOHN - $100; Leven Walker - $1
Exr: Wife DELITHA BRINCEFIELD
Wits: Francis L. Simpson, Joshua Underwood

B:0610 - JAMES G. RICE - 23 July 1829 - Prb Aug 1829
Wife SARAH - balance of my property after debts are paid
Exrs: Stephen D. Rice, Joshua Hightower
Wits: M. R. Moss?, Robert H. Dalton

B:0611 - RODDY HANNER - 4 Aug 1829 - Prb Aug 1829
Son JOHN - land already deeded him, negro boy Ransom, woman Fib
Son ROBERT - land deeded him & tract by Robert Hanner, negro Isaac. Son ELI - land already deeded him
Rodger Kirkman, Alexander Hanner & son JOHN HANNER - trustees & guardian for son ERWIN who is to inherit estate
Ch: JOHN, ROBERT, ELI & IBBY FIELD - inherit estate should ERWIN decease
Dau IBBY FIELD - property I have given her & negro woman Rachel
Negroes Cug, George, Nelly & Martin - to be sold
RODDY HANNER, s/o JOHN - $10; RODDY FIELD, s/o IBBY - $10 DOAK HANNER, s/o ROBERT - $10
Gr dau SALLY FIELD - my bed & furniture
Gr dau SALLY CAROLINE HANNER - $10
ROBERT'S dau SALLY - bed & furniture bought at sale of ELI
Exrs: Son JOHN HANNER, Paul Coble
Wits: Robert Wilson, David Coble, Daniel Coble

B:0612 - JOSHUA JOHNSON - 19 July 1829 - Prb Aug 1829
My lawful heirs - proceed of sale of property
Exrs: John Maris, Jeremiah Mills
Wits: John Gordon, Samuel Couch

B:0613 - SARAH STAFFORD - 29 June 1820 - Prb Aug 1829
Dau POLLY - negro girl Liser; son JOHN - negro boy Davis
Son JAMES - negro girl June; dau SARAH - negro boy Joseph
Dau ANNA MCCLINTOCK - $50
Youngest sons JAMES & JOHN - all the stock

Daus ANNA & RHODA - $100 each
Sons GEORGE, ANDERTON, JAMES & JOHN - balance of estate
Exr: John Stafford appointed by the Court
Wits: Larkin Smith, John Gilchrist

B:0614 - THANKFUL WOODBURN - 11 Aug 1829 - Prb Nov 1829
Negro man Isaac to be free after he has earned $300 and paid it to the exrs; Isaac to receive 3 suits a year, two pairs of shoes & stockings, 1 wool hat, 3 pairs overhalls, 3 shirts, one coat part wool; the hire of Isaac is to be divided between my grand sons
Gr son WILLIAM WOODBURN WILEY, CALVIN HENDERSON WILEY & DAVID WASHINGTON WILEY - $300 when they come of age
Gr dau CATHERINE C. WILEY - household furniture
Dau ANN WILEY - my wearing apparel, cupboard & furniture, if she should have another child; hire of Alfred to be divided between them. Son-in-law DAVID WILEY - $5
Exr: David Wiley appointed by the Court
Wits: Robert Gilmore, David Wiley

B:0615 - NATHAN DONNELL - 5 Aug 1829 - Prb Nov 1829
Wife CHARLOTTE - negro boy Charles, negroes Caleb, Jince & all her children, use of plantation, stock, furniture
Dau MARTHA DONNELL - one bed & furniture
Latham Donnell, s/o Erwin - all my land at the decease or marriage of my wife, negro man Smith, negro woman Jince & her children: Mickey, Milton, Biddy & Amander
Ch of step dau MARTHA, w/o WILLIAM DONNELL - to inherit land if Latham should decease
Latham Donnell, s/o Martha & William - land east of the Big Br
Charlotte Donnell, d/o Martha & William - case of drawers
Joseph Donnell, s/o William & Martha - clock & case, ½ of books
William Donnell, s/o bro JOHN - negro men Ben & Caleb
Bros ANDREW, THOMAS, GEORGE, heirs of JAMES, heirs of ROBERT - each one dollar
Sisters HANNAH DENNEY & JANE DONNELL - each one dollar
Exrs: William Donnell, son of brother JOHN
Wits: John Schoolfield, Senr., John E. Schoolfield

B:0616 - THOMAS HAMILTON - 15 Nov 1820 - Prb Nov 1829
Dau MARY GRAY - negro girl Ruth; son GEORGE - $5
Daus MARGARET, ANN & JANE - negro boys David (by Nance), Spencer and Berrd. Son THOMAS - plantation, smith tools, etc
Exrs: Son THOMAS HAMILTON, Alexander Gray
Wits: John Schoolfield, Joseph Schoolfield

B:0617 - JAMES PHIPPS - 14 Oct 1829 - Prb Nov 1829
Wife ABIGAIL - all my real & personal estate during widowhood
Daus SALLY PHIPPS & ANN MOONEY - each $10
Gr son EDWARD P. GAMBLE - $5
Son BENJAMIN & son-in-law CONRAD RICHARDSON - $1
Ch: JOSEPH, SUSANNAH HAGEY, ABIGAIL PRITCHARD, RACHEL PHIPPS, ANN MOONEY, SALLY PHIPPS, PEGGY RICHARDSON & JAMES PHIPPS - residue of estate
Exrs: Daniel Gladson, James Phipps
Wits: Aaron Phipps, Thomas Rankin

B:0618 - CURTIS JACKSON - 25 Sept 1829 - Prb Nov 1829
Elizabeth and youngest child Lurena - provisions as long as Elizabeth is single; when Lurena is old enough, she & dau Mary to be placed with a nice family & to be schooled
Dau PHEBE, w/o TIMOTHY JESOP - $1 if legally demanded
Dau CATHERINE - $30 over the bed & furniture she has received, her wearing apparel & that of her mother's
Ch: SARAH (w/o KING FISHER), oldest son BOWETOR, 2nd son JACOB, THOMAS, NATHAN, BEULAH (w/o CALEB GORRELL), SUSANNA (w/o TIMOTHY H. JESOP), EDITH (w/o RISDOM CHARLES), REED (w/o JESSE FEREBEE?), CURTIS - each $1 if legally demanded
Exr: Son CURTIS JACKSON
Wits: Richard Mendenhall, James Pitts

B:0619 - Noncupative Will of WILLIAM RANKIN - 17 Sept 1829
Prvd in Court Nov Term 1829 by Samuel E. Donnell & David Wilson
William Rankin related these words on the 7 Sept 1829 and died on the 17th
Wife - proceeds from sale of property after debts are paid

B:0620 - RICHARD DODSON - 17 Sept 1823 - Prb Nov 1829
Wife MARY - all property during lifetime
Youngest son RICHARD - to inherit from wife all lands
Ch: SALLY - 10 sh; CHARLES - $5; MARY - 10 sh; JEREMIAH - 10 sh
Exrs: Wife MARY DODSON, son RICHARD DODSON
Wits: Thomas Edwards, Uriah Stephens, Susannah Edwards

B:0621 - JOSHUA EDWARDS - 29 May 1829 - Prb Nov 1829
Wife ELIZABETH - one feather bed & furniture
Dau POLLY BROWN - $5
Dau NELLY OWENS - bed & furniture, my largest iron pot
Son HARUEL, daus RACHEL LLOYD, MARTHA RUSSELL & HANNAH COOK - each one dollar
Son JOHN - 350 ac tract where I live & all property
Exr: Son JOHN EDWARDS
Wits: Nathan Canady, Charles B. Harris, Charles Bruce

B:0622 - MARY ANN BIZWELL - 12 Feb 1828 - Prb Nov 1829
Sisters ELIZABETH BIZWELL & SUSANNA BIZWELL - 2/3 money, tract whereon I live & all property during life
Nephew ELIZABETH BOOKER - third of money
Exr: Martin Wright, William Weatherly
Wits: William Mills, Robertson T. Weatherly

B:0623 - BARZILLA GARDNER - 1 Sept 1829 - Prb Nov 1829
Wife JEMIMA - home plantation, dwelling house & furniture
Son ELIHU - 100 ac whereon he lives, tin tools
Gr son HENDERSON GARDNER, son of ELIHU - 100 ac on NE of plantation including my old tin shop, tract laid off for son ANNUIL who is now dead
Son NATHAN - 100 ac tract if he returns to Guilford County
Gr son BARZILLA GARDNER, s/o ELIHU - the 100 ac tract if NATHAN hasn't returned when he reaches 21
Daus NIOMI, JEMIMA FORBIS - each $100
Gr ch: LYDIA, FREDERICH & JEMIMA (ch of Judah & Frederich Barnard) - $100 divided among them

Dau EUNICE GARDNER, wife of THOMAS - $200
Gr ch DELPHINE & FLORA GARDNER, daus of BARZILLA - each one share of stock in Cape Fear Navigation Company
Gr gr son BARZILLA BRICKELL, son of ROBERT & REBECCA - my watch
Son ELIHU - to give sufficient support for her condition to black woman Caty who was conveyed to him by Shubel Gardner
Exrs: Son ELIHU GARDNER, nephew GEORGE C. MENDENHALL
Wits: Thomas Stack, Elizabeth Macy, Winsmore Howsen

B:0624 - THOMAS WEBB - 2 Nov 1829 - Prb Feb 1830
Wife SARAH - $4,000, negro boy Nathan, desk, book case, land bought of George Donnell, tract from George Chilcutt adj widow Buckhannon
Brother GILSTRAP - tract whereon he lives & notes against him
WILLIAM WEBB, son of GILSTRAP - tract known as the Wafford place
William Schoolfield - tract whereon he lives bought of Robert Coffey
Noah M. Climer, husband of dau PEGGY or MARGARET, the dwelling home tract bought of Joshua Dee, also tracts bought of Robert C. Rankin and of William Weatherly, the lower still in my still house, still untensils, sorrel mare
John Wharton, husband of sister RHODA - residue of land, $300 to buy a negro woman to help my sister
Ch of bro MEREDITH, dec'd: GINN - a plantation; SAMPE - another tract, $100; and his dau - $100
Slaves: Old Thomas - $75; Jacob, Isaac & David - each $10; Major, Doctor, Little Thomas & Nathan - each $5
Bro SAMEUL - $600 out of band now due me by Joseph Allen
Daugherty's Meeting House - $50
$50 marble to be placed at the head of dec'd wife DORCAS, dec'd bro MEREDITH & his dec'd wife & my own
Exrs: John Wharton, Noah M. Climer
Wits: Mark W. Killingsworth, James Brannock

B:0625 - JOHN THOMPSON - 14 Dec 1829 - Prb Feb 1830
Wife SUSAN & daus MARIAH & ELIZABETH - plantation whereon I live, household furniture, stock, three horses, till daus marry
Wife - six negroes: Drape & his wife Vedda, Hanson & wife Ann, Ming & Harris
Dau MARIAH - negroes Rhoda, Matilda & Isaac
Dau ELIZABETH - Harvey, Anny, Anderson & Bedford
Dau ELIZA WITTY - $300, negroes Esther & Indy lent to her to be inherited by her ch, the land Robert Witty lives on & land John Price lives on
Dau MARTHA HEART - $300; son JOSEPH - $500
Remaining land & slaves to be sold: Dick, Susie, Sam, Boles, Austin, Perry, Moses, Edmond, Henry, Henry son of Rhoda, Harriet & Nelly
Exrs: Wilson Hill to do the business in Louisana; Abraham Given to do the business in this state
Wits: James Cole, Allan Peeples

B:0626 - JOHN WORK - 5 Dec 1829 - Prb Feb 1830
Wife ANNASITTY - sorrell horse, saddle, choice of cows, half the sheep, hogs, one ox, 40 barrels of corn, one fodder house, all wheat, oats, cotton, flax & wool, all the land,

all the nails I have on hand to cover her house, & shingles
Nephew JAMES STAPLETON - horse named Buck, saddle, ox, mattock, hoe, plow, harrow, 20 barrels of corn
Daus ELIZABETH DEWISE & ELENOR MASSEY - each one dollar
Exr: Wife ANNASITTA WORK
Wits: Robert Coffey, B. N. Braswell

B:0627 - RIDLEY BRAZIL - 16 Nov 1829 - Prb Feb 1830
Jane Price - bed & furniture, checked counterpin, blanket
Kipey Brazil - chest, oxen & hooks, part of my clothes, sheets
Jacob Brazil - large white sow; Elijah Brazil - 3 hogs, harrow
Joel Brazil, Pleasant Brazil & James Brazil - one pig each
Elijah Brazil's little ch - the plates, cups & saucers
Elijah Brazil - $1 on Nathaniel Simpson, $1 on William Brown, 50¢ on William Simpson
Exrs: Robert H. Dalton appointed by court
Wits: Thomas Wilson, Nancy Delay

B:0628 - WILLIAM MCCLINTOCK - 19 Dec 1829 - Prb Feb 1830
Daus ISABELLA STAFFORD, MARY VANSTORY, & HENSY WITTY DEANS - each $16
Dau SALLY MCCLINTOCK - $50, sorrell horse named Prince, saddle, bed & furniture, cow named Spot, dutch oven
Sons JAMES - $20; WILLIAM - $150; SAMUEL - 100 ac whereon I live, horse named Jack, saddle, cow & calf, $30, bed & furniture
Exrs: Sons JAMES & WILLIAM MCCLINTOCK
Wits: Willis Satter, Larkin Smith, Moses Gilchrist

B:0629 - THOMAS DILWORTH - 19 Nov 1829 - Prb Feb 1830
Wife SARAH - whole tract on which I live during widowhood
Oldest dau NANCY DILLWORTH - bed, chest & furniture worth $40
Oldest son BENJAMIN & son LINDSAY - each a horse worth $40
2nd dau VIVICY DILLWORTH - bed & furniture, cow & calf worth $40
3rd son GEORGE - horse worth $40
3rd dau FAITHY DILWORTH - bed & furniture, cow & calf worth $40
4th son THOMAS E. - one horse worth $40
4th dau PERLINA I. - bed & furniture, cow & calf worth $40
Each to be paid as they come of age & not before; each to share in my undivided share of my Father's estate
Exrs: Wife SARAH DILLWORTH, son BENJAMIN DILLWORTH
Wits: Joseph Simpson, Ralph S. Simpson

B:0630 - DONALD STEWART, a native of Ballachelick Appins in the Parish of Lismore - Orgglshire, Scotland, but for many years a resident of the United States of America
22 Feb 1822 - Prb Feb 1830
Wife SUSANNA - 300 ac where I reside, stock, negro woman Nancy & her 3 ch: Katty, Donald & Sandy; also Peter, Lucy, Tabby, Anny, Jack, Jeaney, Tom & Henry, Jeaney's child Charles
My sisters in Scotland: Ch of my sister CATHERINE MCKENZIE, ISABELLA ROBERTSON, JANNETT HAMILTON of London - each to receive a fifth of proceeds from sale
Exr: Susan Stewart renounced her right; Henry Humphreys appt
Wits: Prvd by oaths of George Nicks, George Spencer, Richard Wynn

B:0631 - JACOB HUNT - 12 Oct 1829 - Prb May 1830
Ch: REBECCA BALLENGER, WILLIAM, THOMAS, BEULY OGGBURN, HANNAH PERKINS, MARY WHITE & MAHALA WHITE - each one dollar
Wife HANNAH - household furniture, stock
Gr son JAMES HUNT - farming tools, land whereon I live for maintaining my widow
Exr: Gr son JAMES HUNT
Wits: Moses Mendenhall, Nathan Canady

B:0632 - NATHANIEL SIMPSON - 3 Mar 1827 - Prb May 1830
Wife SARAH - the bed we usually sleep upon, her choice of cows, side saddle, 28 ac on western end of tract, dwelling house
Son ROBERT K. - to inherit the 28 ac
Son WILLIAM - already has a tract adjoining the 28 ac tract
Dau SARAH LAIN & sons NATHANIEL & THOMAS ($5) - one dollar
Dau MARY SIMPSON - bed & furniture, heifer or value of $3
Sons NATHAN - $1; JOHN - bed & furniture; WESTLY - $5
Dau SINAH SIMPSON - bed & furniture, sorrell mare, loom, large pot, oven, chest of drawers made by John Adams
Dau ELEBA SIMPSON - bed & furniture, mare colt, loom now in possession of John Work, pot, oven, divide cupboard furniture with Eleba
Ch: JOHN, WILLIAM & ROBERT; daus SINAH & ELEBA - residue of est
Exrs: Sons NATHANIEL & JOHN SIMPSON
Wits: Jeremiah Crowder, Sally Crowder

B:0623 - NATHANIEL KERR - 22 Mar 1830 - Prb May 1830
Wife HANNAH - negro girl Rebecca, side saddle, cupboard & furniture, folding leaf table, walnut chest; wife, oldest dau MALINDA, 2nd dau LUISA, 3rd dau ELIZABETH, son SAMUEL to live together
Son SAMUEL - half of dwelling house, half of land & stock when he becomes 21, all of it at wife's death
Daus MALINDA, LOUISA, ELIZABETH - at 18 a third of the money each from the hiring out of negroes Harry, Jim & Abraham
Exrs: Bro SAMUEL KERR, friend Col James Denny
Wits: John Mitchell, Joseph A. McLean

B:0634 - THOMAS COSBRY, being about to leave the State of N.C. 30 Jan 1829 - Prb in County & State of New York 25 Mar 1830 Probated in Guilford County Court May Term 1830
Nephew THOMAS COSBRY, now residing in Greensborough - house and plantation in Caswell County
Nephew's sister JUDITH BROWN - to inherit if her brother has no heirs. Exr: No one named
Wits: Robert McDowell, James Stean

B:0635 - STEPHEN GARDNER - 3 Dec 1826 - Codicil 6 Mar 1830
Prb Aug 1830. Dau ABEGAIL WORTH of Indiana - $500
Dau MIRIAM GARDNER - $500; dau EUNICE WORTH - $500
Dau RHODA COFFIN - $200
Gr sons JOHN & STEPHEN GARDNER, sons of STEPHEN, dec'd - the land on which their mother, MARY GARDNER lives
Gr son FRANKLIN, son of STEPHEN GARDNER, dec'd - tract in Randolph Co on south side of road from Salem to Fayetteville
Gr dau SALLY COLTRAIN, dau of STEPHEN GARDNER, dec'd - $40

Gr daus ISABELLA, ELIZABETH, & CAROLINE GARDNER ($200) - $100
Sons GEORGE & ABEL - residue of estate
Exrs: Sons GEORGE & ABEL GARDNER
Wits: Judith Mendenhall, Jr., Geo C. Mendenhall, Jno D. Mendenhall, Wm P. Mendenhall
Wits of Cod: Nathan Mendenhall, Asineth Gardner, Jonathan Gardner

B:0636 - EVIN STEPHENS - 1 June 1830 - Prb Aug 1830
Wife NAOMI - plantation, household furniture, stock, farming tools; if she marry: $100, bed & furniture, chest, kitchen furniture
Youngest sons JOHN & ENOCH - to inherit property from wife
Eldest son JOSHUA - $500 of the effects of the Tan yard
Sons JOSHUA & GEORGE - remainder of stock, effects of Tan yard
Exrs: Allen Cook, son JOSHUA STEPHENS
Wits: William Shelley, Jonathan Bond, George Stephens

B:0637 - JOSEPH RUSSELL - 2 July 1830 - Prb Aug 1830
Wife KATTY - negroes Minney, Martha & Kate, household & kitchen furniture & farming tools during widowhood
All my children - property to be divided when Son WILLIAM is 21
Exrs: Wife CATHERINE L. RUSSELL, William Russell
Wits: William Starratt, Andrew Underwood, James H. Davis?

B:0638 - ANTHONY TATE - 27 Aug 1830 - Prb Nov 1830
Wife MARGARET - property belonging to her at our marriage, negroes Phebe & Dysy, horse & saddle
Orphan child POLLY TATE - negroes to be put to hire for her support until she comes of age
Daus SALLY TATE & ISABELLA TATE - proceeds after debts of sale of negroes Bob & William
Dau SALLY - negroes William, Caty, Ann, Bank & Martha
Dau ISABEL - negroes Bob, Nell, Viola, Sina & Charlie
Easther - to be maintained by dau Sally out of estate
Agnes - to be maintained by Isabel out of estate
Exrs: Wife MARGARET TATE, John Lee
Wits: Thomas R. Tate, John Tate, D. W. Simmons?

B:0639 - ELIHU MCKEEVER - 29 May 1830 - Prb Nov 1830
Father TIMOTHY MCKEEVER & mother ELIZABETH MCKEEVER - negroes Charlotte & Thankful
Bro PETER MONNETT - land I bought from him, horse named Rant
Agness Morris & Christopher Monnett - to inherit from my father & mother at their decease
Sister POLLY RUSSOM - $3
Exr: Peter Mennett. Wits: Thomas McCulloch, Eli Edgin

B:0640 - ELIZABETH HARRELL - 18 Sept 1830 - Prb Nov 1830
Son JOSEPH - 10 barrels corn, 10 bu wheat, 300 lbs pork, claim I have against him as Guardian
Dau ABIGAIL PEEPLES - 3 barrels corn, 5 bu wheat, 200 lbs pork
My surviving ch (son HENRY excepted) - residue of estate
Exrs: Sons JAMES H. & JOSEPH HARRELL
Wits: Jonathan W. Parker, Noah M. Clemer

B:0641 - JAMES DICKS - 7 Nov 1822 - Prb Nov 1830
Wife - maintenance of the plantation during widowhood
Son WILLIAM - plantation if he maintains his mother
All my ch: PETER, WILLIAM, FAMOR HODSON, RUTH HODSON, DEBORA HODSON & RACHEL MARMOND? - residue of estate
Exrs: Sons PETER & WILLIAM DICKS
Wits: Jonathan Parker, Martha Parker, Stephen Parker, Abigail Parker

B:0642 - PLEASANT BEVILL - 16 Dec 1816 - Prb Nov 1830
Wife DICEY - all estate during her natural life or widowhood
Dau ELIZABETH BROWN - all the property I have given her
Ch of ELIZABETH BROWN - divide third of personal estate at decease or remarriage of wife
Dau SALLY - third of personal estate
Son ARCHER - third of personal estate, land at mother's death
Exrs: Wife DICEY BEVILL, William McCain
Wits: James Cole, William McCain

B:0643 - SALLY BELL, widow of ROBERT BELL - 30 Jan 1830 - Prb Nov 1830. Gr son ROBERT JOHNSON BELL - horse & saddle, bed & furniture, receive an English education out of my estate
George W. Bell & John Tatum - each one dollar
Ch of George W. Beeson - divide fifth of inheritance I may receive from my father SAMUEL HINSON
Joel Sanders & wife LUCY & son MILTON H. SANDERS - fifth part
Richard G. Beeson & wife Polly - one fifth part
Ch of John Tatum & wife Sally - one fifth part
Dau MARTHA T. BELL - one fifth part
Exr: Son-in-law RICHARD G. BEESON
Wits: John Draughon, John Jones, James York

B:0644 - ROBERT FLEMMING - 2 June 1830 - Prb Feb 1831
Wife ELIZABETH - remainder of estate after debts are paid
Exr: Wife ELIZABETH FLEMMING
Wits: Hamilton Gray, James Gray

B:0645 - JOHN MENDENHALL - 29 July 1826 - Prb Feb 1831
Wife MARTHA - personal estate, maintenance during widowhood
Daus ANNA & MARY - each feather bed & furniture, cow & calf
Father & mother MOSES & DINAH MENDENHALL - have a home on the premises & their maintenance in consideration of father's deed to me of the land whereon I live
Son SAMUEL - all my lands & tenements
Exrs: Wife MARTHA MENDENHALL, son SAMUEL MENDENHALL
Wit: Joseph Hunt

B:0646 - WILLIAM LEWIS - 29 Oct 1830 - Prb Feb 1831
Wife COURTNEY - all property in my possession
Little ch - 3 heads of cattle, 2 horse beasts, farming tools, stock, household furniture
Oldest son LAWRENCE - one shot gun; son ORLANDO - one great coat
Son RHODOLPHUS - six dollars when 21 years old
Exr: Wife COURTNEY LEWIS
Wits: James Chilcutt, Aaron Climer

B:0647 - ANDREW CARMICHIAL - 2 Apr 1829 - Prb Feb 1831
Dau MARY BEESON - my bed & furniture
Gr dau SUSANNAH LAMB - my houses and lands
Gr son JOSEPH THOMPSON - my horse and all my clothes
Dau AGNES THOMPSON - $20, all my corn, cotton, meat & salt
Rest of ch - have already received their portions
Exr: Samuel Lamb
Wits: Adam Hinshaw, John Swindle

B:0648 - WILLIAM LAMBERT - 26 Nov 1825 - Prb May 1831
Wife MARGERY - profits of plantation, personal estate, feather bed & furniture, horse & saddle, linen wheel, cow & calf
Dau ANN - $5, has already received her portion of personal est
Gr son WILLIAM LAMBERT HARVEY - bed & furniture, cow & calf at 21
Dau ABEGAIL - gray horse, saddle, 2 beds, 2 cows, cotton wheel
Exrs: Wife MARGERY LAMBERT, son-in-law JAMES WOODY
Wits: Mederia Hiatt, Catherine Woody

B:0649 - ELIJAH MANSHIP - 11 Apr 1827 - Prb May 1831
Gr dau MARY ANN, NELLY'S dau - negro boy Jo, bed, support by Dorcas, cow
Gr dau MARTHA - bed & furniture
Dau DORCAS - 200 ac of land, negroes Moses & Red for her life then to her children MARTHA & THOMAS
Exr: William Hodson appointed by the Court
Wits: N. Armfield, John Jackson

B:0650 - AMOS KERSEY - 7 Apr 1829 - Prb Aug 1831
Wife ELIZABETH - all moveable effects, profits of plantation, third of profits of the old plantation where Benjamin Kersey did live until gr son BENJAMIN KERSEY is 21
All my children: ISAAC, EZRA, LOIS, JAMES & ELIZABETH - land on Richlands Cr & other property
Gr sons ELWOOD & CHARLES OGBURN - one dollar each
Daus LOIS POTTER & ELIZABETH COFFIN - each $25 worth of property
Exrs: Sons EZRA & JAMES KERSEY
Wits: Stephanus Kersey, Jesse Kersey

B:0651 - HANNAH KERR - 8 July 1831 - Prb Aug 1831
Son SAMUEL - my bed & furniture, all my window curtains for his house when he is 21
All my children - personal property to be sold & proceeds divided when youngest child come of age
Exr: Col James Denny
Wits: Reuben Dick, Samuel Mitchell

B:0652 - ELIZABETH CHARLES - 16 May 1831 - Prb Aug 1831
Son-in-law HENRY CLARY & wife ELIZABETH - $50 note on him
Daus MARY JONES, ANNA RAPER, ELIZABETH CLARY & REBECCA GUYES - my bed clothes and wearing clothes
Son-in-law JACOB GUYES & dau REBECCA - $1, have received theirs
My six sons SMITH, RISDON, JACOB, JOHN, ELISHA & SOLOMAN & my three daus - residue of estate
Exr: Son ELISHA CHARLES
Wits: Elizabeth Lindsay, Phillip Horney

B:0653 - JOHN VANSTORIE - 4 Mar 1829 - Prb Nov 1831
Wife CATHERINE - $1,000, my plantation & plantation called the King Place, also tract on Benagee adj James Stewart that I bought of Robert Rankin, Esq., choice of two negroes
Dau SUSANNAH BEVINGS & her husband, Dr. JAMES BEVINGS - 2 tracts on south side Reedy Fork
Son JOHN - to inherit from his mother, also tract called the William Mackrel place, my shop of Medicine instruments, library
Exrs: Wife CATHERINE VANSTORIE, son JOHN VANSTORIE, William Montgomery. Wits: Isaac Thacker, George Fulton

B:0654 - JOEL S. BEESON - 4 May 1831 - Prb Nov 1831
Wife PERMELIA - all my estate forever unless she has an heir within six months; then share & share alike
Exrs: Wife PERMELIA BEESON & her brother ISAAC SAMPLE of S. C. where part of my business is
Wits: R. G. Beeson, Jesse Sanders, Charles Benbow

B:0655 - JACOB CLAPP, Senr. - 14 Mar 1826 - Prb Feby 1832
Sons GEORGE & LUDWICK - all the tract on which I live
Wife BARBARA - third of said land during her natural life
Dau CATHERINE - $400; heirs of son JACOB - $100; daus BARBARA & MARY - each $100; to all - family book (Dutch title)
Exrs: Christian Clapp, son of Barnett, Christian Foust
Wits: Joseph Gibson, Morrison Gibson

B:0656 - ALEXANDER GRAY, Senr. - 23 Aug 1826 - Prb Feby 1832
Son ALEXANDER - my old plantation that I lived on
Four daus: SARAH DENNY, ANN STARRATT, MARGARET WILSON & ELIZABETH GRAY - proceeds of sale of other property
Sons JAMES & THOMAS - each 50¢
Rebecca Hamilton & Meari (Mary?) Hamilton - each 50¢
Dau JANE DENNY - equal share with the rest of daus
Exrs: Son ALEXANDER GRAY, Robert Rankin
Wits: William Donnell, John Donnell

B:0657 - THOMAS GOSSETT - 24 Oct 1831 - Prb Feb 1832
Wife SARAH - plantation whereon I live, other property
Oldest dau ALSE DEAN - $50, her cow, her loom, her bed
Gr dau MARY RIGGIN - mare, her bed & furniture, cow
Son THOMAS - land & property at decease of my wife
Ch: JOHN, MARTHA HITCHCOCK, EMMA HOSKINS, POLLY JACKSON, heirs of LYDIA CARMICHEAL - have had their share
Exr: Son THOMAS GOSSETT
Wits: Mary Rigans, Joshua Gossett, Jacobs Robbins

B:0658 - CHARLES BRUCE...this Instrument which is written with my own hand...15 June 1830 - Prb Feb 1832 - Tract of 2,000 ac on waters of Sandy River in Carrol County, Tenn to be divided into 6 tracts of 333 1/3 ac each; residue of property to be sold & proceeds divided into 9 parts, called surplus shares
Dau POLLY MURRAY - $20, be exonerated from any payment to firm of Bruce, Murray & Hunter, what she has received, 1 sur share
Son ABNOR B. - 50¢, what has been bestowed on him
Gr son JOHN B. of Darlington, S. C. (son of late son GEORGE) -

1 lot in Tennessee, 1 surplus share
Son CHARLES - what has been given him, negro boy Darwin, negro woman Jenny, $500 for conducting my business, 1 surplus share
Unfortunate son ALFRED - 1 lot in Tenn, $300 for moving expenses, 1 surplus share
Son FELIX M. - 1 lot in Tenn, $100, wagon & 2 horse beasts to aid him in moving, 1 surplus share, provisions for one year
Daus BETSY TATUM, PRISSEY PEEPLES & BECKY HUNTER - ea 1 sur sh
Daus of late dau AGGY JOHNSON: BETSY BRANTLEY, FANNIE K. BRANTLEY, MARY BRANTLY, NAOMI JOHNSON - divide 1 surplus share
Exrs: Abraham Peeples, gr son PINKNEY PEEPLES, Charles Bruce
Wits: D. N. Ogburn, James Cole, Nathan Canady, Edmund W. Ogburn, Robert C. Caldwell

B:0659 - ROBERT GILBREATH - 30 May 1831 - Prb Feb 1832
Ch: oldest son THOMAS, JOHN, JAMES, JAIN LANDRETH & MARY FORBIS - each one dollar
Son WILLIAM - my smith tools; dau CATHERINE GILBREATH - my cow
Sons WILLIAM & JOSEPH & dau CATHERINE GILBREATH - 3 horses, all my lands on the Alamance, all my property
Exrs: Sons WILLIAM & JOSEPH GILBREATH
Wits: John Coe, William Doak

B:0660 - RICHARD SAMPSON - 7 Sept 1827 - Prb Feb 1832
Dau MARGARET SAMPSON - $20, bed & furniture, walnut chest
Dau HANNAH SAMPSON - $10, bed & furniture, bed tray
Daus MARY, JANE, ELIZABETH & SARAH SAMPSON - $10 ea, all furn
Sons NATHANIEL & RALPH - each $5
Son PETER - all the tract on which I live, sorrell horse
Exrs: Sons NATHANIEL, RALPH & PETER SAMPSON
Wits: Nathaniel Sampson, Jeremiah Crowder

B:0661 - ELIZABETH JOHNSON - 2 Oct 1829 - Prb Feb 1832
Nephew ELI EDGIN - 53 ac tract adj Frederich Fentriss
Sister ISABEL JOHNSON - the land I live on
Mary Alexander, Nancy Alexander, Margaret Beard, Mary Johnson & Elizabeth Edgin - proceeds of sale at decease of my sister
William Johnson of Thomas - $10
William Johnson of Sarah Alexander? - $20
Matilda Edgin - one cow or value thereof, $10
Exr: James Polk, Senr. Wits: John Bond, Massey Polk

B:0662 - BENJAMIN KENDALL, Senr. - 29 Aug 1831 - Prb Feb 1832
Dau RUTH HAWORTH - all my land in Randolph Co adj John Bonn & Charles Pittman, note on Joshua Fisher, bedding & furniture
Son SOLOMAN - my clock, note I have on him, my old mirror
Son BENJAMIN - my crop & residue of estate
Exrs: Sons SOLOMAN & BENJAMIN KENDALL
Wits: Zebulon Hunt, Hezkial Hanby

B:0663 - SAMPSON STEWART - __ Jan 1828 - Prb May 1832
Wife CATHERINE - negro woman Lydia, use of house, provisions
Son WILLIAM WILEY - $40, he having received $500
Son ISAAC - all the lands consisting of 3 joining plantations on waters of Alamance Cr part of which was bought of William Wiley, negro girl Esther & negro boy Levi

Dau MARY ANN MATTHEWS - negro girl Hannah
Heirs of dau JANE WILEY, dec'd - $300 divided
Dau MARTHA GULLETT - what she has already received, negro Nance
Gr son JOHN STEWART, son of ISAAC - negro girl Rebecca
My remaining negroes: Rose, Tamar, Jackson, Prude & Eli
- to Isaac if he pays $650
Auxillary Bible Society of Guilford County - $20
Alamance Female Benevolent Society - $10
My old negro woman - $10
Son JOHN in South Carolina - notes due from him
Residue of estate divided among: Wife CATHERINE, son ISAAC, Sampson Stewart Wiley, Sampson Stewart Matthews, Samuel Russel (son of Catherine Russell), John Stewart (son of Isaac), Martha Russell, William A. Stewart
Exrs: Son ISAAC STEWART, Col Matthew Young
Wits: William Sloan, James Robison Sloan

B:0644 - ELAM WHARTON - 14 Feb 1832 - Prb May 1832
Ch of son JOSEPH: ELISA, WARREN, EMILY & GREEN - each $1
Son WILLIAM - plantation bought of Peter Weatherly & Thomas Dick, $100 note on son ROBERT
Son ROBERT - horse, saddle, bed, plantation, third of my mills
Dau MARTHA - maintenance from ROBERT while single, 2 beds & furniture, cupboard, horse & saddle, spinning wheel & cards
All my sons: JESSE, WILLIAM, SAMUEL & ROBERT - my smith shop
Negroes Daniel & Aleys - provided for by my children
Daus JANE ATKINS, IBBA BELL & MARTHA - proceeds of sale
Exrs: Sons JESSE & SAMUEL WHARTON
Wits: John Vanstore, Elisha Wharton
Codicil 3 Mar 1832. Wits: J. A. Foulkes, Elisha Wharton

B:0665 - THOMAS WHITE - 10 Mar 1832 - Prb May 1832
Wife ELIZABETH - maintenance by plantation during widowhood
Son BORDON - plantation at decease or remarriage of my wife
Sons THOMAS - $40; HENRY - $10
Balance of children - divide proceeds of sale
Exr: Son HENRY WHITE. Wits: Henry M. Macy, Reed Swain

B:0666 - JACOB COBLE - 24 Feb 1832 - Prb May 1832
Sons GEORGE - 230 ac where he lives; PETER - 116 ac where he lives; ANDREW - 200 ac where he lives
Daus MARY, JANE & ELIZABETH to live with ANDREW until they marry & be furnished household needs by PETER
Exrs: Sons PETER & GEORGE COBLE
Wits: Samuel McMaster, R. Mayven

B:0667 - WILLIAM POE - 20 Sept 1830 - Prb May 1832
Wife SARAH - maintenance on plantation dw, my bay horse, land to be sold at decease or remarriage of wife & divided
Sons DAVID - $10; MATTHEW - $25; WILLIAM, JAMES & ZADOC - residue of proceeds
Daus RACHEL POE, MARGARET POE, MARY POE, TILLA POE & NANCY POE - each bed & furniture, cow & calf, earthen dish, 6 plates
Dau NANCY POE - $10 when she reaches age of 18
Daus SELAH, SARAH, RACHEL, MARGARET, MARY, TILLA, NANCY - proceeds of sale of household furniture

Exrs: Son WILLIAM POE, Stephen Hussey, Esqr.
Wits: James Poe, Margaret Poe

B:0668 - DAVID MENDENHALL - 25 Apr 1832 - Prb May 1832
Wife MARGARET - all of estate dw to raise my children
My three daus: CLARIA, MARGERY & SARAH
Exr: Father-in-law JESSE MOOR
Wits: Mordecai Mendenhall, Ira W. Mendenhall

B:0669 - WILLIAM BUNCH - 23 Oct 1831 - Prb May 1832
Wife - to hold the land during her life and then:
Dau JUDY MCDORMAN, dau JANE BALLARD, gr son WILLIAM STEPHENS, gr dau GULIAN BUNCH - each a fourth of land where I live
Exr: Son JOHN M. BUNCH who inherits balance or property
Wits: Archibald Wilson, Peter Brim

B:0670 - ROBERT MITCHELL, Senr. - 10 Oct 1829 - Prb Aug 1832
Son ROBERT - upper part of lot in town of Greensboro, all my cooperage tools in my shop in Greensboro
Daus MARY DAWSON & MARTHA MITCHELL - balance of lot, kitchen furn
Exrs: Son WILLIAM MITCHELL, son-in-law KENDAL DAWSON
Wits: William Adams, John C. Horney

B:0671 - BETSEY WILEY - 13 Nov 1832 - Prb Nov 1832
Daus MARY M. WILEY & ISABELLA WILEY (both minors) - household furniture when MARY comes of age
Exr: Father JAMES MILLIS. Wits: William Kirkman, Robert Baitly

B:0672 - JOSIAH MCBRIDE - 24 Sept 1832 - Prb Nov 1832
Daus SALLY, ELSEA & BETSEY - 60 ac land off east side of plantation adj George Gannon, incl the Still house Spring
Son JOSEPH - remainder of my land if he furnishes his sisters each with a horse & saddle worth $50
Dau MARY MCAGBY & her ch - her maintenance this year, privilege to live in the house she lives in or with her sisters
Sons WILLIAM, JOHN, JAMES & ISAIAH - each $2
Daus NELLY, JEAN AKIN, MARGARET FORBIS - each $2
Exrs: Sons JAMES & JOSEPH MCBRIDE
Wits: John Finley, William Sloan

B:0673 - LEVEN WOOLEN - 14 Feb 1832 - Prb Nov 1832
Wife REBECCA - bed & furniture for her natural life
Son WILLIAM BARNS WOOLEN - all my land by paying $5 to each of the rest of the legatees: son LEVEN, dau NANCY WOOLEN, son EDWARD, son BENJAMIN ELLIS WOOLEN, son CHARLES WESTLEY; they also share in proceeds of sale
Exr: John A. Smith. Wits: Martin Weatherly, Green Gordon

B:0674 - JOHN HITCHCOCK - 21 Sept 1819 - Prb Nov 1832
Wife - my bay horse Dick & her saddle, cow & calf, maintenance, the pewter & coffee mill
Son BENEDICK - $10; heirs of son ELISHA, dec'd - $10; son WILLIAM - $10; son ASIAL - $10; son-in-law MICHEAL MCCONN - $10; gr dau SARAH HAYWORTH - $15
Son ISAAC - 80 ac adj Criddleborough lands
Son JOHN - 100 ac where I live, buildings, farming utensils

Gr son JOHN HITCHCOCK, son of BENEDICK - 12 ac where BENEDICK first settled
BENEDICK, WILLIAM, heirs of ELISHA, ASAIL, MCCONN & LEAH HAWWORTH - proceeds of sale of certain goods & chattels
Exrs: Wife & son ASAIL HITCHCOCK
Wits: Jeffery Horney, Josiah Haworth

B:0675 - NANCY LINDSAY - 11 Aug 1832 - Prb Nov 1832
Son WILLIAM - $300, third of my books on the old desk
Son ANDREW - $700 worth of household furniture, third of books
Son DAVID - $300, third of my books on the old desk
Exrs: Sons WILLIAM, ANDREW & DAVID LINDSAY
Wits: A. H. Lindsay, Jesse Shelly

B:0676 - ISAAC CLAPP - 30 Sept 1832 - Prb Nov 1832
Wife CATY - all my property dw for the raising of my children
Exrs: Emanuel Clapp & Augustine Clapp
Wits: David Clapp, George Clapp, Daniel Clapp

B:0677 - GEORGE PARSONS - 17 Jan 1815 - Prb Feb 1833
Wife RUTH - black mare, 2 cows & calves, plentiful maintenance
Son JAMES - my smith tools
Son JOHN - bed & furniture, cow & calf
Gr son JOHN, son of WILLIAM, dec'd - $10
Son EVIN - 150 ac where he lives bought of Daniel Osburn
Son GEORGE - tract bought of Jonathan Parker where he lives
Son THOMAS - 150 ac where I live
Daus MARY WILBOURN & CATHERINE PARKER - $125
Wits: John Bartley, Isaac Frazier

B:0678 - CALEB JESOP - 30 Aug 1832 - Prb Feb 1833
Dau BARSHEBA FOSTER, son CALEB & dau ANN MCCRACKIN - each $1
Wife SUSANNA - all personal estate, mansion house & 42 ac of land on the south side of the Tan yard
Exr: Daniel Coble. Wits: John W. Caldwell, Robt. C. Caldwell

B:0679 - JOSEPH MCLEAN - 20 Mar 1822 - Prb Feb 1833
Son Dr. JOHN MCCLAIN - 228 ac of my plantation surveyed by Joseph Gibson in 1821, clock, $366
Gr son JOSEPH MCLAIN, son of JOHN - $50 for books & schooling
Son MARSHALL - 323 ac of my plantation already surveyed, my cleaning fan, road waggon, Jack Screw, Apple Mill & frames & press, my big Bible
Gr son JOSEPH, son of MARSHALL - $50 for books & schooling
Dau MARY NELSON - $366
Gr son JOSEPH MCLAIN NELSON, son of MARY - $50 books, schooling
Dau JANE DONNELL - $366; her son JOSEPH MCLAIN has his $50
Dau MARGARET MCGANPHREY - $20, saddle, cow, feather bed & furn
Exrs: Bro MARSHALL MCLEAN & son MARSHALL MCLEAN
Wits: Sampson Stewart, Samuel Stewart. Proved in Court by Col Joel McLean as both witnesses had deceased

B:0680 - MARY DODSON - 19 June 1832 - Prb Feb 1833
Son CHARLES - bed & furniture in southeast corner of my house
Dau MARY RICE - 5 earthen plates, cups & saucers, tin ladle,

smoothing iron, knife box, and two chairs
Son JEREMIAH - chest with 2 drawers, 3 pewter plates, two chairs
Son RICHARD - clock & case, our candle lantern, dresser, cupboard, all my bottles & jugs, 2 ovens & 1 shuttle, 2 chairs
Gr dau MARTHA RICE - our chest without feet, my wearing apparel
Exr: Son RICHARD DODSON. Wits: David Caldwell, John Russell

B:0681 - GEORGE FINDLEY - 19 Aug 1819 - Prb May 1833
Sons WILLIAM, JOHN & GEORGE WASHINGTON - divide my land
Wife MARY - possession of the house & improvements, negro Sal
Dau FRANKY FINLEY - bed & furniture, cow
Rachel M. Conney? - if she lives with my family until of age - 2 soots and a wheel
Exrs: Wife MARY FINDLEY, son WILLIAM FINDLEY
Wits: John Cunningham, James Findley

B:0682 - JEHU HANCOCK - 11 June 1833 - Prb Aug 1833
Son JEHU - tract formerly belonging to William Lacky, home plantation, small tract conveyed by William Spruce, bed & furniture, desk, three Windsor chairs
Dau PATSEY ANN HANCOCK - 103 ac that William Stacy is living on, bed & furniture, bureau, chest, side saddle
James Johnson, first son of my step dau DRUSILAH CARFIELD - 80 ac tract of land in Rockingham County
Exrs: George Nicks, Junr. & Jehu Hancock
Wits: William Denny, Joseph Donnell

B:0683 - THOMAS THORNBURG - 1 Aug 1833 - Prb Aug 1833
Wife MARY - use of house & garden, comfortable support dw
Son JOSEPH - remaining portion of land and stock for supporting his mother
Son JAMES - land he has adj JOSEPH, grey horse he now uses
Eldest dau NANCY EVANS & youngest dau POLLY GRAY - each $2
All my ch: JAMES, NANCY, JOSEPH & POLLY - divide household furniture at decease of wife; lots in Greensboro to be sold
Exrs: Son JOSEPH THORNBURG, Jonathan Parker
Wits: William D. Scott, John Carroll, Hiram C. Worth

B:0684 - ISAAC MENDENHALL - 5 May 1832 - Prb Aug 1833
Wife ELIZABETH - 160 ac whereon I live, stock, farming tools dw
Sons JACOB & MILES - proceeds of sale of land after wdhd of wf
Ch: RUTH CARTER, ISAAC, AARON, ZODAC & MORDECAI - each $1, having already given them
Exr: Son MORDECAI MENDENHALL
Wits: Allen W. Tomlinson, Ahimass Kendall

B:0685 - ROBERT STEWART - 26 July 1832 - Prb Aug 1833
Wife MARGARET - plantation for her support & the support of the children while they live with her, mare, stock, slave
Dau PRUDENCE & her husband JOHN AKIN, son SAMUEL, son LINDLEY, dau FENNELL POLK - each $1
Son DAVID C. - half my smith tools, negro boy Green
American Missionary Society - $10, paid by DAVID
Dau MARTHA STEWART - cow she claims, bed & furniture, mare, saddle bought at sale of James Polk, negro girl Rhuhamor
Son ROBERT - half of smith tools, farming tools, horse & saddle,

black girls Beck & Ruth, care of his mother, gun & shot pouch
American Bible Society - $10; Alamance Congregation - $20
Ch: DAVID, MARTHA & ROBERT - my Brown's Family Bible
Exrs: Sons DAVID C. STEWART, ROBERT STEWART
Wits: John Foust, R. Mayben, William Corsbey
Codicil 26 June 1833

B:0686 - JOSEPH OZBURN - 8 June 1833 - Prb Aug 1833
Gr sons GREENVILLE LAMAR & MARTIN ANGEL RIGGINS (minor) - 172 ac whereon I live
Dau ELIZABETH LAMAR - adj tract unless her husband JAMES LAMAR deprives her of the benefit; then she should live with GREENVILLE & GREENVILLE to take possession of the land
Son-in-law HARDY DAVIS - my young stud horse, silver watch, rifle, my still, also share with gr sons a 38 ac tract called the Goldmine Tract
Exrs: Andrew Dillon, David Worth, Junr.
Wits: David Worth, Barnabas Coffin

B:0687 - DANIEL GILLASPIE - 27 Aug 1833 - Prb Nov 1833
Wife LUCRETIA - $100, home plantation, negro man Jack, negro woman Silva, dw, rents of plantation where Council Lyse lives, 10 gallons spirits, household furniture, etc
Dau ELIZABETH NEELEY - $50, plantation at decease of her mother
Gr son DANIEL GILLASPIE NEELEY - plantation from his mother
Son-in-law JAMES NEELEY - negro girl Mary
Gr sons DANIEL A. GILLASPIE, JOHN P. GILLASPIE, WILLIAM S. GILLASPIE (minor sons of JOHN S., dec'd) - 600 ac out of the old plantation whereon Col John Gillaspie died
Gr dau LUCRETIA MINERVA GILLASPIE, MARGARET ELIZA GILLASPIE & NANCY CATHERINE GILLASPIE - each $200
Dau-in-law NANCY GILLASPIE - $20
Daniel J. Hanner, son of John & Ann Hanner - $25
James Daniel Starrett, son of Elizabeth Starrett - $25
Daniel G. Schoolfield, son of John & Nancy Schoolfield - $25
North Buffaloe Church - $50
Negro man Jack - $10 & negro woman Silva - $5, provided they conduct themselves well toward my wife
Negro woman Gemima - to be valued but to stay in the family if she doesn't choose a public sale
Exr: Son-in-law JAMES NEELEY
Wits: Thomas Hamilton, A. E. Hanner

B:0688 - JOHN WHEELER - 10 Nov 1832 - Prb Nov 1833
Wife MARY - $200, use & profit of 8 ac of land agreeable to the lease with son JESSE when he bought the land that 8 ac & the dwelling house be reserved for our lifetime
Esther Stevens - to have home with her mother while single, also after her mother deceases if still single, $50 for services
Dau MARY GORDON & husband JOHN GORDON - $250, note for $400
Dau SARAH VETAW & husband DANIEL VETAW - $125, advances to him
Dau LYDIA SWALLOW & husband WILLIAM - $125, note for $300 that Joseph Caldwell let them have on my account
Son JONATHAN - $500, note of $300, my Fullers Tools if he pays his step mother, MARY, $25 a year
Son JESSE - note for $250, note for $500; pay his mother $25 yr

Gr dau (not named) - $50 over & above her father's estate
Dau KEZIAH SWAIN - $25 annually
Exrs: Sons JONATHAN & JESSE WHEELER
Wits: Nathan Cook, Miriam Chadwick

B:0689 - JOHN PHILIPPY - 26 Oct 1833 - Prb Nov 1833
Wife EVE - household furniture, spinning wheel, half the cotton, flax & linens, German Pray Book, third of proceeds of land
My sons - divide my clothing
Heirs - divide two thirds of proceeds from sale of land
Exr: John Corsby appointed by the Court
Wits: John Foust, Henry Tarkinett

B:0690 - SAMUEL STEWART - 9 Apr 1833 - Prb Nov 1833
Eldest dau FAITHEY REYNOLDS - portion of my land that includes the home, adj Elijah Chillicutt, Nathanial Simpson & William Schoolfield
Dau JANE GANT - land on which she lives
3rd dau MARY STEWART - residue of my land, horse called Buck, 2 beds & furniture, bureau, cow & calf
4th dau DASEY STEWART - negro man Henry, boy Bedford, my horse, Family Bible, bed & furniture, cow & calf
Dau MOURNING STEPHENS - proceeds from sale
Gr son SAMUEL S. GRANT - my shot gun, horn & shot bag
Exr: Elijah Chilicutt
Wits: Branch Gordon, Ralph Gorrell, John David

B:0691 - ROBERT MAYBEN - 17 Aug 1833 - Prb Feb 1834
Wife SALLY - full use of all my lands for the raising of the children while she remains my widow, negro Abie
Daus CAROLINE REBECCA MAYBEN & POLLY ANN SODISKA MAYBEN - plantation bought of Conrad Swing, each a negro
Son WILLIAM MILTON - tract bought of Wm. Shaw, horse & saddle, bed & furniture, to help conduct the store when of age
Son ROBERT LAFAYETTE - tract bought of Daniel A. Wright, black boy Jac, horse & saddle, bed & furniture, cow & calf, table
Dau SARAH JANE MAYBEN - half of tract on South Buffaloe bought of Jonathan Armfield, negro, horse & saddle, etc
Son JOHN QUINCY ADAMS MAYBEN - home tract, horse & saddle, etc
Dau MARY ANN MAYBEN - half of tract on South Buffaloe, etc; all to be given to children at my wife's discretion
Exr: Col. Daniel Clapp
Wits: William Corsbey, John H. Crawford

B:0692 - WILLIAM CASE - 15 Mar 1828 - Prb Feb 1834
Wife CHARLOTTE - use of tract where I live, household furniture
Ch: JONAS, NATHAN, CHARLES, EZEKIAL, SALLY HIGHFILL, POLLY NEAL, CHARLOTTE MATILDA PATTERSON & REBECCA PARRISH - in addition to what I have given them, a new Bible each
Son JESSE - to inherit land from his mother, horse & saddle, bed
Exr: Nathan Canady
Wits: Thomas McMichael, John McMichael, Archibald McMichael

B:0693 - THOMAS STARBUCK - 23 Dec 1833 - Prb May 1834
Wife RACHEL - use of home plantation & tract bought of Benjamin Pitts, household furniture, personal property

Son THOMAS - tract where he resides in Stokes County on Belews Creek adj land of Benjamin Coffin
Son MILTON - land where he lives on waters of Reedy Fork adj lands of Reuben Starbuck
Daus ABEGAIL HENLEY - $50; UNIS STARBUCK - $100, bed, cow, mare
Youngest sons ELWOOD & BEZAIL - lands I have loaned my wife, colt or horse raised out of my stock
Exrs: Wife and son THOMAS STARBUCK
Wits: Charles Benbow, Jane Stanley

B:0694 - ANDREW WILSON, Senr. - 2 Apr 1823 - Prb May 1834
Sons DANIEL, ROBERT, JAMES, WILLIAM, ANDREW, MAXFIELD, & JOHN - each 20 shillings
Son DAVID - my plantation on South Buffaloe, negroes Anne & Jane, household furniture & tools at mine & wife's death
Exrs: Robert Wilson & Andrew Wilson, Junr.
Wits: William Donnell, Andrew Wilson

B:0695 - MARSHALL MCLEAN - 12 Mar 1834 - Prb May 1834
Son DAVID - tract on south side of Alamance on which Aiken McLean now lives
Wife & ch younger than DAVID - to carry on the farm & tanning
Son JOEL - $10; dau JANE SCOTT - $50
Gr son JAMES ROBERT MCLEAN - $10
Exrs: Sons (Col) JOEL MCLEAN & DAVID MCLEAN
Wits: Joseph Gibson, John McLean

B:0696 - HENRY HARRISON - 20 Feb 1834 - Prb May 1834
Wife NANCY - negro woman Lucy, negro man Jesse, boy Elijah, girl Eliza, plantation & house during widowhood
Daus NANCY REYCH? - $5; LUCY KING - $5, negro Hannah
Daus MILLY POTTER - negro Becky, $50; ELIZABETH HOBBS - Charity
Dau TABBY HARRISON - negro Lemuel, $50 out of personal estate
Daus WILLEY PEGRAM & POLLY HARRISON - negro woman Gincey
Dau FANNY LOWE - negro Delilah
Sons JOHN - $200; HENRY - negro boy George
Son-in-law JOHN POTTER - 40 rood(?) of land adj his land
Exr: James Nelson
Wits: Joel Parrish, Thomas Sapp, John Cook

B:0697 - JOHN HUBBARD - 17 Mar 1829 - Prb May 1834
Son JOHN - plantation, stock, tools, wagon & gears, my cross cut saw, household furniture
Son GEORGE - my wearing clothes
Daus SUSANNAH HENLEY, ELIZABETH HAM, ch of deceased dau ANN HENLEY, ch of deceased dau JANE HENLEY, MARTHA SANDERS, JUDITH PITMAN, ch of deceased dau SARAH BOWMAN, JEMIMA VESTAL - each five shillings
Exrs: Stephen Hussey, son John Hubbard
Wits: Stephen Hussey, Eli Hussey, John Hussey
Codicil 23 June 1831 - legacy from Uncle John Couvs? of Charles City Co., Va. to go to dau MARTHA SANDERS

B:0698 - SETH MENDENHALL - 27 Feb 1834 - Prb May 1834
Wife CLARISY - all of estate during widowhood

Ch: REDDICK, NANCY CARLISLE, AZEL, JABIS, MARY MENDENHALL, OLIVIA SPOON & ASHSAH - 8th part each of estate at end of widowhood of my wife
Gr ch: SALLY MENDENHALL, ANN & CLARISY MENDENHALL, daus of WILLIAM, dec'd - 8th part of property
Exrs: Sons REDDICK & JABIS MENDENHALL
Wits: Joseph Hunt, Enos Mendenhall

B:0699 - HENRY B. WATSON - 19 Dec 1833 - Prb Aug 1834
Sister SUSAN WATSON - $100. Sarah Taylor - $10
All my bros & sisters - proceeds of sale of lands & property
Exr: Brother JOHN WATSON to see that graveyard is fenced
Wits: None; proved in Court by Zadoc Stafford

B:0700 - JUDITH WATSON - 20 Jan 1834 - Prb Aug 1834
My mother - my Bible and Hymn Book
Bro JOHN WATSON - $50, 1st & 2nd Vol Henry's Works on the Bible
Bro STEWART WATSON - $50, last Vol on the Bible & 1st on the Testament of Henry's Works
Niece JINCY ANN WATSON, dau of STEWART - $50, 3rd Vol on Bible
Nephew JAMES WATSON, son of STEWART - Bucks Theological Dictionary
Missionary Cause - $100, in the hands of Rev Eli W. Caruthers
Exr: James A. Stewart
Co-signed by David C. Stewart, Jurat

B:0701 - JOEL JOHNSON - 15 June 1831 - Prb Nov 1834
Wife - negro woman Ede, third of land, choice of stock, furn
Sons JAMES & JOHN - divide remaining land; JOHN to have $50 when he comes of age, bed & furniture, etc
Sons JOEL & GANAWAY - divide 269 ac tract on Jacobs Creek in Rockingham Co., furniture
Dau POLLY JOHNSON - $250 when of age, bed & furniture, etc
Exr: Son JAMES JOHNSON
Wits: Isaac Jones, Wm. Maxwell, James Loingile
Codicil 30 June 1832. Wits: Jeremiah Crowder, Peter Phillips

B:0702 - SAMUEL MCCLINTOCK - 11 Oct 1832 - Prb Nov 1834
Wife ANN - plantation, negro Jenny, horse, furniture dw
Ch: JOHN, SARAH GLADSON, MAHALY WEATHERLY - each $1
Dau ISABELLA - negro girl Patsey, horse & saddle, cow
Dau POLLY - negro boy Harper, horse & saddle, cow
Son SAMUEL - negro boy Murphy, horse & saddle, cow
Son JAMES - negro woman Chancey, horse & saddle, cow
Dau PEGGY - negro man Thomas, horse & saddle, cow
Dau FRANCES - negro boy Dempson, horse & saddle, cow
Son GEORGE SANDERS - negro boy Anthony, horse & saddle, cow
Dau RHODA PAMELA - negro girl Kersor, horse & saddle, cow
Sons JAMES & GEORGE SANDERS - the old plantation
Exrs: Wife ANN MCCLINTOCK, son SAMUEL MCCLINTOCK, Nathan Gladson. Wits: Robert R. Prather, Larkin Smith
Codicil 2 May 1834 - Wife & son JAMES have deceased; SAMUEL to receive what they were to inherit except GEORGE SANDERS to receive all the old plantation; son SAMUEL - negro ch Peter, to keep family together & school the younger ones
Wits: Larkin Smith, George D. Wilson

B:0703 - JOHN CHIPMAN - 21 Jan 1830 - Prb Feb 1835
Wife MOLLY - lifetime right of home plantation as agreed when it was sold to sons STEPHEN M. & OBADIAH on 17 Dec 1828
Eldest son JAMES & a son JESSE - $1 & what they have received
Daus DEBORAH WELBOURN, SARAH WHEELER & MARGARET CHARLES - $1 & their share in household property at decease of wife
Gr ch WILLIAM & STEPHEN C. DAVIS, sons of dau MARY DAVIS, dec'd - each $25 & share of household furniture
Son OBADIAH - $1 & share of personal property
Son STEPHEN M. - feather bed & furniture, walnut chest
Dau RACHEL IDOL, w/o BARMITE IDOL - $40 & share in furniture
Dau ANNE CHIPMAN - $125
Exrs: Jesse Chipman, Stephen M. Chipman
Wits: Seth N. Peeples, Joel Chipman, W. H. Hampton, Isaac Odell

B:0704 - WILLIAM ADAMS of Guilford Co & now in City of Raleigh, being in precarious health - 12 Dec 1834 - Prb Feb 1835
Wife MARTHA - negro Manuel & his wife Ruth, negro girl Grace & her child, town lot whereon I live in Greensboro, the meadows within & adj the southside of Town Cooperation. also 45 ac adj Harper Lindsay, during widowhood
Son GEORGE - $5
Son PETER - $100, it being third of capital in store, for his services in the Hatters Shop, half of profits of store
Sons PETER, BENJAMIN & WILLIAM J. & daus MARTHA ANN ADAMS & ELIZABETH HORNEY - residue of estate
Son BENJAMIN - the $500 advanced to him for schooling

Statement of Amount due me from the Store
of which no account has been made

Sale of Boy who came from the Gray Family ----------	$375.00
1 ps land sold to Henry Ryder ---------------------	30.00
1 ps land sold to Edward Ross ---------------------	20.00
1 lot land sold to Andrew Weatherly ---------------	150.00
5 years rent of Shoe Shop to Winbourn -------------	150.00
2 years rent of Hatters Shop to Warren ------------	100.00
2 years rent of house to Blackwell ----------------	45.00
1 year rent of house to Hauschurch? ---------------	30.00
1 year rent of house to Malon ---------------------	30.00
1 year rent of house to Woolen --------------------	30.00
Whole Amt. at different times, as above	$960.00

Exrs: Sons PETER ADAMS, Dr. Benjamin Adams
Wits: Jesse H. Lindsay, Jonathan Parker

B:0705 - JAMES FINLEY - 20 May 1834 - Prb Feb 1835
Daus ELIZABETH WALKER - negro girl Fanny; POLLY MCIVER - negro girl Lucy; son GEORGE B. - $20
Dau NANCY FINLEY - negro man Jeff, girl Hager, wagon, all my horses, any farming tools she wants, stock of cattle
Dau SARAH REED - negro women Tamer & Patience, one red cow
Daus NANCY FINLEY & SARAH REED - divide my land
Exr: Dau NANCY FINLEY
Wits: James Chilcutt, William Vanstorie, Mary Ann Heretage

B:0706 - SAMUEL DEVENNY - 24 June 1825 - Prb Feb 1835

Wife ANN - land, negroes, personal estate dw; then divided equally among her children: HANNAH DEVENNY, ABNER, PITHIAS LUV (LEW?), JESSE, FRANCES BROWN, JEMIMA DEVENNY, BETSY DEVENNY
Son THOMAS - $1; dau LYDIA HUNTER - $1; Jane Grace - $1; ch of Mary Coble - $1; Ann Grace - $1; Samuel - $1
Exrs: Wife ANN DIVENNY & son ABNER DEVENNY
Wits: Jonathan Parker, Jacob Suits

B:0707 - SARAH LANE - 4 Dec 1832 - Prb Feb 1835
Nephew JOHN HOLDER - 25¢; niece NANCY HOLDER - 20¢; bro REUBIN LANE - 50¢; EASTHER LANE - $1; bro JOHN LANE - $10
Sister NANCY LANE - all my land & personal property
Exr: Sister NANCY LANE
Wits: John A. Smith, Aaron Bishop, John Rhodes
"Then came into Open Court Manliff Holstead & his wife Nancy, formerly NANCY LANE, and qualified as Adm."

B:0708 - JAMES CLEMMONS - 16 Dec 1834 - Prb Feb 1835
Wife EASTHER - items formerly belonging to her, $7,000 if estate amounts to $14,000, use of home plantation, small tract bought of Abel Knight, tract bought of Isaac Stanley
Son JOHN DILLON CLEMMONS - $100, one of my best horses, half of my dwelling house on west side of store house, half of plantation; at decease of wife to have use of lands & interest on $7,000, then to his heirs and if no heirs then to James Clemmons (son of JOHN) and James Aurelias Clemmons (son of Benton)
Dau LOUISA BLACKWELL - desk, silver, urn coffee pott, etc
Property to be sold: my interest in the gold mine at Conrad Hill in Davidson Co., tract bought of Paul Coffin, my mills on Mudd Creek
Exr: Brother BENTON CLEMMONS
Wits: James Brindle, Micheal Neugent, John Clemmons

B:0709 - JOHN WATSON - 8 Feb 1835 - Prb Feb 1835
Wife ELLANA - third of land & stock, money on hand, for life
Dau JANE WATSON - $100, bed & furniture, cow named Patte, privilege of living at home during her single state
Dau MARY STEWART - $150; son STEWART - $150
Son JOHNSTON - 30 ac off lower end of McLean tract adj his land, 2/3 of plantation; later the third held by his mother
Exrs: Sons STEWART & JOHNSON WATSON
Wits: Dr. Wm. B. Price, Marshall McLean, Esq

B:0710 - SAMUEL STANLEY - 12 Sept 1832 - Prb Feb 1835
Wife SARAH - home plantation for life, horse, cow, furniture
Son RICHARD - $100, having already given him $150
Son ISAAC - $180, having already given him $70
Son SAMUEL - $1, having already given him $250
Son NATHAN - $1, having already given him $250
Sons JOSHUA, JESSE & WILLIAM - each $250
Dau DORCAS HUNT wife of GEORGE HUNT - $100
Dau MARY MEREDITH, w/o JAMES MEREDITH - $1 as she & her husband do not live together & it might not be properly disposed of
Ch of dau MARY MEREDITH - to divide $100
Dau SARAH HUNT wife of NEESLEY? HUNT - $100
Exrs: Joshua Stanley & William Stanley
Wits: Eleazer Hunt, James Clemmons, Jesse Stanley

B:0711 - WILLIAM GILCHRIST - 29 Aug 1834 - Prb Feb 1835
Wife DELILAH - home plantation, stock, wagon, household furn
My four daus: NANCY N. THOMPSON, POLLY J. TUCKER, PAMILA W. WALKER, ELINOR C. GILCHRIST - proceeds of sale of still house, carpenters tools, and young negroes: Nelson, Ned, Hannah & Emily
Son-in-law THOMAS THOMPSON - divide my clothes among sons-in-law
Gr son WILLIAM G. THOMPSON - my small desk & barbers tools
Exr: Son-in-law THOMAS THOMPSON of Rockingham Co
Wits: Robert Gilchrist, Moses Gilchrist

B:0712 - ELIZABETH KERSEY, widow of AMOS KERSEY - 28 Apr 1835 - Prb May 1835. Son EZRA - bed quilt, blanket, two pillows, oven & hooks, hammock, bolt of flax & cotton linens, sheep
Dau LOUISE POTTER - bed, quilt, blankets, pot & hooks, etc
Dau ELIZABETH COFFIN - one little pot & bale?
Gr dau ELIZABETH KERSY - Bible
Gr son NEWTON KERSY - one horned ewe sheep
My five ch: RUTH BOYDE, EZRAH KERSEY, LOUISE POTTER, JAMES KERSEY, & ELIZABETH COFFIN - proceeds of property sold
Exr: Son EZRA KERSEY
Wits: Eleazer Harlan, John Newman

B:0713 - WILLIAM HIATT - 9 Mar 1835 - Prb May 1835
Sons ALLEN & WILLIAM - all my lands
Wife - maintenance by sons ALLEN & WILLIAM
Dau HANNAH - privilege of the home while single, bed, cow & calf
Sons JAMES, JOB & OTHNEAL - each $10
Exr: John Morris. Wits: Seth Starbuck, Cathbert Hiatt

B:0714 - JOHN FOUST - 10 Apr 1834 - Prb May 1835
Son DANIEL - 100 ac on north end of my tract
Wife PEGGY - maintenance by DANIEL, choice of stock & furniture
Son LEONARD - balance of land provided he pay $20 to my daus
Exrs: Henry Clapp & Daniel Foust
Wits: John Foust, Christian Foust

B:0715 - ISAAC PEARSON - 6 Sept 1834 - Prb May 1835
Wife ELIZABETH - all my lands, bay horse named Miche, stock
Son WILLIAM - horse named Taltun; son JOHN - colt named Jin
All my ch - division of property at decease of wife
Exrs: Wife ELIZABETH PEARSON & son WILLIAM PEARSON
Wits: A.E.D. Tatum, Col Allen Peeples, James Cole

B:0716 - ELISHA BENNETT - 19 Dec 1831 - Prb Aug 1835
Son-in-law THOMAS BRADLOVE - $1; son LEVI - $1; son DAVID - $1
Son-in-law STALEY & dau NELLY - $1; son JOHN - $1
Son DANIEL'S ch: TEMPERANCE & DORRIS MONROE - 1/6 of estate
Elizabeth Shofner, Sally & Peter Coble, son JOHN'S ch - each a sixth part of my estate
Remaining property on Stinking Quarter to be sold
Exr: Son DANIEL BENNETT
Wits: Thomas McCulloch, Samuel Fogleman

B:0717 - DAVID ARCHER - 1 Sept 1834 - Prb Nov 1835
Wife SARAH - use of plantation during widowhood

Daus SARAH ANN ARCHER & FRANCES ARCHER & son WASHINGTON D. - each $100; daus share of household furniture
All my ch: JAMES, WILLIAM, ELIZABETH, MARY, DAVID, ABEL, SARAH ANN, FRANCES & WASHINGTON D. ARCHER - proceeds of sale of my slaves after WASHINGTON D. becomes 18
Negro man Bob - to be free at death or remarriage of widow & use of 10 ac of land
Exrs: Son-in-law DANIEL HOWSEN & Ithamer Hunt
Wits: James Sapp, John Archer, Junr

B:0718 - EDWARD GREEN - 30 Oct 1832 - Prb Nov 1835
Wife MARGARET - all my estate to do with as she pleases except $5 to Rachel Green
Exrs: Wife MARGARET GREEN, sons JAMES, WILLIAM & GEORGE D. GREEN
Wits: William G. Webb, Samplett Webb

B:0719 - THOMAS BROOKSHIRE - 21 June 1835 - Prb Nov 1835
Sons WILLIAM, BENJAMIN, MANNERING & WILEY - each $300
Wife MARY - plantation, household furniture, farming tools dw
My seven daus: JANE LUALLEN, MARGARET BROOKSHIRE, REBECCA NANCE, SARAH NEELEY?, HANNAH HAMMON, MARY HENLEY & OLIVE TUNCANNON - proceeds of sale after decease or remarriage of wife
Exr: Wife MARY BROOKSHIRE appointed by Court with Horace F. Cannon & John W. Caldwell, Esq as sureities
Wits: John W. Caldwell, Robert C. Caldwell

B:0720 - BENJAMIN BEESON - 6 Jan 1831 - Prb Nov 1835
Son RICHARD G. - all my lands & tenements, 2 horses, stock
Ch: ELIZABETH SANDERS (w/o JOHN SANDERS), ISAAC, RACHEL STARBUCK (w/o THOMAS STARBUCK), BENJAMIN, MARY STARBUCK (w/o REUBEN STARBUCK), THOMAS & RICHARD G. BEESON - proceeds of sale of residue of estate
Heirs of son JOHN BEESON, dec'd - 25¢ each
Elijah Boren's children by deceased dau PHEBE - 25¢ each
Exr: Son RICHARD G. BEESON
Wits: John Draughan, David C. Pidgeon

B:0721 - EZEKIAL TURNER - 27 Sept 1832 - Prb Feb 1836
Wife JANE - land dw, horse & saddle, bed, cow, furn for life
Daus MIRIAM & EDITH - each a bed & furniture, cow & calf
Daus MARY YOUNG, RUTH HEDGECOCK & NANCY BUNDY - each $1
Sons WILLIAM, JOSEPH, ABRAHAM & JAMES - $1
Son MILES - one horse the one he now claims
My five sons - proceeds of land at decease or remarriage of wife
Exr: Jacob Hedgecock
Wits: Zebulon Hunt, Henry Frazier

B:0722 - ISAAC MOORE - 6 Dec 1835 - Prb Feb 1836
Wife SARAY - home plantation, tract bought of Elijah Davies, 2 slaves of her choice, stock, household furniture, remaining slaves and Haw River plantation to be sold
Son JOHN - value of $100; all children to be made equal to that as they arrive at the age of 21
Exr: John Moore appointed by Court, bond of $6,000 with Robt Caffey, Levi W. Witty & Henry Moore as sureities
Wits: Col Allen Peeples, James Davis

B:0723 - ANDREW DONNELL - 7 Mar 1833 - Prb Feb 1836
Dau SALLY - $1.25; her daus SINETH & ANN - $50 each; her sons ROBERT - $20; LIAL - $20; MORRISON - $10
Daus PEGGY - $150; NANCY - $150 & part of the land adj Edmund Donnell; HANNAH - $150, clock, land south of NANCY'S land
Sons ADLICE, LATHAM, JOHN, GEORGE - land in Tennessee
Son WILLIAM - $25, land adjoining his land
Buffaloe Congregation - $50; son-in-law THOMAS DONNELL & son WILLIAM to use the money as they please in the congregation
Exr: Son-in-law THOMAS DONNELL & son WILLIAM DONNELL
Wits: Joseph Rankin, John C. Rankin

B:0724 - PHILIP KIMES - 12 Mar 1836 - Prb May 1836
Son CHRISTIAN - tract of land on which he lives
Wife TIRLY - maintenance by Henry
Son HENRY - tract whereon I live & improvements & everything to provide sustenance & comfort for my beloved TIRLY
Daus BARBARA, TIRLY & SALLY - tracts on which they live
Daus CHRISTINA & SALLY - divide the Deamona tract
Sons-in-law ADAM BROWN, PETER FOUST, JOHN HUMBLE, DAVID HUMBLE, & DANIEL SMITH - each $300
Exrs: Sons CHRISTIAN & HENRY KIMES
Wits: William Arter, Peter Rightsell, Frederich Rightsell

B:0725 - JEREMIAH CUNNINGHAM - 16 Aug 1831?(blot) - Prb May 1836
Wife HANNAH - estate in Tennessee by her father, John Cates, choice horse, cow & calf, household furniture
Son JOHN - half of personal estate & what I have given him
Son MATHEW - $400 & what I have given him
Son WILLIAM - $100 & half the land
Son JAMES C. - horse he claims & half the land
Son-in-law JOHN ROBERTS & wife JANE - negro boy child Green
Dau ELIZABETH LANE - share in personal estate
Exrs: James Nelson & John Roberts
Wits: Isaac Cokes, Lemuel Nelson

B:0726 - OBED ANTHONEY - No date - Prb May 1836
Wife CLARY - use & profits of estate during widowhood
Sister-in-law ABIGAIL PIKE - the east room with the fireplace, free firewood & water while single, spinning machine bought of Rhodia Swain, cow & calf, mare colt
Wits: Proved in Court by Jonathan Parker, Senr

B:0727 - AGNES PAMPLIN - 11 June 1836 - No probate date
Dau OLIVE PAMPLIN - land whereon I live, spinning machine, cow
I give to: Matilda White, Sarah Smith, Mary Portice & Robert Pamplin - each $1
Exr: Olive Pamplin (Prb on original will Aug 1836)
Wits: Isardy R. Will Jones, Jesse Harvey, Angelina Luallin

B:0728 - JAMIMA WILSON - 25 Dec 1834 - Prb Aug 1836
Gr son WILLIAM MARSH - all property both real & personal, having already given to the other grand children
Nancy Hodson, widow of Jonathan Hodson - my wearing clothes
Exr: Nathan Armfield
Wit: Thomas Turner

B:0730 - HENRY RIGHTSEL - 13 Apr 1836 - Prb Aug 1836
Son CHRISTION - my land whereon I live west of Fayetteville Road
All my ch: CHRISTIAN, DAVID, DANIEL, PETER, FREDERICH, SARAH RIGHTSEL, BARBARA KIME, ADAM RIGHTSEL, SOPHIA BROWN, PEGGY SHEARER, HANNAH PICKET? and RACHEL RIGHTSEL - division of balance of land on Fayetteville Road & estate
Exr: Eli Coble of Randolph County
Wits: William Smith, Peter Smith

B:0731 - CHRISTIAN FARMER - 20 July 1826 - Prb Aug 1836
Wife ELIZABETH - land & every individual article belonging to me as long as she keeps my name
Heirs: Henry Farmer has had $120; Samuel Farmer has had $120; Peter Farmer has had $116 & must have $4 more; Polly Farmer has had $100 & she must have $20 more; Levi Farmer is to have $120 when he becomes 21
Exr: Joland Clark Wit: Henry Turkenett

B:0732 - SARAH LOVETT - 6 Aug 1835 - Prb Nov 1836
Gr dau SUSANNAH ANN LOVET - cow & calf, bed, basins, chest, etc
Son GEORGE - cow & calf, pewter dish, basins, trunk, bed, etc
Gr dau SARAH HUMPHREY - "one six hundred slay"
Gr dau DEBORAH LOVET - one table
Exrs: Sons GEORGE & JOHN LOVETT
Wits: Christopher Hiatt, Joab Hiatt

B:0733 - ELISHA MENDENHALL of Randolph Co - 7 Aug 1821 - Prb Nov 1836. Wife SUSANNAH - all my lands & tenements forever
Exr: Wife SUSANNAH MENDENHALL
Wits: John P. Carter, B. Elliott, Archibald D. Murphey
Codicil written same day giving Guilford Co as residence:
My wife's niece HESTER MCGEE - $1,000 for her consideration
Sister BETSY WARD - tract bought of Henry Fitchell in Randolph Co
Jonathan Parker - $500 for consideration & kindness
Exrs: Andrew Lindsay, wife SUSANNAH MENDENHALL
Wits: Dr. John A. Mebane. The handwriting of John P. Carter & Archibald D. Murphey proved by oath of John M. Morehead

B:0734 - ROBERT MODERWELL of Greensboro - 20 May 1836 - Prb Nov 1836. Wife MARTHA - house & lots in Greensboro, 120 ac bought of Wm T. Shields & tract bought of Eli Fountain, my third of mill & tract of land in Orange Co., my store in Hillsborough
Robert Moderwell Shields & James Shields - land in Orange Co after decease of my wife
Brother JOHN MODERWELL - $150 yearly, desiring that his brother be brought to this state
Exr: Wife MARTHA MODERWELL
Wits: Col John M. Logan, Robert Mitchell

B:0735 - PRESTON PAISLEY - 20 Sept 1836 - Prb Nov 1836
Wife - one feather bed & furniture
Daus NANCY & BETSEY (minors) - each bed & furniture, horse, saddle & bridle worth $70-$75
Son WILLIAM - land whereon I live, paying his sisters $100 three years after he is 21, furnish maintenance for wife
Exrs: Col Joel McLean, Elisha Wharton, Esqr
Wits: Joseph Gibson, John P. Hanner

B:0736 - JESSE STANLEY - 11 June 1834 - No probate date
Wife PRUDENCE - land whereon I live during widowhood, proceeds of sale of land on head waters of Deep River
Youngest dau PRUDENCE (later called "my unfortunate dau") - good and sufficient maintenance for life
Oldest dau ACHSACK PEGG, w/o ABSALOM PEGG - $5
2nd dau UNITY DENNIS, w/o JESSE DENNIS - $5; son THOMAS - $5
Exr: John Hunt, Wife PRUDENCE STANLEY
Wits: John Draughon, Charles Stanley

B:0737 - JOHN SUMMERS - 2 Apr 1836 - Prb Nov 1836
Daus BETSEY WOODYARD, CATEY STOREY & NANCY SHEPART - property already given them valued at $50 each
Son MARTIN - property already given him valued at $150
Single daus: CEBA, POLLY ANN, PEGGY, PATSEY, ISABEL JANE, SUSAN EMILY & THANKFUL ABIGALE - each a value of $50 in property at marriage
Sons JOHN & PETER RILEY - land on which I live
Wife POLLY - use of land in maintaining herself & family dw, third of land if she married, child's part in personal prop
Exrs: Son MARTIN SUMMERS, Joseph Gibson
Wits: J. P. Gibson, N. A. Hanner

B:0738 - JOHN BOON - 16 Mar 1834 - No probate date
Sons JACOB, JOHN, DAVID, JESSE LEWIS, WILLIAM & CALEB BOON - tracts already conveyed to them & slaves given them
Youngest son CALEB, besides home plantation, negro man Oscar, negro girl Sharte H., 3 yr old filly & saddle, $300 in cash to be put on interest to clothe & educate him
Daus CATHERINE, POLLY, BETSEY, BARBARA, ANN & MOLLY - slaves already given them, $300 each
Wife ANNE - negro girl Saley, $300, bed, cow, spinning wheel
Heirs of dec'd daus CATY & POLLY - each $300
Exr: Son JACOB BOON
Wits: Joseph Gibson, Mary Ann Gibson. Codicil 23 July 1836

B:0739 - JOSHUA UNDERWOOD, Senr. - 7 Oct 1834 - Prb May 1837
Wife MARTHA - all personal estate during life
Gr sons THOMPSON & WILLIAM WESLEY UNDERWOOD, sons of JOSHUA - land whereon I live adj Brooks Watlington, Francis L. Simpson, & Thomas Underwood
Son JOSHUA - my shot gun
Negro boy Jetson sold to Jonathan B. Watlington
All my ch - proceeds of sale of negroes & personal estate after decease of wife, with due regard to charges kept against each one in a book in the hands of Moses Simpson
Exrs: Francis L. Simpson, Edward Watlington
Wits: William Timberlake, John Apple

B:0740 - JOSEPH CLAPP - 21 Aug 1835 - Prb May 1837
Wife SUSANNA - 140 ac whereon I live, slaves Toney, Andy, Madison & woman slaves Hannah, Rose, girls Matilda & Mariah, her choice of a horse beast, 2 cows & calves, 2 ewes & lambs
Son FINLEY E. S. CLAP - plantation at decease of his mother, inheritance of his gr mother PRUDENCE STEWART, horse & saddle
Dau BETSEY ANN CLAP - black girl Becky, horse & saddle, bed & furniture, one end of the house, firewood while single

Dau EUPHANCE STEWART - $100 at her mother's decease to be paid by Wesley McMurry, plus what I have given her
Dau PRUDENCE CORSBY - slave Rose & what I have given her
Son JAMES - slave Madison & what has been given him
Dau SUSAN, w/o WESLEY MCMURRY - yellow girl slave Caroline
Youngest daus PRUDENCE, SUSAN & BETSY ANN - my land
Exrs: Jedidiah Smith, James S. Clap
Wits: Benjamin Ross, John McMurry

B:0741 - GEORGE TWIFORD - 25 Nov 1829 - Prb May 1837
Son-in-law ALLEN POWEL & ELIZABETH his wife - all the money & property I have let him have
Wife DENETINE - balance of estate during life, black woman Cander
Son EDMOND W. - to inherit from my wife
Exr: Wife. Wits: Jonathan Parker, Martha Parker

B:0742 - JAMES DAVIS - 7 Dec 1831 - Prb May 1837
Wife SAPPHIAR - all my lands, adj land where I live, dw
Son MICHAEL COFFEY DAVIS (minor) - to inherit from wife
Son JOHN DAVIS, dau JANE CAFFEY, MICHAEL C. DAVIS - proceeds of sale of personal property at decease or marriage of wife
ROBERT & JANE CAFFEY, my dau - the place I formerly lived; dau JANE'S ch - $475; JANE to have interest until they are of age
Gr son JAMES DILWORTH CAFFEE - $25
Son ROBERT - $1,000 note I have against him
Tombstone to be placed at grave of son JAMES, dec'd
Exr: Wife SAPPHIA DAVIS
Wits: Isaac Moore, John Moore, Christopher Jones

B:0743 - SAMUEL KERSEY - 6 Sept 1837 - Prb Nov 1837
Wife ANNA - my house & one ac of land dq, Bible, bed & furniture
Pamila Matilda Green, dau of Elizabeth Green - $50 to be used for her education
My two sons CLARKSON EWILL & FRANKLIN - residue of estate; to be placed with some decent person to learn a trade, to inherit from wife
Exr: George Albright. Wits: John A. Mabene, Sarah Williams

B:0744 - ROBERT CUMMINS - 15 Dec 1831 - Prb Nov 1837
Son THOMAS - my negro man Ben Black Smith, valued at $450, all my interest in my sister ANN'S slaves at her death besides what I have given him
Son WILLIAM - 5 negroes: Dely, Rose, Calvin, Sally & Abraham, half of smith tools & wheat plus what I have given him
Dau MARY LAW - negro woman Dice & her three ch, $150, bed & furn
Dau ELIZABETH SOCKWELL - 4 negroes: Biddy, Hanna, Ben & Caroline, desk, book case - and then to her children
Ch of dau JANE SIERS - $150 divided among them
Ch of dau ANN ROSE - $100 divided
Ch of dau ISABEL PARMAR? - $200
Gr son ROBERT SOCKWELL, son of dau SALLY - 23 ac adj his father
Other five of SALLY'S ch - $100 divided
Exrs: Son THOMAS CUMMINS, Robert Cummins, John Wharton
Wits: Elisha Wharton, John Ponninger, Jr., John Garrison

B:0745 - WILLIAM STARBUCK - 17 Apr 1837 - Prb Nov 1837

Ch: EDWARD STARBUCK - $1; ch of dau MARY DWIGGINS - 5 sh each; ABIGAIL SIMMONS - $100; PHEBE COFFIN - $1; RHOAD GARBY - $50; DAMARUS FISHER - $100; JANE COFFIN - $100; ANN GARDNER - $100; SALLY DWIGGIN - $100; LYDIA DEEN - $100
Daus now living: ABIGAL SIMMONS, DAMARUS FISHER, JANE COFFIN, AVA GARDNER, & LYDIA DEEN
Exrs: Son-in-law SAMUEL DWIGGINS, gr son-in-law JOHN HUBBARD
Wits: John Hubbard, Abigal Hubbard

B:0746 - MILLY SUITER - 18 Sept 1837 - Prb Nov 1837
Dau ELIZABETH OZMENT - my fancy post bedstead
Dau IBBY HARRIS - $100; dau MARGARET SPENCE - balance of estate
Exr: Dau MARGARET SPENCE
Wits: Col William Denny, James Denny

B:0747 - JARVIS JONES - 11 May 1833 - Prb Aug 1837
Son PINKNEY - my gun, horse colt, farming tools & gears, half my still & tubs, other half at decease of his mother
Daus MARGARET GUNTER, NANCY KIMBRO, SARAH TANSON - have received their full share
Wife - third part of property not given away, my mare
Daus REBECCA JONES & LYDIA JONES - each third of personal prop
Exrs: Wife PRISCILLA JONES, Nathan Mendenhall
Wits: David Beard, Jonathan Mendenhall, William P. Mendenhall

B:0748 - HARMAN HOWLET - 16 Feb 1837 - No probate date
Wife JUDITH - my right in the place where we live, all the pot ware & earthen ware & water vessels, her 2 beds & furniture, wheel & cards, use of one cow, coffee mill, meat on hand, etc
Dau ELIZABETH HOWLET - when she arrives at age of 25, the wheel and cards & sow & pigs from her mother's estate
Daus ANNY WILSON & HANNAH FOSTER - proceeds of sale of personal estate at decease of wife
Son WILLIAM - steer, my part in the cart, one Barshaw plow & gears, 2 horses, a handsaw to furnish firewood for his mother
Son PLEASANT J. - to inherit land from his mother, what he already has, & grind stone, pair of stutgards, work bench in the shop, set of bench planes, fore plane Jack, smooth plane
Son MARBORO T. - other shop tools provided he pay Wilson Hill & Tom $2.80
Son JAMES M. - my bed & bedstead, walnut chest, book case, etc
Son-in-law P. M. FOSTER - my shoe bench & all my shoe tools for him to furnish the old woman in shoes during life
Exrs: Patrick M. Foster who is to attend to the suit now in Equity under the directions of John M. Dick & George Mendenhall; and see that I am buried at home near the Chestnut tree
Wits: Elijah Maye, A. E. D. Tatum

B:0749 - MARTHA FRAZIER - 14 Nov 1825 - No probate date
Gr dau ABIGAIL FRAZIER, dau of JAMES - my bed & furniture, chest containing pewter & other things, looking glass, flax wheel
Son JAMES - spice mortar, remaining household furniture, money due me from Enos Frazier now in hands of William Henry
Dau ABIGALE OZMENT - my large walnut table
Exr: Son JAMES FRAZIER
Wits: William Henry, Soloman Mills, Elender Quait

B:0750 - WILLIAM ARMFIELD - 4 May 1832 - No probate date
Wife ELIZABETH - benefit of dwelling house, furniture & plentiful support of plantation, horse beast, cow & calf
Son ROBERT - stock at decease or remarriage of wife, all my land & farming tools & balance of property
Daus JANE ARMFIELD, RACHEL MACY, MARY MACY, SARAH HIATT & ELIZABETH UNTHANK - each $2
Sons JACOB - $2; WILLIAM - $10
Son ISAAC - $55 to be divided among his children; his son JOAB to have $50; the other $5 divided among the others of his ch: ROBERT, MATILDA EDWARDS, VIRTUEOUS EDWARDS & ELINOR DAUGHERTY
Gr son WILLIAM NELSON ARMFIELD - $55
Exrs: Son ROBERT ARMFIELD, David Edwards
Wits: Alfred Armfield, John Hiatt, J. M. Morehead, Amis Bain
Codicil 22 Jan 1833

B:0751 - LOTTA GOLA, lately from Germany - 11 June 1837 - No prb
All my ch - all my money & property - 200 dollars in German dollars in gold, 53 in American money
$140 due from Christian Gola
Wits: John Fouste, Daniel Fouste

B:0752 - WILLIAM CUNNINGHAM - 17 July 1837 - No probate date
Mother HANNAH CUNNINGHAM - negroes Samuel & Benjamin
Bro JAMES C. - negro Samuel & estate at decease of Mother
Sister JANE ROBERTS - negro Benjamin at decease of Mother
Sister ELIZABETH LOVE - $100 coming to me from father's estate
Exrs: Brother-in-law JOHN ROBERTS, bro JAMES C. CUNNINGHAM
Wits: James Nelson, Benjamin Lancaster, Rodolphus Dodd, Pleasant Parish

B:0753 - SHADRACK OTWELL - 2 Aug 1837 - Prb Aug 1837
Wife ROSINAH - residue of estate after debts and at her decease or remarriage to my dau JANE for her kindness & affection to me in my affliction
Son JAMES OTWELL - $1; dau SARAH HODSON - $1
Exr: William Mills. Wits: John Clark, John Northam

B:0754 - WILLIAM MAXWELL - 6 Feb 1837 - Filed Feb 1837
Wife DEBOLAR - dwelling house & as much cleared land & woodland to afford her comfortable support, $100, negro woman Sal, girl Phillis, half of household furniture, half of stock
Son WILLIAM - half of stock, home plantation to support wife, negro boy Billy, negro girl Estes, $200
Jenny Gordon - 100 ac where she now lives adj William Vanstory
Heirs of deceased dau NANCY LUCIUS; DEBOLAR - negro girl Hamit; FRANCES - negro girl Aley; Wilkins Lucius' dau Mary Fulks that he had by his present wife - negro girl Sary. These slaves all children of Hannah who lives with the Lucius family
Wilkins Lucius - lend him slaves Hannah & Albert; if Hannah has other children, they to be divided among children of his 2nd wife as well as ch of my deceased dau NANCY
Dau SARY MAXWELL - negro woman Beck & her 2 youngest ch named Ansaline & Frank, half of household furniture, 94 ac of land
Dau PATSY BRANNOCK - land whereon she lives, $300
Dau PEGGY YOUNGE - negro boy named Carter

Gr son ALFRED MAXWELL - half of plantation bought of Biswell & Lucius & tract bought from Young, negro boy Harry, negro girl Hannah, Beck's ch, share wagon & smith tools with Wm.
Jenny Gordon, 3 sons of Nancy Lucius dec'd: William, John & James; dau SARY MAXWELL, Peggy Younge, son WILLIAM, dau PATSEY'S heirs, gr son ALFRED MAXWELL - residue of estate
Exr: Gr son ALFRED MAXWELL
Wits: Noah M. Climer, George Fulton

B:0755 - JESSE HASSEL - 27 Nov 1837 - Prb Feb 1838
2 youngest sisters MILINDA & RACHEL HASSEL - all my estate
Exr: Brother BENJAMIN HASSEL
Wits: William Dick, Joseph Newman, Joseph Reynolds

B:0756 - MARY MAGER - 22 June 1837 - Prb Feb 1838
Gr son GREEN MAGER, son of dau PRISCILLA but known as GREEN MAGER - tract I live on known as the Lane tract & proceeds of sale of tract adj William Walker & John Highfill, bed, etc
Dau PRISCILLA, w/o REUBEN LAND - $10, my wearing apparel
Narsissa Land - three cotton frocks
Gr dau LUCY E. DAUGHERTY - $20, my side saddle, bed & furniture
Exr: Elijah Witty. Wits: E. Witty, John Parish

B:0757 - TILMAN HARRIS - 30 May 1831 - Prb Feb 1838
Sons EDWARD, SAMUEL, JONES & GRANDERSON HARRIS - each $1
Daus ELIZABETH R. APPLR, LUCY W. SMITH & SARAH A. HARRIS - ea $1
Son TILMAN HARRIS - one horse, to inherit from wife
Wife SARAH - all of estate of every kind for life
Exrs: Son TILMAN HARRIS, wife SARAH HARRIS
Wits: Crowder & Catherine Russell

B:0758 - TILMAN HARRIS - 30 Jan 1838 - Prb Feb 1838
Peter Apple, my executor & James Smith my son-in-law - 50 ac of land adj Joseph Pritchett
Son TILMAN HARRIS - balance of my land, cattle & hogs
My three ch: PETER APPLE, JAMES SMITH & TILMAN HARRIS - proceeds of sale of personal estate
Exr: Peter Apple. Wit: Joseph C. Pritchett

B:0759 - RICHARD HAWORTH - 2 Dec 1837 - Prb Feb 1838
Wife - mare, side saddle, bed, cow, weaving apparel, clock, loom & tackle, cupboard with 12 lights, 2 tables, 2 fatning hogs, sow & pig, 3 stock hogs for life
Dau ABIGALE - feather bed & furniture & the property she bought at the sale of her Aunt JANE
Daus MARTHA & ELIZABETH - bed & furniture & things they bought at the sale of their Aunt JANE
My ch - everything divided at decease of wife
Exrs: Nathan Mendenhall & Soloman Kendall
Wits: James Sapp, George Mendenhall, Cuthbet Hiatt

END OF BOOK B

C:0760 - PETER SUMMERS - 31 Jan 1837 - No probate date
Son JACOB - land whereon he lives incl the mill on Haw River adj the Mill Dam, also tract in Orange Co that was conveyed to Anthony Coble & me from Israel Holt & later from sd Coble to me. I have given him in all $3,000 & gave him $2,000 more
Son LUDWICK - mill & tract on Reedy Fork on which he lives, tract from Benjamin Allen, $2,000, 1,000 ac in Western District of Tenn bought of A. D. Murphey which is now in litigation
Son PETER - tract where I live which is tract of my father, all other adj lands in Guilford Co bought of Valentine Summers, also tract bought of George Christmon, part of which lies in Orange Co, other tracts & $1,400
Trustees for ch of son ABEL when they come of age: Sons JACOB and LUDWICK - land on Reedy Fork, but if son ABEL would forsake and abandon all habits of intemperance and dissipation, he should be allowed to live on the land with his family
Son JOSHUA - 230 ac of the Crowder tract, negro boy Ned, $1,800
Dau BARBERY - $1,200 she has received & 2 negroes. I now give her all the legacy given me by Anthony Coble of Rock Castle Co., Ky in his last wi-l, also $1,000
Dau ROSA, w/o JACOB CLAPP, & her ch - $1,300, negro girl Nancy, tract on Reedy Fork; these to be held in trust by son LUDWICK for benefit of dau ROSA until JOSEPH CLAPP pays his debts to me & forsakes & abandons his intemperate habits
Dau PEGGY, w/o BATSON GERINGER - having advanced her $3,000 in stock, slaves, etc & the legacy she has received from her grand father WHITESELL, $1,500
Residue of property to be sold & divided betw my ch, excepting son ABEL: Sons JACOB, LUDWICK, PETER & JOSHUA; daus BARBERY & her ch, dau ROSA & her ch, dau PEGGY & dau LUCY
Exrs: Son JACOB & Ludwick Summers
Wits: James W. Doak, D. Thomas, L. A. Holman

C:0761 - ROGER LAYTON - 14 Mar 1838 - Prb May 1838
Wife ANA - house & household furniture, mare, her saddle & bridle, money called hers, viz $113 on interest & $50 more
Dau BETSY FIELD - the Clapp tract she has received & $500 more
Gr son LAYTON FIELD - $50
Son CHARLES LAYTON - the plantation he lives on, $200
Dau POLLY LAYTON - the part of plantation we live on, her mare & colt, 2 cows, 3 sheep, 3 hogs, 2 beds, her wheel, $50, etc
Son JAMES - tract he is improving, $125, bed & furniture, etc
Exrs: Sons CHARLES LAYTON & Absalom Field
Wits: Thomas McCulloch, Leonard Phillippi

C:0762 - ISOM SIKES - No date - Prb May 1838
Wife REBECCA - all my property
Ch of John Forbis: Dolly Ann & John Washington Forbis - to heir whatever is left at decease of wife
Exr: John Forbis. Wits: John Paisley, Hannah Paisley

C:0763 - DANIEL SHERWOOD - 2 Aug 1826 - Prb May 1838
Ch: THOMAS, HUGH, ELIZABETH SWAIN, ELINOR FIELD, DANIEL, BENJAMIN, PRISCILLA SWAIN & JOHN - each $1
Wife - estate dw; if she marries, an equal share with my three daus FANNY, NANCY & ANN SHERWOOD

Exrs: Wife RACHEL SHERWOOD, Roger Layton
Wits: A. West, John Macy, Henry Macy
Codicil 22 Feb 1834 - Dau FANNY has married BRANTLEY YORK; they have dau RACHEL YORK
Wife RACHEL SHERWOOD surrenders her right as executrix and Frederick Fentriss, Esqr is appointed by the Court

C:0764 - GEORGE NICKS - 2 Mar 1838 - Prb Aug 1838
Wife ELIZABETH - during her natural life in lieu of dower - land on which we live devised to me by my father, her choice of household furniture & stock, riding carriage, 5 negroes: Susan, Siller, Milton, William & Rachel, $500; at her decease, to be disposed of in the following manner:
Ch of son JOHN : ELIZABETH & JOHN - negro girl Clarisa, negro boy Nelson
Ch of dec'd dau SARAH GIBSON: ELIZABETH RICHARDSON, ANDREW GIBSON, JAMES A. GIBSON, ALFRED GIBSON, ADALINE GIBSON & JOHN GIBSON - slave Julia
Ch of dau MARGARET : QUINTON N. DAVIE, ASHBURN DAVIE, JOHN C. DAVIE, ELIZABETH DAVIE, LORTORO? M. DAVIE & ch of GEORGE DAVIE, dec'd - negro girl Jediann, negro boy Madison
Gr son CALVIN N. MCADOO, Trustee for my son GEORGE for tract whereon GEORGE lives, slaves Alfred & Letitha
Ch of son GEORGE: THURESA PRYOR, LUCINDA PRYOR, CALVIN NICKS, MALENDA NICKS, SARAH NICKS, ELIJAH NICKS, ELIZABETH NICKS, GEORGE NICKS, PLEASANT NICKS, LAWRENCE NICKS & PARTHENA NICKS
Dau ELIZABETH MCADOO - negro boy Rufus, $75
Son YARBORG - $5
Dau ANNA PHILLIPS - share of residue of estate
Exrs: 2nd son GEORGE, gr son CALVIN N. MCADOO
Wits: James Denny, John A. Gilmer

C:0765 - TRAVIS JONES, Senr. - 1 Oct 1833 - Prb Aug 1838
Wife PATTY JANE - keep her own estate according to our marriage contract
Son CALEB - fifth of personal estate, negro boy Ewel who is to be set free at age 25; 3 old negroes: Phillip, Willy & Lucy to receive the profits of their own labor; Caleb to see that they not suffer
Son-in-law JAMES J. RAGSDILL & wife FANNY - $1; FANNY - negro girl Eliza who is to be set free at the age of 25
Ch of dau ELIZABETH, w/o WYATT PEOPLES - fifth part divided amongst the ch with ELIZABETH as Guardian to have the interest now & negro woman Alice who is to be set free at age of 25
Son-in-law JOHN W. MEDEARES & wife NANCY - fifth part
Son TRAVIS - fifth part, bed, value of what others have received, negro boy William to be set free at 25, negroes Theoderick & Dick; to divide my tract of land with CALEB
Dau NANCY D. MEDEARES - negro girl Sally to be set free at 25
Exr: Son CALEB JONES
Wits: John Pegram, George Pegram

C:0766 - ADAM SCOTT - 1 May 1837 - Prb Aug 1838
Wife POLLY - tract adj Donnell Scott, Denney Line & Nancy Rankin, negro girl Riah, horse & saddle, plow & gears, etc
Step dau POLLY K. THOM - bed & furniture, side saddle, cow

Son ADAM - field on Richland Creek adj his mother, negro boy Pink, half of residue
Son THOMAS - tract adj son ADAM, half of residue
Dau POLLY DONNELL - negro boy Charles; dau ISABELA HALL - negro girl Harriet; dau LOUISA NEELY - negro girl Suck & offspring
Exrs: Sons WILLIAM D. & JOHN SCOTT
Wits: John Rankin, Tabitha Rankin; Codicil 11 June 1838

C:0767 - ROBERT HATRICK - 6 Apr 1827 - Prb Nov 1838
Wife RACHAEL - home plantation, mare named Fly, $50, negro Jim, choice of cows, beds & furniture, etc for life
Dau BETSEY M. HATRICK - bay horse Jack, 2 cows, 2 beds & furniture, chest on wheels, oven & pots, 2 chairs
Dau SALLY G. HATRICK - mare Cate, $50, 2 beds & furniture, etc
Son SAMUEL - 400 ac bought of John Hicks, sorrell horse, beds
Daus BETSEY M., SALLY G., & IBBY HATRICK & ANNE DONNELL - $700
Dau IBBY HATRICK - gray filly, 2 cows, 2 beds & furniture, use of loom to remain in the loom house, share of books
Exrs: Son SAMUEL HATRICK, Col James Denny
Wits: John Hanner, A. E. Hanner
Peter Adams & George Spruce proved handwriting of Robert Hatrick; John M. Logan, CCC proved signatures of John Hanner & A. E. Hanner, both dead

C:0768 - WILLIAM SMITH - 24 Jan 1839 - Prb Feb 1839
Wife EVALINE - all estate both real & personal
Exr: James Sloane
Wits: David Scott, John A. Gilmer, Esqr

C:0769 - JOHN SCHOOLFIELD - 18 Nov 1838 - Prb Feb 1839
Wife MARY B. - money due estate, bed & furniture, side saddle dw
Dau BETSY A. DEANS, sons JOSEPH, WILLIAM & RANKIN C. - each 25¢
Dau SARAH SCHOOLFIELD - bed & furniture, one wheel & side saddle
Dau JANE SCHOOLFIELD - furniture her gr mother gave her
Son DANIEL - black mare Silver & saddle, bed & furniture, land bought of Joseph Brawley
Son SAMUEL D. - $10
Daus ANSELETTA & MARY B. - each bed & furniture, side saddle, wheel at decease or remarriage of their mother
Exrs: Noah M. Climer, Daniel G. Schoolfield
Wits: Emsley Donnell, Latham Donnell

C:0770 - ELISABETH SHOEMAKER - 29 Apr 1823 - Prb Feb 1839
Elijah Shoemaker, son of Leonard - $30; Caty Shoemaker - $20
Slaves Charlotte & Abnor to be set free - all my land if they care for my sister BARBERY SHOEMAKER
Exr: James Chilcut. Wits: Martin Werick, Daniel Werick

C:0771 - CATHERINE VANSTORE - 6 June 1838 - Prb Feb 1839
My gr ch: NANCY, CATHERINE, JAMES, ALBERT, LOUISA, SUSANNAH BIVINGS - share $300
Son JOHN - remainder of property & negroes
Exr: Son JOHN VANSTORE
Wits: Noah M. Climer, Martha Bransmark

C:0772 - JESSE EVANS - 1 Sept 1829 - Prb Feb 1839

Wife DEBORAH - estate as long as she remains the widow of my body
Ch: MARY JESSOP, sons DAVID, JESSE, CALVIN & WILLIAM; also gr dau LOUISA EVANS - each $2
Son JONATHAN P. - all property at death or remarriage of wife
Exrs: Deborah Evans & David Evans
Wits: John Hoskins, Joseph Hoskins

C:0773 - ROBERT THOMPSON - 29 July 1839 - Prb Feb 1839
All lands in county & middle Tenn on Duck River in Maury Co & other property to be sold
Dau LEVINA COFFEE - $800, old mare & colt named Bond
Dau LETTY LEVERTON - $800. Gr dau ZILPHA COFFEY - $50
Dau LEVINA COFFEY - all my bacon for boarding Jackson Lethco; he to have cloth in loom to make him some clothes
Henry Coffey - wheat on hand, rents owed me for corn & fodder
Dau REBECCA GULLET - $25
Gr ch: WILLIAM MCQUISTON, MOSES MCQUISTON & ELIZA MCKIMMEY - $25
Sons SAMUEL - $200, mare & colt, his bed; ROBERT - $1; THOMAS - $50
Harvy & Robert Parker - half of corn & fodder raised on the Russell place
Exr: Son THOMAS THOMPSON
Wits: Noah McClimer, R. Davis

C:0774 - DAN MOSELY - 9 Jan 1839 - Prb May 1839
Rebecca Reece - residue of property after debts are paid
Exr: Edmund W. Ogburn. Wits: Reuben Land, Sarah Sharp

C:0775 - NANCY DONNELL - 8 Sept 1834 - Prb May 1839
Friend Sabra Ann Denny, d/o Col James Denny - all personal estate to be peaceably enjoyed by her for life
Exr: Col James Denny. Wits: Wm. Denny, B. F. McLean

C:0776 - MIAL CARTER - 7 Mar 1839 - Prb May 1839
Sister CLOY - use of plantation during her widowhood & then divided among her ch: ALBERT WALKER, ROBERT WALKER, MIAL WALKER, ELIZABETH WALKER & BARFIELD WALKER
Exr: Albert Walker appointed by the Court
Wit: Thomas Wilson

C:0777 - SAMUEL MITCHELL - 26 June 1839 - Prb Aug 1839
Bro JOSEPH - my houses & lots in Greensboro, half of personal estate; sister MARY PERDUE - balance of money & estate
Friend William L. Gilmer - my gold watch
Friend James Hall - 6 months indulgence in paying the interest
Exr: Friend William L. Gilmer
Wits: D. P. Wier, Jno A. Gilmer, Allan Denny

C:0778 - FREDERICH DEAN - 6 Aug 1839 - Prb Aug 1839
Wife LYDIA - all my estate during widowhood except 177 ac to my son JEPTHA
All my ch - be educated as circumstances permit & to share estate at decease or remarriage of my wife
Exr: Son YANCY DEAN, son-in-law JAMES SHAW
Wits: John Draughan, William Withers

C:0779 - JOHN FOSTER - 26 Mar 1838 - Prb Aug 1839
Dau ABIGAIL STANLEY - $50 that my wife wished her dau to have at her death
Son CRATHAM - $400, wagon, farming tools, household furniture
Gr dau ELMIRA FOSTER, d/o JOSHUA - feather bed & furniture
Son JOSHUA - home plantation, my half of the wheat we had tog
Exrs: Son NATHAN FOSTER, friend Daniel Hobs
Wits: Jonathan Parker, Senr.; Stephen Parker, Martha Parker

C:0780 - JOSEPH PYLE of Orange Co.- 17 Oct 1836 - Prb Nov 1839
Bro JAMES - my saddle; mother ELIZABETH SIMPSON - $10
Sister SARAH HUGHS - $10
Bros MASSE, ENOCH, WILLIAM, WILEY, GEORGE & NATHAN - clothes etc
Exr: Nathan Pyle appointed by Court
Wits: William McKeel, A. N. Brannock

C:0781 - THOMAS GREEN - 3 Oct 1839 - Prb Nov 1839
Daus REBECCA HAMILTON & HANNAH MCLEAN - proceeds of sale of stock, wagon, kitchen furniture
Dau HANNAH MCLEAN - negroes Prince & wife Phebe
Exrs: Gr sons DAVID MCLEAN & JOHN MCLEAN
Wits: Soloman Ness, James Underwood

C:0782 - WILLIAM ALBRIGHT - 13 Jan 1839 - Prb Nov 1839
Sons GABRIEL & JOHN - part of my land, one horse each
Ch of dau CATHERINE SHOVER - 75 ac of land
Sons DANIEL, DAVID, JONATHAN, JACOB & HENRY & son-in-law JOHN SHOVER - have following sums of money: DANIEL - $400; DAVID - $383; JONATHAN - $426; JACOB - $241; HENRY - $420; JOHN SHOVER - $324
Exrs: Son GABRIEL ALBRIGHT, Jeremiah Clapp
Wits: W. Corsby who had died by the time of probate, Samuel Nelson

C:0783 - J. HENRY CLAPP - 9 Nov 1839 - Prb Nov 1839
Wife SALLY - south side of plantation dw adj widow Catherine Clapp, household furniture, etc; remaining property to be sold & divided between my ch, the adult ch furnishing inventory of what they received at marriage, considered to be part of their share
Dau BETSY - $50 more; son ELIA - $250 less & son WILLIAM $80 less than the rest
My minor ch - their shares in hands of exr or guardian
Exr: Son SOLOMAN CLAPP who renounced his right: Adm granted to Col Abram Clapp by the Court. Wit: J. H. Crawford

C:0784 - JOSEPH W. SWAIN - 19 Jan 1840 - Prb Feb 1840
Wife HESTER - all property my wife does not wish to retain, including my land in Shelby Co., Indiana to be sold with proceeds purchasing a good piece of land in Guilford Co for my wife dw
Dau ADALINE - to inherit from my wife; exrs to find a good Christian home for her if wife dies or remarries before she is 20 years old
Exrs: Bros OBED L. SWAIN, AMMIEL G. SWAIN
Wits: Job Worth, Susannah Swain

C:0785 - JESSE IVES - 9 Jan 1840 - Prb Feb 1840
Wife MARIAM - mansion house, land whereon I live, negro woman Harriet & her 2 ch Jonas & Barbary, household furniture, etc
Daus DRUSCILLA & ELIZABETH IVES - inherit from wife at death
Son TIMOTHY - $50; dau LYDIA OZMENT - $20; dau MILBERRY QUAIT - $20; dau PEGGY LINTHCUM - $20
My 7 ch: TIMOTHY, ELUKIEL, LYDIA, MILBERRY, PEGGY, DRUSILLA & ELIZABETH - residue of estate
Exr: John Coe. Wits: Roddy E. Hanner, Abner Weatherly

C:0786 - JAMES STEWART - 20 Oct 1835 - Prb Feb 1840
Son MERRILL - tract whereon I live, my wearing apparel
Gr dau ANN STEWART WASSON - $100
Sarah Casey, my present nurse - bed & furniture, wheel & cards
Nancy Casey, d/o Sarah Casey - one bed & furniture
Dau NANCY WASSOM - residue of estate after debts are paid
Exr: Pleasant Hopkins
Wits: James Brannock, Noah W. Climer

C:0787 - JAMES C. MARTIN - 5 Oct 1837 - Prb Feb 1840
Dau ELIZABETH WILSON - house wherein I have resided a number of years, 20 ac of land adj William Beard's line
Other heirs: Alexander Martin, Sarah Shaw, Anna Pope, Polly S. Thomas, John S. Martin; also John Chadwick & Cyrus Chadwick who are entitled to one share as heirs of Cynthia Chadwick - proceeds of sale of land & remaining property
Exr: Jesse Wheeler. Wits: William Beard, Nathan Beard

C:0788 - BARSHEBA FOSTER - 11 Feb 1840 - Prb Feb 1840
Son HUGH & his heirs - whole of my estate; I have but little to give & he has been a dutiful & affectionate child to me
Exr: Son HUGH FOSTER. Wits: James Wright, Jas. T. Morehead

C:0789 - JOHN SMITH - 8 Jan 1840 - Prb Feb 1840
Dau LEVINA - $40 to make her equal with my other 4 ch which has left me, to wit: LYDIA, JESSE, JOHN & BENJAMIN
Wife - all the land & property dw, then property to be sold & divided between all my children
Exrs: Dau LYDIA SMITH, her son JESSE SMITH
Wits: William Gwin, George Loman

C:0790 - HENRY HUMPHREYS of Greensboro - 11 Feb 1840 - Prb May 1840. Wishes to be buried in the Buffalo Grave Yard
My 3 ch: NANCY TATE, ABSOLAM T. (minor) & SARAH LETITHA HUMPHREYS - cotton factory with all machinery, all land & buildings, Cotton Gin House now converted to a Lumber House, my stables, all my negroes, stock & horse wagon, 100 ac purchased of Washington Adams, 55 ac purchased of the widow Forbis - to be kept together as joint stock for the benefit of all three until LETITHA comes of age
Dau NANCY TATE - the family carriage
Dau SARAH LETITHA HUMPHREYS - money for a gold watch
Son-in-law THOMAS R. TATE - $1,000 annually as manager
Exr: Son-in-law THOMAS R. TATE who is directed to sell the house & lot in Greensboro accepted of William Needham & land deeded to me by William Slade in Rutherford Co, N. C. on Broad River

Wits: Jonathan Parker, John A. Gilmer

C:0791 - JEREMIAH PRITCHETT - 20 June 1837 - Prb May 1840
Wife WINEFRED - plantation & dwelling house & as much of the improvements as she thinks proper to support her & the family, negroes Ross & Frank & Jim & Phillis, stock, furniture, dw
Son WILLIAM - land on which he lives, horse & saddle, bed & furniture, negro boy Morris
Dau PENELOPE PRITCHETT - $100, negro woman Esther & her 3 ch: Watt, Tom & Andy; 3 beds & furniture, bed clothing she makes for herself, set of china, wheel, folding leg table, curtains
Son ROBERT - negro boys Andy & Harry, bed & furniture, horse & saddle now in his possession
Son JEREMIAH - negro boy Tom, 2 horses, bed & furniture, saddle now in his possession, negro boy yet to come
Gr ch: MARTHA JANE & ROBERT AGEE, heirs of dec'd dau MARTHA AGEE - negro woman Mary & all her ch which Philip Agee has
Dau WINIFRED AGEE with her husband - negro girl Susan, bed & furniture, mare & saddle in their possession
Son WEBB - half of plantation at death of his mother, negro Frank; at my death, negro named Martin, $100 in lieu of horse
Son JENKINS - half of plantation at death of his mother, negro Jim, clock & case, $100 in lieu of horse, negro boy Doss
WEBB & JENKINS to manage plantation & live with their mother
Dau POLLY DEAN - negro girl Hannah, 2 beds & furniture, bureau, folding leaf table, wheel, side saddle now in her possession
Ch: WILLIAM, ROBERT, JEREMIAH, WEBB, JENKINS, PENELOPE, & POLLY DEAN - residue of estate
Exrs: Sons WEBB & JENKINS PRITCHETT
Wits: Noah M. Climer, John Vanstorie

C:0792 - ANN DIVENNEY - 30 July 1835 - Prb May 1840
Daus HANNAH & JEMIMA DEVENNY - whole of my estate as willed to me by my late husband SAMUEL DIVENNY
Each of my other children - $1
Exr: Robert Julian. Wits: Dobson G. Burrow, Jesse Julian

C:0793 - DAVID GILLIAM - 24 Sept 1839 - Prb May 1840
Wife SUSANNAH - 100 ac where she lives in Orange Co, stock, furn
Daus MARTHA, SARAH & ELIZABETH - 220 ac where I live, my mill; ELIZABETH to have $40 to make her equal with other girls
My other ch: ROBERT, JOSEPH, HENRY, JAMES, WILLIAM & ANNY BUSICK - divide proceeds of sale after decease of wife
Exr: Son ROBERT GILLIAM
Wits: Caleb Busick, F. L. Simpson

C:0794 - DAVID THOMAS - 2 May 1840 - Prb Aug 1840
Wife PEGGY - plantation, adj tract of land, negro Women Judy & Cealy, boys Soloman & Frank, men Archy & Nell, stock dw
Son ROBERT - $200 has been given him; further sum of $150
Son JOHN C. - part of the Christman tract where he lives adj Greensboro Road, Fayette Road, John Coble, John Christman
Dau MILITIA - have given her $150, now give her $250 more
Dau MARGARET CUMMINS? - have given her $125, give her $250 more
Son ANDREW W. - gray horse Charley valued at $100, $300 more
Son DAN M. - gray horse valued at $75 when of age, $325 more

Dau MARY W. THOMAS - negro girl Delie valued at $300, good horse beast & saddle & furniture to make her equal to the other girls, cow & calf when she leaves her mother
Son WILLIAM W. - negro boy Sam valued at $400, good horse beast
Son DAVID B. - negro boy Jerry valued at $400, good horse beast
Dau SARAH JANE THOMAS - negro girl Jin valued at $300, horse beast & saddle, beds & furniture
Exrs: Widow PEGGY THOMAS, bro JOHN W. THOMAS, son ROBERT THOMAS
Wits: L. W. Lemons?, Samuel E. Brackin, Smith? Lambeth

C:0795 - MARGARET GREEN - 18 Mar 1839 - Prb Aug 1840
Son R. J. & daus JANE & MARGARET GREEN - the tract whereon I live; daus to live in mansion house while single
Son G. D. - to inherit plantation at marriage or death of daus, bay horse named Charlie bought of Hiram Cobb, one red cow, one heifer, my bed & furniture, $49
Dau JANE GREEN - bay horse colt, white faced cow, heifer, $448
Dau MARGARET - roan horse Robb, white cow, heifer, bed, $323
Son WILLIAM - 100 ac on Stage Road from High Rock to Greensboro
Exrs: Sons JAMES, WILLIAM & G. D. GREEN
Wits: William G. Webb, Samplett Webb

C:0796 - MATHIAS SWING - No date - Prb Aug 1840
4 youngest ch: LEWIS, SUSAN SWING, JOSHUA CLAPP & his wife MARY & BARBARA SWING - all my land amounting to 386 ac
Son LEWIS - Lot #1 adj heirs of Robert Mebane, dec'd, Samuel Cotner & Adam Hagey
Dau SUSAN SWING - lot #2 adj Lewis, Adam Hagey & #3
Son-in-law JOSHUA CLAPP & dau MARY - lot #3 adj lot #4 & others
Dau BARBARA SWING - lot #4 adj #3, Adam Hagey & Samuel Coble
My 1st ch: dau PENNY, w/o GEORGE FOUST; & dau ELIZABETH, w/o GEORGE STAYLY - $1 each, having given them their share
Exr: Gr son HENRY SWING
Wits: Eli Euless, Joel Swing

C:0797 - JAMES MCNAIRY - 4 Oct 1840 - Prb Nov 1840
Wife ANN - third of land on which I live, dwelling house, out houses & barn, 2 beds & furniture, my saddle horse for life
Sons PHILLIP J. & WILLIAM - other 2/3 of land, all at decease of wife; PHILLIP to live with wife
Son JAMES, in trust for son BOYD - $2,000, interest to be paid to BOYD from time to time as he requires
Dau SARAH BOWMAN - have given her negro woman Judy & her 2 ch: Martha & George; negro boy Will, other advancements amounting in all to $2,730
Dau MARY HUNT - negro woman Amanda & her child Jesse & boy Hamilton, with other gifts amounting to $1,800, $1,850 more
Son JAMES - $500 & what has already been bestowed on him
Proceeds of sale of slaves & other property to be divided in this manner: Sons JOHN - $1,000; PHILLIP - $1,200; BARTLETT YANCY - $1,700; JOHN - $1,700 more; WILLIAM $1,700; remaining to daus SARAH BOWMAN & MARY HUNT
BARTLETT YANCEY & JOHN - be kept in school & college until they graduate and have a good education
Exrs: Son JAMES MCNAIRY, Milton Hunt, John A. Gilmer
Wits: Dr. I. J. M. Lindsay, Thomas Warren

C:0798 - JEMIMA UNTHANK - 3 May 1837 - Prb Nov 1840
Son JOHN - one brass clock
Dau RACHEL COOK - my bed & furniture & quilt
Gr son ALLEN COOK - one box that my husband had for his papers
Gr dau LYDIA UNTHANK, d/o JOHN - bed & furniture, chest
Son JOHN & dau RACHEL COOK - residue of estate
Exrs: Son JOHN UNTHANK, gr son ALLEN COOK
Wits: John Draughon, Abel Knight
Codicil 23 June 1840

C:0799 - ELIZABETH BALDWIN - 15 June 1840 - Prb Nov 1840
Niece ELIZABETH PITTS - bed & furniture
Niece MARTHA PITTS - case of drawers, table, large pewter dish, one rug
Nephew WILLIAM PITTS - one chest
Nephew E. E. PITTS - walnut candle stand
Br-in-law JAMES GALBREATH - note I have on him for $23
Bros JOHN BALDWIN, JESSE BALDWIN, DANIEL BALDWIN - 50¢ each
Sister JANE GILBREATH & her heirs - share residue of estate with above named nieces & nephews
Exr: Bro-in-law JAMES GILBREATH
Wits: John Stuart, Abigail Hubbard

C:0800 - WILLIAM J. ADAMS of Greensboro - 5 Nov 1840 - Prb Nov 1840
Sister MARTHA A. ADAMS - $300
Sisters MARTHA A. ADAMS, ELIZABETH HORNEY & bro GEORGE ADAMS - remainder of my estate
Exr: John M. Logan
Wits: Jesse H. Lindsay, Peter Doak

* * * *
* * * *

The following is an unrecorded will found in a box of old wills in Rockingham County Courthouse in 1957! The first page is damaged; the other pages are quite legible and the spelling almost perfect. It could well have been written by the devisor.

JOSEPH TATE of the County of Guilford in the Province of North Carolina...3 Mar 1772 - Prb Guilford County May Term 1772
Wife ELLY - all that part of the tract I now live on above a south line made from Dan River, negro man named Ned, negro woman...(torn), negro woman named Hannah...(torn)...Philadelphia mare, side sad...(torn)...set of plow irons and giers
Dau...*torn) ...Perkins - negro woman named...(torn)
Gr son ALEXANDER JOYCE - 40 pounds currency in small yearly payments as shall be required for clothing and schooling
Dau FRANCES RALSTON - negro man Tom
Dau ELIZABETH ROBERTSON - negro named Bob, all that tract of land on both side Rock House Cr adj Charles Mitchell, two bonds for 10 pounds each on James & William Cotton
Dau MARGARET JOYCE - 350 ac in the fork of the Mayo & Dan Rivers where she now lives, use of negro girl Aggie
Son ADAM - land on west side of Dan River & the adj tract of 350 ac on both side of the river, negro man Dickey, negro

woman Jinny, strawberry roan gelding, set of plow irons & giers
Son JOHN - 300 ac tract on east side of Dan River called Mulberry Island, 700 ac adj the same, negro boy Tinker, alias Ned; boy named Peter, man named Will--the same in dispute between Valentine Allen & myself and you are to defend this property at the cost of my estate; bay stallion named Spedillah, gray gelding called Collins, pair of plow irons
Son JOSEPH - 1,000 ac where I live, negro named Bill, boy named Charles, black gelding with a blaze face colt called English colt, plow irons & giers, saddle & bridle, wagon & giers
Dau SARAH TATE - tract on the Great Cr of the waters of the Dan on west side in Surry Co, negro woman Nan, young boldegle mare, side saddle & bridle, two cows & calves
Dau RACHEL TATE - tract on Peters C of the waters of the Dan on east side in Surry Co, negro child Humphrey, three year old colt, side saddle & bridle, two cows & calves
Daus SARAH & RACHEL - tract on east side of Dan River adj the land William Campbell bought of me
To Exrs - 490 ac tract on east side of Dan River called Lad's old place to be sold for paying debts; also bonds on Darby Callahan, Jr; William Campbell, James Presnall, Sr
Ch: ADAM, JOHN, JOSEPH, SARAH & RACHEL - residue after debts
Exrs: Sons ADAM, JOHN, & JOSEPH TATE
Trustees: Alexander Martin, Philemon Deatherage
Wits: Alexander Joyce, Robert Rallston, Samuel Hunter, Constant Perkins, Phil. Deatherage

Note: Thomas Henderson was the first Clerk of Court in Guilford County; then became the first Clerk of Court of Rockingham County when it was formed from Guilford 29 Dec 1785, with the first Court held in Feb of 1786 at the home of Adam Tate.

Since records show Joseph Tate's sons Joseph & John had died before 1785 (apparently intestate and without issue), perhaps one can theorize that the estate was not settled in 1785 and that Thomas Henderson brought the will to Rockingham County. Most of the land involved is in Rockingham County, some being in Stokes County which had not been formed from Surry when the will was written.

MORE ABOUT THE WILL OF JOHN HUNTER, page 25

John Hunter's daughter, Ally Tate, was the same person as Joseph Tate's wife, Elly Tate.

It was known that Alexander and James Martin were nephews of John Hunter and that their mother was Jane Martin. Yet the recorded will of John Hunter named "Sister Jane Markin". A copy of the original will was secured from the Division of Archives & Records in Raleigh and this clearly showed the name to be Jane Martin. This change was made for this volume; however, the names of the slaves are from the recorded will, whereas, some of the names of the slaves differ from those in original will.

GUILFORD COUNTY UNRECORDED WILLS

As found at N. C. Dept. of Cultural Resources
Division of Archives & History
Archives & Records Section
109 East Jones Street
Raleigh, N. C. 27611

Box Number
C. R. 46.801.1 - 1

Testator	Year Probated
Albright, Gabriel	1886
Anthony, Mary	1881
*Beard, Reuben	1841
*Beard, William	1839
*Bevill, Hezekiah	1828
Black, Henry	1881
Brittian, J. M.	1887
Brittain, Joseph	
*Causey, Zebulon	1809
Chichester, John D.	1884
Clapp, Joshua	1884
*Coble, Peter	1816
*Cole, Robert	1816
*Cook, John	1821
*Cook, Margaret	1817
Cooper, Nathan M.	1925
*Coots, James	1820
*Cowin, Elias	1816
&Cummins, Rachel	1816
*Dick, John W.	1822
*Donnell, Robert	1816
*Forbis, Hugh	1816
Gardner, Lydia J.	1900
*Garringer, Andrew	1829
Gibsen, Yancy	1880
Gilham, Sally	1878
Gilmer, Robert	
Gorrell, Parish	1903
*Gossett, Abraham	1822
Graves, David	1870

Box Number
C. R. 801.1 - 2

Testator	Year Probated
*Hamilton, John	1819
*Hardiman, John-Dated	1774
*Harris, Joel	1824
Harris, Peter	1868
*Huffman, Heartwell	1833
Howard, Robert	1893
Ingold, Soloman	1882
Johnson, Joseph	1859
Lane, Isaac	1853
Lindsay, Hiram	1903
*Macy, Henry	1816
Maxwell, James V.	1883
McIver, Mary	1869
*McMichael, Archibald	1818
*McMichael, Charity	1829
McNeely, Lucinda	1900
*Mendenhall, William	1829
Moderwell, Libby	1884
Nelson, Samuel	1870
*Ogburn, William	1828
Parker, W. M.	1903
*Peeples, Lucy	1825
*Perkins, John	1825
Phibbs, William	1871
Popplein, Nicholas	1884
Popplein, Susanna	1884
Rankin, Mary	1897
Raper, Robert C.	1872
Ross, L. G.	1877
Stanley, Abigail H.	1860
*Stanley, Joseph	1840
Thacker, James M.	1856
*Trotter, Josiah	1792
*Weatherley, Isaiah	1818
Wharton, Elisha	1860
*Wilson, Robert	1833
*Wilson, Robert	1821
@Witty, Elijah	1844
Wright, A. S.	1903

*Denotes will abstracted in this volume.

@ This will was recorded in Rockingham County and a copy sent to Guilford County--perhaps for settlement of estate

REUBEN BEARD - 14 Nov 1840 - Prb May 1841
Dau MARY - one good side saddle or its equivalent in value
Dau AGNESS - remainder of estate both real & personal
Rest of my ch - have had their equitable portion
Exrs: Friends Richard B. Armfield, Andrew Lindsay
Wits: Richard Mendenhall, Caleb Beals

WILLIAM BEARD - 13 Oct 1839 -
Son NATHAN - 100 ac of home tract, all my wagon & smith tools
Wife POLLY - use of lands, money, man, stocks & furniture dw
Dau PHEBE WHEELER - $50, making her equal with rest of the ch
Dau RUTH - $100, making her equal with the rest of the ch
Daus LYDIA STANLEY, MARTHA HILL, RACHEL BUNDY, RUTH BEARD & PHEBE WHEELER - each $30
Exrs: Son NATHAN BEARD, wife POLLY BEARD
Wits: Joseph Coffin, L. G. Coffin
18 Nov 1839 - Cyrus P. Mendenhall empowered by the following to contest the will: Polly Beard, Martha Hill, Joseph H. Bundy, William Stanley, Manlove M. Wheeler & William Wheeler

HEZEKIAH BEVIL - 14 Aug 1827 - Prb Aug 1828
Son THOMAS - $20; son ALEXANDER - $100; dau LUCY BEVIL - $50; and dau DOLLY TOMLINSTON - $20
Son PHILIP BEVIL - 281 ac whereon I live, negroes Peter, Moses & Hannah, carpentry & coopers tools, blacksmith tools, still
Exr: Son PHILLIP BEVIL. Wit: Robert H. Dalton

ZEBULON CAUSEY - 13 Mar 1809 - Prb May 1809
Wife DIANER - house, plentiful maintenance, household furniture, sorrel horse called Bret, cow & calf, ewe, sow & pigs
Son ZEBULON - plantation at decease or remarriage of my wife
Sons JOHN & SOLOMAN, dau PEGGY TUCKER - balance of stock & household furniture
Gr dau PEGGY CAUSEY - ten pounds of good new goose feathers
Exr: Son ZEBULON CAUSEY
Wits: Hugh Sherwood, William Fitzgerald

PETER COBLE - 8 Dec 1815 - Prb May 1816
Wife ELIZABETH - all my lands & moveable property except negro Augustine, smith tools & still be sold and divided:
Dau MARY - $100, bed & bedstead she calls hers
Son PETER - $100, colt got by horse called Prospect
Youngest daus SALLY & NELLY - each $100 & enough cash or property to make them equal with those of my ch who have married
All my ch - share in proceeds of sale of estate after death or remarriage of my wife
Son DAVID'S ch: SALLY & DAVID - to have same share that DAVID would have if living
Exrs: Andrew Shatterly & John Black appointed by the Court
Wits: Richard Proctor, Andrew Shatterly

ROBERT COLE - 5 Mar 1813 - Prb Mar 1816
Clarisy McCain, formerly Clarisy Beavil, now w/o William McCain - negro boy 6 or 7 years old named Onder, cow & calf, loom & other property I have given her

Wife DICY COAL - choice of my two stills, all the still tubs, two horse creatures, yoke of oxen, monies from sale of cattle & horses, all of estate
Son JAMES - to inherit at death of my wife
Exrs: Wife DICY COLE, son JAMES COLE
Wits: Hance McCain, William Bevill, James Tomlinson

JOHN COOK - Noncupative Will-9 Aug 1820 - Prb May 1821
Wife DEANNAR - all my estate; at her death:
Son WILLIAM - my land
Daus living at home: NANCY DELILA, DEANNER & JINNA - my property if they take care of WILLIAM
Rest of my ch that is married & left me - have received theirs
Wits: William Neal, John Potter

MARGARET COOK - Noncupative Will - 13 Jan 1817
Rebecca Davey - teakettle, 6 pewter plates, coffee pot, 1 sheet
David Stack - large pot & dutch oven
Isaac Anderson - her bed
Wit: Richard Ozment as certified to James Millis, JP

JAMES COOTS - 27 July 1816 - Prb May 1820
Wife MARY - use of plantation, furniture, negro girl Heger, horse
Gr son JOHN SPENS - negro boy Jo
Eldest dau JINY DILLING - negro girl Elsy
3rd dau LEVINA EYDOLOT - $50
Gr dau MINERVY EYDLOT - negro boy Perry at wife's death
My 5 gr ch: JOHN SPENS, ELVES SPENS, WILLIAM SPENS, BETTY SPENS & MINERVY EYDLOT - money left after debts; their share to be put on interest til they come of age
Exr: Wife MARY COOTS. No witnesses

ELIAS COWEN - 25 Apr 1816 - Prb May 1816
Wife SARAH - shall have her home here if she sees cause to stay & what she brought with her, what has been made since to be divided between her & my dau BETSY
Son ELIAS - my lands by paying the girls $50, use of barn
Dau BETSY - one brown cow & calf, bed and saddle
Son ELISHA - one bed that I left with him
Exrs: Son ELIAS COEN, Samuel Jones
Wits: James Gilbreath, Soloman Turner

RACHEL CUMMINS - 8 Nov 1815 - Prb Feb 1816
Sister MARY ANN CUMMINGS - east end of my land adj Shatrach Lofting & Samuel Cummins, household furniture, cow & calf
Niece MARY AN MCKNIGHT - my other cow
Niece RACHEL MCCALEY - my bed & furniture
Nephews JOHN & JAMES MCCALEY - remainder of land
Bro-in-law WILLIAM MCKNIGHT - negro boy Austin
Exrs: Elisha Wharton, Esqr., William Denton, Esqr.
Wit: James Denny

JOHN W. DICK - 14 July 1822 - Prb Nov 1822
Wife MARTHA W. - all my estate both real & personal
Wits: Robert Thurmon, Lewis Graves, Swepston Wilson

GUILFORD COUNTY, N. C. WILL ABSTRACTS
Unrecorded Wills

ROBERT DONNELL - 22 Sept 1806 - Prb May 1816
Wife ELIZABETH - horse & saddle, her living off the land dw household furniture, bed & furniture, cow
Son EDMUND - tract where I live with a part of tract where son-in-law ELIHU lives on north side Brushy Branch near Andrew Donnell; also my smith tools, wagon & geers, tools, stock
Dau MARY JEAN & son THOMAS - each $5
Exrs: Wife ELIZABETH DONNELL, son EDMUND DONNELL
Wits: Latham Donnell, Thomas Donnell

HUGH FORBUS - 4 Apr 1816 - Prb May 1816
Wife ELIZABETH - 124 ac tract whereon I live, mare named Nell, wagon, smith tools for her and the use of the ch at home, 5 horse beasts for use on plantation, cattle & hogs, furniture
My 4 youngest sons: ELI, DAVID, ABNER & ROBERT - to inherit from wife, and plantation bought of Hendrix
Son JOHN - 150 ac tract on waters of Big Alamance
Daus MARY WILEY, NANCY & ANN FORBIS - each $15 by John, 120 ac on waters of Buffaloe near Wilson's Mill
Son RALPH - 120 ac tract on waters of Buffalo
Exrs: Andrew McGee, John Coe
Wits: Soloman Linthecum, Caty Gilbreath

ANDREW GARRINGER - 15 Nov 1828 - Prb May 1829
Wife AGNESS - $1,000 in silver, plantation, choice of the grown negroes & the small girl named Easther, part of household furniture, tools, stock, all the sugar & coffee on hand, barrel of peach brandy, wool, cotton, flax, etc
Son HENRY - that part of the plantation whereon he lives
Son ANDREW - 490 ac plantation on which he lives
Son JOHN - 233 ac plantation on which he lives
Sons BOSTON & PETER - plantations on which they live
Dau JANE - $150, negro girl Hannah
Dau PEGGY'S 3 ch - the same as PEGGY would get - $150, negro woman Rachel
Dau BETSY - $150, negro girl Alce
Dau BARBRA - $150, negro boy Leven
My negroes Poll & Sam to be sold together
Exrs: Sons PETER & HENRY GARRINGER
Wits: Elisha Wharton, William Rankin

ABRAHAM GOSSETT - 19 Sept 1821 - Prb Nov 1829 - Date on outside of folded will has the probate as Nov 1822
Wife ELIZABETH - 4 cows, all my sheep, one mare, household furniture, loom, spinning wheels, farming utensils, full privilege of all my plantations; my negroes I lend her till youngest son ABRAHAM becomes 21; negro man Isaiah, mulatta woman pat, negro woman Judah
Sons WILLIAM JOHN O. (silver watch) & ABRAHAM - all my lands at decease or marriage of my wife
Daus SUSANNAH & ELEANOR GOSSETT - negro girls Tamar & Tiller
Dau JEAN GOSSETT - negro boy Steve
Gr ch: ABRAHAM GOSSETT, MINERVE, ELIZABETH & ISAAC POTTER - each $100 as they become 21
Son-in-law ISAAC POTTER - $10

Dau SUSANNAH - sorrel mare & saddle that she claims as hers
Dau JEAN - my gray horse & saddle she claims as hers
Dau ELEANOR - $40 & one new saddle
Son ABRAHAM - my rifle gun & saddle, large Bible
Son WILLIAM JOHN O. - 2 vols of Wood & Walker & Whatley? Sermons, & his school books
Daus JEAN & ELEANOR GOSSETT - to have enough to make them equal with dau ANN when she married Isaac Potter
My ch - legacy left them by their grandfather JAMES COLLETT
Exrs: Ezekiel Collett, sons WILLIAM JOHN O. & ABRAHAM GOSSETT
Wits: None. Proved by John Clark, Joash Reynolds, John Gossett, George Parsons, Henry Walton & William John O. Gossett

JOHN HAMILTON - 14 Oct 1818 - Prb Nov 1819
Ch of dau MARY & JAMES MCNAIRY: JOHN H., BOYD, JAMES & AMANDA - each $250 to be paid with interest as they become 21
Daus of dau SARAH DAVIS: HARRIET H. & BETSY ANN - my buffet with all its usual contents
Gr son HAMILTON DAVIS - my riding horse, saddle & bridle
Gr son NATHANIEL DAVIS - my printed books, mare he calls his
Gr son JOHN H. DAVIS - my sword with all my milleterry dress
Gr gr son JOHN H. DICKSON, s/o JOSEPH DICKSON - $50
Gr gr dau BETSY H. DICKSON, dau of DAVID DICKSON - $50
Daus ANN MCNAIRY & SARAH DAVIS - my bonds & proceeds of sale
Exrs: Friends Hance McCain, Senr., William Ryan
Wits: Robert Lindsay, William McCain, Robert Burney

JOHN HARDEMAN - 29 Aug 1774 - No probate date
Son THOMAS - a negro woman & (marked through and not completed)
Wife DORITY - estate both real & personal dw
Ch: ESTER, ELIZABETH, JUDITH, DORITY, JANE, JOHN, EDDY, SUSANNAH - estate to be equally divided after decease or marriage of wife; ESTER'S to be for her lifetime and then heirs
Exrs: Wife DORITY HARDEMAN, Peter Perkins
Wits: Robert Crockett, Salley Crockett, Elizabeth Bostick

JOEL HARRIS - 16 May 1822 - Prb Feb 1824
Wife MARGERY - whole estate as long as she remains my widow
Son HARMON - horse & saddle valued at $100, bed & furn at 19
Dau ELIZABETH BARHAM - bed & furniture at 18
Son MARTIN - horse & saddle worth $100, bed & furniture at 18
Dau CHARITY HARRIS - feather bed & furniture at 18
Son ARTHUR - horse & saddle, bed & furniture at 18
Son JOEL - horse & saddle, bed & furniture at 19
Dau HESTER HARRIS - feather bed & furniture at 18
Older ch at decease of wife - CHARLES B. - $50; SARAH MIDDLETON - $50; HOWEL - $100; LUCY WARREN - $50; & dau AVIS CASE - $100
Minor ch: HARMON, ELIZABETH BARHAM, MARTIN, CHARITY, ARTHUR, JOEL & HESTER - to draw for negroes: Simon, Stephen, Charlot, Adam, Philip, Moses, David & Abraham - also proceeds of sale at decease or remarriage of wife, including sale of land in Rockingham County, to be equally divided
Gr dau ALTHANA HARRIS - $100. Son WILLIAMS ch - $100
Exrs: Nathan Canaday, Howel Harris, Nathan Barham
Wits: William Canady, Charles C. Kellam

GUILFORD COUNTY, N. C. WILL ABSTRACTS
Unrecorded Wills

HARTWELL HUFFMAN - 28 May 1833 - Prb Aug 1833
Wife ELIZABETH - use of all estate dw until my children become of age, provided they have benefit of an education
Exr: Bro JOSHUA CLAPP
Wits: George Huffman, Daniel Brown

ARCHIBALD MCMICHEAL - 23 Sept 1818 - Prb Nov 1818
Wife CHARITY (spelled CHARATEE in will) - all my property both real & personal during life & to be disposed of at her death as she may think proper
Exr: Wife CHAROTEE MCMICHEAL
Wits: Edward Lloyd, James McNairy

CHARITY MCMICHAL - 20 Aug ____ - Prb May 1829
Dau MARGET MCMURREY - beds, household furniture, desk, book case
Gr dau CHARITY MCMURREY - buffet, clock at her mother's death
Genny McMurrey - the old riding chair
Son WILLIAM - my big Bible
Peegy (Peggy?) McMurrey - the money
No exr or wit. James McNairy & Edward Lloyd testified in Court that the will was the handwriting of Charity McMicheal, dec'd. William McMurry was appointed by the Court as Adm.

HENRY MACY - 2 Aug 1812 - Prb May 1816
Wife ELIZABETH - my two East rooms, household furniture, good maintenance provided by my two sons HENRY & THOMAS, including the yearly payment by her son AARON COFFIN
Sons HENRY & THOMAS - all my land; THOMAS to have the homestead
Daus: SARAH ANTHONY, LOUE DAVID, DEBORAH SWAIN & MARY JENKINS - each a sixth part of household furniture at wife's decease
Gr son HENRY SWAIN, s/o dau SUSANNAH SWAIN, dec'd - sixth part
Heirs of dec'd dau PHEBE LEONARD - sixth part
Heirs of dec'd son JOSEPH - third of remainder of estate, along with HENRY & THOMAS MACY
Gr dau SARAH MACY, d/o HENRY - my case of drawers
Exrs: Henry & Thomas Macy
Wits: Jonathan Parker, Henry Davis

WILLIAM MENDENHALL - An oral will presented in Court during May Term 1829 by Asabel (Isabel?) and Nancy Mendenhall who deposed that William Mendenhall had departed this life the 26th of March last at the home of his father, Seth Mendenhall where he had been residing about four weeks and during his sickness had made the following will:
His Father & Mother - to keep his three children and raise and educate them; his father to take what property he had to use for his three children except the interest he had in a saw mill on a branch of Wharre in Randolph Co which was to be sold and put on interest for his children

WILLIAM OGBURN - 14 Oct 1824 - Prb Feb 1828
Son WILKINS - $200
Dau NANCY WATSON - negro woman Fanny & her increase to her & her heirs if any; if not, an equal division between Claboun & Nancy; at her death her part to return back to the old stock;

also 100 ac in Rockingham adj Johnson, John Shelton
Son NICHOLAS - negro boy Lige - residue of the Rockingham Co tract, also tract where he now resides, also tract adj his residence known as the Heath Tract, & part of tract where I reside
All the above property is divised to make the shares of these children equal to the property I have heretofore given my other sons & daus
Heirs of son WILLIAM, dec'd: PRICILLY DONNELL, CHARLES P. OGBURN & EDMOND OGBURN - their father's share in the residue of estate with all my children
Exrs: Son NICHOLAS OGBURN & William Doak
Wit: William Blair

LUCY PEEPLES - 13 Feb 1823 - Prb Aug 1825
Gr son ALPHAR MOORE - $200, my best feather bed & furniture my clock & case, folding table & one cow & calf
Dau ELIZABETH MOORE & her sons & daus; dau POLLY PEEPLES & her sons & daus; & dau SEBEY BOMAN & her sons & daus - proceeds of sale of remainder of property
Exrs: John Moore & James Peeples
Wits: Nathan Canaday, Albena Jonson

JOHN PERKINS - 9 July 1823 - Prb Nov 1825
Only son NEWTON - all my lands & tenements, choice horse, my half of the wagon belonging to me & Shadrack Stanley, farming utensils, cow & calf, sow & pig, third of sheep
Wife DINA - household furniture & ample maintenance from the land during widowhood
Married daus: ANNA DRAUGHON, LAVINNA STANLEY, POLLY WHICKER - each $1; & to BENA LANCASTER - cow & calf which makes their advancement nearly equal
Single daus: BETSY, SARAH & MATILDA PERKINS - each one good horse & saddle, bed & furniture, cow & calf, sow & pig which makes them equal to what married daus have received
Youngest dau PATTY PERKINS - good horse & saddle
Son-in-law JOHN WHICKER - deed to land promised him
Exrs: Bro JARED PERKINS, Moses Mendenhall
Wits: Thomas Thornburg, Gared Perkins

Attached to will above was the following:
"We the heirs and legatees of John Perkins acknowledge this an equal and Just will and we are well satisfied and agreed to all and every devise, therefore are and will remain content therewith. Witness our hands & seals this the 9th of July 1823

Witnesses present:	Signed:
Gared Perkins	Jno Draughn
Thomas Thornburg	Shadrach Stanley
Moses Mendenhall	John Whickear
	Caroline Matilda Perkins
	Sarah x Perkins
	Newton Perkins
	Martha Perkins
	Benjamin Lancaster

GUILFORD COUNTY, N. C. WILL ABSTRACTS
Unrecorded Wills

JOSEPH STANLEY - 24 July 1832 - Prb Nov 1840
Wife PHEBE - all my estate both real & personal dw
Dau MARY - if unmarried at wife's decease or marriage, the profits of the field on southside of land and the orchard field & use of the large room of new part of my house, but at her marriage or decease, the same to be returned to my estate
All my ch - division of remainder at decease or marriage
Exrs: Wife PHEBE STANLEY, son WILLIAM STANLEY
Wit: Jeremiah Hubburd

JOSIAH TROTTER - 25 Feb 1792 - Prb May 1792
Nov Term of Court 1816, Benjamin Trotter, on order issued at last court, came in and qualified as executor
Wife JANE - 300 ac plantation, household goods, stock, negro woman Nancy Beck & girl Nancy Alse, during widowhood
My five daus: NANCY, RACHEL, JANE, BETSY & MARY - household goods, cows, sheep & hogs at wife's decease or marriage
Dau BETSEY - negro woman Beck at wife's decease by paying one fifth of appraisal to her sisters
Dau HANNAH CRANNOR - negro Nancy Alce at decease of wife
Youngest sons JOSEPH, EDWARD & OLDOM - plantation, 100 ac each
Son EPHARIM - 150 ac where he lives on waters of S Buffalo
Son BENJAMIN - 150 ac on waters of S Buffalow I bought from Benjamin Thompson
Son GEORGE - 100 ac on the Rocky Branch adj my line, Frances Cummins & the New Garden Road
Exr: Son BENJAMIN TROTTER
Wits: Benja Thompson, John Hignutt

ISAIAH WEATHERLY - 5 Sept 1817? - Prb Aug 1818
(This will faded and illegible in areas.)
Daus REBECCA _______ & PEGGY _______ - each five shillings
Son ISAIAH - tract of land he now lives on; if he dies without heirs, land to be divided between sons ABNER & WILLIAM
Dau POLLY _______ - the sum of five shillings
Dau LENA WEATHERLY - (too dim to read)
Dau BETSY WEATHERLY - the sum of four dollars
Dau RACHEL LOVETT - sum of five shillings
Son ISAAC - the two tracts of land he now has
Son HENRY - tract of land I purchased from Vincent Russum, also negro boy Eli
Son ABNER - tract purchased of Dennis ______, $200, bed & furn
Son WILLIAM - all remaining part of lands & tenements, 2 beds & furniture, $50, also half my smith tools
Dau ANY WEATHERLY - sum of sixty dollars in cash
Wife NANCY - dw or until WILLIAM becomes of age - negro man Bob; also feather bed & furniture, 2 milch cows, team of horses, & farming tools
Ch: ISAIAH, HENRY, ABNER, WILLIAM, BETSY WEATHERLY, LENA WEATHERLY, RACHEL LOVETT & ANA WEATHERLY - residue of estate
Exrs: Sons ISAAC & HENRY WEATHERLY
Wits: William C. Chapman, Thomas Ozment, William Maben

ROBERT WILSON - 13 May 1821 - Prb Aug 1821
Wife SARAH - all the stock, household furniture, farming tools,

during her life to be hers as she pleases after debts are paid
My two ch DAVID & NANCY WILSON - two notes - one $35 & the other $5 on Samuel Guyer in Washington Co., Indiana in the hands of Nicholas Hubbard
Exrs: Wife SARAH WILSON, NATHAN JOHNSON
Wits: John Davis, James Henderson

ROBERT WILSON - 4 Dec 1833 - Probate not dated
Bro BENJAMIN - sum of $8
Nephew WILLIAM GREEN - $24
Nephews & nieces: JAMES GREEN, WILLIAM GREEN, GEORGE GREEN, MARY GREEN, JANE GREEN & MARGARET GREEN - balance of estate
Exr: Nephew WILLIAM GREEN
Wits: Joseph Jackson, Joshua Gladson
Proven in Court by the oaths of John Green, William Pritchett, & John Starrett who testified to the signatures of Joseph Jackson & Joshua Gladson who had both left the state and Joseph Jackson was believed to be dead.

INDEX OF NAMES

Each name may have several phonetic spellings. Names such as Wright may be spelled as Right. In a few cases various spellings may be grouped, but most of the time they are not.

*Before a page number denotes a will on that page by that person. Index does not give number of times that the name appears on the page.

ADAMS, Benjamin 122; George 122,141; John 108; Martha 122; Martha A. 141; Peter 122,135; Washington 138; William J. 115,*122; William J. 122,*141

ADEAR, Catherine 1; Charles *1; Elizabeth 1; Elliner 1; Ester 1; James 1; Jane 1; John 1; Margaret 1; Mary 1; Sarah 1; William 1

ADES, John 6

ALBERTSON, Phinibas 30,70, 76

ALBRIGHT, Christina 9; Daniel 84,137; David 137; Gabriel 137,143; George 129; Henry 98,137; Jacob 137; John 137; Jonathan 137; Phillip 9; William *137

AGEE, Martha 139; Martha J. 139; Philip 139; Robert 139; Winifred 139

AGNEW, Robert 33

AKIN, AKEN, Jean 115; John E. 117; Prudence 117; William *2

ALCORN, John 17

ALEXANDER, Agness 33; George 2; John 17; Joseph *1,34; Martha 1,2; Mary 113; Nancy 113; William 113

ALLEN, Ann 2; Benjamin 2, 133; Daniel 2; Keziah 2; Mary 2; John Sr. *2; Joseph 2,106; Jemima 2; Valentine 142

ALLISON, Ann 1; Arther 80; Elizabeth 1,80; Isaiah 1; Jain 1; John 1,80; Martha *1; Mary 1; Samuel 1,45,*80

ALTON, James 42

AMICK, Cathering 72; Philip 72

ANDERSON, Ann 102; Isaac 2, 145; Jean 38; James *2; Mary 97; John 2,13,20; Robert 17; Sarah 2,23; William 2,102

ANDREW(S), Benit 2; Jeremiah *2; Louisa 128; Mary 2;

ANDREW(S) cont'd.: Sealey 86; Shadrack 86

ANTHONY, Charlotte 1; Clary 126; Henry *76; Jonathan 1,99; Judah 1; Lydia 1; Mary 1,143; Merat 1; Obed 1,*126; Phebe 1,40; Ruth 1; Sarah 148; Sinthy 75; William 13,76

APPLE, Elizabeth R. 132; John 91,128; Peter 132

ARCHER, Abel 125; Catherine 1; David 1,*124,125; Elizabeth 125; Francis 125; James *1,125; John 1; John Jr. 125; Mary 125; Sarah 1,124; Sarah Ann 125; Thomas 1; Washington D. 125; William 125

ARMFIELD, Alfred 131; Ann 1; David 2,78,79; Elizabeth 1,131; Isaac *1,33, 131; Jacob 1,131; Jane 131; Joab 131; Jonathan *1,119; John 1,17,33,91; Joseph 1,12; Lydia 2; Mary 17; N. 101,111; Nathan 1,2,21,33,83,90,126; Richard B. 144; Robert 131; Sarah 1; Solomon 1,2; William 1,2,21,31, 33,44,53,63,88,101,102, *131; William N. 131; William Sr. *2

ARNETT, Isabel 21

ARTER, William 126

ASHLEY, Mary 46

ATKINS, Jane 114; Sarah 85

AVERY, Waightstill 33

AYDELETT, Eyedlett, Idolet Benjamin *2; David 72; Leven 2; Lucy 2; Martha 72; Mary 13,86; Minervy 145; Obed 60,69; Parker 2; Levina 145; Polly 58; Sarah 2; Shadrach 2; Tabithy 2

AYERS, Gallant 40

AYNERS, Andrew 97

BAILEY, Elizabeth 39

BAIN, Amis 131

BAINES, Sophia 7
BAITLEY, Robert 115
BALDEN, Margret 38
BALDLY, Elijah 6
BALDWIN, Daniel 5,6,10,43,92, 141; Elizabeth 6,28,92, *141; Jane 6,92; Jemima 92; Jesse 6,92,141; John 6,*92,141; Sarah 6; Uriah 5; William *6
BALLARD. Jane 115; Mary 82: Nathan 82; Philip 95; Priscilla 76; Thomas 82: William 22,*82
BALLENGER, Hannah 62; Nancy 45; Rebecca 108
BANNER. Mrs. Polly 60
BARHAM, Benjamin 13; Charles 13: Elizabeth 147; James 27; Nathan 13,147
BARNARD, Benjamin *3; Elihu 100; Elisha 3: Elizabeth 8; Eunice 3,100; Frederich 3, 105; Goram 100; Judah 105; Liben 3: Lebni 76,80,*100; Lyda 3; Mary 3; Matilda 3; Reubin 100; Shubal 3; Timothy 3
BARNES, Elizabeth 6; Jesse 6; John *6
BARNETT. Anne 3; Elizabeth 3; Jean *6; John *3,92,100; Joseph 3; Margaret 3; William 3
BARNEY, Adam 91; David 91; John 91; Jonas 91; Josiah 91; Lydia 93; Mary 91; Odell 91; Rebecca 91; Robert 91: Samuel 91: William *91
BARNHEART, Henry Jr. 89; Henry Sr. 89
BARNHILL, Sarah 3: William *3
BARR, Rev'd. David 55
BARRIETT. Joseph D. 34
BARROW, Mary 75
BARTLETT, C. B. *86
BARTLEY, John 116; Rachel 29
BARNUM, James 16
BARUCH, William 17
BASS, Ann 15
BAYS, Nancy 96; Thomas 95,96
BEACH, Sarah 7
BEALS, Ann 3; Anna 85; Caleb 3.76,85.87.144; Eleazar 3, 85; Jesse *3: John *3,16, 34,76,85; John Jr. 26; Susannah 3,34; William 3
BEALES see BEALS
BEARD, Agness 144; Benjamin 4; David 4,130; George 98; John 83,95; Levina 4; Lydia 4; Margaret 33,113; Mary 144;
BEARD cont'd. Nathan 138,144; Paul 31; Polly 144; Rachel 4; Ruth 144; Reuben 34,143,*144; William *3.4,27,138,143. *144
BEESON, Benjamin 6,22.46, *125; Charity 6; Edward 6; Hasten W. 80; Isaac *5,25,41,46,125; Isabel 85: Jane 80; Joel 80; Joel S. *112; John 22, *80,94,125; John A. 80; Leutisha 80; Martha 6; Mary 6,39,111; Nathaniel 5; Permelia 112; Phebe 5,6; Polly 110; Priscilla 61,80; Samuel 6,22.85; Richard 6,46; R.G. 112; Richard G. 110,125; William 6,42
BELL, Batcey 11; George W. 110; Ibba 114; John 70; Martha T. 110; Nancy 7: Robert 44,46,110; Robert J. 110; Sally *110
BEMBO, ______ 79: Mary 61
BENBOW, BENBO, Ann 94,102; Benjamin 53,*102: Charles 61,94,112,120; David 102: Elizabeth 102; Hannah 94; John 102: Lydia 53,102; Sarah 94; Thomas 28,*94; William 94
BENJAMAM, Ester 63
BENEJAMIN, Thomas 63
BENNETT. Daniel 124; David 124; Elisha 14,*124; Levi 124; Nelly 124; Ruth 30; Temperance 124
BENSON, Ann 94; John *4; John Jr. 4; Phebe 94; Reuben 4,*94,95
BEVILL, Agnes C. 70; Alexander 70,84,144; Alis 84; Archer 110; Clarisy 144; Dicey 110; Elizabeth 84; Hezekiah 46,143,*144; Lucy 144; Lucy A. 84; John 46; Joel T. 84; Philip 144; Pleasant *110; Sally 84,110; Thomas 71, 86,144; Vivant 84; William 46,*84,145
BEVINGS, Dr. James 112; Susannah 112
BILLINGSLEY, Barzil 5; Betsey 23; Elizabeth 5, 21: Clarence 5; Henry 23; James *5,23,50; John J. 5; Martha 5: Mary 5; Samuel 5; Walter 5; William 23

BINER, George 17
BIRD, Wenny 76
BISHOP, Aaron 98,123; Lindsay 98; Mary 45
BISWELL, BYEWELL, BIZWELL, Benjamin *82,102; Elizabeth 82,102,105; Mary Ann 82,*102,105; Susannah 82, 102,105
BIVINGS, Albert 135; Catherine 135; James 135; Louisa 135; Nancy 135; Susannah 135
BLACK, Daniel 77; Henry 143; Rebecca 93; Thomas 12,23
BLACKWELL, Louisa 123
BLAIR, BLEAR, Agnes 5; Andrew 2; Eleanor 18; Hugh 2: James *5,43,94; Jean 2; John *2,5,94; Jonathan 2; Margaret 3; Martha 2.5,94; Mary 5,43; Ruth 94; Samuel 94; Thomas 2,7,18,44,*94; William 94,149
BLESSARD, Parnel 27
BLAYR see BLAIR
BOAK, Robt. 4; John 24
BOCKIN, Lucy 76
BOLES, Elvirah 85; Rachel 85
BOND, John 113; Jonathan 109
BONN, John 113
BOOKER, Elizabeth 105; Martha 82
BOON, Anne 4; Ann 128; Barbara 128; Betsy 128; Caleb 128; Catherine 4,128; Daniel 4; David 128; Jacob *4,128: Jesse Lewis 128; John 4,*128; John Sr. 4,69; Martin 4; Molly 128; Polly 128; William 128
BOREN, Elijah 125; Phebe 125
BOROUGHS, Cornelis 94
BORTON see BURTON
BOSTICK, Elizabeth 147
BOSWELL, Parabow 102
BOURLAND, William 22
BOURMAN, Richard 16
BOURTON see BURTON
BOWEN, Abner 9
BOWMAN, Archalos 61; Edmond 95; Edward 16; Richard 93; Sarah 120,140; Sebey 149; William 93
BOYD, Andrew 4; Ann 44; Catherine *4; James 70
BOYDE, Ruth 124
BOYERS, Jacob 8
BRACKIN, Samuel E. 140
BRADLEY, Sarah 57
BRADLOVE, Thomas 124
BRALEY, Joseph 32
BRANNOCK, A.N. 137; Henry 21;
BRANNOCK cont'd. James 106,138; Patsy 131,132; William 21
BRANSMARK, Martha 135
BRASHER, Asa Jr. 59; Jesse 64; Z.D. 64
BRANTLEY, Betsey 113; Fannie K. 113; Mary 113
BRASWELL, B.N. 107; Blake W. 87; Polly 87
BRAWLEY, Joseph 135
BRAZELL, Jacob 47
BRAZIL, Elijah 107; Jacob 107; James 107; Joel 107; Kipey 107; Pleasant 107; Ridley *107
BREDEN, Alexander *2,3,14; Charles 3; Margaret 3; Mary 3; Robert *3,54; William 2
BRICKEL, Barzilla 106; Rebecca 106; Robert 106
BRIGGANCE, David 29
BRIGHT, Margaret 42; James 42
BRIM, Peter 115
BRINCEFIELD, Clement 103; Delitha 103; John *103; Thomas 103
BRINDLE, James 123
BRISENDRIN, Louisa 75
BRITTAIN, Anne 5; Henry 5; J.M. 143; Joseph 5,29, 143; Robert 34; Ruth 5; William *29
BRITTON, Jane 1; William 9
BROGDON, Anne 6; James *6; Kesia 6; Patiance 6; Reliance 6
BROOKS, David 65
BROOKSHIRE, Benjamin 125; Mannering 125; Margaret 125; Mary 125; Thomas *125; Wiley 125; William 125
BROWDER, Isham 47
BROWN, Adam 9,126; Agnes 35; Benjamin 73; Catherine 9; Charles 94; Comfort 98; Daniel 148; Elias 5; Elizabeth 110; Frances 123; George 5; George L. 28; James 5,76; James Sr. 76; Jane 73; John 4,5,30; Joseph 1,47; Judith 108; Margaret 42; Mary 2,3,22; Matthew *5, 16,18,77; Nancy 98; Nathaniel *4; Polly 105; Rebecca 76; Rebeckah 5; Robert 5; Sally 74; Sarah 76; Sophia 127; Thomas 4, 5,16,35; Westley 98;

BROWN cont'd.
William 4,*5,6,18,67,*73, *98,102,107: Williamson 22,44
BRUCE, Abnor B. 112; Alfred 113; Charles 7,27,64,66, 105,*112,113; Felix M. 113; John B. 112; Nancy 5
BUCHANON, Frances 39; Widow 106
BUCKNER, Aydlett 22; Thomas 22
BULLAR, Anna 46
BULLOCK, Ann Dogged 6; David 6; Edward 5,*6; George 6; John 6; Len 6; William 6; Winnefred 6
BUNCH, Gulian 115; John M. 115; William 61,*115
BUNDAY, Alfred 70; Caleb *70; Joseph 144; Nancy 125; Nathan 70; Sarah *70; Rachel 144
BURKE, Michael 19
BURNEY, Catherine 4,5; Catrin 37; Elizabeth 4,8; John *4,5; Rebeckah 4; Mary 37; Robert 5,147; Samuel 37; William 4,5,32
BUROUGHS, Benjamin 94
BURROW, Catherine 71; Ephraim 9; Eva 9
BURTON, Dorcas 4; Elizabeth 72,73; Isaac 86; Jesse 86; John 72; Richard *4,*72; Sarah *73; William 4,72
BUSICK, Anny 139; Caleb 139; William 72
BYFORD, Quillen 36; Tabitha 53; William 36,*53

CAFFEY, Jane 129; Henry 136; Levina 136
CAKES, Isaac 126
CAIN, Andrew 79
CALDWELL, Alexander 14,39,42, 92; Andrew 91; D. 3; David 83,90,*91,117; Rev. David 21; Edmund 92; James 4,57; John 71; John W. 80,92,116; John W., Esq. 125; Joseph 118; Patsy 92; Rachel 91; Robert 91,92,113; Robert C. 116; Samuel 91; Thomas 92
CALHOUN, Ana 9; Elizabeth 9; Elsaman 8,9; Easter 13; James *8,9,26; Jean *13; Jinnet 8; John 13; John Jonstone 8,9; Mary 9; Nancy 9; Robert 9,13,27; Samuel 8,9,13; Sarah 9
CALLAHAM, Darby Jr. 142
CALLOWAY, Jonathan 16;
CALLOWAY cont'd.
Obidiah 16
CAMPBELL, Archibald 11; James 7,11; John 50,57; Mary *11,57; Moses 5,*7; Polly 11; Rebeckah 7; Robert 81; William 7,142
CANADY, CANNADY, Abigail *77; John 66,77; Nathan 29,77,105,108,113,119, 147,149; William 77,147
CANNON, Horace F. 125
CAPPS, Anny 101; Barbara 14; Bennett 101; Catranena 14; Donley 14; Elizabeth 14; Falty 14; Haines 14; Henry *14; Jacob 14; Magdalina 14; Nancy 101
CARBRY, Thomas *108
CARFIELD, Drusilah 117
CARLISLE, Nancy 120
CARMICHIAL, Andrew *111; Lydia 112
CARNEY, Mary 67
CARR, Betsey 42
CARROL, Elizabeth 56,57
CARROLL, John 117
CARSON, Agnes 43
CARTER, Elizabeth *77; Giles 25; John 3,78; John P. 127; Mial 77,*136; Ruth 117; Samuel 85; Sarah 3; Walker 14
CARUTHERS, Eli W. 121
CASE, Charles 88,119; Charlotte 119; Ezekial 119; Jesse 119; Jonas 88,119; Nathan 119; William *119
CASEY, Nancy 138; Sarah 138
CATES, John 126
CATHEY, John 71
CAULK, Levin 77
CAUSBIE, William 84
CAUSEY, Aaron 21; Charles 64; Dianer 144; John 144; Larkin More 42; Nancy 13, 64; Nehemiah 20,52; Peggy 144; Soloman 144; Zebulon 143,*144
CESENEY, Dolly 29
CESNEY, Stephen 26
CHABERS, John 52
CHADWICK, Cynthia 138; Cyrus 138; John 138; Joshua 22; Miriam 119
CHAMBERS, Elinor *7; Elizabeth 13; John *13; Stuart 7; Thomas 7
CHAMNESS, Joseph 25
CHANCE, Purnel 6
CHAPMAN, Jane 79; William C. *79,150
CHAPPLE, Ambrose 83,*91;

CHAPPLE cont'd.
Delila 91; Sarah 83,91
CHARLES, Anna 9; Edith 105; Elijah 9; Elisha 111; Elizabeth *111; Isaac 9; Jacob 111; Leah 9; Leven C. 27; John 111; Margaret 122; Mary 9; Michael 4; Risdom 105,111; Ruben 9; Sarah 9; Smith 111; Soloman 9,111; William *9
CHATMAN, John 94
CHICHESTER, John D. 143
CHILCUTT, CHILLICUT, Elijah 119; George 106; James 37, 99,110,122,135; John 99; Sarah 52
CHIPMAN, Ann 122; Elizabeth 74; Hannah 74; Hezekiah 74; Jesse 122; James 82,122; Joel 74,122; John 12,*122; Margaret 12; Martha 74; Mary 74; Molly 122; Obadiah 122; Paris *12,69,74; Stephen M. 122
CHRISTMAN, Abraham 7; Anna Maria 7; Balshaster 7; Barbara 7; Catherine; Daniel 7; David 7; Elizabeth 7,94; Ester 94; George 7, 133; Henrick 7; Jacob *7, 27; John 7,14,88,94,139; Joseph 7,*94; Rebecca 7
CHRISTO, Margaret 32; William 32
CHRISTOPHER, Janett 14; Nancy 14; Simon *14
CLAKS, Sary 35
CLAPP, Col. Abram 137; Adam 9; Augustine 116; Barbara 112; Barbery 11; Barmitt 112; Barnay 83; Betsy 137; Betsy Ann 128; Catherine 112,137; Caty 116; Christian 83,112; Christina 11; Daniel 116; Daniel Col 119; David 101; Elia 137; Elizabeth 11; Emanuel 116; Finley E.S. 128; George 11, 112,116; Isaac 11,*116; Henry 124; Jacob 32,36,133; Jacob Sr. *112; James 129; James S. 129; Jeremiah 137; J. Henry *137; John 9,32; John Philip *9; Joseph 97, *128; Joshua 140,143,148; Ludderwich 9; Magdelin 11; Margaret 11; Mary 10,32,112, 140; Philip 11; Rosa 133; Sally 137; Soloman 137; Susanna 128; Tobias 23,24; Tobias Sr. *11; Valentine 9,11; William 137
CLARK, Ann 9,11; Benjamin 78; Catharine 9; Charles 10; Hance *9; Hezekiah S. 78; Jean 9; Jonathan 89; John *10,70,131,147; Joland 127; Joseph 2; Margaret 34; Martha *78; Mary 9,10,23,64,74; Nancy 73; Nathaniel *11; Nicholas 102; Rebecca 2; Ruth 46; Sally 73; William 2
CLARY, Elizabeth 111; Henry 111
CLASS, Jacob 58
CLAYTON, Elizabeth 94; John 94
CLEMMONS, Benton 123; Easter 123; James *123; James A. 123; John 123; John D. 123
CLIFTON, Marget 22
CLEMER, Aaron 99,110; Charles 99; Dudly 99; Elizabeth 98; John *98,99; Seth 99; Sarah 99; Thomas 99; William 99
CLIMER, Margaret 106; Noah M. 106,109,132,135,136, 138,139
CLOMINS, Mary 78
CLORO, Finley A.S. 84; Joseph 84
CLOS, Thomas 42
CLOSS, John 44; Joseph 44
CLOUD, Susan 84
COALING, Robert 14
COASBEE, William 70
COBB, Hiram 140
COBEN, Leven 11
COBLE, Anne 10; Anthony *8,56,114,133; Barbara 102; Catren 23; Caty 60; Daniel 103,116; David 8, 10,103,144; Eli 127; Elizabeth 114,144; Ely 10; Eva 10; Frederich 70; George 8,10,60,*70, 114; Jacob Sr. 32; Jane 114; John 8,10,*14,60, 139; Ludwick 8,*10; Martin 14; Mary 14,70,114, 123,144; Molly 103; Nelly 144; Nicholas 70,71,72; Paul 70,103; Peter 70, 114,124,143,*144; Philip 70; Sally 124,144; Samuel 140; Sarah 10; Sophia 10
COCKRAIN, Martha 43; Robert 43
COE, Avery 13; Hannah 29; Huldah 13; John *13,46, 57,67,78,113,138,146;

COE cont'd.
John Gamble 13; John Jr. 13; Josh Sr. 21,29; Joseph 13; Sarah 13,46
COFFEE, Elizabeth 10; John *7,10; Joshua *10; Lucy 7; Margaret 7; Michael 7; Thomas 7
COFFEY, James D. 129; John 37; Michael 37; Robert 106, 107,125; Zilpha 136
COFFIN, ______ 16; Aaron 8; Abel 10,14,76,92.99; Achsa 9; Adam 8; Alijah *8,12; Anna 76,103; Barnabas 4, 6,8,9,10,12,13,*14,22,28, 30,59,61,118; Benjamin *8, 120; Bethuel 3,8,9,12,39, 41,49,64,69,75,89; David 10; Elihu 9; Elizabeth 8, 9,40,111,124; Esther 9; Ezecil 76; Hannah 40,64, 75,101; James 41; Jane 100, 130; Jethro 10; Job 9; John 10; Joseph 14,76,99, 144; Joseph J. 101; Joseph T. 93; Levi 8,12,40,80; L. G. 144; Libin 8,12; Lydia 10; Mary 8,10; Matthew 9, 10,12,13,30,40,41,67; Miriam 76; Nathan 9; Paul 123; Peter *76; Phebe 8, 14,22,100,130; Pricilla 8,10,12,14; Rachel 8; Rhoda 92.108; Salley 61; Samuel 8,9,*10,12,61; Sarah 87; Stephen 14; Thomas 10; Vestal 9; William 5,8,*9,10, *12,65,101; Zacharias 63, 100
COLE, ______ 84; Dicey 145; James 77,106,110,113,124, 145; Robert 143,*144
COLEMAN, Isaac 71,99; John Jr. 37; Martha 85
COLTRAIN, COALTRAIN, Jane 74; Sally 108; Sarah 74
COLLETT, James 146
COLSTON, Henry 42
COMB, William Jr. 54
COMER, Elizabeth 25; Joseph 25
COMING see CUMMIN(S)
COMPLIN, Annanette 11; Brittain 11; Henry *11; Hooper 11; James 11; Rebekah 11
CONNER, Elizabeth 81
CONNEY, Rachel M. 117
COOK, Abraham *10,22,68; Allen 109,141; Deanar 145; Delila 145; Elizabeth 12; Hannah 105; Isaac 3,10,12;
COOK cont'd.
Jacob 12; James 6,15; Jinna 145; John 10,12, 120,143,*145; John Capt. 47; John Jr. *95; Joseph 12; Margaret 143,*145; Mary 12; Nancy 145; Nathan 10,12.82,92.119; Rachel 141; Ruth 10; Sarah 10; Temri 12; Thomas *11,12; William 12,145
COOPER, Ana 9; David *9, 102; John 9,91; Thomas 9; William 9
COOSY, Levin 73
COOTS, James 143,*145; John 26; Hannah 26; Mary 145
CORSBIE, CORSBEE, CORSBY, Ann 87; Hance *87; John 119; Margaret 87; Prudence 129; W. 45,137; William 10,22,72,87,102, 118.119
CORTNER, Caterena 8; George 8,36,46,56,58; Peter 36
COTNER, Daniel Jr. 9
COTTON, James 141; William 141
COUCH, Charlotte 92; Elizabeth 96; James 92; John 92; Joseph 92; Joshua 92; Mary 92; Mesack *92,96; Phebe 92; Priscilla 92; Sally 92; Samuel 13,92, 103; Waltham 92
COULD, Timothy 91
COVEY, Mary *13; Sarah 11, 73
COWVS, John 120
COWEN, Betsy 145; Elias 143,*145; Elisha 145; Samuel 36; Sarah 145
COX, Abner 6; Burnetty 71; Daniel 6; Jincy 71; John 6; Joshua 6; Martha 6, 32; Mary 21,71; Naomey 25; Neeley 71; Sarah 6; Soloman 6; Thomas *6
CRAFT, Charlotte 8; Gean Charles 8; John 8; John Charles 8; Lydia 8; Marry 8; Nelle 8; John 71; Rebecka 8; Sarah 8,99; Thomas Charles *8
CRANOR, CRANNOR, Hannah 10, 150; John 12; Joseph 10; Joshua 12,102; Moses 10, 12; Phebe 12; Prudence 12; Sarah *12; Thomas *10,12
CRAWFORD, J.H. 137; John H. 119

DENNIS cont'd.
Thomas *15; Unity 128; William *16
DENNY, Agnes 15; Allen 93, 136; Alvan 18; Elijah 98,99; George 15,*18,89, 93; Hannah 10,104; Harriet 93; Isabell 93; Jane 98; Jene 112; Jenny 99; James *14,*15,18,39,42,44,59, 93,99,130,134,145; James Col. 108.111,135,136; James Jr. 67; James Sr. 67; Joseph 75; Mary 14; Mary Ann 98.99; Nancy 93; Peggy 18; Rebecca 98; Sabra Ann 136; Sally 99; Samuel 98; Sarah 112; Thomas 18; Walter 50,98; William 15,18,52.*93,*98, 117.136; William Col. 130
DENTON, Polly 101; William *101; William, Esq. 145
DEPHILL. Thomas 18
DEWEARE, Ezekial 38
DEWISE, Caleb 83; Elijah 83,98; Elizabeth 83,107; Ezekiel 40,*83; Joseph 83; Sarah 83
DIAMOND, DIMON, John 16; Mary 7,17; Patrick *16; Sarah 16; Stuart 16,17; William 17
DICK(S), Ann 69; Elizabeth 16; Hiram C. 97; Isabella 45; James 8.16,18.45,*97, *110; Jane E. 82; Jane M. 97; John 18; John M. 97, 130; John W. 81,82,143, *145; Joshua 3,5,26,27. 69,71; Martha W. 82,145; Nathan 3,25,26,93; Obadiah 41; Obidiah 18; Patsy 97; Peter *16,110; Polly 18; Rebecca 18; Reuben 97,111; Ruth 31; Samuel 18; Seth 69; Thomas 18,64,*81,82, 97,114; William 16,*18, 34,60,76,110,132; Zachariah 16,62
DICKY, Edward 91; Jane 91, 101; John 91; Mary *100; Polly 91; Rebecca 91.100, 101; William 46,57.72,83, *91,100,101
DICKSON, Betsy H. 147; David 147; John 72,147; Joseph 147; Nancy 72; Robert 72; William *72
DILL, Mary 7; Joseph 7
DILLING, Jiney 145; John 90; L. 6
DILLON, Andrew 118;
DILLON cont'd.
Charity 16,*18; Daniel *17; Daniel Jr. 15,16; Hannah 53,63; Isaac 17; Jake 79; Jesse 17,61; Martha 17; Patience 17; Peter *16,17,79; Rachel 79; Sarah 79; Susannah 20; William 17
DINKINS, DENKINS, John 6, 23,71
DILWORTH, Absolam 83; Ann 83; Benjamin 107; Faithy 107; George 107; Jane 83; Lindsay 107; Perlina I. 107; Sarah 83,107; Vivicy 107; Thomas *107; Thomas E. 107
DIVENNY, DEVENNY, Abner 123; Ann 123,*139; Betsy 123; Hannah 123,139; Jemima 139; Jesse 123; Pithias L. 123; Samuel *122,123, 139; Thomas 123
DIX see DICKS
DIXON, Benjamin 6; Major 47
DOAK, Ann 17; Daniel 16; Elizabeth 16; Hannah 16; James 1,16,*18,29; John 2,16,17,18,24; Josiah 17; Jonathan 17; Martha 17, 18; Mary 17,18; Peter 141; Robert *16,17,18; Roddy 17; Thankful 102; William 16,*17,78,102, 113,149; William Jr. 29
DOBINS, Starrett 54
DOBIOS, Jahne 93
DOBSON, Charles 116; Jeremiah 117; Mary *116; Richard 117; William 46
DODD, Rodolphus 131
DODSON, Charles 105; Jeremiah 105; Mary 105; Richard *105; Sally 105; William 105
DONELSON, John 52
DONNELL, Adlice 126; Agness 15; Ann 88; Anna 97; Anne 135; Andrew 77,89,104, *126,146; Betsy 88; Charlotte 104; Daniel 2, 77; Edmund 126,146; Emsley 135; Elizabeth 15, *17,88,146; Erwin 82,104; George 35,106,126; Hannah 82,84,88,89,126; Isabella 35; James 42,88,89,93, 104; Jane 88,89,104,116; John 3,13,15,18,*88,89, 112,126; Joseph 104,117; Joseph M. 116;

DONNELL cont'd.
Lathem 89,104,126,135,146; Latham Sr. 89; Levi 88; Lidia 20; Martha 52,104; Mary 17,88,89; Mary Jean 146; Morrison 90; Nancy 88, 89,*136; Nathan *104; Peggy 126; Polly 135; Pricilly 149; R. 77; Robert 8,17, 18,42,70,89,104,143,*146; Robert Jr. 88; Robert Maj. 89; Robert Sr. 88; Ruth 88; Sally 126; Samuel 17, 84; Samuel E. 105; Thomas 3,17,42,89,104,126,146; William 52,*89,104,112. 120,126
DOWNEY, Elisabeth 51
DOWELL, George 59; John 51
DRAPER. William 62
DRAUGHON, Anna 149; John 110, 125,128,136,141,149
DROG, Jacob 7
DUCK, May 15
DUFF, Abram *16; Elizabeth 43; James 16; Mary 16; Samuel 16; William 16
DUN, William 53
DUNLAP, John *17; Margaret 17; Robert 17
DUNNING, James 34,67
DWIGGINS, Ann 15; Daniel 15; Elizabeth 15: James 15,38; Joseph 15; Lidia 15; Mary 15,38,130; Robert *15; Sally 100,130; Sarah 15; Samuel 15,100,130

EADSLEY, John 5
EDDINS, Sarah 31: William 31
EDWARDS, Abel 40; Ammel 60; David 131; Edward 11,57; Elizabeth 105; Harrison 41; Haruel 105; John 105; Joshua 60,*105; Matilda 131: Susannah 105; Thomas 40,105; Virtueris 131
EKEN, William 47
ELDER, Jean 43
ELDRIDGE, Cathran 62
ELLIOTT, B. 127; John 29,37; Joseph 24; Mary 86; Moses *99; Priscilla 24; Ruth 102; Spencer 99; Thomas *86; Vina 99
ELLIS, Leven 7
EMSLEY, Elamanuel 69
ENDSLEY, Abner 36; Abraham *18,19,46; Elisebeth 19; John 19,66; Mahaly 19; Samuel 19; Sarah 18,19
ENGLESON, Sarah 65
ERVIN, George 18; James 18;

ERVIN cont'd.
Robert *18; Samuel 18
ESTERIG, Henry 29
EUBANKS, Elisebeth 19; Frances 19; George 19; John *19; Ketherine 19; Milton 91; Philip 19,91; Polly 19,91; Rachel 19; Richard 19
EULASS, John 96
EULESS, Eli 140
EVANS, David 136; Deborah 69,136; Calvin 136; Jesse 27,28.30,*135,136; Jonathan P. 136; Louisa 136; Nancy 117; William 136

FAIRBANKS, David 20; Mary 20; Sarah 20; Susannah 20; William *20
FARMER, Christian 72,*127; Elizabeth 127; Henry 127; Levi 127; Peter 127; Polly 127: Samuel 127
FARRINGTON, FERRINGTON. Ann 36; Anna 63; Elizabeth 62; John 62
FENTRISS, Frederich 113; Frederick, Esq. 134
FEREBEE, Jesse 105; Reed 105
FERGUSON, Alexander *77; Samuel 77.78; Sarah 77
FIELD(S), Absolem 70,133; Ann 2,19; Ansyl 55; Benjamin 83: Betsy 133: Charlotte 70; Christopher 70; Elinor 133: Elizabeth 19,83; Elott 83; Hannah 70; Hester 19; Ibby 103; Jane 83; Jeremiah 19,20, 21,70; Jereter 70; Jesey 19; John *10,55,83; Jonathan 21,83; Joseph 19; Layton 133; Lidoak 20; Lydia 70; Mary 19,20,83; Nancy 21,83; Peter *70; Polly 70,83; Rachel 83; Robert 19; Roddy 103: Ruhama 70: Ruth 83; Sally 103; Tabitha 83; Thomas 19; William 19,20, *21,70,83
FINDLEY, FINLEY, Abegail 21; Alcey 21; Becky 80; Betsey 21,80; Eliza 49: Elizabeth 2; Franky 91, 117: George 21,90,*117; George B. 122; George W. 117; Frederich 93; Isabella 1; James 64,117, *122; John 1,2,37,49,70, 74,115,117; Josiah *21;

FINDLEY, FINLEY cont'd.
Lettis 21; Mary 117; Nancy 122; Polly 21; Rachel 21; William 48, 92,117
FIPPS, Aaron 32; Christian 32
FISHER, Anne 82; Damarus 130; Daniel *20; Hanner 20; John 20; Jonthan 20; Joshua 113; King 105; Mary 20; Molloston 20; Nathan 20; Sarah 20,105; Theodoria 20; Thomas 20
FITCHELL, Henry 127
FITZGERALD, William 144
FLACK, Andrew 20,75; Dorcas 20; Elisha *20; Hannah 20; James 20; Jane *20; Jean 50; Jenny 20; Susan 17; Thomas 20,74
FLEMING, Alexander 21; Betsy 21; Boniah 21; Elizabeth 110; James 21; Robert *21, *110; Samuel 24; Sarah 21; Silas 21; William 51
FLEMON, Elizabeth 13
FLERE, Jane 19; Judith 19; Thomas *19
FLUKE, William 72
FOGLEMAN, George 46; Mulkia 46; Samuel 124
FOLGER, Reuben 80
FORBIS, Abner 146; Ann 19, 20,21,146; Arthur *19, *20; David 146; Dolly Ann 133; Eli 21,146; Elizabeth 19,20,24,68,146; Finley S. 59; George 3,47; Hugh 21, 143,*146; Jane 84; Jemima 105; Jeremiah 42; Jeremy 21,52; Jessey 21; John 19, 21,34,37,133,146; John Washington 133; Liddy 21; Margaret 115; Marthy 19; Mary 1,19,21,113; Nancy 146; Poley 21; Ralph 24, 146; Rebeccah 21; Robert 146; Widow 138; William *19,21,34
FORD, Elizabeth 12; Henry 10,12; Moses 12; Prudence 12; Sarah 12; Thomas 12; William 12
FORGUSON, John 27
FOSTER, Barsheba 116,*138; Elmira 137; Cratham 137; Hannah 130; Hugh 65,138; John *137; Joshua 137; Nathan 137; Patrick M. 130
FOULKES, John A. 85; J.A. 114
FOUNTAIN, Andrew 94; Eli 95;
FOUNTAIN cont'd.
John 95; Sally 95; Samuel *95; William 95
FOURHAND, David *20; Garisies 20; Gordin 20; John 20; Moley 20; Owing 20; Prudence 20; Thomas 20
FOUST, Christian 112,124; Daniel 124,131; George 140; John 118,119,*124, 131; Leonard 124; Peggy 124; Penny 140; Peter 126
FOWLER, John 12
FRAZIER, Abel *76; Abigail 130; Abner 74; Enos 74, 130; Isaac 58,74,116; Henry 125; James 34,45, *74,130; John 76; Martha 74,76,*130; Mary 76; Polly 100; Rachel 76; Rebecca 76; Sarah 76; Soloman 74; William 74
FULKERSON, Abram 7; Fredrick 7; Mary 7
FULTON, Alexander 77,87; Elizabeth 68; George 87, 11,132; James 91,94; James Capps 87; Mary 86; Samuel *86,87; Sols 20; Thomas 87

GALBREATH, James 13,141; Robert 1
GALLOWAY, Charles 15; James 15
GAMBLE, Edward P. 104; Hannah 13
GANNON, Nancy 24
GARBY, Rhoas 130
GARDNER, Abel 109; Abigail 1,3; Ann 100,130; Anne 74; Annuil 105; Asineth 109; Barzella 74,*105; Carolina 109; Deborah 74; Delphine 106; Eliab 27; Elihu 105; Elizabeth 74, 76,109; Eunice 61,106; Flora 106; George 79,109; Henderson 105; Hezekiah 28,76,*78; Isaac 41,74; Isabella 109; James 74; Jane 78; Jemima 74,105; Jesse 74; John 108; Jonathan 76,79,109; Lydia 78; Lydia J. 143; Mary 74,108; Miriam 108; Nancy 79; Nathan 105; Niomi 105; Obed 74,78,101; Rachel 74; Richard *76, 79; Sarah 78; Shubel 106; Silvanis 17,79; Stephen 1,3,4,74,79,*108;

GARDNER cont'd.
Stephen Jr. 1; Susannah 74; Thaddeus 74; Thomas 106; Thomas C. 79; William 6,*74
GARRINGER, Andrew 143,*146; Agness 146; Barbra 146; Betsy 146; Boston 146; Henry 146; John 146; Jane 146; Peggy 146; Peter 146
GARRISON, John 129
GARROTT, William 47
GATES, Charles 33
GAYRE, Mary 99
GERINGER, Baston 133; Peggy 133
GIBBONS, Patrick 78: Sophia 78
GIBSON, Adaline 134; Alfred 134; Andrew 4,32,90,134; Elizabeth 49,90; Henry 55; James 34,90; Jane 90; John 134; John F. 90; Joseph 75,90,96,101,112,120, 127,128; Joseph, Esq. 75, 89; J.P. 128; Mary Ann 128; Morrison 112; Moses 49,90; Nancy 90; Sarah 134; Widow 18; Yancy 143
GIFFORD, Eunice 22; Hannah 22; Jonathan *22; Mary 22; Sarah 22; William 22,57
GILBERT, Edward 54; Josiah 30
GILBREATH, Catherine 113; Caty 146; James 113,145; Jane 141; John 113; Joseph 113; Peggy 96; Robert 9, *113; Thomas 113; William 113
GILCHRIST, _____ 24; Davidson 95; Delilah 124; Elinea C. 124; James 95; John 12,23, 25,32,39,45,51,57,68,71, 77,*95,104; John Jr. 89; Moses 32,45,89,95,107,124; Patrick D. 25; Robert 25, 31,39,95,124; Samuel *25, 31,39,95; William 25,82, 95,*124
GILL, Thomas 25
GILLASPIE, _____ 24; Charles Joseph 23; Daniel 17,23,50, 81,*102,*118; Daniel A. 118; Daniel Col. 34,37,44; Daniel Sr. 3; Elizabeth 23; James 102; James S. 23,58; John 16,*23,102: John Col. 17,63,118; John S. 81,118; John Sr. 89; John Rev. 23; Lucretia 118; Lucretia M. 118; Margret 23,44; Margaret E. 118; Nancy 78,118;
GILLASPIE cont'd.
Nancy C. 118: Patrick 102; Robert 31,78,102
GILLIAM, David 7,*139; Elizabeth 139; Henry 139; James 139; Joseph 139; Martha 139; Sarah 139; Susannah 139; Robert 139; William 139
GILMER, John A. 134,136, 139,140; John A., Esq. 135; William L. 136
GILMORE, Robert 104; Robert S. 74
GIRM, Abraham 97
GISPED, Rebekah 31
GLADSON, Ann 23; Daniel 23,104; John 23; Joshua 23,151; Levin 23,92; Nathan *23,121; Sarah 121
GLAS, GLASS, GLESS, GLOSS, Adam 72; Barbara 8; Barbery 23; Christen 23,24; Crisley *24; David 71; Eve 8,72; George 23,24; Inland Philpenah 24; John 72: Mary 24,72; Molly 72; Pall *72; Philip *23,24; Powel 23
GLENN, John 55; Joseph
GLOVER, Richard 4
GLOVYER, Christian 51; Richard 51
GOACHEN, Rachel 55
GOARDIN, John 61
GOBAL, Jacob 24; George 24
GOFF, Elender 72; Samuel 72; Steven 66
GOLA, Christion 131; Lotta *131
GOODING, Margaret 55
GOODRICH, Rebecca 79
GORDON, Branch 87,119; Charity 98; Charles 59; Green 115; James 84; Jenny 131,132: John 103, 118: Mary 118
GORMET, John 91
GORRELL, Agnes 70; Catherine 24,70; Finley W. 84; David 24,59,84; James 24; Jenney 70; Margaret 24; Mary 24; Mary Ann 70; Parish 143: Ralph 16,*24, 33,37,43,54,58,63,70,119; Robert 16,24,37: Uphane 84; William 24,*70
GORDY, Eunice 24; Isaac 24; Moses *24; Polly 24
GOSSETT, Abraham 143,*146, 147: Alice 67; Eleanor 146,147; Elizabeth 146; Jean 146,147; Joshua 112;

HANNAH, HANNER cont'd
Matilda 79; Melinda 78; N.A. 128; Nancy 48; Robert 2,3,34,*78,81,103; Roddy 20,51,*103; Roddy E. 138; Roddy, Esq. 59; Roddy Sr. 17; Sarah 59, 84; Sally C. 103; William 78
HARBIN, George 73
HARDEMAN, Dority 147; Eddy 147; Elizabeth 147; Ester 147; Jane 147; John 143, *147; Judith 147; Susannah 147; Thomas 147
HARDIN, Catharine 29; Charles *29,51; Elizabeth 45; Jean 29; John 29; Rebeckah 29; Stewart 29
HARGROVE, Jesse 28; Martha 28; Naomi *28; Samuel 28,69
HARLAN, Eleazer 124; Stephen 88
HARRELL, Abegail 85; David 37,*84,85; Elizabeth 37, 85,*109; Henry 85,109; James H. 109; Joseph 85, 109; Rachel 85; Stephen 85
HARRILL. David *91; Harvey 91
HARRIS, Althana 147; Arthur 147; Charity 147; Charles B. 105,147; Christopher 26; David *28; Edward 132; Elizabeth 28; Granderson 132; Hannah 25,26,27; Harmon 147; Hester 147; Howel 147; Ibby 130; James 29; Joel 37,47,143,*147; John 25, 116; Jones 132; Margery 77,147; Martin 147; Nelly 27; Obadiah 12,22,28; Peter *27,143; Polly 10; Robert 25,26; Samuel 132; Sarah 132; Sarah A. 132; Thompson *25; Tilman **132; William 66,147
HARRISON, Henry *120; John 120; Julianna 71; Nancy 120; Polly 120
HART, Henry 19,94
HARTIN, Stephen 71
HARTLEY, Francis *27; Sarah 27
HARVEY, Elizabeth 99; Isaac 71; Jesse 126; John *29,95; Mary Ann 95; Nancy 29; William 31,74,*99; William L. 111
HASSEL, Benjamin 132; Jesse *132; Milinda 132; Rachel 132
HATTEN, Sally 99
HATRICK, Betsey M. 135;
HATRICK cont'd.
Ibby 135; Rachael 135; Robert 59,*135; Sally G. 135; Samuel 93,135
HAUSCHURSH ?, _____ 122
HAWORTH, HAYWORTH, Abegale 132; Deborah 97; Elizabeth 28,132; George 29; Hannah 29; Henry 87; Jane 28; Josiah 116; Leah 116; Martha 132; Mary 29; Micajah 29; Phebe 28; Rachel 28; Richard 28, 29,*132; Ruth 113; Sarah 115; Soloman 28; Stephano 39; Stephanus *28
HAYES, Isaac 3; James 64; John 27; Patrick *27; Rebeccah 27
HAYNES, Lucy *75
HEALY, Hugh 30; Jesse 30; John *30; Mary 30; Phebe 30
HEART, Martha 106
HEATH, _____ 149; Allen 124; Ambrose 99; Charlotte 32; Charlotty 42; Cathbert 124; Delilah 25,31, 32; Elizabeth 32; Hannah 124; Henry 31; Jacob *32; James 124; Jestin 32; Job 124; John 32,*32; Keziah 32; Levina 32; Mary 32,53; Nancy 32; Othneal 124; Ralph 32; Robert 32; Samuel 31,*32; Sarah 25,32; Smith *31, 53; Tabitha 31; William *31,*124
HEDGECOCK, Jacob 125; Ruth 125
HELLAN, James 43
HELLIT, Polly 80
HEMRY, Mary 12
HENDERSON, Daniel 28; Elizabeth 58; James 151; John *28; Michael 66; Rebeckah 28; Thomas 28,142; Thomas Esq. 21; William 28
HENDRICKS, Hendnay 34; James 34; Mary 34
HENDRIX, Mary 25; Samuel 25
HENRY, Ann 62; William 130
HENLEY, Abegail 120; Ann 120; Henry 75; J.H. 57; Hezekiah 75; Jane 120; John 75; Joseph 75; Mary 75,125; Rebecca 75; Susannah 120
HERETAGE, Mary Ann 122
HESTER, Ann 71; Elizabeth 71; Patsy 71; Stephen 71

HIATT, HIETT, Aaron 30; Amos 27; Asher 26,27; Bennajah 30,68; Christopher 26,*27, 127; Cuthbet 132; Enos 59; Esther 27; Ford 25; George *31; Isaac 59; Isom 30; Joab 127; Joel 30,35; John 27,31,131; Joseph 34; Lydia 27; Martha 31; Mary 26; Mederia 111; Nathan *26; Rebecca 30; Silas 30; Sarah 25,131; Susanna 25; Susannah 31; William 25,26,27,*30, 31,68
HICKS, Eleanor 56; Elizabeth Rees 57; John 135
HIGHFILL, Delly 75; Hezekiah *75; John 75,132; Sally 119; William 75
HIGNUTT, John 150
HIGHTOWER, Joshua 103
HILL, Ann 55; Elizabeth 26; Isaac *26; Martha 144; Richard 26; Sarah 26; Wilson 106,130
HILTON, Abraham 28; Alexander 78; Ann Elexander 28; Elexander 28; Hannah 28,78; James *28; John 28; Mary 28; Peter 28; Prissals 28; Samuel 78; Stephen 28; William 28
HIMPBELL, Samuel Sr. 83
HINCHMAN, William 95
HINDS, John 25; Joseph *25; Levi 25; Simeon 25; Susanna 25
HINSHAW, Adam 111
HITCHCOCK, Asial 115,116; Benedick 115,116; Elisha 115; Hannah 30; Isaac 115; John *115,116; Martha 112; William *29
HOBBS, Daniel 93,137; Elixabeth 120; James 93
HOBBY, Daniel 71
HODGE, John 47
HODGIN, Samuel W. 95
HODGINS, Anne 25; Robert 25
HODGSON, Amos 29; Ann 13; Deborah 30; Elizabeth 63; George *25,29,*30; Hugh 18; Isaac 30; John 25,*29,58; Jonathan 17,44; Joseph 25, 29,66; Mary 29,63; Rachel 30; Robert 25; Susannah 30; William 30,58,66; Zachariah 30
HODSON, Any 31; Charity 31; David *31; Debora 110; Elizabeth 31; Ester 38; Famor 110; George 98; Hester 31; Hur 31; Jane 75;
HODSON cont'd.
Jesse 31,76; Jonathan 31, 126; Margaret 31; Martha 31; Mary 31; Nancy 126; Polly 94; Rachel 31; Rebecca 31; Richard 18, 31; Robert *31,88; Ruth 42,110; Sarah 31,131; Simmeon 31; Soloman 79; Thomas 31,76; William 95, 98,111
HOFHAINS, Barbara 27; Christian 27; Christina 27; David 27; Elizabeth 27; Jacob *27; Mallison 27; Mary Elizabeth 27; Philip 27
HOGGATT, Agnes 25; Ann 63; Anthony 26; David 26; Deborah 38; Hannah 26; Isiah 30,31; Jesse 86; John 26; Joseph 26,*30; Malen 30; Margaret 26, 63; Mary 26; Nathan 30; Pheby 30,31; Philip *26, 30; Sarah 31; Stephen 26; Stephanus 30; William *26,30; Zimri 30,31
HOLDER, John 98,123; Nancy 98,123
HOLDERNESS, James 33
HOLEMAN, Esther 94; Spencer A. 94
HOLIDAY, Ann 13
HOLLAND, James 58; Joshua 66; Stephen 77
HOLMAN, James 19; L.A. 133
HOLMES, Elizabeth 50
HOLSTEAD, Manliff 123; Nancy L. 123
HOLT, Israel 133; Micheal 103
HOLTON, Dinah 29; Lewis *29
HOMER, William 5
HOOD, John 47
HOPKINS, Pleasant 138
HORNE, Judith 62
HORNEBY, Ebenezer 70
HORNEY, Anna 81; Dovis 85; Elizabeth 122,141; Hannah 12; Kersiah 84; James 85; Jared 84; Jason 84; Jeffery 78,81,*84,85,116; John *85; John C. 81,115; Jonathan 85; Manlove 31, 81,84; Mary 12,85; Nancy 81,84; Pamela 81; Paris 85; Philip 27,78,*80,81, 84,85,111; Philip Jr. 84; Sally 81; Samuel 30,81; Sarah 84,85; Soloman 85; Stephen 85; Terresa 81

HOSKINS, Ann 28; Arnold *28; Eli 28; Elizabeth 28; Ellis 28; Emma 112; Hannah 28: John 3; Nelly 28; Jean 28; John 28,136; Joseph *28,136; Mary 28
HOULSTON, Soloman 27; Thomas *27
HOUREN, Sarah 12; Winsmore 10,12
HOWARD, Robert 143
HOWELL, Hannah 34; John 8, 29,34,40; Mary 34
HOWLET, Ann 47; Elizabeth 130; Harmon 47,*130; James M. 130; J.H. 47; Judith 130; Pleasant J. 130; Marboro T. 130; William 130
HOWREN, Winsmore 60
HOWSEN, Daniel 125; Winsmore 106
HUBBARD, Abigal 130; Abigail 141; Elizabeth 59; George 67,120; Jane 59; Jeremiah 76,150; Judith 59; John 61, *120,130; Martha 59; Nicholas 151; Sarah 59; Susanna 59
HUDDLESTON, Elizabeth 27; Hannah 27; Jonathan 27; Levinah 27; Lydia 27: Mary 27; Rachel 27; Sarah 27; Seth *27; Stephenson 22
HUFFMAN, Catherine 32; Elizabeth 148; George 101,148; Heartwell 143; John 32; Oliver 101
HUGHES, Sarah 101,137
HUGHS, Sally 38
HULLUM, Henery 64
HUMBLE, David 126; John 126
HUMPHREY(S), Absolom T. 138; Henry 79,83,107,*138; Lanham 73; Letitha 138; Sarah 127
HUNT, Ebenezer 30; Elazer 56; Eleazer 123; Barnabas 14; Dorcas 123; Elisebeth 14; Hannah 5,108; Isaiah *87; Ithamar 81; Ithamor 88; Jabez *30; Jacob 29,62,65, *108; James 108; Jesse 87; Joel 6,87; John *29,83,128; Joseph 76,97,110,121; Libin 13; Martha 96; Mary 87; Meriam 87,88; Miriam 13; Milton 140; Nathan 30,97, 100; Neeley 123; Phebe 14; Polly 29; Prissila 30; Prudence 62; Sally 29; Samuel 31; Sarah 123; Semira 30; Starret 29;
HUNT cont'd. Thomas 9,71,78,87,108; Thomas T. 97,100; William 29,35,65,69,87,108; Zebulon 30,97,113,125
HUNTER, Alexander 25; Becky 113; Edward 25; James 24, 25,65; John *25,142; Lydia 123; Samuel 42,64, 75,93,142
HUSE, Mary 33
HUSEY, Anne 25; Christopher *25; Stephen 25
HUSSEY, Ann 87; Bathalder 8; Eli 120; Eliza 87; Henry 87; John 6,65,87, 120; Jonathan 87; Joseph 87; Lydia 87; Mary 78, *87; Rebeckah 87; Stephen 6,86,120; Stephen, Esq. 115; Thomas 87; William 87
HUSTON, John 44; Levenus 44; Levi 49,73,74,90
HUTCHINSON, Widow 18
HUTTON, Arnold 29; Elizabeth 29; George *29; Jemima 29; Lydia 29; Mary 29; Ruthy 29; Sarah 6; William 29

IDDINGS, James 101; Jonathan 101; Joseph 39,40, *101; Joshua 101; Mark 101; William 101
IDOL, Barnite 122; Rachel 122
INGLE, Adam 32,101; Barnabas 32; Barnell *101; Caty 101; David 101; George *32; Jacob 32; Lovinia 32; Ludwick 32; Margaret 32; Philipina 32; Reuben 101; Sally A. 101; Sophia 32
INGOLD, Soloman 143
IRELAND, Sarah 86
IRWIN, Abel 80; Elizabeth 80; George 80; James 80; John 80; Mary 78; Nancy 80; Robert 80; Samuel *80
ISLEY, Christen 32; David 101; Elizabeth 32; Lodwich *32; Palliser 32
IVES, Drucilla 138; Elizabeth 138; Elukiel 138; Jesse *138; Mariam 138; Timothy 138

JACKSON, Andrew 33; Ann 64; Anny 100; Bowetor 105; Catherine 105; Craft *98;

JACKSON cont'd.
Curtis *105; David 33,*34; Edward 100; Elizabeth 73, 105; Gabriel 33; Gabrel 34; Jacob 105; James *33, 34; James Jr. 7; James Sr. 7; Joel 98; John 34,100, 111; Joseph 34,100,151; Lurena 105; Margaret 33; Mary 105; Nancy 98; Nathan 105; Polly 112; Rebecca 90; Sarah 34; Thomas 105; W. 35; William *33,*34,98
JAMES, John 86
JAMISON, Elizabeth 34; George *34
JANSON, Jane 19
JEAN, Edmund 38; Eliza 79; Sally 49; William 48
JENKINS, Carolus 1; Daniel 32; Demery *75; Ephraim *34; Hur 32; John 32; Joel 1; Lettis 32; Mary 148; Nancy 83; Peter 75; Thomas *32; William 3,34
JENNINGS, Miriam 57; Nancy 57
JESOP, JESSOP, Caleh *116; Elias 92; Josiah 82; Liddy 78; Mary 80,136; Phebe 105; Rachel 10; Susanna 105, 116; Timothy 105; Will 78
JESTER, Elizabeth 87; Henry 55; Isack 22; John 87; Maikel *87; Margaret 87; Phebe 87; Rebecca 87; William 87
JOB, John Jr. 9
JOHNSON, _____ 149; Abigail 72; Aggy 113; Alexander *33.*72; Ana 30; Caleb 34; Caty 72; Charles 85; Elenor 40; Elisabeth 30,33,93,*113; Esebell 34; Ganaway 121; George 34,56,59,72,*92; Hannah 85; Isabell 93,113; James *34,48,72,73,117,121; Jane 95; Jennett 33; Joel 33,*121; John 33,*72,121; Joseph 60,143; Joshua 34, 73,85,*103; Margaret 85; Mary 33,85,113; Miriam 85; Nancy 7; Naomi 113; Nathan *85,151; Nelly 72; Pleasant *33; Polly 121; Rebeckah 85; Robert 43,77; Sarah 33, 75,85,93; Soloman 34; Tarlton 9,*85; Thomas 8, 33; William 30,72,89,113
JONES, Betsy 63; Caleb 134; Christopher 129; Deborah 73; Elichores 73; Elizabeth 103; Isaac 121;
JONES cont'd.
Isardy R.W. 126; Jarvis *130; John 80,110; John W. *73; Judson 73; Lydia 130; Mary 111; Patty 134; Pinkney 130; Priscilla 130; Rebecca 130; Richard 73; Robert 73; Samuel 145; Soloman 63; Thomas 46; Travis 48,80; Travis Sr. *134
JONSON, Albena 149
JONY, Ory 41
JORDAN, Elizabeth 7; Mary 33; Michael *33; Notty 7
JOY, Deanna 38
JOYCE, Alexander *33,55, 141,142; Andrew 33; Elijah 33; Elisha 33; Elizabeth 33; Esther 33; James 15,33; Jane 33; John 33; Joseph 33; Margarett 33,141; Mary 33; Robert 33; Sarah 33; Thomas 33
JULIAN, Jesse 139; Robert 139
JULEN, Peter 24
JUSTICE, Garrison 77

KARR, John 86
KECK, Henry 11
KELHAM, Charles C. 77; Dinnah 77
KELLAM, Charles C. 147; Gustus 35; Elizabeth 35; Ester 35; Harvy 35; Henry 35; John *35,63; John Pursel 35; Joshaway 35; Samuel 30,35; Shadrack 35
KELLEY, Edward 101
KENDALL, Ahimass 117; Benjamin 113; Benjamin Sr. *113; Soloman 113,132
KENDLE, William 99
KENNEDY, William 19
KERR, Alise 71; Ann 16; Catherine *35; David *35; Elizabeth *35,108; Hannah 108,*111; Isbell 35; James 35,96; John 35; Luisa 108; Malinda 108; Margaret 35,96; Nathaniel *96,*108; Samuel 96,108, 111; Thomas 35; William 35,71,96
KERSEY, Aeazer 14; Amos 71, *111,124; Anna 129; Benjamin 111; Clarkson 129; Eleazer *71,85; Elizabeth 71,85,111,*124; Enoch 71; Ezra 111,124; Franklin 129;

KERSEY cont'd.
Isaac 111; James 111,124; Jesse *88,90,111; Moses 71; Newton 124; Samuel *129; Stephanus 111; Stephen 71; Thomas 86; William 71,76,88
KILLEY, KILLY, David 51; Lydia 51
KILLINGSWORTH, Mark W. 82, 84,92,106; William 23
KIMBRO, Nancy 130
KIME(S), Barbara 126; Christina 126; Dolly 72; Henry 126; Philip 51,60, *126; Sally 126; Tirly 126
KING, Abigail 37; John 94; Lucy 120; Peter 7; William 37,67,85
KIRKMAN, Eleanor 14,35; Elijah 34; Elisha 34; George 34,100; James *34; Mary 34; Peter *34,99; Polly 100; Rodger 34,103; Roger 20; Sarah 34; Thomas 22, 62; Thomas S. 34; William 34,35,99,100,115
KISLER, Mary 96
KNIGHT, Abel *35,123,141; Abel Jr. 88; Abel, 3rd 13,87; Andrew 35; Elizabeth 56; Jonathan 35; Samuel 35; Thomas 35; William 94
KNOTT, Justain 11,13,45,46; Nancy 11

LACKEY, Adam 5,*37,43; Alexander 37; Martha 37, *81; William 37
LACY, Anne 41
LAD(D), _____ 142
LAIN, Sarah 108
LAKEY, John *36; Rachel 36; William 36
LAMAR, Elizabeth 118; Greenville 118; James 118
LAMB, _____ 16; Isaac 29; John 38; Rachel 62; Robert 25,29,*38,62; Salathiel 101; Samuel 29,38,39,41, 111; Simeon 38; Susannah 111
LAMBERT, Abigail 111; Ann 111; Margery 111; Smith 140; William *111
LAMCASTER, Benjamin 131,149
LANDRETH, Asa 37; Francis 36; Jain 113; Jedidiah 36; John 37.69,78.88; Martha 37; Semor 37; Simon 88; Thomas 1.31,*36,37,50
LAND, Ansel 95; James 26; Narsissa 132; Priscilla 132; Reuben 132,136
LANE, Easter 123; Esther 98; Isaac 143; John 123; John Sr. *97.98; Nancy 98; Reuben 97,98,123; Sarah *123; Sary 98; Tidmore 53; William 41
LANIER, Andrew 94
LARKINS, John 12
LATRELL, Elizabeth *94; Lucy 94; Presley 94; Samuel 94; Sarah 94
LATTA, John 90
LAUGHTON, Nancy 102
LAURANCE, John 54
LAW, Andrew *37; Elizabeth 37; James 37; Margaret 37; Mary 129; Rachel 37; Robert 37,96
LAWERY, George 75
LAWRANCE, Adam 58
LAWRENCE, Ann 37; Caleb 37; John *37
LAYTON, Ana 133; Charles 133; James 133; Polly 133; Roger *133,134
LECKY, William 117
LEE, Elizabeth 25; Frances 25; Henry *37; John 25, 37,109; Joshua 37; Robert 25; Sarah 37
LEMONS, John 81; L.W. 140; Martha 81; Sarah 103
LEONARD, James 42; Jane 90; Malinda 90; Phebe 148; Sarah 90; William 90
LETHCO, Jackson 136
LEVERTON, Letty 136
LEWARK, Elijah 52; Joseph 52
LEWIS, Barberry 36; Courtney 110; Lawrence 110; Mary Elizabeth 36; Orlando 110; Philip *36; Rhodolphus 110; Sarah 53; William *110
LILLARD, Moses 7
LINDLEY, Martha 75
LINDSAY, A.H. 116; Andrew 69,77,82,116,127,144; Anne E. 77; A.T. Harper 76,77; David 116; Easter 69; Elizabeth 69,111; Hiram 143; Dr. I.J.M. 140; Jane 69; Jenna 69; Jesse H. 77,122,141; John 69; John Sr. 43; Letty 76; Mary 69,77; Nancy 69,*116; Robert 43,60,65,*69,*76, 77; Samuel 9,29,32,48,69; Sarah 69; Susannah 69;

LINDSAY cont'd.
Thomas 82; William 69,116
LINEGAR, LENEGAR, Elizabeth 85,*95; Isaac *75,96; Rosannah 76,*85
LINTHICUM, Peggy 138; Richard *79; Sarah 79; Soloman 146
LINVILLE, Nancy 93; Thomas 95
LISTER, Joseph 12; Mary 12
LITTELL, James 43
LLOYD, Edward 148: Rachel 105; Thomas 102
LOCKMAN, Christopher 36
LOFTING, Shadrach 145
LOGAN, John M. 135,141; John M. Col. 127
LOINGILE, James 121
LOMAN, Adam *37,38: Andrew 37: Elizabeth 37; George 37,138
LOMAX, Ann 36; James 36; Robert 36; Terrence 36; Thomas 36; William *35
LOMEY, John 19
LONEY, Susanna 6
LONG, Catherine 58: Eder. 8; John 51
LORIMER, Hugh 36; James 36; Mary 36; Samuel *36
LOVE, Elizabeth 126,131; John 27; Sarah 13
LOVET, Deborah 127; George 127; John 127; Rachel 150; Sarah 29,*127: Susannah A. 127
LOVEY, Edward *36; James 36; John 36; Mary 36; Sarah 36
LOVIL, William 7
LOW, Cunrod 36; David *36, 90; Eve 36; Lisabeth 36; Ludwick Capt. 89; Robert 11; Ruth 80; Samuel 36
LOWE, Eve 71; Fanny 120; Tidwell 5; Thomas 4
LOWDER, Joel 91
LOWERY, Andrew 59; Mary 59
LUALLIN, Angelina 126
LUALLEN, Jane 125
LUCAS, James 92; John 92; Wilkins 92; William 6, 68,*92
LUCIS, Debolar 131; Frances 131; James 132; John 132; Nancy 131,132; Sary 131; Wilkins 131: William 32
LUDENEMA, Catherine 34

MACKREL, William 112
MACY, Abigail 38,40; Anna 38; Anne 41; David 38; Deborah 76; Dinah *38,41; Elizabeth 106,148:
MACY cont'd.
Enoch 10,38,*41,53,65; Hannah 38; Henry 41,71, 134,143,*148; Henry M. 114; Isaac 38; Jemima 61; John 41,134; Joseph 148; Mary 131; Matthew 10,38, *40,56,61; Miriam 41; Nathaniel 15,39,40,76; Paul 15,39,61,64,76; Paul Jr. 40; Rachel 131; Sarah 38,41,148; Stephen 41; Thadeus 38,41; Thomas 148; Zacheus 40
MAGER, Green 132; Jacob 33; Mary *132
MAGUAR, T. 32
MAJORS, Margaret 40; Thomas *40
MAKELLHATTEN, Abraham 14
MALON, _____ 122
MALOY, James 51
MANLOVE, George 4; Jonathan 84; William 84
MANSHIP, Dorcas 111; Elijah 34,*111; Jane 93; Martha 111; Mary Ann 111; Nelly 111
MARIS, John 96,103,124; Rachel 96
MARCELLIOTT, Jane 56
MARLEY, Robert 21
MARONEY, Elizabeth 39; Isaac 39; John 39,40: Lyda 39; Nathan 39; Noah 91; Rachel 39; Ruth 39; William *39
MARMOND, Rachel 110
MARSH, Leonard 67: William 126
MARSHALL, Martha 53
MARTIN, Alexander 15,25, 138,142: Elizabeth 99; Enoch 102: Ezekial W. 102; Francis 39; Governor 92; Henry 39; James 25,*39,142; James C. *138; Jane 25,142; John 39; John S. 138; Joshua *102; Mary 39
MASON, Abraham 41; Rachel 41; Reuben 41
MASSEY, Elenor 107; Elizabeth 83; John 68; Nathan 68; Thomas 68
MATTHEWS, David 45; Hugh 68; Mary 68.76; Mary Ann 114; Sampson S. 114; William 56,72,79
MAXWELL, Alfred 132: Debolar 131; James 51,70,77; James V. 143; John *77; Martha 51; Mary 24;

MCIVER, Mary 143; Polly 122
MCKEEL, William 137
MCKEEN, Alexander 18,36; Mary 18
MCKEEVER, Elihu *109; Timothy 109
MCKIMMEY, Eliza 136
MCKENEY, Catey 45; Demsey 45; Elizabeth 45; Fanny 45; George *45; Jarrat 45; Lettia 45; Polly 45
MCKENNA, Charity; Gideon *45; James 45; Shadrack 45; William 45
MCKINNEY, Demsey 80; George 49; Nancy 49
MCKINSEY, William 64
MCKENZIE, Catherine 107
MCKNIGHT, Alexander *42; Ann 80; Catrine 42; Elizabeth 42; Hannah 39, 42; Hugh 42; Jean 42; John *42,92; Mary 69; Mary An 145; Robert 42,68; Samuel W. 80; William *42, 145
MCLEAN, B.F. 136; Catey 91; David 120,137; Dorcas 45; Elizabeth 45; Hannah 137; Jane 91; Jean 45; John *45,120,137; John Dr. 116; John M. 19; Joel 120; Joel Col. 116,128; Joseph 45, *116; Joseph A. 108; Joseph Sr. 45; Margaret 45; Marshall 40,45,96,116,*120; Marshall. Esq. 123; Mary 42; Moses 42; Nancy 45; Nelly 45; Polly 45,96; Robert 45,129; Thomas 40, 45,89
MCMASTER, Samuel 114
MCMICHAEL, Archibald 119, 143,*148; Charity 143; Charoty *148; John 119; Thomas 64,72,119; William 148
MCMILLICAN, Samuel 28
MCMIN, Daniel 20,34; Philip P. 24
MCMURPHY, Anny 97
MCMURRY, Charity 148; Elizabeth 4,44,97; Hannah 44; James 27,42,43,*44,55; Jean 43,44; John 28,*42. *43,44,81,97,129; Marget 148; Mary 4; Nathaniel 4; Peggy 148; Robert 43; Susan 129; Uphial 44; Wesley 129; William 42,65,72
MCNAIRY, Amanda 147; Ann 140; Bartlett Yancy 140; Boyd 140,147;
MCNAIRY cont'd. James 95,*140,147,148; John 140; John H. 147; Mary 147; Phillip J. 140; William 140
MCNEELY, Lucinda 143; Thomas 25,70
MCQUISTON, Moses 136; William 136
MCWHICKER, Samuel 96
MEARS, Elizabeth 39; Zedock *39
MEBANE, MABENE, John A. 129; John A. Dr. 127; See also MAYBEN
MEDARIS, Charles *38; Elizabeth 38; John 38; Thomas 38
MEDEARIS, _____ 79; John 45,48,76; John W. 134; Massey 48; Nancy D. 134
MEDLIN, Sarah 16
MEINER, Jean 26; Henry 26
MEINING, Ludwig 7
MENDENHALL, Aaron 16,*39, 40,41,47,63,117; Abigail 41; Achsah 121; Ailee 4; Ann 41,121; Anne 110; Asenath 39; Azel 121; Betty 41; Beulah 39,96; Charity 39,40,48; Claria 115; Clarisy 120,121; Cyris P. 144; Daniel *74; Dinah 39,50,110; Deborah 74; Elijah 74; Elisha *127; Elizabeth 117; Enos 39,96,121; Esther 74; George 41,27,130,132; George C. 94,106,109; Hannah 41; Ira W. 115; Isaac 39,40,52,96,*117; Isabel 148; Isaiah 74; Jabis 121; Jacob 117; James 39,*41,59,74,81; Jemima 41; John 34,*40, 41,*110; Jno. D. 109; Jonathan 74,130; Judith 41,92; Judith Jr. 109; Lydia 74; Margaret 115; Margery 115; Marmaduke 88; Martha 110; Mary 40, 41,48,74,110,121; Mary Jane 39; Mary T. 81; Miles 117; Miriam 39,40, 41; Mordecal 39,*40,85, 96,115,117; Moses 39, *41,48,108,110,149; Nancy 148; Nathan 41,73, 74,83,92,94,95,98,109, 130,132; Paris 74; Phebe 39,50,*96; Rachel 64; Reddick 121; Richard 41, 81,87,144;

MENDENHALL cont'd.
Richard, 2nd 41,105; Ruth 39,96; Sally 121; Samuel 110; Sarah 115; Seth 39, 96,*120,148; S.G. 94; Stephen 40; Stephen G. 95; Susannah 41,127; Thomas *39,40; William 41,94,121, 143,*148; William P. 130; Zodac 117
MENNETT, Peter 109
MEREDITH, James 123; Mary 123
MIDDLETON, George 79; Sarah 147
MILEHAM, Ann 40; Ebenezer 38; Elizabeth 38; John 38; Joseph 40; Mary 38; Samuel *38,40; Sarah 38, 40; Walter 17,*40,51; Valentine 17,40,51
MILFORD, Elizabeth 7
MILLAR, Jonathan 31
MILLIKEN, Benjamin 3; Margaret 3; Mary 4
MILLIS, Betsy 102; Edward *73; James 14,35,73,80, 115,145; James, Esq. 86; N. 31,100; Nancy 91,100; Nickoson 34,73; Nicholas 80; Rachel 73; William 100
MILLS, Amos 56,*96; Benoni 18; Beroni 16; Betsy 96; Catherine 41; Charity 18; Elizabeth 96; Hannah 28, 75; James 39,47,71; Jeremiah 96,103; Jonathan 12, 96; Joseph 6,28; Margaret 41; Nathan 96; Rachel 96; Ruth 96; Selah 76; Solomon 95,130; William *41,105,131; William Jr. 44
MILLSAP, Thomas 62
MINER, Elizabeth 71; Levin 66; Mars 71; Meares *71
MINZES, Sally 100
MITCHEL, MITCHELL, Adam 38; Henry 27; John 43,108; Joseph 136; Margarete 38; Martha 115; Rebecca 38; Robert *38,115,127; Robert Sr. *115; Samuel 91,111,*136; William 115
MODERWELL, John 127; Libby 143; Martha 127; Robert 95,*127
MONTGOMERY, Charlotte 38; David 38; Elizabeth 38; George 42; Hannah 39; Irvin 42; James *38,42; Jane 38; Jean 39; John 38,39; Levi 42; Lydia 38;
MONTGOMERY cont'd.
Margrett 38; Mary 38,39, 42; Rebeccah 18,39,42; Robert 42; Samuel 42; William 18,38,*41,42,82, 112; William Sr. *39
MONNETT, Christopher 109
MONROE, Dorris 124
MOOD, Alexander 42
MOODY, Thomas 55
MOONEY, Ana 104
MOOR, Jesse 115; Julius E. 93
MOORE, Alphar 149; Arno 48; Elija 93; Elizabeth 149; Hannah 93; Henry 125; Isaac *125,129; J. 11; James 93; John 18,41,48, 51,77,80,93,125,129,149; Joshua 30,85; Judith 50; Joshua 85; Nathaniel 39, 51; Patsy 73; Saray 125; Thomas 31,41,82; William 48,*93
MORDOCK, John 28
MOREHEAD, Agnes 49,50; Ann Quail 50; John M. 127, 131; James T. 138
MORELAND, Elizabeth 46; Francis 46; Jane 46; Thomas *46; William 46
MOREMEN, William 6
MORGAN, Elias 76; Enos 76, 99; Green 76; Hubikkuk *42; James 42; John 42, 55; Kershew 76; Martha 76; Mary 76; Nancy 42; Thomas 19,76; Timothy *76
MORRIS, Aaron 75; Agness 109; Curtis 7; George 7; Jane 75; John 40,*75; Judy 7; Silas 75
MORRISON, David 100; Effy 100; Elizabeth 100; John 16; Katherine 100; Kenneth 100; Malcum *100; Mary 41; Rebecca 100
MORROW, David 23; Samuel 42
MORTIMER, David 75
MORTON, John 7
MOSELEY, Dan *136
MOSS, M.R. 103
MOUNT, Elinor 7; John 26
MOWERS, Phebe 97
MUCKSH, John Matthew 7
MULLOY, Daniel 40; Edward *40; James 40; Jane 40; Jeremiah 40; Ruth 40
MURPHEY, A.D. 133; Archibald D. 127
MURRAY, Bruce 112; Polly 112

PARKER cont'd.
Howell 52,70,87; John 49; Jonathan 42,49,53,86,110, 116,117,122,123,127,129, 139,148; Jonathan Sr. 126,137; Jonathan W. 109; Martha 110,129,137; Polly 75; Rhoda 50; Robert 136; Stephen 110,137; W.M. 143
PARKHILL, John 47; Martha 47; Nancy 47; William *47
PARMAR, Isabel 129
PARMOR, Sarah 94
PARSONS, Charity 49; Eleanor 49; Evin 116; George 49, *116,147; James 49,100, 116; John 49,116; Katherine 49; Mary 49,100; Patience 49; Robert 116; Ruth 49, 116; Thomas 116; William *49,116
PARRISH, Joel 120; Noel 37, 64; Rebecca 119
PATTERSON, Andrew 73; Caty 81; Charlotte M. 119; Elizabeth 88; George *73; Joseph 79; Margaret 81; Matty 73; Michael 73; Molly 73; Nancy 81; Nathaniel B. 81; Rebeckah 73; Robert 73; Thomas 88; William 58,*81; William H. 81; Wilson 88; Young *88
PAYNE, Anny 41; Benjamin 41; Roda 41
PEACE, Joseph 70; Silas 67,70
PEARCE, Mary 54; Silas 34; Windsor 54
PEARSON, John 124; Elizabeth 124; Isaac *124; William 124
PEAY, George 7; George Sr. 25
PEEBLES, PEEPLES, PEOPLES, Abigail 109; Abraham 11,68, 83,85,87,113; Allan 106; Allen Col. 124,125; Catherine S. 80; Caty 49; David 7; Drury 8,46,49,77; Drury W. 80; Edward R. 87; Elizabeth 134; Elizabeth F. 87; Frederich 47; Harbert 49; Hebert *79; Hebert Jr. 80; Hubbard 7,68,*871 James 149; Jehu *49; Joel W. 78,80; John R. 80; Lucy 143,*149; Martha Ann 80; Nathaniel 49; Pinkney 113; Polly 149; Prissey 113; Robert G. 79, 80; Sally 79; Sally W. 79, 80; Seth 49; Seth N. 122; Uriah 80; Wyatt 19,49,76, 134; Wyatt M. 79,80
PEGG, Absolam 128; Achsack 128; Elizabeth 85; John 79,98; Martin 13; Valentine 13,59
PEGRAM, Edward *48; George 134; John 134; Patsey 45; Patty 48; Willey 120
PEIRCE, Bryan 67
PENDY, Jemima 50
PENNINGTON, Isaac 40
PERDUE, Mary 136
PERKINS, (Name torn) 141; Ann 48; Betty 48; Betsy 149; Caleb *47; Constant 142; Dina 149; Faithey 87; Hannah 108; Isaac 44, 47,48; Jared 47,48,149; John 47,48,143,*149; Joseph *48; Joseph Jr. 47; Martha 149; Mary 47, 48; Newton 149; Patty 149; Peter 147; Perinah 44; Thomas 47,48
PETTEGREW, Hans 34
PETTY, Elias (94; James 94, *99; Rachel 94; Rutherford 90; Samuel 94,99; Watson 94,99; William 94,99
PHIBBS, William 143
PHILIPPY, Eve 119; John *119
PHILLIPPI, Leonard 133
PHILLIPS, Anna 134; Hulda 60; Peter 121
PHILPOTT, Charles 47; David *47; Edward 47; Elizabeth 47; John 47; Mary Ann 47; Nathan 47
PHIPPS, Aaron 104; Abigail 104; Benjamin 104; James *104; Joseph 104; Rachel 104; Sally 104
PICKET, Hannah 127
PIDGEON, David C. 125; Samuel 50
PIGGOTT, William 30
PIKE, Abigail 126
PILKINGTON, Edely 32; Larkin 72; Nancy 72
PINNELL, Francis W. 95,96
PIRCHESON, James 78
PITMAN, Judith 120
PITTMAN, Charles 113
PITTS, Benjamin 119; E.E. 141; Elizabeth 123,141; James 105; Martha 141; Sarah 92; William 141
PLUNKET, Catherine *48; Caty 48; Is. 48; John 98; Mary 98; Rosanna 98; T.J. *98; Thomas 48,98; William 3,*48,98

POE, Betsy 49; David 114; Gabril 49: James *49,114, 115; John 49; Margaret 114, 115; Mathew 114; Matildy 49; Nancy 49,114; Polly 49; Rachel 114; Reney 49; Sarah 49,114; Selah 114; Tilla 114; William 49, *114,115; Zadoc 114
POLK, Fennell 117: James 117; James Sr. 86,113; Massey 113; Rebeccah 53
PONNINGER, John Jr. 129
POPE, Anna 138; George 56
POPPLEIN, Nicholas 143; Susanna 143
PORTER. Ann 47; Harry 43; Henry *49; Hugh 47; James *47,*49; Jane 37; John 48,*74; Margaret 48; Martha 74; Samuel *48; Vilet 47; William 23
PORTICE, Mary 126
POTTER. Abraham 47; Ailce 47; Elizabeth 146; Ephraim *47; Henry 35; Isaac 146; John 47,120,145; Joseph 47; Lois 111; Louise 124; Martha 47; Mary 35; Milly 120; Minerve 146; Robert Gwin 23; Sarah 47; Zadock 35
POWEL, Allen 129; Elisebeth 19,129
POWELL, Sarah 55
PRATHER, J.L. 97; Robert R. 121
PRATT, James 54; John 55
PRESNALL, James Sr. 142
PRICE, David 41; Jane 107; John 106; Meredith 76; Polly 41; Price, Wm. B. Dr. 123
PRICHET see PRITCHETT
PRITCHARD, Abegail 104
PRITCHETT, Alexander 64; Elizabeth 47; Ezekiel *47; Hessie 47; Isaac 47; Jenkins 139; Jeremiah 67, *139; John 31,47; Joseph 7,132; Penelope 139; Robert 139; Sarah 47; Sary 7; Unity 47; William 16,139, 151; Winafred 139; Webb 139; Zachariah 47; Zebulon 47,48
PROCTOR, Richard 144
PRYOR. Lucinda 134; Thuresa 134
PUTALE, Fill 42
PYLE, Enoch 137; George 137; James 137; Joseph *137; Masse 137; Nathan 137;
PYLE cont'd. Wiley 137; William 137
PYATT, John 63

QUAIL, David 49; Elizabeth 49,50; Isbel 49; James 49; Margaret 49; Robert 49; Samuel 49; William *49
QUAIT, Elender 130; Milberry 138
QUART, Ellender 100
QUENER, Cathren 48

RAGSDILL, Fanny 134; James J. 134
RALPH, Elizabeth 6
RALLSTON, Robert 142
RALSTON, Frances 141
RAMEY, Benja. 4; William 4
RAMSEY, Robert *51
RANKIN, Agness 52; Ann 53; Ana 52; Elisabeth 52; George 51,92,93,102; Isabel 51,72; Hannah *53, 58; James *97; Jency 52; Jennet 13; Jennie 52; John 3,15,20,52,*53,59, 92,97,99,135; John C. 126; John Sr. 52; Joseph 52,85,126; Lydia 72; Margaret 58,68; Mary 58, 143; Nancy 102,134; Polly 53,72; Robert 20,39,42, *51,52,53,68,72,85,97, 112; Robert C. 91,106; Robert, Esq. 112; Samuel 53,59; Sarah 52; Tabitha 68,135; Thankful 72; Thomas 52,97,104; William 13,*52,53,97,*105,146
RAPER, Anna 111; Elizabeth 22,51; Jacob 51; Robert C. 153; Thomas 51; William *51
RAY, Elizabeth 97; William 34
RAYE, Susannah 64
RAYL, RAIL, George 27,39; George Jr. 67; Hannah 77; Jean 5; William 16
REA, Margaret 50; William *50
READ, Nancy 13
READDUCK, John 1
REAGON, James 66; John 54
RECORDS, Ananias *52; Mary 52
REECE, John 57; Rebecca 136
REED, Agness 50; Henry *50; Sarah 122; William 50
REES, John 51

REEVES, James *50; Jeremiah 50; Malachia 50; Michel 50; Milisent 50; Thomas 46; William 50,51
REID, Joseph 100
REITZEL, Adam *51; Christopher 51; George 51; Henry 51; John 51; Margret 51; Mike 51
REYCH, Nancy 120
REYNOLDS, RENNOLDS, RANNOLDS Ann 38; David *53; Faithey 119; Jeremiah 25,53; Joash 31,147; John 53; Joseph 132; Lewis 29; Nancy 29; Rezin 53; Rhoda 97; Susannah 53
RHODES, Absalom 51; Fortune 50; Hezekiah 21,50; John *50,51,123; Joseph 50; Samuel 51; Sarah 51
RICE, James G. *103; Mary 55, 116; Martha 117; Sarah 103; Stephen D. 103
RICHARDSON, Elizabeth 134; Peggy 104
RICK, RICKS, Aaron 30; Betsey 86; Ed 100; Edward 67,86; Gwinn 86; Hannah 86; James *86; Jane 96; Jenny 75; Jonas 70; Nancy 86; Phebe 63,96; Thomas 86
RIED, Sarah 10
RIGGINS, Martin A. 118; Mary 112
RIGHT, Deborah 42
RIGHTSEL, Adam 127; Christian 127; Daniel 127; David 127; Frederich 126,127; Henry *127; Peter 126,127; Rachel 127; Sarah 127
RILEY, Joseph 70
ROBBINS, Jacob 112
ROBERTS, Jane 126,131; John 126,131; Prudence 25
ROBERTSON, Elizabeth 141; Henry C. 100; Isabella 107; James 53; Nathaniel 53; Suca *53
ROBINS, Bithiah 46; Frances 46
ROBINSON, Elino 3; James 3; Naomy 5; Nicholas 40; Rebekah 5; William 65
ROCHELLE, Christian *100
ROGERS, Ann 71; Elizabeth 71; Jacob 9,*71; Jamimah 71; Rachel 71
ROPER, John 1; Soloman 41; William 41
ROS, John 23; Rebeckah 23
ROSE, Ann 129; Henry 20; Mary 71; Nancy J. 53;
ROSE cont'd. William 48,53
ROSS, Andrew 50; Benjamin 101,129; Grizzald 56; Henry 21,43,50; James 50, 52; Jean 50,56; John 40, *50,*52; Jonas 64; Joseph 81; Levi 40; L.G. 143; Margret 50; Mary 33,35, 38,40,50,52,64; Nancy 50; Rebecker 50; Susannah 40,52,56; Thomas 20,50,52,56; Trainai 40
ROYALL, John D. 100
RUCKMAN, Isaiah 53; Joseph *53; Sarah 53
RUDDUCK, Jane 50,52; John *50,57; John Jr. 50; Mary 52; Ruth 50; William 50,52,96
RUDOCK, John 28
RUKE, Stephen 51
RUMLEY, Elijah 6
RUSSELL, Adell 98; Alexander 51,52,53; Andrew 60,*101; Anna 101; Catherine 109,114,132; Christian 60; Crowder 132; Daniel 101; David 51,52,80; Delilah 50; Elijah 101; Elinor 51; Elizabeth 101; George 80; Hepseybah 38; James 51, *52,58,101; Jesse 52; John 51,117; Joseph *109; Judith 80; Leah 78; Lucretia 52; Martha 52, 105,114; Mary 101; Nancy 51,101; Matthew 19; Robert 51,*52; Robert W. 52; Samuel 114; Sarah 80, 101; Susanna 52; Thomas 52; Timothy *80; William *51,*52,80,109
RUSSOM, Polly 109; Rachel 86
RUSSUM, Vincent 150
RYAN, Ellener 51; Ginnia 51; John *51,55,56; Margaret 51,57; Robert 44, 51,83; William 44,51,57, 73
RYDER, Henry 122

SALGRAVE, James 59
SAMPLE, Isaac 112
SAMPSON, Hannah 113; Jane 113; Margaret 113; Mary 113; Nathaniel 113; Peter 113; Ralph 113; Richard *113; Sarah 113

SANBURG, LIMEBURY???, Catheran 96; George 96; Daniel 96; Susannah 96
SAND, Susana 82
SANDERS, David 59,61; Elizabeth 61,125; Forrest 59; Hezekiah *61; James 22,59; Jane 59,75; Jemima 59,61, 75; Jesse 59,61,80,112; Joel 56,*61,110; John 6, *56,*59,61,125; Joseph 59; Lucy 110; Martha 61,120; Martha S. 61; Mary 61,75; Milton H. 110; Rebeckah 61; Sarah 50,61,75; Susannah 59,67; Thomas 61,80
SANFORD, Richard 66
SAPP, Benjamin 60; Dorothy 60; Howel 13; James 60,125; Robert *60; Samuel 60,77, 87; Sarah 13,60; Thomas 120
SATTER, Willia 107
SAUNDERS, David 75; Martha *74
SCALES, Agness 55; Alfred 85; Betsy 55; David 55; Henry 55; James 55; John 55; Joseph *54,55; Mary 54; Nathaniel 55; Robert 55; Thomas 55
SCHOOLFIELD, Agness 97; Anseletta 135; Daniel 135; Daniel G. 118; Jane 97, 135; John 97,104,118,*135; John E. 104; John Sr. 104; Joseph 104,135; Mary 99; Mary B. 135; Nancy 118; Rankin C. 135; Samuel D. 135; Sarah 135; William 106,119,135
SCOTT, Adam 57,*134,135; Adw. 71; David 135; Donnell 134; Gabriel 42,54; Hannah 55; Jane 120; John *54,79, 135; Jinet 54; Margaret 54, 57; Mary 55,57; Martha 54; Matthew 42; Nancy 54,57,58; Polly 134; Rebeckah 57,*58; Rebeccah M. 59; Robert *55; Samuel 54,57,59; Tenny 54; Thomas 42,54,55,57,58,135; William 10,21,39,42,43,50, 51,54,*57; William D. 117, 135
SEARCY, Keron 54; Kerizia 54; William *54
SEPRATT, Jane 27
SETTLE, Josiah 2
SHAFNOR, George
SHANNON, Ann 59; Isabella 59; Soloman 56; William 56,*59
SHARBROUGH, Joseph *57; Malakia 57; Perthenia 57
SHARP, Agnes 54; Cathren 54; Elizabeth 54; Isham 54; James 54; John *54; Mary 54; Richard 54; Robert 99; Samuel 54; Sarah 136; Sary 54; Susannah 54
SHATTERLY, Andrew 14,144; George 71,102; John 103; Micheal *102; Milly 102
SHAVER, Conrad 58; Catherine 58; Elizabeth 58; Jacob 58; Laish 58; William *58
SHAW, Ann 102; Benjamin 56; Betsy 58; Elizabeth *101; Finley 101,102; Hugh 43, 58; James 136; John 58; Joseph 102; Nancy 58; Patrick *58; Robert 56; Sarah 56,138; William *56,58,76,102,119
SHEARMAN, Benjamin 21
SHEARER, Peggy 127
SHELLY, Betsy 57; Elinnor 57; Francis 57; James 55, *57; Jane 4; Jeremiah 47, 55; Jesse 116; Jesy 55; John *55,57; Mary 55,57; Nathan 55; William 57,109
SHELTON, John 149
SHEPARD, Sarah 60
SHEPHARD, Nancy 128
SHERMAN, Samuel 34
SHERWOOD, Ann 133; Benjamin 133; Daniel 59,*133; David 34,72; Fanny 133; Hugh 133,144; John 133; Nancy 133; Rachel 134; Thomas 133
SHIELDS, James 127; Robert M. 127
SHILCOTT, Deborah 68
SHOE, Henry 72
SHOEMAKER, Adam 60; Barbara 60; Barbery 135; Caty 60, 135; Cemratt 60; Christian 60; Daniel 60,88; Elijah 89,135; Elizabeth 60,*135; George 60,69; Jacob 60; John 60; John 60; Marry 60; Susannah *60
SHOFNER, David 98; Elizabeth 124; Nancy 98
SHORT, Jean 89; Margaret 89
SHOVER, Catherine 137; John 137
SHRIFT, Margaret 5
SHUTTERLING, Molly 8
SIERS, Jane 129
SIGFRIED, Catherine 58; Henerich *58; John 58

SIKES, Isom *133; Rebecca 133
SILLIVAN, Hannah 39; James 83,84; Joel 14; Joseph 86; Levi 56; Levicy 86; Mary 86; Sarah 86; Soloman *86; William 51,56
SIMMONS, Abigail 130; D.W. 109; William 22
SIMONS, Elizabeth 4
SIMPSIN, Thomas 56,57
SIMPSON, Anna 62; Eleba 108; Ellener 62; Elizabeth 57, 137; F.L. 139; Francis L. 103,128; James 62; John 108; Joseph 107; Mary 93, 108; Moses 128; Nathan 108; Nathaniel 40,56,57, 107,*108,119; Peter 62; Peter Ryan 57; Pharby 62; Ralph S. 107; Richard *56,57,62; Richard Sr. *61; Robert K. 108; Sarah 108; Selah 61; Sinah 108; Thomas 108; Vincent 73; Westly 108; William 38, 46,57,62,107,108
SIMS, Isabell 84; Rufus 82
SKEANS, Alexander 103
SLADE, William 138
SLICK, Thomas 31
SLOAN, James 2,135; James R. 114; William 114,115
SMITH, Abraham 55; Adam 60; Alexander 15,33; Anderson 93; Andrew 65; Ann 32; Arthur 54; Benjamin 138; Charles 55; Daniel 126; David 60; Elizabeth 58; Eri 70; Evaline 135; Jacob 60; James 13,28,132; Jane 97; Jedidiah 129; Jesse 94,138; John 37,38,44,*55, 60,*138; John A. 115,123; Joseph 58,*60; Joshua 15, 55; Larkin 60,104,107,121; Levina 138; Lisabeth 8; Lucy W. 132; Lydia 41,138; Mary 13,70; Martha 100; Molly 60; Nancy 22; Nathaniel 60; Nickolas 33,60; Peter *60,127; Philip 60; Robert *54,58; Sally 60; Samuel 54; Sarah 126; Sarah Powell 55; William 44,54,*58,70,127,*135
SMITHSON, Barbra 57
SNOLEY, David 30
SOCKWELL, Elizabeth 129; Sally 129; Robert 129
SPARR, John 95
SPENCE, Charles 22; George 107; John 20; Nathan 20;
SPENCE cont'd.
Sally 91; Sidney 20
SPENSE, Betsy 145; Elves 145; John 145; Margaret 130; William 145
SPIKERMAN, Elizabeth 59; William 59
SPINKS, Amy 54; Bowley 54; Enoch *53,54; Garrett 54; John 54; Martha 54; Lewis 54; Sarah 54
SPOON, Olivia 121
SPRINGER, Sarah 40
SPRUCE, Betsy 77; Elizabeth 59,*86; Sally F. 86; George 59,77,86,135; John 59; John H. 77; Joseph 59,77; Maday 2; Quinton 59,77; Sarah 59,*77; Simpson 77; Thomas 59, 77; William *59,77,117
STACK, David 56,145; Elijah *56; Rachel 56; Sarah 78; Thomas 56,106
STAFFORD, Anderton 71,104; Betsy 73; George 71,104; Henrietta 68; Isabella 107; James *71,103,104; John 71,103,104; John B. 95; Joseph C. 95; Polly 71,103; Sarah 6,71,*103; Rhoda 104; Zadoc 121
STALKER, Deborah 57; Elizabeth 57; George *57; Hannah 57; John 57; Jonathan 57; Lydia 57; Nathan 57; Rachel 57; Rebeckah 57; Thomas 57
STANDLEY, Jesse 10; Jonathan 1; Sarah 1
STANFIELD, Grace 57; Rachel 57; William 57
STANFORD, Jenny 45
STANLEY, Abigail 64,137; Abigail H. 143; Agness 56; Anthony 79; Barnabas 14; Charles 128; Catherine 79; Edward 56,64; Elizabeth 56; Henry 56; Huldah 14; Isaiah 76,79, 123; James 79; Jane 120; Jemima 62; Jessa 56; Jesse 14,79,80,100,123, *128; Joseph *150; Joshua 123; Judith 56; Lavinna 149; Lydia 144; Mahlon 79; Mary 150; Micajah 62,*79; Michael 20,79; Nathan 123; Phebe 28,56, 150; Prudence 128; Richard 23,56; Robert 56; Samuel *123; Sarah 41,123; Shadrach *56,149;

STANLEY cont'd.
Strangeman 16,18,20,62, 65,79; Thom 41; Thomas 128; William 79,123,144, 150; Zachariah 40
STANTON, Abigail 38; Ruth 68
STAPLETON, James 107
STARBUCK, Avis 61; Benjamin 61; Bezail 120; Charles 61,82; Daniel 61; Drocas 61; Edward 130; Elizabeth 61; Elwood 120; Eunice 61; Gayer *61; Hezekiah 6,16, 20,31,56,61,63; Hephzebah 80; Jean 63; John 61; Lathmon 6; Lathum 61; Lydia 61; Mary 61,125; Matthew 14,*61; Milton 120; Pamely 61; Paul 61; Peter 22,61; Rachel 61,119,120,125; Reuben 61,120,125; Ruth 61; Seth 61,124; Unis 120; Thomas 61,98,*119,120,125; William 6,9,20,61,62,63, 67,*129
STARNES, Ebenezer 53; Peter 53
STARR, Abner 89; Adam 11,36, *89; Caty 89; Barbary 89; David 89; Elizabeth 89; Henry 89; John 36; Mary 89; Susannah 89
STARRETT, STARRATT, Ann 112; Anny 99; Benjamin *54; Betsey 23; Betsy Ann 99; Elizabeth 118; Hanna 54; Hester 54; James 54,*58; James D. 118; James Hall 58; Joanna 54; John 17,50,58,151; J.H. 24; John Tobius 54; Mary 54; William 58,109; William F. 54
STAYLY, Elizabeth 140; George 140
STEAN, James 108
STEARNS, Isaac 53; Sarah 53; Shubal *53
STEPHENS, Enoch 109; Evin *109; George 96,109; Jehu 96; John 109; Joshua 109; Mary 10; Mourning 119; Naomi 109; Uriah 105; Ursley 31; William 115
STEPHENSON, Alexander 55; Ann 55; Ann Jr. 55; Hugh 55; John 34,55,56,59; John Jr. 55; Matthew *55; William 55
STEVENS, Esther 73,118; John 1
STEVENSON, Ann *57; Hugh 93; John 57
STEWART, Adam Lackey 81; Agness 24; Catherine 113,114; Dasey 119; David C. 117,121;
STEWART cont'd.
Donald *107; Elizabeth 75; Eapharus 59; Euphance 129; Finley *59,81; Finley G. 59; Hannah 29; Isaac 113,114; James 59, 84,112,*134; James A. 84,121; Jehugh 29; Jennet 59; John 24,59,61,84,114; Lindley 117; Margaret 81, 117; Martha 81,117; Mary 119; Merrill 138; Prudence 59,81,*84,128; Ralph 24; Robert 59,74, 84,117,118; Robert S. 84; S. 24; Sampson 5,74,*113, 116; Samuel 17,116,117, *119; Susanna 59,107; Wiley 53; William W. 114
STOCKTON, Daniel D. 100
STOKES, John 102; Thomas 102
STONE, John *60; Salathiel 16,60
STOREY, Catey 128
STRADER, Adam 75,88
STRAIN, Sarah 77
STUBBLEFIELD, Edward 47
STUART, Adam Lackey 37; Amos 99; Andrew 5; Elizabeth 85; George 40; Henry 1; Jehu 99; John 9,10, 27,74,85,92,*99,141; John Jr. 12; Jonathan 27; Mary 3; Meriam 99; Moses 27; Rachel 99; Robert 37, 99; Samuel 70; Sarah 12, 99; Susanna 62; Temple 62; Zebulon 96
SUITS, Casper 64; Frederich 103; Jacob 123
SUITER, Milly *130
SULGRAVE, Catherine 59; James 59
SULLEN, Ann or Nancy 59; Barbary 59; John *59; Margaret 59
SULLIVAN, Caleb 60; Daniel *59; David 60; Edward 60; Elenar 51; Florence 60; Joel 60; Henney 60; John 60; Margaret 60; Mary Ann 60; Nancy 60; William 60
SUMMERS, Abel 133; Barbery 133; Ceba 128; Isabel J. 128; Jacob 133; John *128; Joseph 33; Joshua 133; Ludwick 133; Martin 128; Patsey 128; Peggy 128; Peter 32,*133; Peter R. 128; Polly Ann 128; Susan E. 128; Thankful A. 128; Valentine 133

SUTZ, Adam 57; Christian 57; Frederich 57; Jacob *57, 58; Margaret 58; Mary 58; Tobias 58
SWAIM, Daniel 70; Marion 38; William 70
SWAIN, Adaline 137; Ammiel G. 137; Charles 97; Cynthia 92; Deborah 148; Elisia 92; Elizabeth 133; Eunice 92; George 11,97; Henry 148; Hester 137; Iven 92; Jethro 92,103; Joseph *103; Joseph W. *137; Keziah 119; Michael 26; Miriam 80; Nancy 97; Narsissa 92; Obed 103; Obed L. 137; Priscilla 144; Rebecca 97; Reed 80,114; Rhoda 92,126; Silvanas *92; Susannah 137, 148; Thomas 31,73,93; Zacheus *97
SWALLOW, Lydia 118; William 118
SWEET, John 41
SWIFT, David 20; Thomas 53
SWIGETT, Elisebeth 6; Lucy 6; Rodey 6
SWINDLE, John 111
SWING, Barbary 9,32,140; Conrad 119; Eve 32; George 52, 56; Henry 140; Joel 140; John 56,58; Lewis 140; Ludwick *56; Mathias 9,56,*140; Susan 140
SWISHER, Jacob 36; John 36

TALBOT, John 4,41,50
TALBERT, Mary 77
TALLEY, John 63; Mary 63; Nicholas *63
TANSON, Sarah 130
TARKINETT, Henry 119
TATE, Adam 141,142; Ally 25, 109,142; Elly 141,142; Anthony *109; Easther 109; Isabella 109; John 109,142; Joseph *141,142; Margaret 109; Nancy 138; Polly 109; Rachel 142; Sally 109; Sarah 142; Thomas R. 109, 138
TATEMAN, Henry 93
TATUM, A.E.D. 124,130; Betsy 61,113; Edward *63; Harbert 63,64,77; Henry 63,75,77; John 110; Jonathan 22; Sally 110; Sebon 77; Sihon 63,64; Sucky 63,64
TAYLOR, Alexander 63; Edward Tatum 37; John 62,63; Lydia 63; Mary *63; Nathan 63; Ruth 63; Sarah 121;
TAYLOR cont'd. Simcon 62,63; Thomas 62, 63
TEASE, William 18,41
TELFORD, Isabell 58
TERRELL, Deborah 13,14
TERRY, Thomas 5
THACKER, Isaac 112; James M. 143
THARP, Elizabeth 13,46; James 28,75; Laban 63; Mary 84
THOM, also written TOM, TOME, Ann 24; Catron 69; Catherine 91; Daniel 91; Ebenezer 91; Elinor 35; Harper 69; Jane 91; John 2,35,*91; John H. 79; Mary 91; Nancy 69; Nelly 91; Polly K. 134; Polly Porter 69; Samuel 24; William 68,73,91
THOMAS, Andrew W. 139; Benjamin 62; D. 133; Dan M. 139; David 88,91,*139; David B. 140; Elijah 62; Francis 62; Hannah 98; Isaac 62; James *62; John 39,47,62; John C. 139; John W. 140; Mary Ann 47; Mary W. 140; Militia 139; Milly 62; Molly 39; Peggy 91,139, 140; Robert 139; Sarah Jane 140; Stephen 62; William 94; William W. 140
THOMPSON, Joseph 106,111; Margaret 64; Mariah 106; Nancy N. 124; Robert 44, 52,64,*136; Samuel *64, 136; Susan 106; Thomas 136; William F. 63; William G. 124
THORNBERRY, Rachel 102
THORNBURGH, Ann 63; Benjamin 64; Edward 53,63; Elizabeth 67; Hannah 62; Henry 26,62; Isaac 63; James 3,10,41,62,*64, 117; Joseph 26,29,33,62, *63,117; Joseph Jr. 15; Martha 62,64; Mary 62, 64,117; Richard 64; Ruth 62; Thomas 41,50,*62,64, 65,*117,124,149; Thomas Jr. *62; Walter 26; William 29,61,78
THORPE, Aaron 11; Alse 13; John 11
THRIFT, Abraham 26; Susannah 26
THURMAN, Robert 145

TILLEY, George *63; Nancy 63
TIMBERLAKE, William 128
TIMSON, Elisabeth 53
TOMLINSON, Allen W. 117; Dolly 144; James 72.84, 98,145; John 40,50,84, 98; Polly 72; William 50,86
TOUCHSTONE, James 2,*64; Sarah 64
TROLLINGER, Barbara 75; Frederich *75
TROTTER, Benjamin 10,150; Bennet 78; Edward 150; Edward O. 78; Elizabeth 95; Epharim 150; Ephraim *78; George *83,150; Hardin 78; Jane 150; John 83; Joseph 150; Nancy 150; Oldom 150; Polly 78; Rachel 150; Rubin 78; Sarah 83; Shadrack 78
TROXLER, Eli 101; John 101
TUCKER, Abbit 64; Anderson 64,65; Diana 64; Elizabeth 64; Ezekial *125; John 64; Leah 64; Levi *64; Mary 64; Patty 65; Peggy 64, 65,144; Polly J. 124; Sarah 64; Zodac 64,65
TULFORD, Thomas 54
TUMBLESON, John 35
TUNCANNON, Olive 125
TURKENETT, Henry 127
TURNER, Abraham 125; Edith 125; James 125; Jane 125; Mary *90; Miles 125; Miriam 125; Soloman 145; T.G. 47; Thomas 65,126; William 125
TWIFORD, Denetine 129; Edmond W. 129; Elizabeth 86; Edward W. 86; George *129; Jonathan *86; Robert 86
TYER, Frederich 65

UNDERHILL, John 67
UNDERWOOD, Andrew 109; Elizabeth 85; James 137; Joshua 13,103,128; Joshua Sr. *128; Lilly 103; Martha 128; Thompson 128; Thomas 128; William W. 128
UNTHANK, Allen 8,34,65,*88; Anna 78,88; Betsy 89; Eli 89; Elizabeth 131; Hannah 65; Jemima 88,*141; Jonathan 65,88; Joseph 5,*65, *89; Josiah 49,65,78,88, 89; Judith 65; Lydia 141; Mahaly 89; Mary 65; Rachel 88; Rebeckah 89; Ruth 88; Sally 89; Sarah 65;
UNTHANK cont'd.
Timple 89; William 88, 89; William, Esq. 88

VANSTORY, VAN STORRE, etc. Cathren 66; Catherine 112.*135; John 66,*112, 114,135,139; Mary 107; William 122
VAUGHAN, George 26; Kinchin 64; Mary 26; Tabitha 64
VERNON, James 33
VESTAL, Jemima 120
VETAW, Daniel 118; Sarah 118
VICKERY, Christopher 70; Elizabeth 46
VOWELL, William 53

WADDELL, Elizabeth 66; James *66
WAFFORD, Sally 73; Sarah 73; Levina 73; William 73
WAGGONER. Fatty 14
WAGNER, Adam 37; George 37
WAGOMAN, Christian 49
WALKER, Adam 15; Albert 136; Barfield 136; Betsy 93; Cloe 77; Cloy 136; David 25; Eliner 66; Elizabeth 25,43,122,136; Hannah 67; Henderson 93; Jacob 64,75; James 66; Joel 25; John 6,25,66, 68,77,*90; John Hunter 25; John Jr. 6; Kesia 98; Leven 68,90,103; Matildy 93; Mial 136; Nancy 88; Pamila W. 123; Richard *66; Robert 136; Samuel 93; Sarah 67; Thomas 55; William 25,73,132; William T. 93
WALL, Rebeccah 100
WALLACE, Elizabeth 17; Sarah 17; William 23
WALTON, Alse *66; Henry 47; John 38,66; Nathaniel 38,66
WANICK, Charity 88; David *88; Elizabeth 88; Jesse 88; Polly 88
WARD, Betsey 127; James 82
WARREN, _____ 122; Soloman 11,76; Thomas 140
WASON, Margaret 4
WASSON, WASSOM, Ann S. 138; Nancy 138
WATLINGTON, Brooks 128; Edward 128; Jonathan B. 128

WILLEY cont'd.
Emelia 66; James 45; John 66; Prichard 66; Thomas W. 66
WILLIAMS, Andrew 34,60; Bartholomew 27; Buly 89; Catherine 40; Dolly 11; Elizabeth 34; Jane 102; Jesse 26,28,53,62; John 30; Margaret 25; Richard 8,30,65,68; Sophia 11; Sarah 129; William 46,62
WILLIS, Joel 68; Mary 2; Rodger 2
WILLOW, Jn 31
WILSON, Agness 13; Allen *66; Allan 102; Andrew 10, 13,51,*120; Andrew Sr. *120; Anny 130; Archer 23; Archibald 23,115; Benjamin 17,58,151; Charles 13; Daniel 13,120; David 105, 120,151; Elizabeth 138; George D. 121; George, Esq. 33; Henry 90; Isabella 59; Jacob 26; James 11,14,17,31,33,66,101,*102, 120; Jane 59,66,102; Jeane 25; Jemima 90,102, *126; John 66,89,120; Jonathan *67,69,*90; Letha 90; Margaret 112; Mary 43,51; Mary Ann 18; Maxwell 51,120; Michael 28, 79,*90; Nancy 67,90,151; Pamela 93; Robert 13,67, 75,103,120,143,*150,*151; Reuben 88; Sarah 150; Swepston 145; Thomas 23, 24,102,107,136; Unis 90; Will 90; William 67,120; William R. 51
WINBOURN, ______ 122
WINCHESTER, John 102; William 73
WINEGARDNER, Joseph 36
WINN, Martha *100; Peter 100; Richard 100
WIRICK, George 94; Mary *93; Peggy 94
WITHERS, William 136
WIT, Elizabeth 65
WITT, Esther 65; Jean 65; John 65; Margaret 65; Mary 65; Michael *65; Rachel 65; Rosanah 65
WITTY, Elijah 132,143; Eliza 106; Levi W. 125; Mary 5; Robert 106
WOFFORD, William 73
WOLFINGTON, David 90; Isaac 90; Jane *90; Samuel 90
WOLLUN, John 51
WOMACK, Adam 54
WOOD, John 25
WOODBURN, Ann 67,88; Arthur 67,*69,88; David 88; Evelina 88; Hannah 88; Jesse S. 88; John 88; Margaret 88; Martha 68; Mary 88; Patsy 69; Robert 88; Tabitha E. 69; Thankful 67,*104; Thomas *88; Watson 69; William *67, 69,88
WOODSIDE, Hannah 66; James 66; John *66; Robert 66; Samuel 66; William 66
WOODY, Catherine 111; James 111
WOODYARD, Betsey 128
WOOLEN, ______ 122; Benjamin E. 115; Edward 115; Charles W. 115; John 32; Levin 31,*115; Nancy 115; Rebecca 115; William Barns 115
WOOTEN, Phebe 67
WORK, Annasitty 106,107; Elizabeth 67; Henry 23, 51,67; Jean 67; John *66, *68,87,*106,108; Polly 68; Margaret 12,66,67; Sarah 67
WORTH, Abegail 108; Daniel 8,38; David 53,60,72,93, 94,103,118; David Jr. 118; Eunice 94,108; Francis *67; Hiram C. 117; Job 8,30,60,137; Lydia 103; Mary 67; Reuben 103; William 67,92,94,99; Yeno 38
WORTHENTON, John 19
WHITSEL, Daniel 14
WRIGHT, A.S. 143; Alexander 66; Daniel A. 119; Dianna 66; Elijah 66; James 65, 138; James Jr. *66; James Sr. 66; Jane 66; John *65; Levin 20; Lucy 66; Lyda 66; Martin 82,105; Micajah 66; Prudence 66; Rebeckah 69; Richardson 96; Robert 65; Thomas *69; Whiley 69; William 66
WRIGHTSEL see RIGHTSEL, Henry 60
WYRICK see WIRICK,WERICK, Jacob 101
WYNN, Richard 107

YAKS, YATES, Johnson 100
YARBROUGH, Archibald 26

INDEX OF DEVISORS NAMING SLAVES

SANDERS, Joel 61
SCALES, Joseph 54
SCOTT, Adam 134; Robert 55
SHOEMAKER, Elizabeth 135; Susannah 60
SMITH, Joseph 60; William 58
SPINKS, Enoch 53
SPRUCE, Elizabeth 86; Sarah 77
STAFFORD, James 71; Sarah 103
STARR, Adam 89
STEWART, Donald 107; Finley 59; Prudence 84; Robert 117; Sampson 113
SUMMERS, Peter 133
TATE, Anthony 109; Joseph 141
TATUM, Edward 63
THOM, John 91
THOMAS, David 139
THOMPSON, John 106
TROTTER, Josiah 150
TWIFORD, George 129; Jonathan 86
WEATHERLY, Edward 67; Isaiah 150
WEBB, Thomas 106
WELBORN, Thomas 65
WHARTON, Elam 114; Watson 68
WILEY, David Senr. 68; Robert 79
WILSON, Andrew Senr. 120
WINN, Martha 100
WOODBURN, Thankful 104
WORK, John 68
WRIGHT, John 65; Thomas 69

IN RESEARCHING SLAVES, it could be wise to order a copy of the original will. In the few cases that the slaves named in the recorded will have been checked against the names of slaves in the original will, there has been some variation.

www.ingramcontent.com/pod-product-compliance
Lightning Source LLC
Chambersburg PA
CBHW021906020426
42334CB00013B/497

* 9 7 8 0 8 9 3 0 8 3 5 2 6 *